T0342475

Programming the Internet of Things

An Introduction to Building Integrated, Device-to-Cloud IoT Solutions

Andy King

Beijing · Boston · Farnham · Sebastopol · Tokyo

Programming the Internet of Things

by Andy King

Copyright © 2021 Andrew D. King. All rights reserved.

Published by O'Reilly Media, Inc., 1005 Gravenstein Highway North, Sebastopol, CA 95472.

O'Reilly books may be purchased for educational, business, or sales promotional use. Online editions are also available for most titles (*http://oreilly.com*). For more information, contact our corporate/institutional sales department: 800-998-9938 or *corporate@oreilly.com*.

Acquisitions Editor: Melissa Duffield
Development Editor: Sarah Grey
Production Editor: Christopher Faucher
Copyeditor: Arthur Johnson
Proofreader: Piper Editorial Consulting, LLC

Indexer: Ellen Troutman-Zaig
Interior Designer: David Futato
Cover Designer: Karen Montgomery
Illustrator: Kate Dullea

June 2021:   First Edition

Revision History for the First Edition

2021-06-10:   First Release
2022-08-26:   Second Release
2023-09-29:   Third Release

See *http://oreilly.com/catalog/errata.csp?isbn=9781492081418* for release details.

The O'Reilly logo is a registered trademark of O'Reilly Media, Inc. *Programming the Internet of Things*, the cover image, and related trade dress are trademarks of O'Reilly Media, Inc.

The views expressed in this work are those of the author, and do not represent the publisher's views. While the publisher and the author have used good faith efforts to ensure that the information and instructions contained in this work are accurate, the publisher and the author disclaim all responsibility for errors or omissions, including without limitation responsibility for damages resulting from the use of or reliance on this work. Use of the information and instructions contained in this work is at your own risk. If any code samples or other technology this work contains or describes is subject to open source licenses or the intellectual property rights of others, it is your responsibility to ensure that your use thereof complies with such licenses and/or rights.

978-1-492-08141-8

[LSI]

Table of Contents

Part I.   Getting Started

Part II. Connecting to the Physical World

Part III.   Connecting to Other Things

Part IV.   Connecting to the Cloud

Foreword

The Internet of Things has the potential to become one of the most disruptive technological advances of our time. With more than 50 billion devices expected to come online over the next few years, the IoT will have a profound impact on every industry. Exciting new connected devices and supporting systems will be developed to solve problems in medicine, transportation, agriculture, housing, energy, manufacturing, and more. Many of these projects are already under way, and most companies are eager to expand their products and capabilities to leverage the IoT.

Built on advancements and cost reductions in sensing, metrology, microelectronics, wireless communications, cloud services, and the expansion of the World Wide Web, the Internet of Things is at the intersection of multiple technologies developed over the last few decades. While this breadth introduces several challenges, it also offers the opportunity to architect and develop software across traditional career boundaries. The IoT pushes practitioners outside of their comfort zones to explore the full spectrum of software engineering. In most cases, a solution touches all levels of the stack: starting with bare-metal code on constrained devices, then aggregated through more capable edge nodes before heading northbound to the cloud. This means the designer must have enough expertise at each level to understand the protocols, languages, patterns, and frameworks available to build a stable and scalable system.

In *Programming the Internet of Things*, Andy lays out a carefully crafted guide to building an end-to-end IoT system. By working step by step through the text and leveraging the thorough reference materials, you will implement a versatile testbed built on patterns and protocols used in real commercial IoT systems. I encourage you to invest in the optional hardware components. One of the most rewarding aspects of this field is the integration of software and the physical world. The simple act of controlling an LED from the cloud or capturing indoor environmental conditions will have you hooked on the IoT.

The organization of this book and its reference materials shows the significant practical experience Andy has, not only in the IoT, but also in software engineering and architecture overall. The steps are deliberately designed to follow the process of a real software engineering project, backed by the Kanban-style management system utilized by most software development teams. If you complete each exercise in combination with the supporting reference material, you will gain a better understanding of the IoT—with the bonus of familiarizing yourself with processes and best practices common across software development in general.

While Andy covers the IoT down to the implementation level, I think this book also provides valuable guidance for the technology leader. By working through the software architecture that is the core of most IoT systems, you will gain a better understanding of the complexities involved in their implementation. Each exercise contains valuable insights regarding the challenges, risks, and trade-offs involved in that segment of the system.

I strongly advise readers to pay close attention to the numerous callouts and references regarding security in the Internet of Things. As with any technology, the pressure to deliver a solution can often overshadow the need for robust security. Deficient security has already been the downfall of many IoT systems. As this technology becomes more prevalent, it will become part of many critical systems. It is vital that security becomes one of the first considerations in any IoT project; it should be continually revisited throughout the lifecycle of the solution.

Programming the Internet of Things provides a road map for developers of all skill levels to break into one of the fastest-growing fields in software engineering. I encourage you to work through this content carefully and think about how you could apply solutions based on similar principles to problems in your life. I look forward to seeing the projects created by the technologists who get inspired by this content and dive into building the IoT.

— Tim Strunck
Director of Software Engineering
Atom Power
Charlotte, North Carolina
April 2021

Preface

The Internet of Things (IoT) is a complex, interconnected system-of-systems composed of different hardware devices, software applications, data standards, communications paradigms, and cloud services. Knowing where to start with your own IoT project can be a bit daunting. *Programming the Internet of Things* is designed to get you started on your IoT development journey and shows you, the developer, how to make the IoT work.

If you decide to stay with me through this book, you'll learn how to write, test, and deploy the software needed to build your own basic, end-to-end IoT capability.

Who Is This Book For?

Programming the Internet of Things is, at its core, a book about building IoT solutions —from device to cloud.

This book was primarily written as a teaching guide for my Connected Devices course at Northeastern University, and for any students interested in learning how to program IoT solutions. While it's structurally focused on assisting students and practitioners, it can also be helpful for those interesting in learning more about IoT concepts and principles.

Throughout the book, you will find step-by-step guidelines for building your own end-to-end IoT capability, with exercises within each chapter that build on one another to help you cement your knowledge of the IoT. If you're more interested in the concepts, however, that's perfectly fine! You can learn about the *what* and *why* but move quickly through the *how* and skip the exercises, if you'd prefer.

As an educator and a consultant, I've structured the content so it can be used as a road map for teaching introductory IoT programming courses, with the intent of stepping through key concepts and gradually building a base of knowledge in this important area. Whether you're a college-level instructor or a student looking to develop your skills in the IoT, I hope you'll find this book helpful in building your course and knowledge.

Lastly, I leave most of the specific instructions and details to the existing specifications and open source APIs. While some parts of the book might serve as a high-level reference, a majority of the content here focuses on helping you leverage such information to build the solution you need. We're fortunate to have access to well-written protocol specifications and a vibrant open source community, and I'm grateful to those who have championed these efforts.

To the Programmer

If you're embarking on your own IoT learning journey as a practitioner, I assume you're mostly interested in expanding your skill set. Perhaps you've witnessed the growth of IoT opportunities and want to be part of this important technology evolution. Over the years, I've found the step-by-step, "build from the ground up" approach to implementing integrated and open IoT solutions to be most helpful in understanding the complexities of this area, and so I follow this model throughout the book.

The programming examples you'll encounter here are constructed from my own journey in learning about the IoT, and many have evolved from lab module assignments in the graduate-level Connected Devices course I teach as part of Northeastern University's Cyber Physical Systems program.

Each chapter and exercise set builds on the one before, so if you are just starting out with the IoT and are unfamiliar with how an end-to-end IoT system comes together through software, I'd recommend walking through each as-is, working through each exercise in the order given. It's best to consider application customizations only after you've mastered each chapter.

If you're an experienced programmer and are using this book as a reference guide, you may find you can skip over some of the basic development environment setup procedures and simply skim through some of the programming exercises; however, I do recommend you work through the requirements specified in each, even if you choose to use your own design.

To the Instructor

The contents that underpin this book have been used successfully in my graduate-level Connected Devices course for the past few years. This book is the formalization of these lecture notes, presentations, examples, and lab exercises and is structured in much the same way as my course.

I originally designed the class as an introduction to the IoT, but with student input and suggestions from my teaching assistants, it quickly morphed into a project-oriented software-development course. It's now one of the final required classes for students wrapping up their master's degrees in the Cyber Physical Systems program. The goal of the course is to establish a strong baseline of IoT knowledge to help students move from academia into industry, bringing foundational IoT skills and knowledge into their respective organizations.

This book is structured so it can be used as a reference guide or even as a major component of a complete curriculum, to help you with your own IoT-related course. The content is focused on constructing an end-to-end, open, and integrated IoT solution, from device to cloud, using a "learn as you build" approach to teaching. Since each chapter builds on the preceding one, you can use this book to guide your students in building their own platform from the ground up.

You can remain up to date with the online exercises by reviewing the Programming the IoT Kanban board (*https://oreil.ly/programming-iot-kanban*).[1] Other relevant content useful for teaching and explaining some of the concepts in this book can be found on the book's website (*https://programmingtheiot.com/programming-the-iot-book*).

To the Technology Manager or Executive

The contents of this book should help you better understand the integration challenges inherent to any IoT project and should provide insight into the skill sets your technology team(s) will need to succeed across your IoT initiatives.

If you're part of this group, my assumption is that you're mostly concerned with understanding this technology area as a whole—its integration challenges, dev teams' setup requirements and needs, team skill sets, business user and stakeholder concerns about the IoT, and the change-management challenges you may encounter as you embark on your organization's IoT journey.

For technology executives and managers, you don't need to implement the exercises yourself, but it will be helpful to read through the entire book so you understand the challenges your team will likely encounter.

For business stakeholders interested mostly in understanding what the IoT entails, I recommend reading—at a minimum—the overview section at the start of each chapter and then focusing on the final chapter, which discusses a handful of practical cases, scenarios, and implementation suggestions.

---

1 All the exercises in this book are adapted from my Programming the IoT Kanban board and are used with my permission.

What Do I Need to Know?

Although the exercises in this book assume that you have some experience writing software applications in Python and Java, most do not require sophisticated programming skills or a formal computer science background. Most exercises do, however, require that you're comfortable developing code in an integrated development environment (IDE); reading, writing, and executing unit tests; running applications from the command line; and configuring Linux-based systems via a shell-based command line.

If you intend to complete the optional exercises listed in the Kanban board (*https://oreil.ly/programming-iot-kanban*) or at the end of some of the chapters, you'll need to be comfortable building Python and Java applications from scratch with little to no guidance.

All exercises are preceded by a target state design diagram for the specific task at hand that details how any new logical components you build should work with the existing components you've already developed. Most are simple block diagrams that show the basic relationships among the components of the application.

 Many of the diagrams are not designed to fit into a specific documentation methodology and show only a high-level view of the components and their basic interactions. Some diagrams do require additional specificity, and in such cases I include one or more Unified Modeling Language (UML)–based class diagrams to clarify the intention of the design.[2]

How Is This Book Arranged?

This book will take you through building an end-to-end, full stack, and integrated IoT solution using various open source libraries and software components that you'll build step by step. Each component will be part of the larger system, and you'll see how the components interconnect with and map into an end-state architecture as you work through each chapter's exercises.

In each chapter, I'll provide a brief introduction to that chapter's topic along with some helpful background material, which will include some pertinent definitions. I'll also summarize why the topic is important and what you can expect to learn, and that will be followed by programming exercises relevant to the topic. Many chapters end

---

2 The Appendix provides a basic UML representation for each exercise. The latest UML specification can be found on the Object Management Group (OMG) website (*https://www.omg.org/spec/UML*).

with additional exercises you can choose to implement as well, further cementing your knowledge of the chapter's topic.

I have grouped like chapters together and have used this scheme to establish the four parts of the book: Part I, "Getting Started"; Part II, "Connecting to the Physical World"; Part III, "Connecting to Other Things"; and Part IV, "Connecting to the Cloud". I'll discuss each part and chapter in a bit more detail here and then provide some background on the IoT itself.

Each part or chapter begins with a haiku that attempts to capture the essence of what you'll learn and some of the challenges you'll likely encounter. How did this come to be? In my early days as a software developer, one of the teams I worked with had a policy: if you committed code that caused the nightly build to break, you had to write a haiku related to the issue and email it to everyone on the team. While you probably won't encounter many broken nightly builds as you work through the exercises in this book, you should feel free to write your own haiku as you make and learn from your mistakes!

Part I, "Getting Started"

In this section, we build our initial foundation for IoT development. You'll start by creating a development and testing environment and then wrap up the section by writing two simple applications to validate that your environment is working properly.

- Chapter 1, "Getting Started" is the longest chapter in the book. It lays the foundation for your end-to-end solution and will help you establish a baseline of IoT knowledge. It will also guide you in setting up your workstation and development environment so you can be productive as quickly as possible. In this chapter, I cover some basic IoT terms, create a simple problem statement, define core architectural concepts, and establish an initial design approach that I'll reference as the framework for each subsequent exercise.

 The IoT consists of a plethora of heterogeneous devices and systems, and there are many tools and utilities available to support development and system automation. I use open source tools and utilities throughout the book. These represent a small subset of what is available to you and shouldn't be taken as carte blanche recommendations; you may have your own preferences. My goals are simply to keep the content well-bounded and inform a generalized development and automation approach that will help you implement the exercises successfully.

- Chapter 2, "Initial Edge Tier Applications" covers setting up your development environment and your approach to capturing requirements and then moves into coding. Here you'll create your first two IoT applications—one in Python and the other in Java. These are quite simple but set the stage for subsequent chapters. Even if you're an experienced developer, it's important to work through the exercises as given so we're working from the same baseline going forward.

Part II, "Connecting to the Physical World"

This section covers a fundamental characteristic of the IoT—integration with the physical world. While the exercises focus on simulation and hardware emulation, the principles you'll learn—how to read sensor data and trigger an actuator (virtually)—will be helpful should you decide to use real hardware in the future.

- Chapter 3, "Data Simulation" explores ways you can collect data from the physical world (sensing) and trigger actions based on that data (actuation) using simulation. You'll start by building a set of simple simulators, which you'll continue using throughout each subsequent exercise. While very basic in design, these simulators will help you better understand the principles of collecting data and using that data to trigger actuation events.

- Chapter 4, "Data Emulation" expands the simulation functionality you developed in Chapter 3 to emulate sensor and actuator behavior. This chapter remains centered in the virtual world through the use of an open source hardware emulator you can run on your development workstation.

- Chapter 5, "Data Management" discusses telemetry and data formatting, including ways to structure your data so both humans and machines can store, transmit, and understand it easily. This will serve as the foundation for your interoperability with other "things."

Part III, "Connecting to Other Things"

This is where the rubber meets the road. Part III focuses on integration across devices: to be truly integrated, you'll need a way to get your telemetry and other information from one place to another. You'll learn about and utilize application layer protocols designed for IoT ecosystems. I'll assume your networking layer is already in place and working, although I'll discuss a few wireless protocols along the way.

- Chapter 6, "MQTT Integration–Overview and Python Client" introduces publish/subscribe protocols—specifically, Message Queuing Telemetry Transport (MQTT), which is commonly used in IoT applications. I'll walk through a select set of specification details and explain how you can begin building out a simple abstraction layer that allows you to easily interface with common open source libraries, beginning with Python.

- Chapter 7, "MQTT Integration–Java Client" continues to build on your knowledge of MQTT by digging into an open source library that allows you to connect your Java applications to an MQTT server. You'll use this protocol in the exercises and tests you'll run at the end of the chapter to integrate with the Python code you developed in Chapter 6.

- Chapter 8, "CoAP Server Implementation" focuses on request/response protocols —specifically, the Constrained Application Protocol (CoAP), also commonly used in IoT applications. The big difference here is that you'll start with Java and build a CoAP server using another open source library. Optional exercises are also provided to build a CoAP server in Python.

- Chapter 9, "CoAP Client Integration" continues with CoAP but focuses on building the client code you'll use to connect to your newly developed Java server. This client code, written in both Python and Java, will enable you to support device-to-device communications using CoAP as the protocol.

- Chapter 10, "Edge Integration" centers on integration, enabling you to connect your two applications to each other using either MQTT or CoAP. I'll include exercises for each protocol, which will help you decide which one may be most relevant for your solution. Much like Chapter 9, this chapter will require implementation work in both Python and Java.

Part IV, "Connecting to the Cloud"

Finally, at the "top" of the integration stack, you'll learn how to connect all your IoT device infrastructure to the cloud by using your gateway application as a go-between for your cloud functionality and all your devices.

This section covers basic cloud connectivity principles and touches on various cloud services that can store, analyze, and manage your IoT environment. You'll build the same simple cloud application across each platform.

- Chapter 11, "Integrating with Various Cloud Services" discusses the key concepts of connecting your IoT solution into the cloud and explores various cloud-integration exercises you can implement using the MQTT protocol. Since there are many books and tutorials available for these platforms, I'll simply review these capabilities rather than going into detail on building anything specific. The exercises help you choose which cloud platform you'd like to use in your own implementation.

- Chapter 12, "Taming the IoT" examines the key enablers of an IoT solution and maps these into a few simple IoT use cases that I've found particularly helpful to preparing my Connected Devices course. I'll cover the overall problem statement, expected outcome, and high-level notional design approach.

My hope is that this book's approach will allow you to understand and create an integrated IoT system, end to end.

Some Background on the IoT

Here's a brief summary of how the IoT got to this point.

Computing took a big step forward with the invention of the transistor in the 1950s, followed in the 1960s by Gordon Moore's paper describing the doubling of transistors packed in the same physical space (later updated in the 1970s).[3]

With modern computing came modern networking, and the beginnings of the internet, with the invention of the ARPAnet in 1969.[4] This led in the 1970s to new ways to *chunk* or packetize data using the Network Control Protocol (NCP) and Transmission Control Protocol (TCP) via the Internet Protocol (IP) and leveraging existing wired infrastructure. This was useful for industry, allowing electrical industrial automation to move down the path of centralized management of distributed, connected systems. Supervisory Control and Data Acquisition (SCADA) systems—ancestors of machine-to-machine (M2M) technologies that led to the IoT—emerged from their proprietary roots, and programmable logic controllers (PLCs)—initially invented just prior to the ARPAnet—evolved to take advantage of TCP/IP networking and related equipment standards.[5]

The 1980s introduced the User Datagram Protocol (UDP)[6] and the birth of what many of us experienced as the early modern internet—the World Wide Web (WWW), invented in the late 1980s by Tim Berners-Lee.[7]

This time period has also been an important enabler for what would eventually be known as the Industrial Internet of Things (IIoT), a subset of the IoT and an important part of the IoT's evolution.

---

3 *Encyclopaedia Britannica Online*, s.v. "Moore's law" (*https://oreil.ly/6sqQr*), by the editors of *Encyclopaedia Britannica*, last updated December 26, 2019.

4 *Encyclopaedia Britannica Online*, s.v. "ARPANET" (*https://oreil.ly/tHVZq*), by Kevin Featherly, last updated March 23, 2021.

5 Simon Duque Antón et al., "Two Decades of SCADA Exploitation: A Brief History" (*https://doi.org/10.1109/AINS.2017.8270432*), in *2017 IEEE Conference on Application, Information and Network Security (AINS)* (New York: IEEE, 2017), 98–104.

6 John Postel, "User Datagram Protocol" (*https://tools.ietf.org/html/rfc768*), Internet Standard RFC 768, August 28, 1980.

7 For further reading on Tim Berners-Lee's WWW proposal, please see *https://www.w3.org/History/1989/proposal.html*.

I'm sure you've noticed a common theme: a problem is followed by a technology innovation (often proprietary) to address the challenge, which then becomes standardized or is superseded by one or more standards, leading to wide adoption and further innovation.

This brings us to the era of the IoT. In the 1980s and early 1990s, the first connected devices emerged, including an internet-connected toaster demonstrated by John Romkey and Simon Hackett at Interop 1990.[8] In 1991, users of the computer lab near the Trojan Room at the University of Cambridge set up a web camera to monitor the coffeepot— because who wants to make a trip only to find the pot empty?[9]

More devices followed, of course, and I'd guess even more were built and connected as experiments in college labs, dorms, homes, apartments, and businesses. All the while, computing and networking continued to become more inexpensive, powerful, and of course smaller. Kevin Ashton is widely believed to have coined the phrase *Internet of Things* in 1999, when he presented on the topic at Proctor & Gamble.[10]

Fast-forward to 2005, when the Interaction Design Institute Ivrea in Italy gave us the inexpensive, designed-for-novices Arduino single-board computer (SBC),[11] opening the door for more people to build their own sensing and automation systems. Add easily accessible storage and the ability to analyze data through services reachable from anywhere on the internet, and you have the underpinnings of an IoT ecosystem: that is, a lot of individually unique things that can be connected to each other to serve a larger purpose.

Yet to view the IoT as a bunch of things that connect the physical world to the internet does not do the IoT justice. I believe the essence of the IoT, and a key driver behind its complexity, is *heterogeneity*: dissimilarity and wide variation among device types, features and capabilities, purposes, implementation approaches, supported protocols, security, and management techniques.

Complexity Redefined

So, what exactly is the Internet of Things? It's a complex set of technology ecosystems that connect the physical world to the internet using a variety of edge computing devices and cloud computing services.

---

8 See an explanation at "The Internet Toaster" (*https://oreil.ly/VxRcP*).

9 *Encyclopaedia Britannica Online*, "Know Your Joe: 5 Things You Didn't Know About Coffee" (*https://oreil.ly/j7pVk*) (2. The Watched Pot), by Alison Eldridge, accessed January 18, 2021.

10 Kevin Ashton, "That 'Internet of Things' Thing" (*https://oreil.ly/BqzmG*), *RFID Journal*, June 22, 2009.

11 You can read a brief summary of the Arduino's birth in the Computer History Museum's Timeline of Computer History (*https://oreil.ly/Qv6AW*).

For the purposes of this book, we'll use some slightly simplified definitions. *Edge computing devices* refers to the embedded electronics, computing systems, and software applications that either interact directly with the physical world through sensors and actuators or provide a *gateway*, or bridge, for those devices and applications to connect to the internet. *Cloud computing services* refers to computing systems, software applications, data storage, and other computing services that live within one or more data centers and are always accessible via the internet.

Going forward, I'll refer to these two areas by their representative *architectural tier*—that is, *Cloud Tier* for cloud computing services, and *Edge Tier* for edge computing devices. Architectural tiers separate the key functionality of an IoT system both physically and logically—meaning, for example, that all sensing and actuation take place in the Edge Tier, and all long-term storage and complex analytics take place in the Cloud Tier.

 For those interested in a deeper study of architecture and related standards, there are many organizations actively participating in and publishing content related to these areas. A few to start with are:

- The European Telecommunications Standards Institute (ETSI) (*https://www.etsi.org*), a Europe-based standardization organization

- The International Telecommunication Union (ITU) (*https://www.itu.int/en/Pages/default.aspx*), the United Nations' agency for information and communication technologies

- The Internet Engineering Task Force (IETF) (*https://www.ietf.org*), a global internet standards body

- The Industry IoT Consortium (IIC) (*https://www.iiconsortium.org*), an organization of businesses and organizations focused on the IIoT

The IIC has published a variety of useful documents. Of particular interest is the *Industrial Internet Reference Architecture*, which discusses a framework and common vocabulary for IIoT systems and has heavily influenced my thinking on the topic of IoT architecture.[12]

---

12 *The Industrial Internet of Things, Volume G1: Reference Architecture* (*https://www.iiconsortium.org/IIRA.htm*), Version 1.9 (Needham, MA: Industrial Internet Consortium, 2019).

Creating Value

The real value in any IoT system is its ability to provide an improved or enhanced outcome via integration of the physical and logical worlds and the collection and analysis of time-series data.

Let's take a simple example from an appliance-laden residential kitchen. If, for example, I can measure the inside temperature of a refrigerator every minute, I can determine how long the items stored in the refrigerator have been exposed to a given temperature. If I sample the inside temperature only once a day, I don't have adequate detail to make that determination.

Of course, if other systems can't understand the data I collect, it's pretty much useless. Although individually each part may be unique and not dependent on another part, building integratable IoT solutions requires you, as the developer, to think carefully about how their design (and data) for each part of an IoT system might interact with other systems (and other developers).

Another key part of the value chain is *scalability*. It's one thing to build a system that supports a handful of inputs but another thing altogether to handle thousands, millions, or even billions of inputs. Scalability—the ability of a system to handle as much or as little information as we want—is what gives the IoT its true power. For example, a scalable cloud system that supports the IoT is one that can handle a single gateway device sending it data, or thousands (or millions or billions) of inputs, without failing.

It's probably clear by now that in building an integrated IoT system, you will need to deal with significant nuances at each step. You can't expect plug 'n' play or even consistent behaviors from the systems that send you data. What's more, even if you try to write your code generically enough to function the same way from one hardware device to another, it might not always work across every platform.

 It's not possible for one book to cover all specialized platforms, nor is it easy to write consistent, semi-low-level code at the device level that doesn't need to be optimized for every device. While every device may have differences that we need to account for when we create (and test) our solutions, the code samples I provide in this book are portable (with some minor exceptions) and usable across most systems that can run a Java Virtual Machine or Python 3 interpreter.

Living on the Edge

With all the power and flexibility of the Cloud Tier, an IoT solution generally exhibits the greatest complexity at the edge, which is where most (and often all) of the system's heterogeneity lives. The two categories of devices this book will focus on are constrained devices and gateway devices.

To grossly oversimplify: *constrained devices* have some power, communications, and processing limitations, whereas *gateway devices* generally do not.

I'm leaving out the nomenclature of "smart devices" on purpose, since it's becoming less clear how to best define "smart" versus "not-so-smart" devices.

One way to view a constrained device is as a low-power (sometimes battery-operated) SBC that either reads data from the environment (such as temperature, pressure, or humidity) or triggers a mechanical action (such as opening or closing a valve).

The IETF provides detailed definitions and terminology for various "Constrained Devices or Nodes" in RFC 7228.[13] It is *not* the intent of this book to alter these definitions in any way—I simply use the terms *constrained device* and *constrained device app* to separate the intended functionality of the constrained device from the gateway device, while implying the nature of each type of device (in short, that the former has more technical limitations than the latter).

A gateway device may also be implemented as an SBC but is much more powerful: it can communicate with many different constrained devices and has enough processing power to aggregate the data from these other devices, perform some analytics functions, and determine when (and how) to send any relevant data to the cloud for further storage and processing.

Figure P-1 envisions a notional IoT systems architecture that represents the relationships between these device types within the Edge Tier and the services and other functionality that live within the Cloud Tier.

---

13 Carsten Bormann, Mehmet Ersue, and Ari Keränen, "Terminology for Constrained-Node Networks" (*https://tools.ietf.org/html/rfc7228*), IETF Informational RFC 7228, May 2014, 8–10.

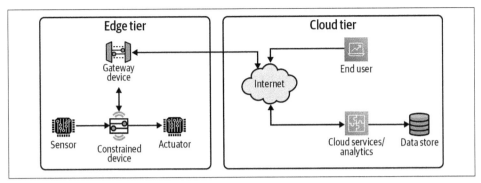

Figure P-1. Notional IoT system architecture

For the purposes of this book, I'll qualify these devices as follows:

- Gateway devices focus primarily on processing, interpreting, and integrating edge data and interacting with the cloud. They perform "at the edge" analytics, convert and/or transform protocol stacks, determine how messages should be routed (if at all), and, of course, connect directly to the internet and the various cloud services that make the IoT useful for business stakeholders.

- Constrained devices handle only sensing and/or actuation and control while processing messages for themselves, passing messages along if the right communications protocol is implemented, and sending messages to a gateway device. In short, their abilities are limited, and they may not be able to connect directly to the internet, relying instead on a gateway device for cloud connectivity.

Can a constrained device connect directly to the internet? Sure, if it contains a TCP/IP stack, has a routable IP address that's accessible to and from the public internet, and has the appropriate communications hardware to talk to the internet.

For the purposes of this book, however, I'll narrow the category of constrained devices to these two limitations:

- They do not support packet routing directly to or from the public internet (although let's assume they support both TCP/IP and UDP/IP) and must interact with a gateway device to be part of any IoT ecosystem.

- They do not contain adequate computing resources to intelligently determine complex courses of action based on the data they collect.

I'll focus on the "constrained device to gateway device to cloud connection" paradigm throughout the book, although there are other viable edge computing models that may be more suitable for your specific use case.

Conclusion

What it all means is this: as we make better computing devices that are smaller, faster, and cheaper, use them to interact with the physical world, and connect them (or their data) to the internet for processing using cloud services, we can derive insights that help deliver better business outcomes.

Thanks for reading!

Conventions Used in This Book

The following typographical conventions are used in this book:

Italic

Indicates new terms, URLs, email addresses, filenames, and file extensions.

`Constant width`

Used for program listings, as well as within paragraphs to refer to program elements such as variable or function names, databases, data types, environment variables, statements, and keywords.

`Constant width bold`

Shows commands or other text that should be typed literally by the user.

`Constant width italic`

Shows text that should be replaced with user-supplied values or by values determined by context.

This element signifies a tip or suggestion.

This element signifies a general note.

This element indicates a warning or caution.

Using Code Examples

Supplemental material (code examples and documentation templates) can be found online at *https://github.com/programming-the-iot*. The code samples in this book are licensed under the MIT License (*https://www.mit.edu/~amini/LICENSE.md*).

If you have a technical question or a problem using the code examples, please send email to *bookquestions@oreilly.com*.

This book is here to help you get your job done. In general, if example code is offered with this book, you may use it in your programs and documentation. You do not need to contact us for permission unless you're reproducing a significant portion of the code. For example, writing a program that uses several chunks of code from this book does not require permission. Selling or distributing examples from O'Reilly books does require permission. Answering a question by citing this book and quoting example code does not require permission. Incorporating a significant amount of example code from this book into your product's documentation does require permission.

We appreciate, but generally do not require, attribution. An attribution usually includes the title, author, publisher, and ISBN. For example: "*Programming the Internet of Things* by Andy King (O'Reilly). Copyright 2021 Andrew D. King, 978-1-492-08141-8."

If you feel your use of code examples falls outside fair use or the permission given above, feel free to contact us at *permissions@oreilly.com*.

O'Reilly Online Learning

For more than 40 years, *O'Reilly Media* has provided technology and business training, knowledge, and insight to help companies succeed.

Our unique network of experts and innovators share their knowledge and expertise through books, articles, and our online learning platform. O'Reilly's online learning platform gives you on-demand access to live training courses, in-depth learning paths, interactive coding environments, and a vast collection of text and video from O'Reilly and 200+ other publishers. For more information, visit *http://oreilly.com*.

How to Contact Us

Please address comments and questions concerning this book to the publisher:

O'Reilly Media, Inc.
1005 Gravenstein Highway North
Sebastopol, CA 95472
800-889-8969 (in the United States or Canada)
707-829-7019 (international or local)
707-829-0104 (fax)
support@oreilly.com
https://www.oreilly.com/about/contact.html

We have a web page for this book, where we list errata, examples, and any additional information. You can access this page at *https://oreil.ly/programming-the-IoT*.

For news and information about our books and courses, visit *http://oreilly.com*.

Find us on Facebook: *http://facebook.com/oreilly*

Follow us on Twitter: *http://twitter.com/oreillymedia*

Watch us on YouTube: *http://youtube.com/oreillymedia*

Acknowledgments

I think we're all on a perpetual path of finding ourselves, whether through career, connection, or missional work. The specific twists and turns God has led me through, and the mentors and companions He's put in my life, represent the window through which I've experienced His love for me. It goes without saying that this book would never have happened if it weren't for the patience, critiques, encouragement, and expertise of family, friends, and colleagues who were willing to join me on this journey. I'll attempt to acknowledge everyone who's influenced me and impacted this writing, but I'm afraid I'll inadvertently miss some callouts. Please forgive any unintended oversights.

I started programming at the age of 12 or so, after my dad brought home an Atari 400 that a friend had lent him. After digging into BASIC for a bit (and losing all my work after each power cycle), my parents bought me my own Atari 800XL with tape storage (remember that?), which we subsequently upgraded to 5¼" floppy disk storage and eventually enhanced with a blazingly fast 1200 Kbps modem. Thanks, Mom and Dad. Dad...wish you were still here with us.

Fast-forward 25 years, and I (eventually) became a programmer and computer scientist. But how did this project start? My friend Jimmy Song, author of *Programming*

Bitcoin (O'Reilly), connected me to the O'Reilly Media team after I reached out one day and said, "I'm thinking of writing a book..." I truly appreciate Jimmy's candid advice, feedback, and encouragement throughout this journey.

Of course, the genesis of this book's lab module content is my Connected Devices course at Northeastern University. As such, I am very fortunate to work with some amazing colleagues in academia, such as Dr. Peter O'Reilly, Director of the Cyber Physical Systems program at Northeastern University's College of Engineering, who brought me onboard to teach Connected Devices. Dr. Rolando Herrero, also from Northeastern, was one of the earliest reviewers of the book's content. His expert knowledge of IoT systems and protocols was immensely helpful in shaping the form and function of the material. Working with both Peter and Rolando as friends and colleagues on building an IoT discipline has been one of the highlights of my career, and I'm deeply thankful to both for their mentorship.

To all the Connected Devices graduate students I've had the privilege to teach and collaborate with, a huge thank you! The content in this book and the exercises in each chapter have been inspired by your feedback, suggestions, requests, commentary, and tolerance of my silly dad jokes. You are the primary reason this book came to fruition and are why I get to live my passion for teaching (and not as a stand-up comedian).

Many of the teaching assistants for the course provided book commentary and review and helped me address disconnects between the prose and online exercises. A heartfelt thank you to these amazing colleagues: Cheng Shu, Ganeshram Kanakasabai, Harsha Vardhanram Kalyanaraman, Jaydeep Shah, Yogesh Suresh, and Yuxiang Cao. I am glad to have worked with each of them and deeply appreciate their contributions to the course's success.

Some of my industry friends and colleagues provided detailed feedback and commentary on the pre-final draft. Tim Strunck, an expert in commercial IoT solutions engineering, provided a rich set of feedback on overall flow and technical content—I'm grateful for his friendship and keen insights, along with the amazing Foreword to this book. Steve Resnick, Managing Director at a large consulting firm and author of two books of his own, shared his executive perspective and advice on flow, form, and content, helping me to provide further clarity on key concepts. Ben Pu provided a fresh set of eyes on the overall book, which helped me view it through a lens that enabled me to connect with future readers. I'm thankful to have a network that includes professionals like Tim, Steve, and Ben, and I'm very appreciative of their quick-turn feedback and inputs.

To all my colleagues and friends at O'Reilly Media—wow, what a team! Mike Loukides, VP and Intake Editor, who spent hours on video conferences, emails, and phone calls and helped shape the proposal and get it through the intake process. Melissa Duffield, VP of Content Strategy, who worked with me on the marketing angle and pushed it through the green-lighting process in record time. Cassandra

Furtado, who patiently responded to all my initial questions. Chris Faucher, who transformed my manuscript into a book. Virginia Wilson, who helped manage the schedule and tech review process. Arthur Johnson, who, as copyeditor, caught and corrected many prose and formatting consistency foibles. And of course, Sarah Grey, who, as Development Editor, helped me think through the organization of the material and make it real. I have tremendous respect for each of them, and for their professionalism, support, responsiveness, and comradery throughout this project.

A great deal of open source software and open specifications were used in the preparation of this book, its examples, and exercises. I'd like to thank the developers of and contributors to each of these projects.

Most of all, thanks to my wonderful wife, Yoon-Hi, and incredible son, Eliot: you two are the rocks in my life, and I don't know how I would've even started down this path without your encouragement and support. Thank you for all the reviews, wordsmithing conversations (and edits), challenges, support, and belief! You pulled me out of valleys and pushed me up hills. You're both amazing, and I love you more than I can possibly express.

## PART I

Getting Started

Introduction

I must move forward.
However, where do I start?
First things first—setup.

The preface introduced some basic IoT principles and concepts but probably left much to be desired in terms of what the IoT is, how it works, and what you can do about it. This section won't explain everything there is to know about the IoT as an ecosystem of widely divergent devices and capabilities; instead, I'll focus on a basic set of core concepts to help you create a mental map of how the IoT can help you solve a variety of problems.

The process I'll walk through in this section and use throughout the book is the same one I use to help my students better understand the IoT and—perhaps most importantly—how to build a simple, end-to-end IoT solution, from device to cloud.

What You'll Learn in This Section

Chapters 1 and 2 are focused on three primary topics: (1) problem definition and functional categorization, (2) development environment setup, and (3) building the initial edge tier applications. You'll learn about each of these as I define a simple IoT problem, create an architecture baseline to address the problem, and discuss the design philosophy that will drive the suggested implementation path. That path begins with the construction of two simple applications: the gateway device application and the constrained device application. Ready? Let's get started.

## CHAPTER 1

Getting Started

IoT Basics and Development Environment Setup

A path lies ahead,
Brambles and thorns, then it clears.
Almost there. Patience.

> **Fundamental concepts**: Identify a problem area to tackle and define an architecture as the baseline for your IoT solution; set up an IoT-centric development environment that supports multiple deployment options.

You've likely gathered by now that the Internet of Things can be vast, unwieldy, and very difficult to tame. To plan a way forward, we'll first want to identify a problem area to tackle and then create an architecture from which to design and build our IoT solution.

Let's start with a few key questions to establish a baseline: What problem are you trying to solve? Where does it start and end? Why does it require an IoT ecosystem? How will all of the pieces work together to solve this problem? What outcome can you expect if everything works as designed? We'll explore each of these questions in detail, and along the way we'll construct an end-to-end, integrated IoT solution that meets our needs.

What You'll Learn in This Chapter

To help you really understand how an IoT system can and should be constructed, I'll dig into some basic architectural concepts based on the preceding questions and use this as the basis for each programming activity. From there, you'll build a solution that addresses the problem layer by layer, adding more functionality as you work through each subsequent chapter.

It goes without saying, of course, that the right development tools will likely save you time and frustration, not to mention help you with testing, validation, and deployment. There are many excellent open source and commercial development tools and frameworks available to support you.

If you've been a developer for any length of time, I expect you have your own specific development environment preferences that best suit your programming style and approach. I certainly have mine, and while the examples I present will be based on my preferred set of tools, my goal in this chapter is not to specify those you must use but to help you ramp up IoT development in a way that enables you to move out quickly and eventually choose your own tools for future development projects.

The concepts I present will be what matter most; the programming languages, tools (and their respective versions), and methods can be changed. These concepts represent some of the fundamentals of consistent software development: system design, coding, and testing.

Defining Your System

Creating a problem statement is probably the most important part of this puzzle. Let's start by drafting something that is reasonably straightforward but is enough to encompass a variety of interesting IoT challenges:

> I want to understand the environment in my home, how it changes over time, and make adjustments to enhance comfort while saving money.

Seems simple enough, but this is a very broad goal. We can narrow it down by defining the key actions and objects in our problem statement. Our goal is to isolate the *what*, *why*, and *how*. Let's first look at the *what* and the *why* and then identify any action(s) that the design should consider as part of this process.

Breaking Down the Problem

The exercises in this book will focus on building an IoT solution that can help you understand your home environment and respond appropriately. The assumption is that you'll want to know what's going on within your house (within reason) and take some sort of action if it's warranted (for example, turn on the air conditioning if the temperature is too hot).

This part of your design approach considers three key activities:

Measure: Collect data

Let's define this in terms of what can be sensed, like temperature, humidity, and so on. This is centered on the capture and transmission of *telemetry* (measurement data). The action—or rather, the action category—will be named *data collection* and will include the following data items (you can add more later):

- Temperature
- Relative Humidity
- Barometric Pressure
- System Performance (utilization metrics for CPU, memory, storage)

Model: Determine relevant changes from a given baseline

To decide which data is relevant and whether or not a change in value is important, we need not only to collect data but also to store and trend time-series data on the items we can sense (like temperature, humidity, etc., as indicated in the preceding definition). This is typically known as *data → information conversion*. I'll refer to this category as *data management*.

Manage: Take action

We'll establish some basic rules to determine whether we've crossed any important thresholds, which simply means we'll send a signal to something if a threshold is crossed that requires some type of action (for instance, turning a thermostat up or down). This is typically known as *information → knowledge conversion*. I'll refer to this category as *system triggers*.

In my university IoT course, I talk about Measure, Model, and Manage often. To me, they represent the core aspects of any IoT design that ultimately drive toward achieving the system's specified business objectives, or outcomes.

Defining Relevant Outcomes

Now that we know what steps we need to take, let's explore the *why* portion of our problem statement. We can summarize this using the following two points:

- *Increase comfort:* Ideally, we'd like to maintain a consistent temperature and humidity in our living environment. Things get a bit more complicated when we consider the number of rooms, how they're used, and so forth. I refer to this action category as *configuration management*, and it goes hand in hand with both data management and system triggers.

- *Save money:* This gets a bit tricky. The most obvious way to save money is to not spend it! Since we'll likely need to allocate financial resources to heat, cool, or humidify a given area, we want to optimize—not too much (wasteful), and not too little (we could end up with frozen water pipes in the winter). Since we might have some complexity to deal with here—including utility costs, seasonal changes, and so on, as well as anything related to configuration management—we'll probably need some more advanced analytics to handle these concerns. I'll call this action category *analytics*.

You've likely noticed that each step in the *what* and *why* sections has an action category name that will help with the solution design once we move on to the *how*. As a reminder, these categories are data collection, data management, system triggers, configuration management, and analytics. We'll dig further into each of these as part of our implementation approach.

Although the problem statement seems rather banal on the surface, it turns out that the things you'll need to do to address the problem are actually quite common within many IoT systems. There's a need to collect data at its source, to store and analyze that data, and to take action if some indicator suggests doing so would be beneficial. Once you define your IoT architecture and start building the components that implement it—even though it will be specific to this problem—you'll see how it can be applied to many other problem areas.

Let's take a quick look at a simple data flow that represents this decision process; in the data flow diagram depicted in Figure 1-1, each action category is highlighted.

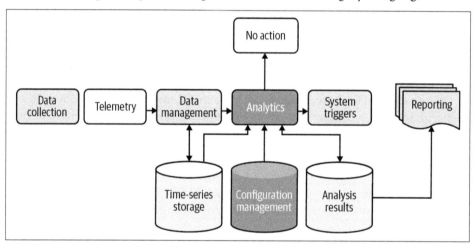

Figure 1-1. Simple IoT data flow

Most IoT systems will require at least some of the five action categories I've called out. This means we can define an architecture that maps these into a systems diagram and then start creating software components that implement part of the system.

This is where the fun starts for us engineers, so let's get going with an architecture definition that can support our problem statement (and will in fact be reusable for others).

Architecting a Solution

Organization, structure, and clarity are hallmarks of a good architecture, but too much can make for a rigid system that doesn't scale well for future needs. And if we try to establish an architecture that will meet all our plausible needs, we'll never finish (or perhaps never even get started)! It's about balance, so let's define the architecture with future flexibility in mind, but let's also keep things relatively well bounded. This will allow you to focus on getting to a solution quickly, while still permitting updates in the future. But first, there are a few key terms that need to be defined to help establish a baseline architectural construct to build your solution on.

As you may recall from Figure P-1 in the preface, IoT systems are generally designed with at least two (and sometimes three or more) architectural tiers in mind. This allows for the separation of functionality both physically and logically, which permits for flexible deployment schemes. All of this is to say that the cloud services running within the Cloud Tier can, technically speaking, be anywhere in the world, while the devices running within the Edge Tier must be in the same location as the physical systems that are to be measured. Just as Figure P-1 implies, an example of this tiering may include a constrained device with sensors or actuators talking to a gateway device, which in turn talks to a cloud-based service, and vice versa.

Since we need a place for these five categories of functionality to be implemented, it's important to identify their location within the architecture so we can have some things running close to where the action is, and others running in the cloud where you and I can access (and even tweak) the functionality easily. Recalling the Edge Tier and Cloud Tier architecture from the preface, let's see how to map each of the action categories from the *what* and *why* into each tier:

- Edge Tier (constrained devices and gateway devices): Data collection, data management, device triggers, configuration management, and analytics
- Cloud Tier (cloud services): Data management, configuration management, and analytics

Why do the Edge Tier and Cloud Tier include similar functionality? This is partly out of necessity, but also because, well, we can. The technical boundaries and separation of responsibilities between edge and cloud are becoming fuzzier as computing power increases and as business needs dictate "as close to the edge as possible" computation and analytics capabilities. For instance, some autonomous decisions may not require messages to traverse the internet out to the cloud and back again, as the Edge Tier can manage them directly (and should in some cases). So it's important to account for this capability whenever and wherever reasonable.

Figure 1-2 shows how the simple data flow from Figure 1-1 fits within a tiered architecture.

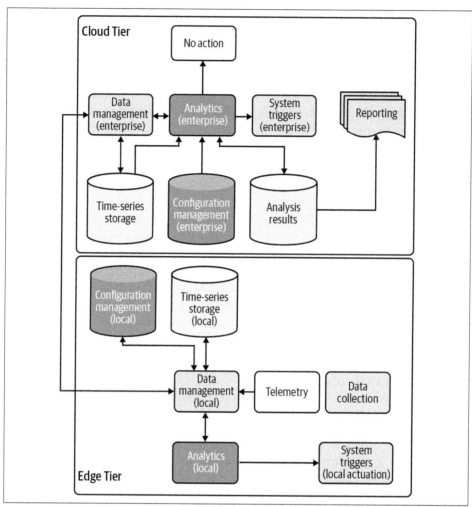

Figure 1-2. Notional IoT data flow between the Edge and Cloud Tiers

Again, notice that we have some shared responsibility, where some of the action categories are implemented within both tiers. Normally, duplication of effort is a bad thing—but in this case, it can be an advantage! Analytics can be used to determine whether a trigger should be sent to a device based on some basic settings—for example, if the temperature in your home exceeds 30°C, you'll probably want to trigger the HVAC straight away and start cooling things down to, say, 22°C. There's no need to depend on a remote cloud-based service in the Cloud Tier to do this, although it would be useful to notify the Cloud Tier that this is happening, and to perhaps store some historical data for later analysis.

Our architecture is starting to take shape. Now we just need a way to map it to a systems diagram so we can interact with the physical world (using sensors and actuators). It would also be good to structure things within the Edge Tier to avoid exposing components to the internet unnecessarily. This functionality can be implemented as an application that can run either directly on the device or on a laptop or other generic computing system with simulation logic that can emulate sensor and actuator behavior. This will serve as the basis for one of the two applications you'll develop, beginning in this chapter.

Since you'll want to access the internet eventually, your design should include a gateway to handle this need and other needs. This functionality can be implemented as part of a second application you'll begin developing in this chapter. This application will be designed to run on a gateway device (or, again, on a laptop or other generic computing system). Your Gateway Device Application and Constrained Device Application will comprise the "edge" of your IoT design, which I'll refer to as the Edge Tier of your architecture going forward.

You'll also want to deploy analytics services, storage capabilities, and event managers in a way that's secure but accessible from your gateway device and also by human beings. There are many ways to do this, although I'll focus on the use of one or more cloud services for much of this functionality.

Figure 1-3 provides a new view that will give further insight into what you're going to build and how you can begin incorporating the five action categories I mentioned. It represents, in grey boxes, cloud services within the Cloud Tier and the two applications within the Edge Tier that will contain the functionality of your constrained device and your gateway device, respectively.

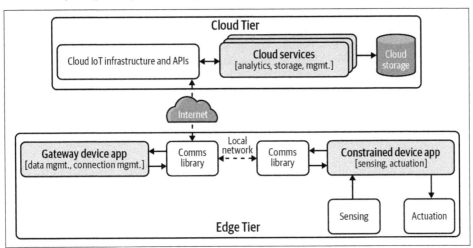

Figure 1-3. Notional IoT simplified logical architecture with Edge and Cloud Tiers

Let's dig into each a bit further:

Constrained Device Application (CDA)
You'll build this software application to run as part of a simulated constrained device within your development environment, and it will provide data collection and system triggers functionality. It will handle the interface between the device's sensors (which read data from the environment) and actuators (which trigger actions, such as turning the HVAC on or off). It will also play a role in taking action when an actuation is needed. Eventually, it will be connected to a communications library to send messages to, and receive messages from, the gateway device app.

Gateway Device Application (GDA)
You'll build this software application to run as part of a simulated gateway device within your development environment, and it will provide data management, analytics, and configuration management functionality. Its primary role is to manage data and the connections between the CDA and cloud services that exist within the Cloud Tier. It will manage data locally as appropriate and will *sometimes* take action by sending a command to the constrained device that triggers an actuation. It will also manage some of the configuration settings—that is, those that represent nominal ranges for your environment—and will perform some initial analytics when new telemetry is received.

Cloud services
All cloud services applications and functionality often do much of the heavy data processing and storage work, as they can theoretically scale ad infinitum. This simply means that, if they are designed well, you can add as many devices as you want, store as much data as you want, and do in-depth analysis of that data—trends, highs, lows, configuration values, and so on—all while passing any relevant insights along to a human end user, and perhaps even generating Edge Tier actions based on any defined threshold crossing(s). Technically, cloud services within an IoT environment can handle all the action categories previously mentioned, with the exception of data collection (meaning they don't perform sensing or actuation actions directly). You will build some cloud services to handle this functionality but mostly will utilize those generic services already available from some cloud service providers.

Putting it all together into a detailed logical architecture, Figure 1-4 shows how each major logical component within our two architectural tiers interacts with the other components.

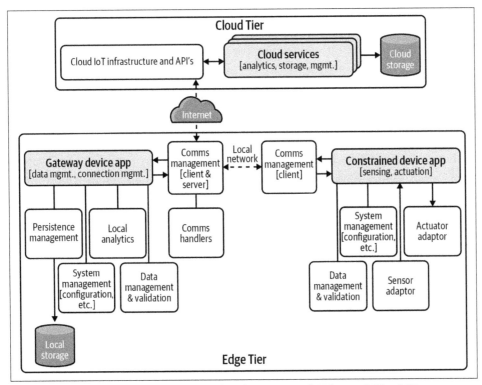

Figure 1-4. Notional IoT detailed logical architecture with Edge and Cloud Tiers

We'll use Figures 1-3 and 1-4 as our baseline architecture for all the exercises in this book.

Now that we have a handle on what we're up against, let's get our development environment set up so we can start slinging code.

Setting Up Your Development and Test Environment

Building and deploying code across different operating systems, hardware configurations, and configuration systems is no walk in the park. With typical IoT projects, we have to deal not only with different hardware components but also with the myriad ways to develop and deploy across these platforms, not to mention the various continuous integration/continuous deployment (CI/CD) idiosyncrasies of the various cloud service provider environments we often work within.

With all these challenges, how do we even get started? First things first—what problem are we trying to solve? As a developer, you want to implement your IoT design in code, test it, package it into something that can be easily distributed to one or more systems, and deploy it safely. We can think of our development challenges in terms of build, test, and deploy phases that also map into two architectural tiers: Edge Tier (telemetry generation and actuation) and Cloud Tier (remote compute infrastructure). I'll cover the functionality within the Cloud Tier later in Part IV, while Parts I, II and III will focus on the Edge Tier.

Although the Edge Tier of a typical IoT ecosystem could have specialized hardware to deal with, for our purposes, you can simulate much of the required system behavior, and even emulate some hardware components within your local development environment. This will make deployment much easier and is perfectly fine for all the required exercises in this book.

There are many ways to get up and running with IoT development. The exercises in this book focus on building an integrated simulated deployment approach, mentioned next. Hardware integration is completely optional, and is out of scope for the book, but will be very briefly referenced as an optional exercise in Chapter 4.

Integrated simulated deployment
> This approach doesn't require any specialized device and allows you to use your development workstation (laptop) as both gateway device and constrained device. This means you'll run your GDA and CDA in your local computing environment. You'll emulate your sensing and actuation hardware by building elementary software simulators to capture this functionality within your CDA. All of the book's required exercises, with the exception of the optional Chapter 4 exercises posted online (*https://oreil.ly/Zm4Po*), should be implementable using this deployment approach.

Separated physical deployment
> This requires a hardware device, such as a Raspberry Pi, that gives you the ability to connect to and interact with real sensors and actuators. Although many off-the-shelf single-board computing (SBC) devices can be used as full-blown computing workstations, I'll refer to this as your constrained device, and it will run your CDA directly on the device. As with the integrated simulated deployment approach, you'll run the GDA in your local computing environment.

As referenced in the preface, the IETF RFC 7228 document defines various classes of constrained devices (also referred to as *constrained nodes*). These classes include Class 0 (very constrained), Class 1 (constrained), and Class 2 (somewhat constrained).[1] For our purposes, we'll assume our CDA can run on Class 2 or even more powerful devices, which typically support full IP-based networking stacks, meaning the protocols we'll deal with in this book will generally work on these types of devices. Although it's technically feasible to connect Class 2 devices directly to the internet, all of the examples and exercises will interact indirectly with the internet via the GDA.

Blended physical deployment

This approach is nearly identical to the separated deployment approach but will run both your CDA and your GDA on the SBC device. This technically means you can choose to deploy each app to a different SBC, although it isn't necessary for any of the exercises listed.

While the exercises in the book focus on the integrated simulated deployment approach, if you choose either of the last two paths for your deployment, there are a wide range of inexpensive SBCs that may work for you. The only exercises in this book that require hardware are the optional exercises in Chapter 4, and while you could possibly implement these on other hardware platforms, they are designed with the following hardware in mind: Raspberry Pi Model 3 or 4 and the Sense HAT board (which connects to its general-purpose input/output [GPIO] and uses the Inter-Integrated Circuit [I2C] bus for device communications). If you select a different device for these exercises, you may want to consider one that includes the following: GPIO functionality, I2C, TCP/IP and UDP/IP networking via WiFi or Ethernet, support for a Linux-based operating system (such as Debian or a derivative), and support for both Python 3 and Java 11 (or higher).

The exercises in the book will focus on the integrated simulated deployment path. Part II introduces the concept of integration with the physical world, and I'll address some hardware integration concepts in Chapter 4 while maintaining focus on simulated data and emulated hardware.

Irrespective of the selected deployment path, all exercises and examples assume you'll do your development and deployment on a single workstation. This involves a three-step process that includes preparing your development environment, defining your testing strategy, and identifying a build and deployment automation approach. I'll cover the basics of these steps to get you started in this chapter but will also add to

---

1 Carsten Bormann, Mehmet Ersue, and Ari Keränen, "Terminology for Constrained-Node Networks" (*https://tools.ietf.org/html/rfc7228*), IETF Informational RFC 7228, May 2014, 8–10.

each as you dig into later exercises that have additional dependencies and testing and automation needs.

 You may already have experience developing applications in both Java and Python using your own development environment. If so, be sure to review the first step—preparation of your development environment—to ensure that your development environment, including your operating system, Java runtime, and Python interpreter, are all compatible with the exercise requirements.

Step I: Prepare Your Development Environment

Recall that your CDA will be written in Python, and your GDA will be written in Java. While this technically means that any OS supporting Python 3.7 or higher and Java 11 or higher may work for most exercises, there are some Linux-specific dependencies you should be aware of prior to setting up your development environment:

- Chapter 4: The hardware emulator I'll discuss in this chapter requires a Unix-based environment along with an X11 server to support its graphical user interface (GUI). Linux and macOS should work, whereas Windows will require Windows Subsystem for Linux (WSL)[2] plus an X11 server.

- Chapter 8: The Python-based CoAP[3] server is an optional exercise and has been partially tested with the Java client from Chapter 9 on Windows 10, macOS, and Linux. As of this writing, you'll probably need to run these tests within a Linux-based environment.

- Chapter 9: Some of the Python-based CoAP client exercises currently depend on Linux-specific bindings. As of this writing, you'll probably need to run these tests within a Linux-based environment.

Although I'll discuss setup for Linux, macOS, and Windows, I'd suggest you use Linux as your development environment to avoid some of the integration challenges I just mentioned. Be sure to read through PIOT-CFG-01-001 (*https://oreil.ly/PrtRU*) for more information on operating environment setup and library compatibility considerations. Many of the open source libraries the exercises depend on are actively maintained; however, this is not universally the case. Please be sure to check each library for the latest tested version, its license and usage, and its operating environment compatibility constraints.

---

2 Learn more about WSL and how to install it on your platform at *https://oreil.ly/YK9Rb*.

3 CoAP, or Constrained Application Protocol, is a messaging protocol that I'll discuss in Part III (specifically, in Chapters 8 and 9).

Most of my own development is done on Windows 10, with a majority of application execution and testing done using WSL with an Ubuntu 20.04LTS kernel. If you must use a non-Linux operating environment, you can still build your end-to-end IoT solution by skipping the exercises in Chapter 4, Chapter 8, and Chapter 9 and relying instead on the data simulators described in Chapter 3 and the MQTT[4] protocol for connectivity. Be sure to read through them all, however, as each will provide further insights into how to evolve your applications in the future.

You can make sure your workstation has the right stuff installed to support these languages and their associated dependencies by following these steps:

1. Ensure Python 3.7 or higher is installed on your workstation (the latest version as of this writing is 3.10, although my original development and testing was primarily done within WSL using Python 3.8.5). To check if it's already installed, do the following:

    a. Open a terminal or console window and type the following (be sure to use two dashes before the parameter)

        i. Linux/macOS:

            ```
            $ python3 --version
            ```

        ii. Windows:

            ```
            C:\programmingtheiot> python --version
            ```

    b. It should return output similar to the following:

        ```
        Python 3.8.5
        ```

    c. If the version returned is less than 3.7, or if you get an error (e.g., "not found"), you'll need to install Python 3.7 or higher. Follow the instructions for your operating system (Windows, macOS, Linux) at *https://www.python.org/downloads*.

In some cases, you may need to download the source code for Python and then build and install the executables. Check out the instructions at *https://devguide.python.org/setup/* if you need to go down this path. As a heads-up, this process may take a while.

---

4 MQTT, or Message Queuing Telemetry Transport, is a messaging protocol that I'll discuss in Part III (specifically, in Chapters 6 and 7).

2. Ensure pip is installed on your workstation. If not, you can install pip by down-loading the bootstrapping and installation script (*https://bootstrap.pypa.io/get-pip.py*). If you're using WSL or Ubuntu, you may need to install pip using the apt package manager.

    a. Open a terminal or console window and type the following (again using two dashes before the parameter):

    ```
    $ pip --version
    ```

    b. It should return output similar to the following:

    ```
    pip 21.0.1
    ```

    c. If pip is not installed, or if your version is out of date, use Python to execute the pip installation script. Type the following command:

        i. Linux/macOS:

        ```
        $ python3 get-pip.py
        ```

        ii. Windows:

        ```
        C:\programmingtheiot> python get-pip.py
        ```

3. Ensure Java 11 or higher is installed on your workstation (the latest version of OpenJDK as of this writing is JDK 18). You can check if it's already installed, or install it if not, using the following steps:

    a. Open a terminal or console window and type the following (there are two dashes before the parameter, although it will likely work with just one):

    ```
    $ java --version
    ```

    b. It should return something like the following (make sure it's at least Java 11):

    ```
    openjdk 14.0.2 2020-07-14
    OpenJDK Runtime Environment (build 14.0.2+12-Ubuntu-120.04)
    OpenJDK 64-Bit Server VM (build 14.0.2+12-Ubuntu-120.04, mixed mode,
    sharing)
    ```

    c. If you get an error (e.g., "not found"), you'll need to install Java 11 or higher. Follow the instructions for your platform (Windows, macOS, or Linux) on the OpenJDK website (*https://openjdk.java.net/install*).

4. Ensure Git is installed on your workstation. If not, you can install Git easily enough. Go to "Installing Git" (*https://oreil.ly/cmRX3*) and review the instructions for your specific operating system.

A prerequisite for any of the exercises in this book, and for setting up your development environment, is a basic understanding of Git, a source code management and versioning tool. Many IDEs come with source code management already enabled via an embedded Git client. In a previous step, you installed Git via the command line so that you can run Git commands independently of your IDE.

For more information on using Git from the command line, see the Git tutorial documentation (*https://git-scm.com/docs/gittutorial*).

 You can use Git as a stand-alone source code management tool on your local development workstation and manage your source code in the cloud using a variety of free and commercial services. GitHub[5] is the service I use to host the code repositories and latest exercise instructions (which also embed many of the solutions). Be sure to follow along with the book's Kanban board (*https://oreil.ly/programming-iot-kanban*) while you go through each exercise in this book, as it will contain the latest information.

5. Create a working development directory, and download the source code and unit tests for this book:

   a. Open a terminal or console window, create a new working development directory, and then change to that directory. Then type the following:

      i. Linux/macOS:

      ```
      mkdir $HOME/programmingtheiot
      cd $HOME/programmingtheiot
      ```

      ii. Windows:

      ```
      mkdir C:\programmingtheiot
      cd C:\programmingtheiot
      ```

   b. Clone the following two source code repositories for this book by typing the following (you can also simply clone the repositories from within the IDE):

      ```
      $ git clone https://github.com/programmingtheiot/python-components.git
      $ git clone https://github.com/programmingtheiot/java-components.git
      ```

6. Set up your Python environment. It's usually easiest, but not required, to use a virtual environment for isolating your Python dependencies and libraries.

   There are a handful of ways to establish a virtual execution environment for Python on your system, and my goal in this step isn't to discuss them all. Python 3.3 or higher provides a virtual environment module, so you don't have to install virtualenv unless that's your preferred approach for Python virtualization. You can read more about using the venv module at *https://docs.python.org/3/library/venv.html*.

   a. Create a virtual Python environment. Open a terminal or console window, change your directory to your desired virtual environment installation path

---

5 More information can be found on the GitHub website (*https://github.com*).

(for example, *$HOME/programmingtheiot/piotvenv*, although you can choose any directory you'd like), and create a virtual environment (venv) as follows:

    i. Linux/macOS:

```
$ python3 -m venv $HOME/programmingtheiot/piotvenv
```

    ii. Windows:

```
C:\programmingtheiot> python -m venv C:\programmingtheiot\piotvenv
```

b. Install the requisite Python modules. You can do this by typing the following:

    i. Linux/macOS:

```
$ cd $HOME/programmingtheiot
$ . piotvenv/bin/activate
(piotvenv) $ pip install -r ./python-components/requirements.txt
```

    ii. Windows:

```
cd C:\programmingtheiot
C:\programmingtheiot> piotvenv\Scripts\activate.bat
(piotvenv) C:\programmingtheiot>
pip install -r .\python-components\requirements.txt
```

c. Ensure your virtualenv can be activated. You can `activate` (using the activate script) and then `deactivate` virtualenv (using the deactivate command) from your command line easily enough:

    i. Linux/macOS:

```
$ . piotvenv/bin/activate
(piotvenv) $ deactivate
```

    ii. Windows:

```
C:\programmingtheiot> piotvenv\Scripts\activate.bat
(piotvenv) C:\programmingtheiot> deactivate
```

At this point, your development workstation is mostly configured. The next step is to configure your development environment and clone the sample source code for the book.

Configuring an integrated development environment (IDE)

There are many excellent tools and IDEs that help you, the developer, write, test, and deploy applications written in both Java and Python. There are tools that I'm very familiar with and work well for my development needs. My guess is you're much the same and have your own tool preferences. It doesn't really matter which toolset you use, provided the tools meet some basic requirements. For me, these include code highlighting and completion, code formatting and refactoring, debugging, compiling and packaging, unit and other testing, and source code control.

I developed the examples in this book using the Eclipse IDE (*https://www.eclipse.org/ide*) with PyDev (*https://oreil.ly/YjLFD*) installed, as it meets the requirements I've specified and provides a bunch of other convenient features that I regularly use in my development projects. You may be familiar with other IDEs, such as Visual Studio Code (*https://code.visualstudio.com*) and IntelliJ IDEA (*https://www.jetbrains.com/idea*), both of which also support Java and Python. The choice of IDE for the exercises in this book is, of course, completely up to you.

If you're already familiar with writing, testing, and managing software applications using a different IDE, most of this section will be old hat. I do recommend you read through it, however, as this section sets the stage for the development of your GDA and CDA.

Set up your Gateway Device Application project

The first step in this process is to install the latest Eclipse IDE for Java development. You can find the latest download links for Eclipse at *https://www.eclipse.org/downloads*. You'll notice that there are many different flavors of the IDE available. For our purposes, you can simply choose "Eclipse IDE for Java Developers." Then follow the instructions for installing the IDE onto your local system.

Once installed, launch Eclipse, select File → Import, find Git → "Projects from Git," and click Next.

Select "Existing local repository" and click Next. If you already have some Git repositories in your home path, Eclipse will probably pick them up and present them as options to import in the next dialog (not shown). To pull in the newly cloned repository, click Add, which will take you to the next dialog, shown in Figure 1-5. From here, you can add your new Git repository.

On my workstation, the repository I want to import is located at *E:\aking\programmingtheiot\java-components*. Yours will most likely have a different name, so be sure to enter it correctly! For Windows examples, I'll mostly stick with the path *C:\programmingtheiot*.

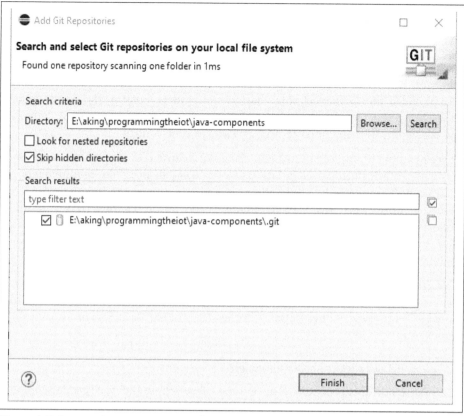

Figure 1-5. Import `java-components` *from your local Git repository*

Click Finish, and you'll see your new repository added to the list of repositories you can import. Highlight this new repository and click Next. Eclipse will then present you with another dialog and ask you to import the project using one of several options, as shown in Figure 1-6.

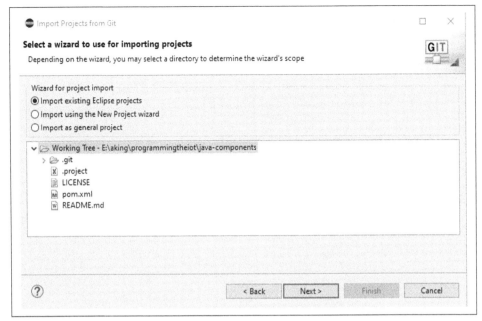

Figure 1-6. Import `java-components` *as an existing Eclipse project*

You now have a choice: you can import `java-components` as an existing Eclipse project using the new project wizard, or as a general project. Unless you want to fully customize your project environment, I'd recommend the first option—importing an existing Eclipse project. This process will look for a `.project` file in the working directory (which I've included in each of the repositories you've already cloned), resulting in a new Java project named `java-components`. If you'd prefer to create your own project, you can remove this and import as a new project using the appropriate wizard.

Click Finish, and you'll see your new project added to the list of projects in the Eclipse Package Explorer, which by default should be on the left side of your IDE screen. If you don't immediately see your project in the Package Explorer, simply change the IDE's perspective to 'Java' (or 'Python' for the CDA).

Your GDA project is now set up in Eclipse, so let's explore the files inside. Navigate to this project in Eclipse and click on the caret (>) symbol to expand it further, as shown in Figure 1-7.

Figure 1-7. GDA project now set up and ready for use

 What if you don't like the project name? No problem—you can right-click the `java-components` name, select Rename, type the new name, and click OK. Just know that I'll continue to refer to the project by the original name throughout the book :).

You'll notice that there are already a number of files included in the project—one is `GatewayDeviceApp` in the `programmingtheiot.gda.app` package, and the other one, at the top level, is called *pom.xml*. The `GatewayDeviceApp` is a placeholder to get you started, although you may replace it with your own. I'd recommend you keep the naming convention the same, however, as the *pom.xml* depends on this to compile, test, and package the code. If you know your way around Maven already, feel free to make any changes you'd like.

Bear in mind that if you plan on building your GDA from the command line, you'll need to install Maven (*https://maven.apache.org*) if it's not already installed in your environment.

For those of you less familiar with Maven, the *pom.xml* is Maven's primary configuration file and contains instructions for loading dependencies, their respective versions, naming conventions for your application, build instructions, and of course packaging instructions. Most of these dependencies are already included, although you may want to add your own if you find others to be useful. You'll also notice that Maven has its own default directory structure, which I've kept in place for the Java repository. To learn more about these and other Maven features, I'd recommend you walk through the five-minute Maven tutorial (*https://oreil.ly/oLetb*).

Now, to make sure your GDA development environment is setup properly, you can build and run the GDA from within the IDE (this has been tested within Eclipse). Simply do the following:

1. Make sure your workstation is connected to the internet.

2. Run your GDA application within Eclipse.

    a. Right-click on the project `java-components` again and scroll down to "Run As," and this time click "Java application."

    b. Check the output in the console at the bottom of the Eclipse IDE screen. The output similar to the following:

    ```
    Jul 04, 2020 3:10:49 PM programmingtheiot.gda.app.GatewayDeviceApp
    initConfig INFO: Attempting to load configuration.
    Jul 04, 2020 3:10:49 PM programmingtheiot.gda.app.GatewayDeviceApp
    startApp INFO: Starting GDA...
    Jul 04, 2020 3:10:49 PM programmingtheiot.gda.app.GatewayDeviceApp
    startApp INFO: GDA ran successfully.
    ```

If you choose to build the GDA and run it from the command line, you'll need to tell Maven to skip the tests, since they'll fail (as there's no implementation to test as of yet). Within a Linux shell, you can use the following command from within your GDA's top level source directory:

```
$ mvn install -DskipTests
```

At this point, you're ready to start writing your own code for the GDA. Now let's get your development workstation set up for the CDA.

Set up your Constrained Device Application project

This process will mimic the GDA setup process but requires the addition of PyDev to Eclipse. Here's a summary of activities to get you started.

If it's not already running, launch the Eclipse IDE. In a separate window or screen, open your web browser and navigate to the PyDev Python IDE for Eclipse download page (*https://oreil.ly/4Je1X*); drag the PyDev "Install" icon from the web page and drop it near the top of the Eclipse IDE (you'll see a green "plus" icon show up, which is the indicator that you can drop it into the IDE). Eclipse will then automatically install PyDev and its dependencies for you.

Once PyDev is installed, you can switch the Python interpreter to use the venv (or virtualenv) environment if you chose to create it in the previous section. Select Preferences → PyDev → Interpreters → "Python Interpreter." Eclipse will present a dialog similar to that shown in Figure 1-8.

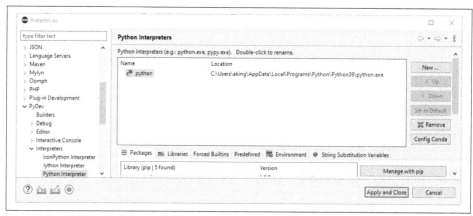

Figure 1-8. Add a new Python interpreter

Then add a new interpreter using the "Browse for python/pypy.exe" selection and provide the relevant information in the next pop-up window. Once complete, select the venv (or virtualenv) interpreter and click Up until it's at the top of the list. At this point, venv (or virtualenv) will be your default Python interpreter, as Figure 1-9 indicates.

Click "Apply and Close."

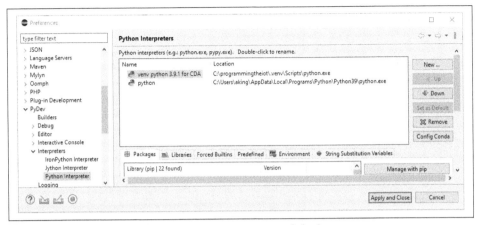

Figure 1-9. Virtualenv Python interpreter now set as default

Once these steps are complete, select File → Import and import the python-components Git repository you've already cloned from GitHub. Again, this is nearly identical to the previous steps shown in Figures 1-5, 1-6, and 1-7, except you'll import the python-components Git repository you cloned from GitHub.

On my workstation, the repository I want to import is located at:

C:\programmingtheiot\python-components

As with the GDA, your repository name will likely be different, so be sure to use the correct path. I've also included the Eclipse .project file within this repository, so you can import it as an Eclipse project. This one will default to Python, so it will use PyDev as the project template. Again, you can import any way you'd like, but my recommendation is to import it as you did with the GDA.

Once you complete the import process, you'll notice a new project in your Package Explorer named python-components. You now have the CDA components set up in your Eclipse IDE.

To view the files inside, navigate to python-components and click on the caret (>) to expand it further, as shown in Figure 1-10.

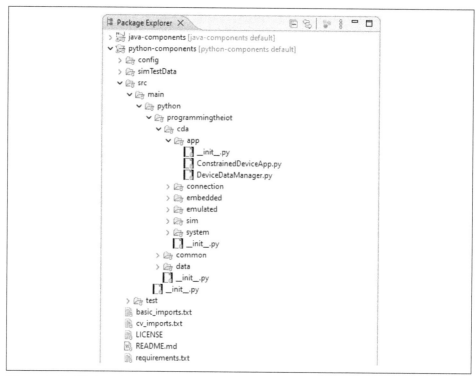

Figure 1-10. CDA project now set up and ready for use

You'll notice that there are already many Python files included in the project, one of which is `ConstrainedDeviceApp.py` in the `programmingtheiot.cda.app` package, which is the application wrapper for the CDA. There are also *__init__.py* files in each package; these are empty files the Python interpreter uses to determine which directories to search for Python files (you can ignore these for now). Much like the GDA example previously given (and written in Java), the `ConstrainedDeviceApp` is simply a placeholder to get you started.

There are also two .txt files: *requirements.txt* and *basic_imports.txt*. These should be the same - I had created the second to disambiguate with other requirements files that are not in use for this version of the book. The *requirements.txt* file will be used to install library dependencies required to support the upcoming CDA programming exercises.

If you've worked extensively with Python, you're likely familiar with the PYTHONPATH environment variable. Since I've attempted to keep the GDA and CDA packaging scheme similar, you may need to tell PyDev (and your virtualenv environment) how to navigate this directory structure to run your application. Make sure the *src/main/python* and *src/test/python* paths are both set in PYTHONPATH by doing the following: right-click "python-components," select "PyDev - PYTHONPATH," and then click "Add source folder," as shown in Figure 1-11. Select the *python* folder under *main* and click Apply. Do the same for the *python* folder under *test*. Click "Apply and Close" to finish.

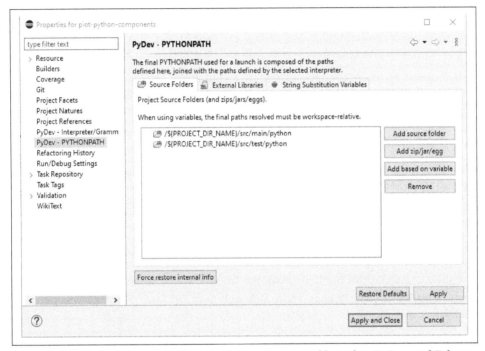

Figure 1-11. Updating the PYTHONPATH environment variable within PyDev and Eclipse

Run your CDA application within Eclipse.

1. Right-click on the project "python-components" again, scroll down to "Run As," and this time click "Python Run."

2. Check the output in the console at the bottom of the Eclipse IDE screen. As with your GDA test run, there should be no errors, with the output similar to the following:

```
2020-07-06 17:15:39,654:INFO:Attempting to load configuration...
2020-07-06 17:15:39,655:INFO:Starting CDA...
2020-07-06 17:15:39,655:INFO:CDA ran successfully.
```

Application configuration

After running the CDA and GDA, you've likely noticed the log messages related to configuration, and of course you recall the discussion of configuration management earlier in this chapter. Since you'll be dealing with a number of different configuration parameters for each application, I've provided a basic utility class within each code repository to help with this—it's named ConfigUtil.

In Python, ConfigUtil delegates to its built-in configparser (*https://oreil.ly/4MuGf*) module, and in Java, ConfigUtil delegates to Apache's commons-configuration library (*https://oreil.ly/ev5un*). Both will allow you to load the default configuration file (*./config/PiotConfig.props*) or a customized version.

The easiest way to ensure each repository's default configuration file is loaded correctly by the CDA and GDA is to update the DEFAULT_CONFIG_FILE_NAME config/PiotConfig.props' property to reference the fully qualified (absolute) file name for *PiotConfig.props* in each repository's ConfigConst class (found in the ./programmingtheiot/common directory in each repository).

Here's a Windows-specific example of the CDA's updated DEFAULT_CONFIG_FILE_NAME property after modification (you'll need to change to map to your own file and use a different path naming convention if/when using WSL or Linux, of course):

```
DEFAULT_CONFIG_FILE_NAME = "C:\programmingtheiot\python-components\config\
   PiotConfig.props"
```

For the exercises in this book, many of the "consts" you'll need are already defined in each repository's ConfigConst class, although you can (and probably will need to) add your own.

The format of the configuration file is the same for both the CDA and the GDA. Here's a brief sample from the CDA's *PiotConfig.props*:

```
[ConstrainedDevice]
deviceLocationID = constraineddevice001
enableEmulator   = False
enableSenseHAT   = False
enableMqttClient = True
enableCoapClient = False
enableLogging    = True
pollCycleSecs    = 60
testGdaDataPath  = /tmp/gda-data
testCdaDataPath  = /tmp/cda-data
```

And here's a snippet from the GDA's *PiotConfig.props*:

```
[GatewayDevice]
deviceLocationID          = gatewaydevice001
enableLogging             = True
pollCycleSecs             = 60
enableMqttClient          = True
enableCoapServer          = False
enableCloudClient         = False
enableSmtpClient          = False
enablePersistenceClient   = False
testGdaDataPath           = /tmp/gda-data
testCdaDataPath           = /tmp/cda-data
```

Notice that the sections are designated by a keyword contained in brackets, and the properties are in key = value format. This makes it easy to add new sections and key/value pairs alike.

One special case that's addressed in each implementation of `ConfigUtil` is the ability to define—and load—a separate configuration file that contains credentials or other sensitive data that should not be part of your repository's configuration. Each section allows you to specify a value for `credFile`, which is a key that maps to a local file that can and should be outside of your repository.

 If you look at *PiotConfig.props* for the CDA and GDA, you'll likely notice it contains a `credFile` entry for some sections. The reason for this is to move password references, user authentication tokens, API keys, and so forth out of the main configuration file so it can be referenced separately. It's very important to keep secrets such as these out of your repos—you should NEVER commit usernames, passwords, private keys, or any other sensitive data to your Git repository. If you need a way to store this type of information, you may want to carefully read through the article "Encrypted Secrets" (*https://oreil.ly/PZye4*) to learn more about this process in GitHub. Secure storage of credentials is an important topic, but one that's outside the scope of this book.

The configuration approach I've described here is rather basic and is designed only for testing and prototyping purposes. If you've been programming for a while, you may already have an application configuration strategy and solution in place. Feel free to adapt the configuration functionality I've introduced here to suit your specific needs.

At this point, both your GDA and your CDA should be set up and working within your IDE, and you should be familiar with how the configuration logic functions. Now you're ready to start writing your own code for both applications!

Before we jump into the exercises in Chapter 2, however, there are two more topics we should discuss: testing and automation.

Step II: Define Your Testing Strategy

Now that your development environment is established for your GDA and CDA, we can discuss how you'll test the code you're about to develop. Obviously, good testing is a critically important part of any engineering effort, and programming is no exception to this. Every application you build should be thoroughly tested, whether it works completely independently of other applications or it is tightly integrated with other systems. Further, every unit of code you write should be tested to ensure it behaves as expected. What exactly is a unit? For our purposes, a unit is always going to be represented as a function or method that you want to test.

 What's the difference between a function and a method? To grossly oversimplify, a function is a named grouping of code that performs a task (such as adding two numbers together) and returns a result. If the function accepts any input, it will be passed as one or more parameters. A method is almost identical to a function but is attached to an object. In object-oriented parlance, an object is just a class that's been instantiated, and a class is the formal definition of a component—its methods, parameters, construction, and deconstruction logic. All of the Java examples in this book will be represented in class form with methods defined as part of each class. Python can be written in script form with functions or as classes with methods, but I prefer to write Python classes with methods and will do so for each Python example shown in this book, with only a few exceptions.

Unit, integration, and performance testing

There are many ways to test software applications and systems, and there are some excellent books, articles, and blogs on the subject. Developing a working IoT solution requires careful attention to testing—within an application and between different applications and systems. For the purposes of the solution you'll develop, I'll focus on just three: unit tests, integration tests, and performance tests.

Unit tests are code modules written to test the smallest possible *unit of code* that's accessible to the test, such as a function or method. These tests are written to verify that a set of inputs to a given function or method returns an expected result. Boundary conditions are often tested as well, to ensure the function or method can handle these types of conditions appropriately.

A unit of code can technically be a single line, multiple lines of code, or even an entire code library. For our purposes, a unit refers to one or more lines of code, or an entire code library, that can be accessed through a single interface that is available on the local system—that is, a function or a method that encapsulates the unit's functionality and can be called from your test application. This functionality can be, for example, a sorting algorithm, a calculation, or even an entry point to one or more additional functions or methods.

I use JUnit (*https://junit.org/junit4*) for unit testing Java code (included with Eclipse), and Python's unittest framework[6] for unit testing Python code (part of the standard Python interpreter, and available within PyDev). You don't have to install any additional components to write and execute unit tests within your IDE if you're using Eclipse and PyDev.

In your GDA project, you've likely noticed two directory structures for your source code: one for Java source code located in *./src/main/java*, and another Java unit test code located in *./src/test/java*. This is the default convention for Maven projects, and so I've opted to use the same directory naming convention for the CDA as well (swapping "java" with "python," of course).

You may have noticed that the CDA and GDA projects contain a *./src/test/python* directory and a *./src/test/java* directory, respectively. I provide most of the unit tests and many integration tests for you to use to check whether your implementation works, broken down by each chapter. These will work for the core exercises, although they are not intended to cover every possible edge case. For additional test coverage, and for all of the optional exercises, you'll have to create your own unit and/or integration tests.

Here's a simple unit test example in Java using JUnit that checks whether the method addTwoIntegers() behaves as expected:

```
@Test
public int testAddTwoIntegers(int a, int b)
{
    // TODO: be sure to implement MyClass and the addTwoIntegers() method!
    MyClass mc = new MyClass();

    // baseline assertions
    assertTrue(mc.addTwoIntegers(0, 0) == 0);
```

---

6 Detailed information on Python 3's unittest library can be found in the unittest documentation (*https://oreil.ly/Sqm5Z*).

```
    assertTrue(mc.addTwoIntegers(1, 2) == 3);
    assertTrue(mc.addTwoIntegers(-1, 1) == 0);
    assertTrue(mc.addTwoIntegers(-1, -2) == -3);
    assertFalse(mc.addTwoIntegers(1, 2) == 4);
    assertFalse(mc.addTwoIntegers(-1, -2) == -4);
}
```

What if you have a single test class with two individual unit tests, but you only want to run one? Simply add `@Ignore` before the `@Test` annotation, and JUnit will skip that particular test. Remove the annotation to reenable the test.

Let's look at the same example in Python, using Python 3's built-in unittest framework:

```
def testAddTwoIntegers(self, a, b):
    // TODO: be sure to implement MyClass and the addTwoIntegers() method!
    MyClass mc = MyClass()

    # baseline assertions
    self.assertTrue(mc.addTwoIntegers(0, 0) == 0)
    self.assertTrue(mc.addTwoIntegers(1, 2) == 3)
    self.assertTrue(mc.addTwoIntegers(-1, 1) == 0)
    self.assertTrue(mc.addTwoIntegers(-1, -2) == -3)
    self.assertFalse(mc.addTwoIntegers(1, 2) == 4)
    self.assertFalse(mc.addTwoIntegers(-1, -2) == -4)
```

The unittest framework, much like JUnit, allows you to disable specific tests if you wish. Add `@unittest.skip("Put your reason here.")` or `@unittest.skip` as the annotation before the method declaration, and the framework will skip over that specific test.

 Unit tests within the `python-components` and `java-components` repositories can be run as automated tests either from the command line or within the IDE. That is, you can script them to run automatically as part of your build, and each will either pass or fail, depending on the implementation of the unit under test.

Integration tests are super important for the IoT, as they can be used to verify that the connections and interactions between systems and applications work as expected. Let's say you want to test a sorting algorithm using a basic data set embedded within the testing class—you'll typically write one or more unit tests, execute each one, and verify all is well.

What if, however, the sorting algorithm needs to pull data from a data repository accessible via your local network or even the internet? So what, you might ask? Well, now you have another dependency just to run your sort test. You'll need an integration test to verify that data repository connection is both available and working properly before exercising the sorting unit test.

These kinds of dependencies can make integration testing challenging with any environment, and even more so with the IoT, since it's sometimes necessary to set up servers to run specialized protocols to test our stuff. For this reason, and to keep your test environment as uncomplicated as possible, all integration tests will be manually executed and verified.

Manual execution and verification means that the integration tests within the python-components and java-components repositories are designed to be executed by you from the command line and must be observed to determine success or failure. While some can technically be exercised from within your IDE and can even be included within an automated test execution environment, others require some setup prior to execution (described within the test comments itself or within the requirements card for the module being tested). I'd suggest you stick with executing them from the command line only.

Finally, performance tests are useful for testing how quickly or efficiently a system handles a variety of conditions. They can be used with both unit and integration tests when, for instance, response time or the number of supported *concurrent* or simultaneous connections needs to be measured.

Let's say there are many different systems that need to retrieve a list of data from your data repository, and each one wants that list of data sorted before your application returns it to them. Ignoring system design and database schema optimization for a moment, a series of performance tests can be used to time the responsiveness of each system's request (from the initial request to the response), as well as the number of concurrent systems that can access your application before it no longer responds adequately.

Another aspect of performance testing is to test the load of the system your application is running on, which can be quite useful for IoT applications. IoT devices are generally constrained in some way—memory, CPU, storage, and so forth—whereas cloud services can scale as much as we need them to. It stands to reason, then, that our first IoT applications—coming up in Chapter 2—will set the stage for monitoring each device's performance individually.

Since performance testing often goes hand in hand with both integration and unit testing, we'll continue to use Maven and specialized unit tests for this as well, along with open source tools where needed.

The performance tests within the python-components and java-components repositories are all designed as manual tests and must be observed to determine success or failure, in much the same way as the integration tests previously described. Again, automation is technically feasible but is outside the scope of this book. Be sure to review the setup procedures for each test prior to execution, which are described as part of the exercise or contained within the requirements card for the module.

There are many performance testing tools available, and you can also write your own. System-to-system and communications protocol performance testing is completely optional for the purposes of this book, and I'll only briefly touch on this topic in Chapter 10. If you'd like to learn more about custom performance testing, you may want to look into tools designed for this purpose, such as Locust (*https://oreil.ly/ x6z6x*), which allows you to script your own performance tests and includes a web-based user interface (UI).

Testing tips for the exercises in this book

The sample code provided for each exercise in this book includes unit tests, which you can use to test the code you'll write. These unit tests, which are provided as part of the java-components and python-components repositories you've already pulled into your GDA and CDA projects (respectively), are key to ensuring your implementation works properly.

Some exercises also have integration tests that you can use as is or modify to suit your specific needs. I've also included some sample performance tests you can use to test how well some of your code performs when under load.

Your implementation of each exercise should pass each provided unit test with 100% success. You're welcome to add more unit tests if you feel they'll be helpful in verifying the functionality you develop. The provided integration tests and performance tests will also be helpful validation tools as you implement each exercise.

Remember, tests are your friend—and like a friend, they shouldn't be ignored. They can surely be time consuming to write and maintain, but any good friendship takes investment. These tests—whether unit, integration, or performance—will help you validate your design and verify your functionality is working properly.

Step III: Manage Your Design and Development Workflow

So you've figured out how you want to write your code and test it—terrific! But wouldn't it be great if you could manage all your requirements, source code, and CI/CD pipelines? Let's tackle this in our last step, which is all about managing your overall development process workflow. This includes requirements tracking, source code management, and CI/CD automation.

You're probably sick of me saying that building IoT systems is hard, and that's largely because of the nature of the Edge Tier (since we often have to deal with different types of devices, communication paradigms, operating environments, security constraints, and so on). Fortunately, there are many modern CI/CD tools that can be used to help navigate these troubled waters. Let's look at some selection requirements for these tools, and then explore how to build out a CI/CD pipeline that will work for our needs.

Your IoT CI/CD pipeline should support secure authentication and authorization, scriptability from a Linux-like command line, integration with Git and containerization infrastructure, and the ability to run pipelines within your local environment as well as a cloud-hosted environment.

There are many online services that provide these features, some of which also provide both free and paid service tiers. When you downloaded the source code for this book, you pulled it from my GitHub repositories using Git's clone feature. GitHub is an online service that supports overall developer workflow management, including source code control (using Git), CI/CD automation, and planning.

Each exercise will build, test, and deploy locally but will also assume your code is committed to an online repository using Git for source code management. You're welcome to use the online service of your choice, of course. For this book, all examples and exercises will assume GitHub is being used.[7]

 There are lots of great resources, tools, and online services available that let you manage your development work and set up automated CI/CD pipelines. Read through this section, try things out, and then as you gain more experience, choose the tools and service that work best for you.

Managing requirements

Ah yes—requirements. What are we building, who cares, and how are we going to build it? Plans are good, are they not? And since they're good, we should have a tool that embraces goodness, with features such as task prioritization, task tracking, team collaboration, and (maybe) integration with other tools.

The CDA and GDA repositories both include shell implementations (and some complete implementations) of the classes and interfaces you'll complete by following each

---

7 You can learn more about GitHub and its hosting features and create a free account on the GitHub website (*https://github.com*).

chapter's coding exercise requirements. All of the requirements—including some informational notes—can be found in another GitHub repository I've made available in the Programming the IoT project (*https://oreil.ly/programming-iot-kanban*). This is the best place to start, as it provides an ordered list of activities in columns and rows, as is typical in a Kanban board.

 From time to time, I'll make updates to the Kanban board (*https://oreil.ly/programming-iot-kanban*) exercises and instructional cards, along with tweaks to the supporting Python and Java source code repositories. As such, the Kanban board will have the most up-to-date information on any exercises discussed in the book. If you find any discrepancies between the book and online GitHub content, defer to the latter, which should be the most accurate.

The specific requirements within each column are captured as *cards* and actually reference "Issues" from the `book-exercise-tasks` repository (*https://github.com/programming-the-iot/book-exercise-tasks*) I've created to make centralized requirements management easier. You can easily drill down into any of these requirements by clicking on the name or by opening it in a separate tab.

The naming convention for each card should be relatively easy to understand: {book}-{app type}-{chapter}-{number}. For example, PIOT-CDA-01-001 (*https://oreil.ly/U8p3a*), which refers to Programming the Internet of Things (PIOT), Constrained Device App (CDA), Chapter 1 (01), requirement no. 1 (001).

That last number is important, as it indicates the sequence you should follow. For example, requirement no. 2 (002) would follow requirement no. 1 (001), and so on. The contents of each requirement contain the implementation instructions that you, the programmer, should follow, followed by the tests you should execute to verify the code works correctly.

There are two special numbers to keep in mind, although they, too, follow the sequence. All tasks ending with "000" are setup-related tasks, such as creating your branch. All tasks ending with "100" are merge- and validation-related tasks, such as merging your chapter branch into your primary and verifying that all functionality works as expected.

All of these cards and notes are organized into the book's Kanban board (*https://oreil.ly/programming-iot-kanban*), with a single column for each chapter, so that you can see all the things that need to be implemented for each chapter's exercises. You've probably heard of Agile[8] project management processes such as Scrum and Kanban.

---

8 You can find out more by reading the Agile Manifesto (*https://agilemanifesto.org*).

With a Kanban board, the idea is to select a card, start working on it, and—once it's tested, verified, reviewed, and committed—close it out.

Even though you can't pull down the cards I provide and close any of these issues, they are available for you to review and track on your own as you move through the exercises in each chapter. I'll discuss a way to manage your CDA and GDA requirements within your own repositories beginning in Chapter 2, when you start writing code; for now I'll provide a quick overview of how I've set up requirement cards (which are just references to one or more repositories' issues) within the Programming the IoT Kanban board (*https://oreil.ly/programming-iot-kanban*).

 I'm managing the activities for this book within a Kanban board, too. Each card on the board represents a task I or one of my team members needs to complete. A card moves to "Done" only after the team agrees it is complete.

GitHub provides an "Issues" tab to track requirements and other notes related to your repository. Figure 1-12 shows the task template I used for each requirement throughout the book. This is the stuff that goes into each task and can contain text, links, and so on. Notice that each of the requirement cards I've created contains five items: Title, Description, Actions, Estimate, and Tests.

Figure 1-12. Task template

Most of these categories are self-explanatory. But why only three levels of effort for *Estimate*? In this book, most of the activities should fall into one of the following "level of effort" categories: 2 hours or less (Small), about half a day (Medium), or about one day (Large). Keep in mind these are approximations only and will vary widely depending on a variety of factors.

For example, a "task" with the name *Integrate IoT solution with three cloud services* certainly represents work that may need to be done, but judging by the name only, it's clearly way too big and complicated to be a single work activity. In this case, I may create multiple Issues, with a set of tests specific to each one. In other cases, I may have multiple modules that are each very basic with similar implementations—all of which would be contained within the same Issue. I try to keep each Issue self-contained as much as possible.

Figure 1-13 shows an example of the template filled in with highlights from the first coding task you'll have—creating the Constrained Device Application (CDA).

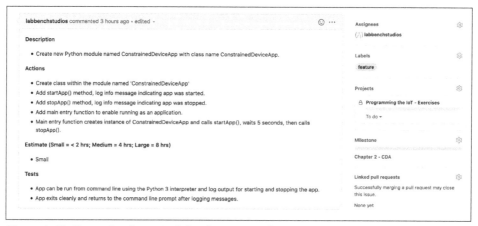

Figure 1-13. Example of a typical development task

And Figure 1-14 shows the result of adding the task as a Kanban card. This card was generated automatically after aligning the task to a project. Notice it's been added to the "To do" column on the board, since it's new and there's no status as of yet. Once you start working on the task and change its status, it will move to "In progress."

Again, the requirements are already written for you and are contained within the Programming the IoT Kanban board (*https://oreil.ly/programming-iot-kanban*), but now you should have a better idea of how these requirements are defined, and even a template for creating your own, should you decide to do so.

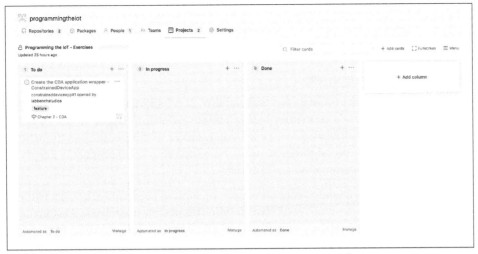

Figure 1-14. The new example task added into the Kanban board

Next, let's get your remote Git repositories set up.

Setting up your remote repositories

There are many excellent cloud-based Git repository services available. As I mentioned, I'm using GitHub, and so I've provided some optional instructions here to help you get started:

1. Create a GitHub account. (If desired, create an organization associated with the GitHub account.)

2. Within your account (or organization), create the following:

    a. A new private project named "Programming the IoT – Exercises"

    b. A new private Git repository named "java-components"

    c. A new private Git repository named "python-components"

3. Update the remote repository for both "java-components" and "python-components."

    a. From the command line, execute the following commands:

    ```
    git remote set-url origin {your new URL}
    git commit -m "Initial commit."
    git push
    ```

    b. IMPORTANT: Be sure to do this for both "java-components" *and* "python-components," using the appropriate Git repository URL for each!

Once you complete these tasks, your Git repositories will be in place, and you will have the ability to manage your code locally and synchronize it with your remote instance.

Code management and branching

One of the key benefits of using Git is the ability to collaborate with others and synchronize your local code repository with a remote repository stored in the cloud. If you've worked with Git before, you're already familiar with remotes and branching. I'm not going to go into significant detail here, but they're important concepts to grasp as part of your automation environment.

Branching is a way of enabling each developer or team to segment their work without negatively impacting the main code base. In Git, this default main branch is currently called "master" and is typically used to contain the code that has been completed, tested, verified, and (usually) placed into production. This is the default branch for both "java-components" and "python-components," and while you can leave it as is and simply work off this default branch, that's generally not recommended for the reasons I've mentioned.

Branching strategies can differ from company to company and from team to team; the one I like to use has each chapter in a new branch, and then once all is working correctly and properly tested, the chapter branch gets merged into the master. From there, a new branch is created from the merged master for the next chapter, and so on.

This approach allows you to easily track changes between chapters, and even to go back to the historical record of an earlier chapter if you want to see what changed between, say, Chapter 2 and Chapter 5. In Eclipse, you can right-click on the project (either "java-components" or "python-components") and choose Team → "Switch To" → "New Branch" to establish a new branch for your code.

I'd suggest you use the naming convention of "chapter*nn*" for each branch name, where *nn* is the two-digit chapter number. For instance, the branch for Chapter 1 will be named "chapter01," the Chapter 2 branch will be named "chapter02," and so on. It's useful to have a branching strategy that allows you to go back to a previous, "last known good" branch, or at least to see what changed between one chapter and the next. I've documented the chapter-based branching strategy within the requirements for each chapter as a reminder.

> The gory details on Git branching and merging are outside the scope of this book, so I'd recommend reading the guide "Git Branching—Basic Branching and Merging" (*https://oreil.ly/cJHBv*) if you'd like to dig into them.

Thoughts on Automation

Although outside the scope of this book, automation of software builds, testing, integration, and deployment is a key part of many development environments. I'll discuss some concepts in this section but won't be tackling this in this current book release.

Automated CI/CD in the cloud

Within Eclipse, you can write your CDA and GDA code, execute unit tests, and build and package both applications. This isn't actually automated, since you have to start the process yourself by executing a command like `mvn install` from the command line or by invoking the Maven install process from within the IDE. This is great for getting both applications to a point where you can run them, but it doesn't actually *run* them—you still need to manually start the applications and then run your integration and/or performance tests.

As a developer, part of your job is writing and testing code to meet the requirements that have been captured (in cards on a Kanban board, for example), so there's always some manual work involved. Once you know your code units function correctly, having everything else run automatically—say, after committing and pushing your code to the remote dev branch (such as "chapter02," for example)—would be pretty slick.

GitHub supports this automation through GitHub actions.[9] I'll talk more about this in Chapter 2 and help you set up your own automation for the applications you're going to build.

Automated CI/CD in your local development environment

There are lots of ways to manage CI/CD within your local environment. GitHub actions can be run locally using self-hosted runners, for example.[10] There's also a workflow automation tool called Jenkins (*https://www.jenkins.io*) that can be run locally, integrates nicely with Git local and remote repositories, and has a plug-in architecture that allows you to expand its capabilities seemingly ad infinitum.

---

9 GitHub actions (*https://docs.github.com/en/actions*) is a feature available within GitHub that allows customized workflows to be created for those who have an account within GitHub.

10 Self-hosted runners, part of GitHub actions, allow you to run your action workflows locally. There are caveats, of course, and security considerations. You can read more about self-hosted runners in the GitHub actions documentation (*https://oreil.ly/VPlkb*).

There are lots of great third-party Jenkins plug-ins and other utilities that I've found useful for my own build, test, and deployment environment, but you should do your own research to determine which ones are actively maintained and will add value for your specific environment. It's easy to introduce system compatibility issues and even security vulnerabilities if you're not fully aware of what a product will or will not do. It's ultimately your responsibility to make this decision.

Once it is installed and secured, you can configure Jenkins to automatically monitor your Git repository locally or remotely and run a build/test/deploy/run workflow on your local system, checking the success at each step. If, for example, the build fails because of a compile error in your code, Jenkins will report on this and stop the process. The same is true if the build succeeds but the tests fail—the process stops at the first failure point. This ensures your local deployment won't get overwritten with an update that doesn't compile or fails to successfully execute the configured tests.

Setting up any local automation tool can be a complicated and time-consuming endeavor. It's super helpful, however, as it basically automates all the stuff you're going to do to build, test, and deploy your software. That said, it's not required for any of the exercises in this book, and so I won't go into it here.

Containerization

You've likely heard of *containerization*, which is a way to package your application and all its dependencies into a single image, or *container*, that can be deployed to many different operating environments. This approach is very convenient, since it allows you to build your software and deploy it in such a way as to make the hosting environment no longer a concern, provided the target environment supports the container infrastructure you're using.

Docker[11] is essentially an application engine that runs on a variety of operating systems, such as Windows, macOS, and Linux, and serves as a host for your container instance(s). Your GDA and CDA, for example, can each be containerized and then deployed to any hardware device that supports the underlying container infrastructure and runtime.

It's worth pointing out that containerizing any application that has hardware-specific code may be problematic as it will not be portable to another, different hardware platform (even if the container engine is supported). If you want your hardware-specific

---

11 You can read more about containerization concepts and Docker containerization products on the Docker website (*https://www.docker.com/resources/what-container*).

application to run on any platform that supports Docker, that platform would require a hardware-specific emulator compatible with the code developed for the application.

For example, if your CDA has code that depends on Raspberry Pi–specific hardware, that is less of a concern for us at the moment, since you'll be emulating sensors and actuators and won't have any hardware-specific code to worry about until Chapter 4 (which, again, is optional). I'll discuss this more in Chapter 4, along with strategies to overcome hardware specificity in your CDA.

When using CI/CD pipelines in a remote or cloud environment, you'll notice that these services will likely deploy to virtual machines and run your code within a container that includes the required dependencies, all configured as part of the pipeline. For many cases, this makes perfect sense and can be an effective strategy to ensure consistency and ease of deployment. The caveat is that the target platform must support the container runtime environment you want to deploy. Cross-platform languages can make this easier, but it is a pain point that I don't expect to go away any time soon.

To keep things simpler, I won't walk through using containerization within your development environment and as part of your workstation, even though there are many benefits to doing so. The primary reason is that it adds another layer of complexity to manage initially, and I want to get you up and running with your own applications as soon as possible.

Programming Exercises

All the work you've done up to this point is to prepare you to build your CDA and GDA. You have some initial background in the IoT and a development environment setup and are ready to code. So far, so good, right?

If you look through your code base, you'll see that you have a bunch of components already in place. In fact, most are just shell implementations of the components that are required for both the CDA and the GDA. But how are they all supposed to eventually work together?

The remaining chapters of the book will walk you through the requirements documented in the Programming the IoT Kanban board (*https://oreil.ly/programming-iot-kanban*) to achieve this end state. Figures 1-15 and 1-16 depict the overall design approach we'll follow to get there for the CDA and the GDA, respectively.

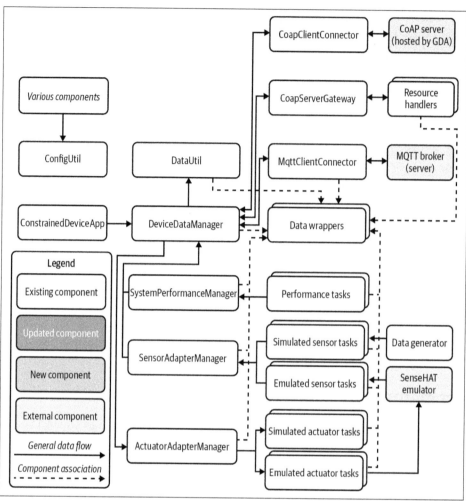

Figure 1-15. CDA end-state design

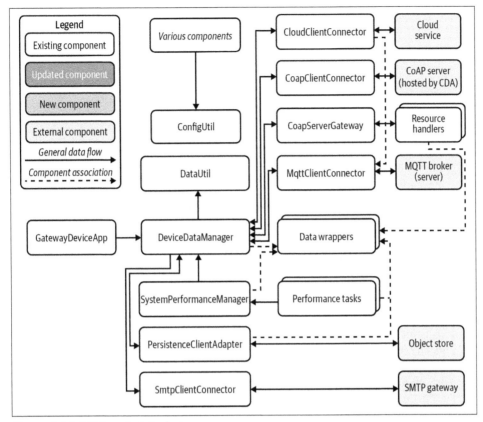

Figure 1-16. GDA end-state design

Looks like a ton of work! But don't worry—we'll take things step by step. Each chapter adds more functionality to each of these diagrams using the color coding in the legend (for existing, new, and changed components), along with drilling down into each area that the chapter addresses.

Let's take a look at the specific designs of the CDA and GDA that are relevant for this chapter and walk through the exercises (there's only one for each application). You can review the details for each online: PIOT-CDA-01-001 (*https://oreil.ly/U8p3a*) for the CDA and PIOT-GDA-01-001 (*https://oreil.ly/JG3c6*) for the GDA.

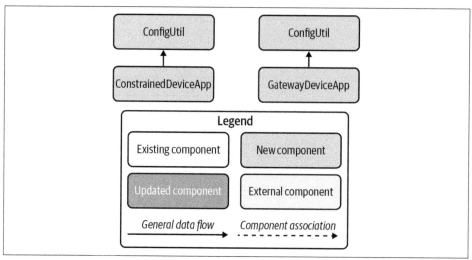

Figure 1-17. CDA design for Chapter 1 (left) and GDA design for Chapter 1 (right)

These look a bit more tractable! In fact, you've already completed the first—and perhaps most important—of them all and implemented all the requirements for Chapter 1! All that remains is to test them out. In the Test section of each requirement card, you'll see that you need to execute each application as a manual integration test.

Testing the Constrained Device App

For the CDA, navigate to the *./src/main/python/programmingtheiot/part01/integration/app* path. You'll see the ConstrainedDeviceAppTest. After you've executed this test, your output should look similar to the following:

```
Finding files... done.
.
2020-12-30 13:54:32,915 - MainThread - root - INFO - Testing ConstrainedDeviceApp
class...
2020-12-30 13:54:32,915 - MainThread - root - INFO - Initializing CDA...
2020-12-30 13:54:32,915 - MainThread - root - INFO - Starting CDA...
2020-12-30 13:54:32,916 - MainThread - root - INFO - Loading config:
../../../../../../../config/PiotConfig.props
2020-12-30 13:54:32,917 - MainThread - root - DEBUG - Config:
['Mqtt.GatewayService', 'Coap.GatewayService', 'ConstrainedDevice']
2020-12-30 13:54:32,917 - MainThread - root - INFO - Created instance of
ConfigUtil: <programmingtheiot.common.ConfigUtil.ConfigUtil object at
0x0000026B463E0E48>
2020-12-30 13:54:32,917 - MainThread - root - INFO - CDA started.
2020-12-30 13:54:32,917 - MainThread - root - INFO - CDA stopping...
2020-12-30 13:54:32,917 - MainThread - root - INFO - CDA stopped with exit code 0.
----------------------------------------------------------------------
Ran 1 test in 0.002s

OK
```

You may notice numerous module loading log output statements (which I've excluded)—that's OK. If your output generally follows the pattern shown here, you can move on to testing the GDA.

Testing the Gateway Device App

To test the GDA, navigate to the *./src/main/java/programmingtheiot/part01/integration/app* path. You'll see the GatewayDeviceAppTest. Your output will look a bit like the following:

```
Dec 30, 2020 1:45:50 PM programmingtheiot.gda.app.GatewayDeviceApp <init>
INFO: Initializing GDA...
Dec 30, 2020 1:45:50 PM programmingtheiot.gda.app.GatewayDeviceApp parseArgs
INFO: No command line args to parse.
Dec 30, 2020 1:45:50 PM programmingtheiot.gda.app.GatewayDeviceApp startApp
INFO: Starting GDA...
Dec 30, 2020 1:45:50 PM programmingtheiot.gda.app.GatewayDeviceApp startApp
INFO: GDA started successfully.
Dec 30, 2020 1:45:51 PM programmingtheiot.gda.app.GatewayDeviceApp stopApp
INFO: Stopping GDA...
Dec 30, 2020 1:45:51 PM programmingtheiot.gda.app.GatewayDeviceApp stopApp
INFO: GDA stopped successfully with exit code 0.
```

If your output looks similar, then you're ready to *actually* start writing code.

Conclusion

Congratulations—you've just completed the first chapter of *Programming the Internet of Things*! You learned about some basic IoT principles, created a problem statement to drive your IoT solution, and established a baseline IoT systems architecture that includes the Cloud Tier and the Edge Tier.

Perhaps most importantly, you now have the shell of two applications in place—the GDA and the CDA—which will serve as the foundation for much of your IoT software development throughout this book. Finally, you set up your development environment and workflow; learned about requirements management; explored unit, integration, and performance testing; and considered some basic CI/CD concepts to help automate your builds and deployment.

You're now ready to start building real IoT functionality into your CDA and GDA using Python and Java. If you're ready to move on, I'd suggest you grab some water or a good cup of coffee or tea, and then we'll dig in.

## CHAPTER 2

Initial Edge Tier Applications

Building Two Simple IoT Monitoring Applications

I must have data!
How much memory remains?
I dare not look. Sigh.

Fundamental concepts: Build two IoT performance monitoring applications—one as an IoT gateway, and the other as an IoT constrained device.

This chapter focuses on the initial steps to getting your IoT solution up and running. You'll build on these in the upcoming chapters, so setting the basic design in place now is very important. The overall architecture presented in Chapter 1 provides the initial guidance you'll need to start coding your IoT solution, and we'll keep building on that as we blaze ahead in this chapter and beyond. I'm sure you're anxious to start building out your own solution based on what you'll learn, but it's important to take things one step at a time.

We'll start by adding some simple functionality to the two applications you created in Chapter 1: the Gateway Device App (GDA) that will run on your "gateway device," and the Constrained Device App (CDA) that will run on your "constrained device."

What You'll Learn in This Chapter

This is the beginning of your official coding journey with the IoT. You'll learn how to define a detailed design for both your GDA and your CDA, separate the logical components of your design, and implement the framework for these two applications in Java and Python, respectively.

Right now, these two applications are very simple, but they'll serve as important foundation layers for your overall solution. You'll see how the design for each will evolve a bit in each subsequent chapter, providing more functionality with each step along the way.

Design Concepts

Remember the problem statement from Chapter 1? Let's briefly review it now:

> I want to understand the environment in my home, how it changes over time, and make adjustments to enhance comfort while saving money.

If you think about all the things your applications will need to do to address this problem and also consider the importance of testing system behavior and performance, there are some important capabilities you'll want to "bake in" from the start.

You'll also want to ensure your application can be extended without redesigning it if possible. Of course, it's highly unlikely any of us can design a system that will never need to be changed! That said, there are three design principles we can keep in mind that will help mitigate redesign and refactoring work (also known as "technical debt"):

1. *Modularity:* Create software components that perform a particular task (or closely related tasks). The concept behind modularity should be *separation of concerns*, a term often used in computer science and application design to define how a system should be architected.[1] In short, create software modules that serve very specific purposes. Don't boil the ocean.

2. *Interfaces:* Well-defined interfaces, or *contracts*, can make a software design both elegant and efficient. Poorly designed interfaces can break it. Interfaces provide the rules for interacting with modules and provide some sanity around how a system should behave.

3. *Validation:* I've talked quite a bit about testing already, and validation is certainly a part of testing the quality of a given system. Validation includes checks and balances that enforce certain behaviors within a system, including its nominal operating conditions, excluding those that could cause problems (or harm). For instance, a test may permit a wide range of values, such as passing a maximum temperature value of 100°C into an emulator. However, if that emulator is an abstraction for a home heating system, a more reasonable maximum value will

---

1 It's believed that Dr. Edsger W. Dijkstra coined the term separation of concerns in the mid-1970s to define the ordering (and categorization) of thought. See the E. W. Dijkstra Archive (*https://oreil.ly/QdyXX*) for more information.

likely be much lower. The system must be smart enough to deal with this and act accordingly (e.g., discard the value, logging a warning or error message).

These design principles will begin to show up in this chapter as you dig into the first set of exercises for the CDA and GDA. But first let's do some administrative work.

Tracking Your Requirements

As I mentioned in Chapter 1, keeping track of the issues you'll be implementing is a good idea. How you manage this is up to you; there are many ways to keep tabs on what work you're tackling, and a plethora of online tools you can use to do so.

GitHub has an issues tracker built into each repository, of course, which you can use, or you can even create a separate repository to track issues that span both the CDA and the GDA (which is actually how the requirements listed in book-exercise-tasks are managed).

As a convenience, I've created a separate repository that contains just 12 issues—one for each chapter (or rather, for each Lab Module, as they're labeled). You can use this repository if you'd like—each issue contains a simple checkbox for each exercise within each Lab Module, whether for the CDA, the GDA, or both.

Figure 2-1 shows the checklist for Lab Module 01 (*https://oreil.ly/DwXOG*); I've even clicked the box for PIOT-CDA-01-001 (*https://oreil.ly/U8p3a*), which is the first (and only) task for the CDA from Chapter 1 (chapter numbers and Lab Module numbers are synchronized, as I'm sure you've figured out by now).

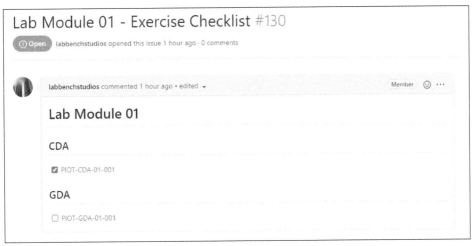

Figure 2-1. Lab Module 01 exercise checklist

You can access the checklist repository (*https://github.com/programming-the-iot/book-exercise-checklists*) and create your own issues repository within each application to help you track any design or implementation issues that need to be resolved.

With your checklist now in place, you can review the tasks that are part of the Chapter 2 – Create Initial Apps column in the Programming the IoT project (*https://oreil.ly/5b4Gx*). You'll notice that the "000" task number is a simple task designed as a reminder to create a branch aligned to the current chapter. You can do this now by following the guidelines discussed in PIOT-CDA-02-000 (*https://oreil.ly/2LUhT*). All other tasks for the CDA (PIOT-CDA-02-001 through PIOT-CDA-02-007 (*https://oreil.ly/DDOpt*)) pertain to implementing the Chapter 2 CDA functionality. Let's discuss each in turn.

Programming Exercises

Here's where you get to (finally) start coding! In these exercises, you'll dig into the requirements that discuss system performance and how to add this capability into your CDA and GDA.

System performance is one part of your system validation—it allows you to track how much memory, CPU, and even disk storage is being used by the system each IoT application runs within. Further, the design of this capability will begin to exercise the principles of modularity and interface definition I mentioned earlier in this chapter. You'll see how you can apply these concepts across not only the exercises within this chapter but all the other chapter exercises as well.

Eventually, it should be clear how you can add even more functionality to your CDA and GDA by following these principles.

The first step in designing both the GDA and the CDA is to create an application wrapper that can determine what features need to be loaded and then launch those features consistently. Since this is already provided for you with the exercise in Chapter 1, we can dig into the specific functionality for each application.

Figures 2-2 and 2-3 show the system performance manager design for the CDA and GDA, respectively.

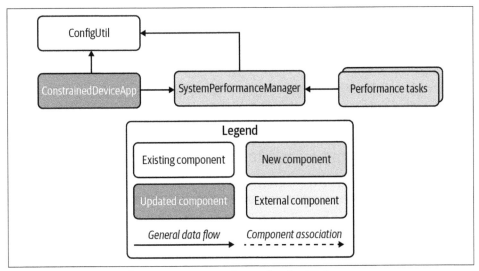

Figure 2-2. System performance manager design for the CDA

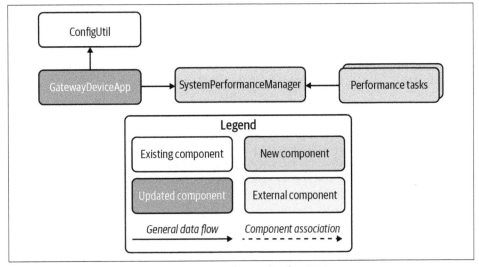

Figure 2-3. System performance manager design for the GDA

These designs are a bit different from those shown in Figures 1-15 and 1-16, right? You'll see in Chapter 3 how this is "corrected," and yes, it does mean that a very, very small amount of technical debt is being introduced in this chapter (where the application wrappers for the CDA and GDA each talk directly to `SystemPerformanceMan ager`, as opposed to `DeviceDataManager`). The purpose behind this is more educational—that is, it's intended to help you quickly build and get some functional capability in place that doesn't require much rework to integrate with the final end-state design.

Before we dig into coding, I want to quickly note that your initial GDA and CDA designs for this chapter will look very similar to each other. They'll collect some basic telemetry, which for now will include just CPU utilization and memory utilization, and simply log the data to the console. It won't be long before you'll have both applications talking to each other.

Add System Performance Tasks to the Constrained Device Application

Take a look at the Chapter 2 requirements (*https://oreil.ly/DDOpt*) listed for the CDA. Review each requirement carefully (all of them start with PIOT-CDA-02). Notice that PIOT-CDA-02-000 (*https://oreil.ly/2LUhT*) instructs you to check out a new branch for this chapter, and each subsequent requirement instructs you to create (or more accurately, edit) the modules related to this chapter's tasks.

ConstrainedDeviceApp is the entry point for the application and creates the instance of, and manages, SystemPerformanceManager. There are also two other performance task components: SystemCpuUtilTask and SystemMemUtilTask. As their names imply, these are components that will collect—you guessed it—system CPU utilization and system memory utilization. These components will be managed by System PerformanceManager and run as asynchronous threads that update one of the methods you'll define within SystemPerformanceManager.

 If you're already familiar with Python development and comfortable implementing your solution from Figure 2-2, you can walk through the requirements labeled as PIOT-CDA-02-{number}, and simply review this section to verify your implementation is correct. I'd recommend you do walk through Constrained Device App Testing Details, however, as it will provide some insights into the unit test framework that's part of your code base.

With your branch checked out, let's dig into this chapter's requirements for the CDA.

Review the Constrained Device Application module

To get started, let's walk through the PIOT-CDA-02-001 (*https://oreil.ly/yMZzc*) requirement activities from the Programming the IoT project. I've included most of the detail for this particular card here, although going forward, I'll simply summarize the actions and reference the card by name and link:

- Create a new Python package in the `programmingtheiot\cda` source folder named `app` and navigate to that folder. Again, this has already been done for you if you've cloned the repository as instructed in Chapter 1.

- Import the Python `logging` module: `import logging`.

- Create a new Python module named `ConstrainedDeviceApp`. Define a class within the module by the same name of `ConstrainedDeviceApp`.

- Add the `startApp()` method, log an info message indicating the app was started.

- Add the `stopApp()` method, log an info message indicating the app was stopped.

- Add the main entry function to enable running as an application. It will create an instance of `ConstrainedDeviceApp`, call `startApp()`, wait 60 seconds, and then call `stopApp()`, as follows:

```
def main():
    cda = ConstrainedDeviceApp()
    cda.startApp()

    while True:
        sleep(60) # 1 min, or make it 2 min's (120) if you'd prefer

    cda.stopApp()

if __name__ == '__main__':
    main()
```

To test your implementation, simply follow the test procedure listed in the card:

- Run the `ConstrainedDeviceAppTest` unit tests. The log output should look similar to the following (you can ignore the timestamp, obviously, as well as the non-INFO messages—these are generated when invoking Run as → Python unit-test within Eclipse):

```
Finding files... done.
Importing test modules ... done.

2020-07-20 10:08:20,169:INFO:Initializing CDA...
2020-07-20 10:08:20,169:INFO:Loading configuration...
2020-07-20 10:08:20,169:INFO:Starting CDA...
2020-07-20 10:08:20,169:INFO:CDA started.
2020-07-20 10:08:20,169:INFO:CDA stopping...
2020-07-20 10:08:20,170:INFO:CDA stopped with exit code 0.
----------------------------------------------------------------
Ran 1 test in 0.001s

OK
```

These steps are already implemented for you in the code you've cloned and are given here only to help familiarize you with the formatting for future requirements. You'll eventually connect the `ConstrainedDeviceApp` to `SystemPerformanceManager` and hook up the start and stop functions accordingly.

Follow the Test instructions to execute the `ConstrainedDeviceAppTest` integration test (there's only one). Check the output in your IDE console—it will look similar to what I've included here from the original requirement card.

Your `ConstrainedDeviceApp` is beginning to come together, but you still need a way to collect data and generate your first telemetry data.

Create and integrate the system performance manager module

The next requirement is to create—or rather, to update—the `SystemPerformanceMan ager` class. As the description for PIOT-CDA-02-002 (*https://oreil.ly/Ng3ce*) states, this requirement instructs you to "Create a new Python module named `SystemPerfor manceManager` with class name `SystemPerformanceManager`." Since the shell for `Sys temPerformanceManager` already exists, you'll simply have to edit the existing class. Be sure to read through the other class initialization logic in the PIOT-CDA-02-002 (*https://oreil.ly/Ng3ce*) card before moving on.

It's important to note that this component actually lives in the "system" folder, whereas the CDA application from the previous chapter's exercise is in the "cda" folder. Your import statements will need to reflect this and the other directories for the modules your implementation uses.

After creating the constructor, the key activities for `SystemPerformanceManager` involve two simple tasks: adding a log message to `startManager()` indicating the manager started and adding another to `stopManager()` with the opposite message.

Once this is done, you can implement the `SystemPerformanceManagerTest` integration test, with the log output looking similar to what's listed in the card:

```
2020-07-06 21:03:03,654:INFO:Initializing SystemPerformanceManager...
2020-07-06 21:03:03,655:INFO:Started SystemPerformanceManager.
2020-07-06 21:03:03,656:INFO:Stopped SystemPerformanceManager.
```

This next task is also straightforward. With the basics of `SystemPerformanceManager` implemented, it's time to tie it into the CDA. Review the actions in the PIOT-CDA-02-003 card (*https://oreil.ly/ClKYa*) for integrating this module into your CDA.

The description instructs you to "Create an instance of `SystemPerformanceManager` within `ConstrainedDeviceApp` and invoke the manager's start/stop methods within the app's start/stop methods." Let's take a look at the actions listed in the card:

- Create a class-scoped instance of SystemPerformanceManager within the Con strainedDeviceApp constructor called sysPerfManager using the following:

  ```
  self.sysPerfManager = SystemPerformanceManager()
  ```

- Edit the startApp() method to include a call to self.sysPerfManager.startMan ager().

- Edit the stopApp() method to include a call to self.sysPerfManager.stopMan ager().

Once you've completed these tasks, you can again run the CDA integration test, ConstrainedDeviceAppTest. It will still call the startApp() and stopApp() methods on ConstrainedDeviceApp, but this time it will generate some additional output, similar to the following:

```
Finding files... done.
Importing test modules ... done.

2020-07-20 10:23:00,146:INFO:Initializing CDA...
2020-07-20 10:23:00,147:INFO:Loading configuration...
2020-07-20 10:23:00,260:INFO:Starting CDA...
2020-07-20 10:23:00,260:INFO:Started SystemPerformanceManager.
2020-07-20 10:23:00,260:INFO:CDA started.
2020-07-20 10:23:00,260:INFO:CDA stopping...
2020-07-20 10:23:00,260:INFO:Stopped SystemPerformanceManager.
2020-07-20 10:23:00,260:INFO:CDA stopped with exit code 0.
----------------------------------------------------------------
Ran 1 test in 0.115s

OK
```

Pretty simple, right? OK—almost there. Let's create the different modules that will actually do the system monitoring next and get them connected to the SystemPerfor manceManager. You can see where I'm going with this, right?

Create the system utility task modules

Some of the system utility functionality can be abstracted into a base class, which is described in PIOT-CDA-02-004 (*https://oreil.ly/H3djs*). If you're using the sample code from python-components, the shell of this class—BaseSystemUtilTask—is provided, although it requires you to complete the implementation.

It includes a constructor that accepts two parameters—name and typeID—and defines three methods: getName(), getTypeID(), and getTelemetryValue(). The constructor parameters will be passed in by the subclass, and the getName() and getTypeID() methods will return these values.

You can implement these now, along with the constructor logic that will set the appropriate class-scoped variables, based on the detail provided in PIOT-CDA-02-004 (*https://oreil.ly/H3djs*).

The getTelemetryValue() method is technically a *template* method—that is, a function that's declared in a base class that a subclass must implement. I've provided the implementation for you—it simply passes, as the subclass will need to implement its own specific functionality for this method.

There are no unit tests to run, so let's move on to the next set of requirements. This is where you can begin collecting some real metrics. The SystemCpuUtilTask module, described in PIOT-CDA-02-005 (*https://oreil.ly/s2N94*), will retrieve the current CPU utilization across all cores, average them together, and return the result as a float.

For this module and the next, you can use the *psutil* (*https://psutil.readthedocs.io/en/latest*) library. Again, the module is already created for you, so you will need only to ensure that the import statements are correct and then implement the following requirements:

 You may recall that *psutil* was one of the libraries you imported when you set up your virtualenv environment and used pip to install *basic_imports.txt*. This library gives you the ability to monitor system metrics, such as CPU utilization and memory utilization. You'll likely notice that some functions are system dependent and may not return the expected result if your system doesn't support those particular calls.

- Make sure you've imported *psutil*.
- In the constructor, call the base class (with parameters specific to this class) using the following code:

```
super(SystemCpuUtilTask, self).__init__( \
  name = ConfigConst.CPU_UTIL_NAME, \
  typeID = ConfigConst.CPU_UTIL_TYPE)
```

- You may recall that BaseSystemUtilTask defines a template method named getTelemetryValue(self) -> float:, which should be implemented in the subclass using the following *psutil* command: return psutil.cpu_percent().

The call to cpu_percent() will aggregate all cores into a single CPU utilization percentage, which makes life rather easy for you as a developer. This class essentially boils down to returning the value of this single line of code.

I'm sure you're wondering why the base class abstraction exists at all, since it's not really saving much in terms of coding. The point of this exercise is not only to obtain the CPU utilization but also to establish a pattern of *separation of control* or *separa-*

tion of key functions so they can be managed and updated separately from the rest of the application's logic. Introducing `BaseSystemUtilTask` provides a window into this concept.

As with any software design, there's a balance between complexity, clever coding, and just getting it done. I'll attempt to strike that balance throughout the book. You may have different ideas—that's great! I encourage you to consider how else you might implement each exercise to meet your specific needs. This is part of what makes programming creative and fun.

Once you've completed the implementation, run the unit tests specified in PIOT-CDA-02-005 (*https://oreil.ly/s2N94*) within the `SystemCpuUtilTaskTest` test case. If all is well, these tests should pass with flying colors.

The next module—`SystemMemUtilTask`, described in PIOT-CDA-02-006 (*https://oreil.ly/Jhfmi*)—follows the same pattern as `SystemCpuUtilTask`, so I'll spare you the reiteration.

Simply replace the `getTelemetryValue(self) -> float:` implementation with this one line of code:

```
psutil.virtual_memory().percent
```

This will retrieve the current virtual memory utilization and return the result as a float. There are other properties you can extract from the call to `virtual_memory()`, and you're welcome to experiment. For now, just return the percent utilization.

Make sure your `SystemMemUtilTaskTest` unit tests all pass before moving on. And now, let's connect both `SystemCpuUtilTask` and `SystemMemUtilTask` to `SystemPerformanceManager`.

Reading a single value from a sensor (emulated or real) is good but insufficient, since you'll want to monitor these values over time to see whether they change. Even after connecting `SystemCpuUtilTask` and `SystemMemUtilTask` into `SystemPerformanceManager`, you'll want to process their data on a recurring basis.

There are many ways to do this in Python: you can build your own scheduling mechanism using Python's concurrency library or leverage one of many open source libraries to do this for you. I've included APScheduler (*https://pypi.org/project/APScheduler*) in *basic_imports.txt*; it provides a scheduling mechanism that will suit our purposes rather well.

Python provides two mechanisms for running code in a way that appears to execute simultaneously with other code. One is using concurrency, and the other is using multiprocessing. The former is handled using threads, whereas the latter is handled using separate child processes. One key difference is that Python threads actually get run in sequence using the same processor core as the main application, but they happen in such a way as to appear to be running simultaneously. Multiprocessing allows for true parallelism, where the code written using the multiprocessor library can be distributed to run on a separate processor core, which can execute in parallel to other code in a different processor core. The CDA-specific exercises and samples within this book will assume that threaded concurrency in Python is sufficient for our needs, and so I won't discuss multiprocessing for any CDA development.

Integrate the system utility tasks with the system performance manager

Things get a bit more interesting now that you're going to integrate a couple of components but also run a scheduler to poll for updates. The `SystemPerformanceManager` will need to access the `SystemCpuUtilTask` and `SystemMemUtilTask` at a regular interval, checking for new data. Eventually you'll integrate even more functionality, but for now you can simply poll each for the latest telemetry value and log it using the logger.

Here's a summary of the actions necessary to complete `SystemPerformanceManager`, taken from PIOT-CDA-02-007 (*https://oreil.ly/4pMCp*):

- Update the imports and add a constructor that will use a configured polling rate and create class-scoped instances of `self.cpuUtilTask`, `self.memUtilTask`, and `self.scheduler`. You'll then add a job to the `scheduler` within the `SystemPerformanceManager`. A simple implementation approach is shown below. A more advanced approach is included within the PIOT-CDA-02-007 (*https://oreil.ly/4pMCp*) card, which you may want to consider as it's more effective at handling potential timing issues and race conditions.

  ```
  self.scheduler.add_job( \
    self.handleTelemetry, \
    'interval', \
    seconds = self.pollRate)
  ```

- Finally, add the start and stop functionality into the `startManager()` and `stopManager()` methods.

For the first bullet, you can use code that looks similar to the following:

```
import logging
```

```
from apscheduler.schedulers.background import BackgroundScheduler

from programmingtheiot.common.IDataMessageListener import IDataMessageListener

from programmingtheiot.cda.system.SystemCpuUtilTask import SystemCpuUtilTask
from programmingtheiot.cda.system.SystemMemUtilTask import SystemMemUtilTask

from programmingtheiot.data.SystemPerformanceData import SystemPerformanceData

class SystemPerformanceManager(object):
  def __init__(self):
    configUtil = ConfigUtil()

    self.pollRate = \
      configUtil.getInteger( \
        section = ConfigConst.CONSTRAINED_DEVICE, \
        key = ConfigConst.POLL_CYCLES_KEY, \
        defaultVal = ConfigConst.DEFAULT_POLL_CYCLES)

    self.locationID = \
      configUtil.getProperty( \
        section = ConfigConst.CONSTRAINED_DEVICE, \
        key = ConfigConst.DEVICE_LOCATION_ID_KEY, \
        defaultVal = ConfigConst.CONSTRAINED_DEVICE)

    if self.pollRate <= 0:
      self.pollRate = ConfigConst.DEFAULT_POLL_CYCLES

    self.scheduler = BackgroundScheduler()
    self.scheduler.add_job( \
      self.handleTelemetry, \
      'interval', \
      seconds = self.pollRate)

    self.cpuUtilTask = SystemCpuUtilTask()
    self.memUtilTask = SystemMemUtilTask()

    self.dataMsgListener = None
```

First, you'll notice the sample code pulls in a couple properties from the configuration file via ConfigUtil. This configuration utility code is provided as part of python-components, so you don't have to do anything except use it as is. I'll talk in much more depth about ConfigUtil and *PiotConfig.props* (the configuration file) in the introduction to Part II and in Chapter 3. Essentially, you're just retrieving the poll rate for the scheduler and a string value named "locationID" for later use (in Chapter 5).

The scheduler initialization leverages the previously referenced APScheduler library, which provides a mechanism for scheduling a background process to poll a method named handleTelemetry() at regular intervals (hence the poll rate property). I'll also discuss this in more detail in Chapter 3, as you'll use the same mechanism for polling sensor simulator tasks.

 There are many ways to schedule a background job in Python, including the method shown in the previous example. Be sure to review the Kanban board (*https://oreil.ly/programming-iot-kanban*) for updates to the sample code and pay particular note to the suggestions called out for this (PIOT-CDA-02-007 (*https://oreil.ly/4pMCp*)) and other Python-specific job scheduling exercises.

The last bullet—adding the start and stop functionality—needs to start and stop the scheduler. You can implement this using code similar to the following:

```
def startManager(self):
  logging.info("Started SystemPerformanceManager.")

  if not self.scheduler.running:
    self.scheduler.start()
  else:
    logging.warning( \
      "SystemPerformanceManager scheduler already started. Ignoring.")

def stopManager(self):
  logging.info("Stopped SystemPerformanceManager.")

  try:
    self.scheduler.shutdown()
  except:
    logging.warning( \
      "SystemPerformanceManager scheduler already stopped. Ignoring.")
```

With your implementation complete, you can now run the integration tests specified within PIOT-CDA-02-007 (*https://oreil.ly/4pMCp*), which simply requires you to execute the SystemPeformanceManagerTest. It should pass and generate a bunch of log output as shown within the card. Here's a sample:

```
Finding files... done.
Importing test modules ... done.

2020-12-29 14:43:18,520:SystemPerformanceManagerTest:INFO:Testing
SystemPerformanceManager class...
  .
  .
  .
2020-12-29 14:43:18,623:SystemPerformanceManager:INFO:Started
SystemPerformanceManager.
2020-12-29 14:43:18,626:base:INFO:Added job
"SystemPerformanceManager.handleTelemetry" to job store "default"
  .
  .
```

```
.
2020-12-29 14:43:23,629:SystemPerformanceManager:INFO:CPU utilization is 10.1
percent, and memory utilization is 79.1 percent.
.
.
.
2020-12-29 14:44:18,631:base:INFO:Scheduler has been shut down
--------------------------------------------------------------------
Ran 1 test in 60.112s

OK
```

Congratulations! You've just completed the first iteration of the CDA. It's a stand-alone Python app, with a small suite of unit and integration tests for you to build on over the next chapters.

Now let's move on to the GDA and start writing some Java code.

Add System Performance Tasks to the Gateway Device Application

Your GDA will need the same three components as your CDA: an application wrapper, a system performance manager, and components to read the system performance data that will comprise your GDA's telemetry.

 In IoT systems, the gateway device may or may not generate its own telemetry (although it generally should). The example you'll build within this book generates only its own system performance telemetry. The constrained device, implemented as the CDA, will be responsible for generating not only its specific system performance telemetry but any sensor-specific telemetry as well.

Although the GDA doesn't have much to do right now, it will eventually process the data from the CDA, using it to make decisions about any requisite actions, and send its own telemetry—along with the CDA's—to the cloud for further processing. Figure 2-4 provides further detail on the GDA's system performance design.

Notice the additional metric the GDA collects. In Chapter 5, I'll discuss local caching of messages, so disk utilization will be an important metric to track. In Chapter 6 and beyond, I'll dig into passing messages between devices (and eventually the cloud in Chapter 10), so tracking network utilization will be pretty useful as well. Although network bits in and bits out are not expressed in Figure 2-4, you can add them as optional tasks.

Aren't there tools for monitoring system performance? Yes, and you should use them when they make sense. Devices that are part of the IoT Edge Tier aren't always easy to manage, nor are they always able to participate in network monitoring environments.

This doesn't mean we need to build everything from scratch! But we will anyway. Because we can. And it's fun :).

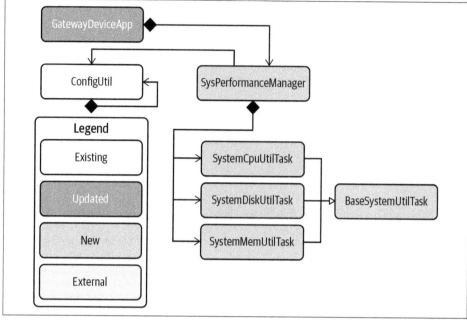

Figure 2-4. Detailed design UML for the GDA

Back to Figure 2-4. Notice that GatewayDeviceApp is the entry point for the application and creates the instance of, and manages, SystemPerformanceManager, which is similar to the CDA design. We also have a SystemCpuUtilTask and SystemMemUtil Task, along with the SystemDiskUtilTask that will be useful to your design later.

 It almost goes without saying, but if you're already familiar with Java development and comfortable implementing your solution from the design in Figure 2-4, feel free to do so. But be sure to look carefully at the requirements in the next section first.

You'll recognize these next steps, of course, because you already did something similar for the CDA. Since the GDA repository is different from the CDA repository, you may want to set up your issue tracker separately. Again, you can simply use the exercise checklist I've already provided.

You'll notice that the Programming the IoT Kanban board (*https://oreil.ly/programming-iot-kanban*) has a bunch of optional requirements within some chapters (indicated by the optional label), and called out in the exercise checklists. You can either ignore these or choose to implement them. I created them for my graduate course, and I hope you'll find them useful for your own study of this subject.

Notice the first actual requirement for the GDA is to create a branch for GDA-specific updates related to this chapter, as indicated in PIOT-GDA-02-000 (*https://oreil.ly/HE3iy*). Again, you'll follow this pattern for each chapter and application.

Let's start with the application wrapper for the GDA.

Review the Gateway Device Application module

Much like with the CDA, the GDA application module requirements are described in PIOT-GDA-02-001 (*https://oreil.ly/Pqaxf*). As I've stated previously, the shells of most classes are already provided for you—they just require the implementation details. In other cases, such as the GDA application module, much of the basic implementation is already in place, although you'll need to update it later in this chapter.

For now, simply verify that the code implements the requirements listed in PIOT-GDA-02-001 (*https://oreil.ly/Pqaxf*) and run the integration test as specified—`testRunGatewayApp()`—by using the JUnit 4 Runner. If you're using Eclipse as your IDE, simply right-click on `GatewayDeviceAppTest` and select "Run As → JUnit Test." You should get a green bar along with sample output similar to the following (timestamps will obviously be different):

```
Sep 05, 2020 5:48:10 PM programmingtheiot.gda.app.GatewayDeviceApp <init>
INFO: Initializing GDA...
Sep 05, 2020 5:48:10 PM programmingtheiot.gda.app.GatewayDeviceApp parseArgs
INFO: No command line args to parse.
Sep 05, 2020 5:48:10 PM programmingtheiot.gda.app.GatewayDeviceApp initConfig
INFO: Attempting to load configuration: Default.
Sep 05, 2020 5:48:10 PM programmingtheiot.gda.app.GatewayDeviceApp startApp
INFO: Starting GDA...
Sep 05, 2020 5:48:10 PM programmingtheiot.gda.app.GatewayDeviceApp startApp
INFO: GDA started successfully.
Sep 05, 2020 5:49:15 PM programmingtheiot.gda.app.GatewayDeviceApp stopApp
INFO: Stopping GDA...
Sep 05, 2020 5:49:15 PM programmingtheiot.gda.app.GatewayDeviceApp stopApp
INFO: GDA stopped successfully with exit code 0.
```

Embedded within the module are a few commented "TODO" lines of code as placeholders for you to eventually add more functionality. As it stands, your `GatewayDeviceApp` has some neat stuff in it, but it's not very useful as an IoT gateway application. Let's start working on the other components to bring this app to life.

Create and integrate the system performance manager module

You're about to see a pattern emerge between the CDA requirements you just implemented and the GDA. We'll see the code bases and designs diverge once you move into Part III, where you'll not only build client communications capabilities between the two applications but also implement your own server.

For now, let's blaze ahead with building out the SystemPerformanceManager in the GDA. As the description for PIOT-GDA-02-002 (*https://oreil.ly/qhUgg*) states, this requirement instructs you to "Create the SystemPerformanceManager module." Since the shell for SystemPerformanceManager already exists, as does the *programmingtheiot\gda\system* package, you'll simply have to edit the existing class.

The requirements listed under "Actions" are similar to those you found when creating the SystemPerformanceManager for the CDA, and include the following:

- Create a default constructor and create the initial start and stop manager methods.

- The start and stop methods—startManager() and stopManager()—should each log an info message indicating the manager was started or stopped.

Once this is done, you can implement the SystemPerformanceManagerTest integration test, with the log output looking similar to what's listed in the card:

```
Jul 19, 2020 12:58:42 PM programmingtheiot.gda.system.SystemPerformanceManager
startManager
INFO: SystemPerformanceManager is starting...
Jul 19, 2020 12:58:42 PM programmingtheiot.gda.system.SystemPerformanceManager
stopManager
INFO: SystemPerformanceManager is stopped.
```

This next task is also straightforward. Now that you have the basics of SystemPerformanceManager implemented, it's time to tie it into the GDA using the requirements listed in PIOT-GDA-02-003 (*https://oreil.ly/UKLhG*).

The description indicates you'll need to create an instance of SystemPerformanceManager within GatewayDeviceApp and invoke the manager's start/stop methods within the app's start/stop methods.

To do so, follow the actions listed in the requirements card, as follows:

- Create a class-scoped variable named sysPerfManager.

- Create an instance of SystemPerformanceManager within the GatewayDeviceApp constructor called this.sysPerfManager. For now, just use "10" as the parameter to the constructor (you can change this if you'd like).

- Edit the startApp() method: add a call to sysPerfManager.startManager().

- Edit the `stopApp()` method: add a call to `sysPerfManager.stopManager()`.

The final step is to run the GDA integration test—`GatewayDeviceAppTest`. It works in the same manner as the `ConstrainedDeviceAppTest` and will generate log output similar to the following:

```
Jul 19, 2020 1:01:38 PM programmingtheiot.gda.app.GatewayDeviceApp <init>
INFO: Initializing GDA...
Jul 19, 2020 1:01:38 PM programmingtheiot.gda.app.GatewayDeviceApp parseArgs
INFO: No command line args to parse.
Jul 19, 2020 1:01:38 PM programmingtheiot.gda.app.GatewayDeviceApp initConfig
INFO: Attempting to load configuration: Default.
Jul 19, 2020 1:01:38 PM programmingtheiot.gda.app.GatewayDeviceApp startApp
INFO: Starting GDA...
Jul 19, 2020 1:01:38 PM programmingtheiot.gda.system.SystemPerformanceManager
startManager
INFO: SytemPerformanceManager is starting...
Jul 19, 2020 1:01:38 PM programmingtheiot.gda.app.GatewayDeviceApp startApp
INFO: GDA started successfully.
Jul 19, 2020 1:01:38 PM programmingtheiot.gda.app.GatewayDeviceApp stopApp
INFO: Stopping GDA...
Jul 19, 2020 1:01:38 PM programmingtheiot.gda.system.SystemPerformanceManager
stopManager
INFO: SytemPerformanceManager is stopped.
Jul 19, 2020 1:01:38 PM programmingtheiot.gda.app.GatewayDeviceApp stopApp
INFO: GDA stopped successfully with exit code 0.
```

If your test was successful, you can move on to creating the system utility task modules for the GDA.

Create the system utility task modules

This is the first abstraction you'll create for the GDA—again, the first of many. As with the other classes described, the shell is provided for you if you're using the sample code in `java-components`. The requirements for this abstraction—`BaseSystemU tilTask`—are described in PIOT-GDA-02-004 (*https://oreil.ly/T615m*).

Notice the class-scoped variables for name and `edu`—be sure to set those within the constructor and then implement their corresponding getter methods: `getName()` and `getTypeID()`.

Last, much like the `getTelemetryValue()` method in the CDA's version of this class, the `getTelemetryValue()` method is also a template method. The difference is that in Java, we can enforce the implementation strategy, as the base class is abstract, and the template method is as well. This means any subclass must implement the template method.

The next step is to create the `SystemCpuUtilTask`, described in PIOT-GDA-02-005 (*https://oreil.ly/EGsuz*). This module will derive from `BaseSystemUtilTask`, and as such, it needs to do two things:

- Call the super class constructor with the appropriate name and `typeID` (retrieved from `ConfigConst`).
- Override the `getTelemetryValue()` template method from the base class with the correct implementation for CPU utilization retrieval.

To retrieve system CPU utilization, you can use the Java management interface.

To start, make sure you've imported the following:

```
import java.lang.management.ManagementFactory;
```

Next, retrieve the system load average, log the value, and then return it as a float, using the following code to retrieve the value:

```
ManagementFactory.getOperatingSystemMXBean().getSystemLoadAverage()
```

Run `./system/SystemCpuUtilTaskTest`. If your operating system supports retrieval of CPU load, the `testGetTelemetryValue()` unit test should pass while displaying values greater than 0.0% and (likely) less than 100.0%.

If your operating system doesn't support this feature (and some systems don't), each test will return a negative value (usually "–1.0"), as follows:

```
Test 1: CPU Util not supported on this OS: -1.0
Test 2: CPU Util not supported on this OS: -1.0
Test 3: CPU Util not supported on this OS: -1.0
Test 4: CPU Util not supported on this OS: -1.0
Test 5: CPU Util not supported on this OS: -1.0
```

Once you've completed the implementation, run the unit tests specified in PIOT-GDA-02-005 (*https://oreil.ly/EGsuz*) within the `SystemCpuUtilTaskTest` test case, which should pass with flying colors.

Not surprisingly, the next module—`SystemMemUtilTask`—follows the same pattern as `SystemCpuUtilTask`, although you need to do a little more work to calculate system memory utilization.

As PIOT-GDA-02-006 (*https://oreil.ly/xFc5c*) states, you'll need to ensure the class derives from `BaseSystemUtilTask` and imports the following:

```
import java.lang.management.ManagementFactory;
import java.lang.management.MemoryUsage;
```

Once you've done this, update `getTelemetryValue()` with the following code:

```
MemoryUsage memUsage = ManagementFactory.getMemoryMXBean().getHeapMemoryUsage();
double memUtil = ((double) memUsage.getUsed() / (double) memUsage.getMax()) *
100.0d;
```

This will retrieve the current JVM memory utilization and return the result as a double, which you can log and then cast to float and return. Make sure your `SystemMemU tilTaskTest` JUnit tests all pass before moving on.

Before connecting both `SystemCpuUtilTask` and `SystemMemUtilTask` to `SystemPer formanceManager`, let's take a look at running repeatable tasks in Java.

Although your GDA isn't collecting sensor data, it clearly needs to gather and assess its own system performance (such as CPU and memory utilization, of course). This type of functionality is typically collected in the background at regular intervals, and as with Python, Java provides options for creating polling systems.

Fortunately, there's no need to import any separate libraries, because this is built into the core Java Software Development Kit (SDK).

 Java's concurrency library is quite powerful and allows you to use a basic `Timer` functionality as well as a `ScheduledExecutorService` (you can also create your own threaded polling system if you really want to, of course). We'll use `ScheduledExecutorService`, as it provides a semiguaranteed way to poll at regular intervals while handling most of the complexity for us. Modern Java virtual machines will handle the load distribution across the CPU architecture, meaning it will utilize multiple cores if at all possible.

Integrate the system utility tasks with the system performance manager

This particular exercise is a bit more involved, even though it doesn't take many lines of code to complete. This is because you'll be using both concurrency and a *Runnable* implementation, the latter of which is just an interface definition for a method that can be invoked one or more times by a Java thread.

The details are documented in PIOT-GDA-02-007 (*https://oreil.ly/w8TXR*), but let's walk through each action in the requirement card:

- Add the following import statements:

```
import java.util.concurrent.Executors;
import java.util.concurrent.ScheduledExecutorService;
import java.util.concurrent.ScheduledFuture;
import java.util.concurrent.TimeUnit;
import java.util.logging.Logger;

import programmingtheiot.common.ConfigConst;
import programmingtheiot.common.ConfigUtil;
```

```
import programmingtheiot.common.IDataMessageListener;
import programmingtheiot.common.ResourceNameEnum;
import programmingtheiot.data.SystemPerformanceData;
```

- Add the following class-scoped variables:

```
private ScheduledExecutorService schedExecSvc = null;
private SystemCpuUtilTask sysCpuUtilTask = null;
private SystemMemUtilTask sysMemUtilTask = null;

private String   locationID = ConfigConst.GATEWAY_DEVICE;
private Runnable taskRunner = null;
private boolean  isStarted  = false;
private int      pollRate   = ConfigConst.DEFAULT_POLL_CYCLES;
```

- Create a public method named handleTelemetry() and add the following code, and then log a debug message with the CPU and memory utilization values:

```
cpuUtilPct = this.cpuUtilTask.getTelemetryValue()
memUtilPct = this.memUtilTask.getTelemetryValue()
```

- Add the following to the constructor. Notice the use of ConfigUtil to retrieve the poll rate, much like you did with the CDA. I'll discuss the use of ConfigUtil (and the configuration file, *PiotConfig.props*) in the introduction to Part III:

```
this.pollRate =
  ConfigUtil.getInstance().getInteger(
    ConfigConst.GATEWAY_DEVICE,
    ConfigConst.POLL_CYCLES_KEY,
    ConfigConst.DEFAULT_POLL_CYCLES);


if (this.pollRate <= 0) {
  this.pollRate = ConfigConst.DEFAULT_POLL_CYCLES;
}

this.locationID =
  ConfigUtil.getInstance().getProperty(
    ConfigConst.GATEWAY_DEVICE,
    ConfigConst.DEVICE_LOCATION_ID_KEY,
    ConfigConst.GATEWAY_DEVICE);

this.schedExecSvc   = Executors.newScheduledThreadPool(1);
this.sysCpuUtilTask = new SystemCpuUtilTask();
this.sysMemUtilTask = new SystemMemUtilTask();

this.taskRunner = () -> {
  this.handleTelemetry();
};
```

- Within the startManager() method, add the following:

```
if (! this.isStarted) {
  ScheduledFuture<?> futureTask =
    this.schedExecSvc.scheduleAtFixedRate(
      this.taskRunner, 0L, this.pollRate, TimeUnit.SECONDS);

  this.isStarted = true;
}
```

- Within the `stopManager()` method, add the following:

  ```
  this.schedExecSvc.shutdown();
  ```

You may have noticed the retrieval of "locationID" from the GDA's configuration (which was also the case for the CDA's `SystemPerformanceManager` implementation). I'll address this in Chapter 5, as alluded to previously. For now, just leave the code in place.

To test all of this new goodness, you need only to run the `GatewayDeviceAppTest` unit test named `testRunTimedGatewayApp()` and follow the preceding instructions under the Test section.

 JUnit unit tests can be included or excluded in a test run by using the `@Test` annotation before the unit test method. You can simply comment it out or uncomment it as desired. Note also that unit tests are not designed to run in any particular order—you should expect a random order and write your tests as stand-alone.

On successful execution, your log output for this test will look similar to the following:

```
Jul 19, 2020 1:53:19 PM programmingtheiot.gda.app.GatewayDeviceApp <init>
INFO: Initializing GDA...
Jul 19, 2020 1:53:19 PM programmingtheiot.gda.app.GatewayDeviceApp parseArgs
INFO: No command line args to parse.
Jul 19, 2020 1:53:19 PM programmingtheiot.gda.app.GatewayDeviceApp initConfig
INFO: Attempting to load configuration: Default.
Jul 19, 2020 1:53:19 PM programmingtheiot.gda.app.GatewayDeviceApp startApp
INFO: Starting GDA...
Jul 19, 2020 1:53:19 PM programmingtheiot.gda.system.SystemPerformanceManager
startManager
INFO: SystemPerformanceManager is starting...
Jul 19, 2020 1:53:19 PM programmingtheiot.gda.app.GatewayDeviceApp startApp
INFO: GDA started successfully.
Jul 19, 2020 1:53:20 PM programmingtheiot.gda.system.SystemPerformanceManager
handleTelemetry
INFO: Handle telemetry results: cpuUtil=-1.0, memUtil=0.1469148
Jul 19, 2020 1:53:50 PM programmingtheiot.gda.system.SystemPerformanceManager
handleTelemetry
INFO: Handle telemetry results: cpuUtil=-1.0, memUtil=0.1469148
```

```
Jul 19, 2020 1:54:20 PM programmingtheiot.gda.system.SystemPerformanceManager
handleTelemetry
INFO: Handle telemetry results: cpuUtil=-1.0, memUtil=0.1469148
Jul 19, 2020 1:54:24 PM programmingtheiot.gda.app.GatewayDeviceApp stopApp
INFO: Stopping GDA...
Jul 19, 2020 1:54:24 PM programmingtheiot.gda.system.SystemPerformanceManager
stopManager
INFO: SystemPerformanceManager is stopped.
Jul 19, 2020 1:54:24 PM programmingtheiot.gda.app.GatewayDeviceApp stopApp
INFO: GDA stopped successfully with exit code 0.
```

Notice that it's quite extensive! This is because you're not only doing a bunch of interesting things, but you're also running the app for over a minute.

If your test run yields similar output, you can really celebrate. You've just completed the first iteration of both IoT Edge Tier applications—the GDA and the CDA. As a final step, be sure to merge your CDA and GDA branches back into each respective repository's main branch following the steps listed in PIOT-CDA-02-100 (*https://oreil.ly/ECOVS*) and PIOT-GDA-02-100 (*https://oreil.ly/Hr5Hv*).

The rest of this book is about adding functionality to these applications, connecting them together, and eventually hooking everything up to a cloud service. Buckle up!

Additional Exercises

Figure 2-4 depicts the GDA's design with three system performance tasks (CPU utilization, memory utilization, and disk utilization). While disk utilization isn't critical right now, you may want to tackle it at this time. Additionally, see if you can add two other tasks, SystemNetInTask and SystemNetOutTask, using the patterns for System CpuUtilTask, SystemMemUtilTask, and SystemDiskUtilTask.

In fact, it's not a bad idea to implement the network utilization tasks for the CDA as well (SystemDiskUtilTask is less relevant, as your CDA won't be storing much [if any] data).

Conclusion

This wraps up Part I of *Programming the Internet of Things*—well done! The preface, Chapter 1, and Chapter 2 all helped you get started on your IoT journey. You learned about the IoT ecosystem along with a bit of history, some terminology, and some architectural concepts to help you better understand how these pieces all fit together. If you're a developer and tackled the exercises, you also learned how to collect some basic system performance data using two apps—the CDA (written in Python) and the GDA (written in Java).

You're now ready to add some important functionality to your CDA and GDA applications and eventually connect them to each other and to the cloud.

## PART II

Connecting to the Physical World

Introduction

To be real or not.
Must I live simulated?
You can always choose.

Connecting computers to the physical world can be tricky. This is because computers use digital signals (*binary data*, or 1's and 0's), but the physical world operates on ranges of inputs and outputs (*analog data*), which can represent all kinds of things, such as temperature, wind speed and direction, or degrees of force.

Yet a big part of the IoT is connecting computers to the physical world and the internet to solve problems (as with automatic climate control), right? This connectivity starts at the Edge Tier, where our software (the CDA in this case) interprets this physical world input (sensing) and converts it into the 1's and 0's our computing systems understand. It can also take those 1's and 0's and convert them into commands that can be sent to turn on, turn off, or adjust another physical system (actuation).

Sensing is the process of interpreting a mechanical input signal by converting it into electricity (and eventually into digital signals—i.e., those 1's and 0's I mentioned previously). *Actuation* is the converse of sensing: the process of converting an electrical signal into a mechanical output.

Depending on the sensor and actuator, how this happens may vary dramatically. For the purposes of this book, you'll just need to collect the data from a sensor "source" and send a command to an actuator "target." To keep things simple and maintain our focus on building out the Edge Tier software applications, our goal will be to simulate —or *emulate*—this physical world interaction.

Fortunately, this is relatively easy to do. The sensor-source input ranges and relevant actuation triggers for the target output device can be stored within a configuration file and processed by the software you'll develop for your CDA and GDA. You'll start this process in Chapter 3 by building a simple simulator capability and carry it forward into Chapter 4 by incorporating a software emulator that allows manual control over the process—all without relying on any specific hardware.

Finally, in Chapter 5, you'll build some of the integration underpinnings that will allow your CDA and GDA to "talk" with each other.

What You'll Learn in This Section

This section will begin to address all three key activities discussed in Part I: Measure (data collection), Model (data management), and Manage (system triggers). However, most of the focus will be on data collection, at least initially. I'll dig further into the simpler aspects of data management and system triggers in Chapters 4 and 5 and then discuss an integrated approach in Chapter 10.

Chapters 3 and 4 will show you how to add functionality to the CDA to collect data from simulated and emulated sensors, store and interpret that data within data object wrappers, and convert that data to and from JSON (JavaScript Object Notation).[1] This will be really important for integration not just with the GDA in Chapter 5 and Part III but also with the cloud in Part IV, beginning with Chapter 11.

Chapter 5 brings the GDA back into the picture and adds similar data-object-wrapper and JSON-conversion functionality into its capabilities. This will be important not only for connecting the applications to each other and eventually to the cloud but also for performing some basic analytics within the Edge Tier on the GDA directly. I'll also introduce local storage mechanisms for the GDA using Redis (*https:// redis.io*), an in-memory data cache.

Before we get started, let's discuss configuration.

Application Configuration Review

In Chapter 1, I discussed the "common" package in the cloned Python and Java Git repositories. The configuration utility—ConfigUtil—and its "consts" class—Config Const—deserve a quick review.

---

1 For more information about JSON, see IETF RFC 4627 (*https://www.ietf.org/rfc/rfc4627.html*). For a summary of JSON and a list of libraries that support JSON conversion, I've found *https://www.json.org* to be very helpful.

You may recall that `ConfigUtil` is a very simple abstraction (really a delegate) to the Python and Java libraries that I'll use for the remaining chapters to manage configuration logic. In both repositories, `ConfigUtil` is implemented using a *Singleton*[2] design pattern. This generally works well for logging and configuration purposes, since you'll typically be writing log messages to a single file or reading configuration data from a single file. In the forthcoming code examples and exercises, you'll use `ConfigUtil` rather extensively. It's a very convenient way to load up parameters that are well suited for some degree of customization without requiring code modifications.

The Singleton design pattern has been hotly debated for as long as I can remember. I'll leave the debate to various internet forums; I use it where I believe it adds value and clarity to the design.

Using the same configuration style with both applications affords tremendous flexibility, since you'll have to maintain only one format for configuration files. That said, it does make sense to host the configuration file for each app in a different location, if for no other reason than to ensure that a tweak to one doesn't negatively affect the other.

You might want to review (again) the sample configuration files for the CDA and GDA, which are located in the *./python-components/config* path for the CDA and the *./java-components/config* path for the GDA, both are named *PiotConfig.props*.

The exercises in Part II will rely on some of the configuration parameters specified in both configuration files, so let's take a quick look at the relevant entries. In the `Con strainedDevice` section of the CDA's *PiotConfig.props*, notice the configurable limits specified for humidity, pressure, and temperature:

```
# configurable limits for sensor alerts
humiditySensorFloor   = 35.0
humiditySensorCeiling = 45.0
pressureSensorFloor   = 990.0
pressureSensorCeiling = 1010.0
tempSensorFloor       = 15.0
tempSensorCeiling     = 25.0

# configurable limits for actuator triggers
handleTempChangeOnDevice = True
triggerHvacTempFloor   = 18.0
triggerHvacTempCeiling = 22.0
```

---

2 Erich Gamma et al., *Design Patterns: Elements of Reusable Object-Oriented Software* (Boston: Addison-Wesley, 1994).

Notice the various …`SensorFloor` and …`SensorCeiling` settings under the "configurable limits for sensor simulation"? These key/value pairs establish the baseline settings, or lowest (floor) and highest (ceiling) settings, for each sensor. There are also threshold crossing parameters used to trigger an HVAC[3] alert (`triggerHvacTempFloor` and `triggerHvacTempCeiling`), along with Boolean flags indicating whether the application should take action.

One important aspect of collecting and then acting on sensor data is dealing with *hysteresis*, which is essentially a lagging effect that is influenced by a system's inputs.[4] Consider the following, for instance: if you're tracking temperature, you probably don't want your thermostat to signal your HVAC on and off every time the ambient temperature oscillates slightly above or slightly below a given value. It would be better to track the gradual decrease or increase in ambient temperature and then run the HVAC for a period of time to bring the temperature back into a nominal range.

This is a feature that would be useful in any heating or cooling system, as it would prevent the system from turning on and off rapidly based on minor fluctuations in the sensor reading. I'll address this using a simple set of configuration properties, although you're welcome to introduce advanced features into your own code.

Regardless of how you choose to handle hysteresis, some threshold crossings are best handled as close to the reading as possible, whereas others should be managed further upstream by the GDA or even in the cloud. As such, it's important to include these floor and ceiling settings in the configuration files for both applications.

Speaking of the GDA, here are some of the existing trigger values in its *PiotConfig.props* file, contained within the `GatewayDevice` section:

```
# configurable limits for actuator triggers
enableHandleHumidityChangeOnDevice = True
triggerHumidityFloor   = 30.0
triggerHumidityCeiling = 40.0
```

I'll reference these configurable floor and ceiling settings at various points throughout Chapters 3, 4, and 5 as part of the Model and Manage design characteristics of your system. Of course, you're welcome to adjust these to your specific needs or even to add others as appropriate. If you do so, you might also want to add the property key and some floor and ceiling boundary values within `ConfigConst` to ensure proper validation limits in your code.

---

3 Heating, ventilation, and air conditioning—I'll use "HVAC" to refer to any system that controls heating and cooling, although it's not intended to imply the use of one type of system or another.

4 *Merriam-Webster*, s.v. "hysteresis (*n.*)", accessed February 13, 2021.

## CHAPTER 3

Data Simulation

Sensing and Actuation Using a Data Generator and Simulator

Is it real or fake?
A matter of perception.
Do I act or not?

Fundamental concepts: Design and build logical components that plug into your IoT applications and can interact with the emulated sensors and actuators.

Processing data from sensors and sending commands to actuators are important capabilities of an end-to-end IoT system. Sensors and actuators, as you'll soon see, are truly the "edge of the edge," serving as the final interface between the physical and logical worlds.

Sensing and actuation *capabilities* introduce a conundrum, however: there are myriad types of hardware that support this type of functionality, each with its own set of interface requirements. To mitigate this, and to stay within the realm of programming in support of our initial use case, this chapter will focus on using data simulation and hardware emulation to provide the "physical world" interface needed to program the IoT.

What You'll Learn in This Chapter

This chapter focuses on measuring and (to a lesser degree) modeling the data you generate as part of a simple sensor and actuator simulation environment you'll build for the CDA. The generated data will represent a small handful of environmental sensors, and you'll learn how to process simple threshold crossings to trigger simulated actuation events.

As a reminder, this chapter and Chapter 4 focus exclusively on the CDA, so all of the code will be written in Python.

Simulating Sensors and Actuators

To simulate a sensor, there are a few things you'll need to know, including:

- the data type representing the value it will generate
- the type of sensor and its purpose (which can be represented via a name and an ID value)
- the range of data the sensor can support

There will be similar settings for the actuator, except that you won't be collecting data from it—you'll send it one or more commands (such as an ON or OFF signal), and perhaps even a value and some other information (such as state data) to go along with the command.

Finally, you'll need access to a data source that your simulated sensor logic can use. There are many ways to integrate a data source within the CDA, so I'll posit the data itself must be local to the CDA. This means that you'll essentially have two options: use a fixed data set for each sensor (which can simply be stored in the filesystem), or generate a dynamic data set relative to each sensor. For my Connected Devices course, I use the latter, and I rely on a simple module I've included within the `python-components` source tree located within the *./src/main/python/programmingtheiot/cda/sim/SensorDataGenerator.py* file called `SensorDataGenerator`.

Before we get started, be sure to follow the steps listed in PIOT-CDA-03-000 (*https://oreil.ly/N2H1j*) and check out a new branch for this chapter.

Generating Simulated Data Using a Sensor Data Generator Class

`SensorDataGenerator` is a relatively simple class that you can use to generate data sets representing the sensor measurements your CDA will collect, such as temperature, pressure, and humidity. It relies on the NumPy (*https://numpy.org*) package to generate a series of float values within a given range over a period of time. It also allows you to introduce varying degrees of *noise*, or fluctuations, and apply them to each data value.

While this is a very basic approach to generating simulated data, designed for testing and prototyping purposes, it will provide sufficient variety in each sensor's data to trigger actuation events based on the configuration properties set within *PiotConfig.props* for both the CDA and the GDA. Combining this class with the configuration bounding values provides an initial *model* capability that encapsulates the limits, ranges, and time entries for the data we'll work with in this chapter.

You're welcome to create your own model if you like, but I'll use `SensorDataGenerator` throughout this section to create the data sets needed for each exercise.

If you examine the code, you'll notice that `SensorDataGenerator` implements six methods that can be used to generate values for temperature, pressure, humidity, or any other float-based range, including one that will render an on-screen graph of the data (for visual validation purposes). This latter method—named `generateOnScreen Graph()`—uses Matplotlib[1] to generate the static graph visualization.

The data generation methods `generateDailyEnvironmentHumidityDataSet()`, `generateDailyEnvironmentPressureDataSet()`, `generateDailyIndoorTemperature DataSet()`, `generateDailyMonitorTemperatureDataSet()`, and `generateDailySen sorDataSet()` all return a `SensorDataSet` instance that contains all the timestamp and float value entries generated by the method calls mentioned.

Each of these methods is parameterized, so you can easily customize the output by setting the range (floor and ceiling values), sinusoidal type (approximated), noisiness level (my own levels range from 0% to 100%), the number of items in the set, and whether or not to use second-level granularity (the default is one sample per minute). You can review the documentation in the python-components repository (*https:// github.com/programming-the-iot/python-components*).

The `generateOnScreenGraph()` call accepts the `SensorDataSet` instance, along with your choice of labels for the y-axis and x-axis.

Let's look at some examples of data set visualizations I've created using this library. In Figure 3-1, you can see there's a bit of noise, included to show what you might expect from a temperature sensor that might oscillate between 1% and 2% of the real temperature value for each reading. Over time, you can see the overall floor is about 18°C, with a ceiling of about 22°C and the temperature gradually increasing from its starting point of about 20°C to its maximum in hour 7, followed by its low in hour 19.

---

1 John D. Hunter, "Matplotlib: A 2D Graphics Environment" (*https://matplotlib.org*), *Computing in Science & Engineering* 9, no. 3 (2007): 90–95.

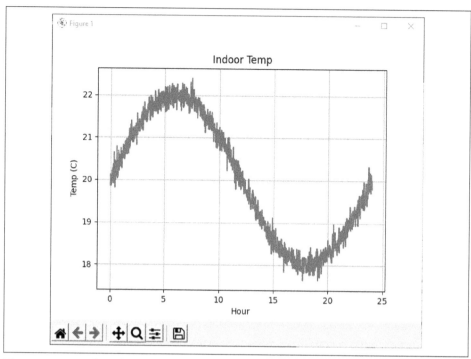

Figure 3-1. Sample indoor temperature range using `generateDailyIndoorTemperature` `DataSet()`

As you can see, this data set provides simulated temperature data that looks reasonable and will suit our testing needs. If you want to simulate a heating system actuation event (such as turning the heating system on and moving hot water through the radiator system in a given room), all you need to trigger it is to set the floor to, say, 19°C. By hour 14 or 15, the event will be generated. This means you can simulate both the sensor reading data and the actuator triggering event using a simple set of simulated data, all contained within the CDA.

Let's take a look at just one more data sample and then dig into some coding exercises.

Figure 3-2 depicts another graph—this one representing humidity over time—in an arc. Humidity levels rise from about 35% relative humidity to as high as about 45% relative humidity before dropping back down again. In this case, I passed in a lower noise value to the method to simulate a cleaner value reading from the humidity sensor. Either way, the trend is clear and provides ample opportunity to set a ceiling value from which to switch on a dehumidifier or an air-conditioning system via an actuation event.

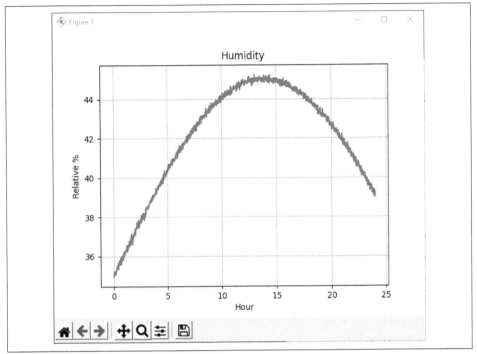

Figure 3-2. Sample indoor humidity range using generateDailyIndoorHumidityData Set()

Programming Exercises

Recall that the overall designs of the Edge Tier applications focus on sensing and actuation (within the CDA) and integration with the cloud and some analytics functionality (within the GDA). This means that the CDA is about to get more complicated, so it will be helpful to look at the application design along with the modules you'll be updating.

Integrating Sensing and Actuation Simulation Within Your Application Design

Figure 3-3 depicts the Constrained Device App with simulated sensing and actuation functionality.

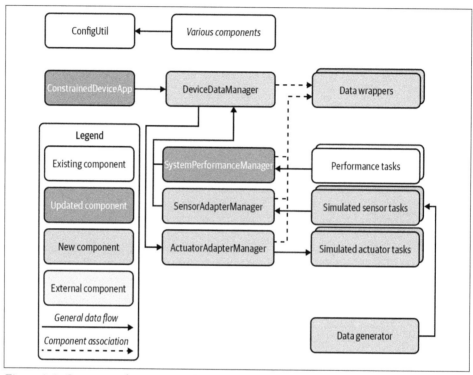

Figure 3-3. Constrained Device Application simulator design

In Figure 3-3, you can see that we're embarking on a more involved software engineering effort—one that will require a deeper dive into data management, capability abstractions, and callbacks. No worries, though! I'll break these parts down piece by piece, so it should be quite manageable.

One way to implement all this functionality is to begin at the top and work our way down to the data structures. Implementation-wise, however, it's easiest to work from the bottom up, because the components at the top—DeviceDataManager and more—all depend on these lower-level structures and classes being in place.

Figure 3-4 shows a UML representation of some of the components that need to be implemented and their relationships. This pattern represents just two instantiation use cases between the DeviceDataManager, the SystemPerformanceManager, and the SensorAdapterManager (temperature simulator task only). The other sensor simulator tasks and `ActuatorAdapterManager` instantiation sequences will adhere to the same pattern.

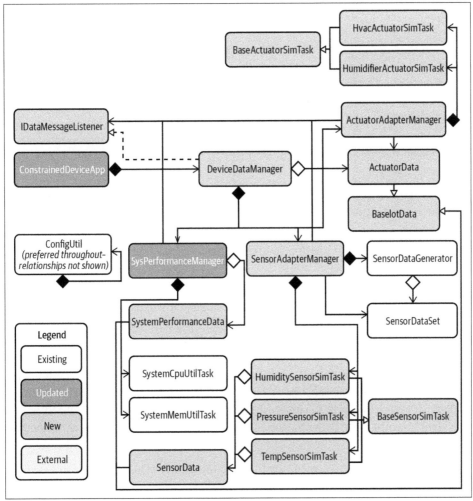

Figure 3-4. Constrained Device Application simulator UML

We'll start with these data structures and the tasks that use them. Before we start, though, be sure to read through PIOT-CDA-03-000 (*https://oreil.ly/N2H1j*) and check out a new branch for this chapter.

Representing Sensor and Actuator Data Within the Application

Before we go further, let's take a step back and consider how all this data will be stored internally and subsequently passed on to the GDA (and the cloud). Since there are similarities between the properties of a simulated sensor and those of an actuator (as well as with the system performance data you're already collecting), you can abstract much of this functionality into a base class. These properties include the following:

- A unique device name. This will be used to identify the physical device instance, represented as a string value. It could take many forms, such as a serial number or network address, for example. For the CDA, you can just use "constraineddevice" or "constraineddevice001" (which is what I've chosen for my implementation).

- An ID to represent the sensor or actuator type. This will be represented as an integer (which can be used to map to a string-based name within each application).

- A timestamp. This will be stored internally as an ISO 8601[2] time/calendar representation and generated when the data container is initialized (or updated).

- Relevant location information. This can be a bit complicated, so let's keep things relatively simple and use float values to store decimal latitude, decimal longitude, and elevation in meters above (or below) sea level (note that a float value will provide sufficient precision for the purposes of the exercises in this book).

- An error indicator flag. This is a boolean value that will default to False.

- A status code. This will be used to represent the current status of the sensor or actuator and will default to 0.

Abstractions can be helpful, but you also need some boundary values, default values, and preset names for the sensors, actuators, and system performance data. You'll see in Part III—specifically in Chapter 10—how these presets can be centralized within the GDA, but for now they can simply be accessed as "consts" in the ConfigConst class.

Let's look at the first requirement for this chapter: PIOT-CDA-03-001 (*https://oreil.ly/ HthCm*).

Create Data Containers to Support Data Collection and Actuation

It can be challenging to determine the appropriate level of detail for each data collection activity in any system, never mind for an IoT edge device that might have many different types of data to handle. The options seem to be endless—ranging from

---

2 The ISO 8601 standard (*https://oreil.ly/ppMNf*) is an internationally recognized specification representation for time and calendar information.

values with varying degrees of precision (integer or floating point—and if the latter, how many decimals?) to text-based representations with different encoding schemes.

Let's keep things simple and assume that all sensor and actuator data values will be represented as 32-bit float values. We'll trust that the precision afforded by the Python 3 float and Java 11 float are sufficient for our needs.

 In Python 3, you can use the decimal module (*https://oreil.ly/rFtAj*) for greater precision if that's important to your application. The use cases discussed in this book won't need that degree of specificity, so a float will suit our purposes.

With this simplified approach to storing values in mind, you can see that the requirements listed in PIOT-CDA-03-001 (*https://oreil.ly/HthCm*) may seem a bit pedantic and perhaps tedious, but the implementation should be relatively straightforward. Let's start with the base class—BaseIotData.

Abstracting shared properties within a base class

BaseIotData is a container for all the common properties that we'll store for all sensor, system performance, and actuator data. These properties include the following:

- name (string, e.g., tempsensor)
- typeID (integer)
- timeStamp (string, e.g., 20201129T18:48:15Z)
- locationID[3] (string, e.g., constraineddevice001)
- latitude (float)
- longitude (float)
- elevation (float)
- hasError (boolean)
- statusCode (integer)

The constructor for BaseIotData accepts the parameters name and typeID, whereas statusCode is set after initialization via the setter method. The hasError fl ag is set to True only if statusCode is set to anything less than 0 (you can change this to align with an alternative error tracking scheme if you'd prefer). The timeStamp variable is

---

3 It can be helpful (and even required) to use a globally unique identifier (GUID), or universally unique identifier (UUID), to represent the unique device ID as part of your telemetry structure. Throughout this book, I'll use the locationID for this purpose, along with human-readable names such as "constraineddevice001."

set at initialization and whenever the data is updated via the `updateTimeStamp()` method.

Implement the sensor and actuator data structures

With `BaseIotData` in place, it's time to create the subclasses that will store the telemetry and command information (`SensorData` and `ActuatorData`, respectively). These classes have some similarities—both require a value (as a float) and need access to the same functionality that's stored in `BaseIotData`. To create these as subclasses, simply derive from `BaseIotData` and implement the additional functionality within each. They'll inherit the base class functionality automatically.

The actions listed in PIOT-CDA-03-001 (*https://oreil.ly/HthCm*) describe the implementation requirements for each. Let's first examine `SensorData`, which inherits from `BaseIotData`.

First, import both `ConfigConst` and `BaseIotData`:

```
import programmingtheiot.common.ConfigConst \
  as ConfigConst
from programmingtheiot.data.BaseIotData \
  import BaseIotData
```

Declare the class and inheritance scheme:

```
class SensorData(BaseIotData):
```

`SensorData` now inherits from `BaseIotData`, so it needs to call its constructor from within the constructor and initialize the class-scoped value parameter, as follows:

```
def __init__(self, \
  typeID: int = ConfigConst.DEFAULT_SENSOR_TYPE, \
  name = ConfigConst.NOT_SET):
    super(SensorData, self).__init__( \
      name = name, typeID = typeID)

    self.value = ConfigConst.DEFAULT_VAL
```

Implement the accessor methods that will get and set the value:

```
def getValue(self) -> float:
  return self.value

def setValue(self, val: float):
  self.updateTimeStamp()
  self.value = val
```

Before moving on to the final action, let's look back at `BaseIotData` for just a moment. Notice that it contains a method named `updateData(self, data)`, and that its only parameter is "data." It will check if "data" is not None and is also a type of `BaseIotData`; if both are true, it will set the local parameters using the values within

data, update the timestamp, and then call the "private" method _handleUpdate
Data(data), which will, by default, simply pass.

The subclass can and should implement this so that it can update its own local
parameters accordingly.

For SensorData, the implementation is relatively simple, since the base class did most
of the work for us. That said, you should still check if data is valid and is also of type
SensorData, since—technically speaking—a "private" method in Python (which is, by
convention, preceded by a single "_") can still be called externally.

Implement _handleUpdateData() in SensorData:

```
def _handleUpdateData(self, data):
  if data and isinstance(data, SensorData):
    self.value = data.getValue()
```

Now that SensorData is complete, let's move on to ActuatorData. I won't go into the
same level of detail, since it's nearly identical. The main differences are:

- The constructor should call the BaseIotData constructor using Config
  Const.DEFAULT_ACTUATOR_TYPE as the typeID.

- Within the constructor, declare the class-scoped variables of self.command,
  self.value, and self.stateData.

You'll then create accessor methods for the class-scoped variables and implement
_handleUpdateData().

Going in the order just given, the code within the constructor will look similar to the
following:

```
self.command = ConfigConst.DEFAULT_COMMAND
self.value = ConfigConst.DEFAULT_VAL
self.stateData = None
```

Next, implement the accessor methods. These will follow the same pattern as Sensor
Data; just remember to implement accessors for the command and stateData[4] in
addition to the value.

Finally, implement the _handleUpdateData() method. You can follow this pattern
provided if you'd like:

```
def _handleUpdateData(self, data):
  if data and isinstance(data, ActuatorData):
```

---

4 The stateData property is mostly a placeholder for future content that might be relevant for an actuation event
  —such as one that displays a message to an LED display (the stateData would then contain the message
  content).

```
self.value = data.getValue()
self.command = data.getCommand()
self.stateData = data.getStateData()
```

That was easy, right? We're almost done—just one more data container remains: `SystemPerformanceData`.

Implement the system performance data structure

`SystemPerformanceData` is a bit different, because it has two values—one for CPU utilization, and the other for memory utilization. Fortunately, it still follows the same pattern as `SensorData` and `ActuatorData`. It also inherits from `BaseIotData`, so the class declaration will follow the same implementation approach as `SensorData` and `ActuatorData`.

The constructor doesn't need any parameterization, however, since `SystemPerforman ceData` knows what it is. It can call the `BaseIotData` constructor with a more specific name and `typeID` and declare its class-scoped variables:

```
def __init__(self):
  super(SystemPerformanceData, self).__init__( \
    name = ConfigConst.SYSTEM_PERF_NAME, \
    typeID = ConfigConst.SYSTEM_PERF_TYPE)

  self.cpuUtil = ConfigConst.DEFAULT_VAL
  self.memUtil = ConfigConst.DEFAULT_VAL
```

With the constructor complete, you can add in the accessor methods for getting and setting the CPU utilization and memory utilization values.

Finally, just like you did with `SensorData` and `ActuatorData`, add in the `_handleUpda teData(data)` method, as follows:

```
def _handleUpdateData(self, data):
  if data and isinstance(data, SystemPerformanceData):
    self.cpuUtil = data.getCpuUtilization()
    self.memUtil = data.getMemoryUtilization()
```

Let's run the unit tests in the python-components repository and the *./src/test/python/ programmingtheiot/part02/unit/data* package—specifically, the three test case files named for the data containers they test: *ActuatorDataTest.py*, *SensorDataTest.py*, and *SystemPerformanceDataTest.py*.

These are very simple unit tests and are designed only to verify that the basic functionality of each class—`ActuatorData`, `SensorData`, and `SystemPerformanceData`—performs as expected.

If you're using the Eclipse IDE with PyDev, here's a sample of the console output you might see if all the `ActuatorDataTest` unit tests execute successfully:

```
Finding files... done.
Importing test modules ... done.

2020-11-29 16:22:51,217:ActuatorDataTest:INFO:Testing ActuatorData
class...
------------------------------------------------------------------
Ran 3 tests in 0.001s

OK
```

Assuming each unit test passes, the next step in the process is to add the sensor and actuator simulator tasks (requirements PIOT-CDA-03-002 (*https://oreil.ly/mOVRM*) through PIOT-CDA-03-005 (*https://oreil.ly/jPfPb*)). I'll walk you through it and then show you how to integrate them all into your CDA application in PIOT-CDA-03-006 (*https://oreil.ly/w2NR7*) through PIOT-CDA-03-008 (*https://oreil.ly/qihSP*).

Simulating Sensors

Now that your data containers are in place, let's put them to use and start building out the sensor simulation infrastructure. This will allow you to generate a steady stream of (simulated) sensor data information that can be stored within `SensorData` for easy processing within the CDA.

Beginning with PIOT-CDA-03-002 (*https://oreil.ly/mOVRM*), you'll move up the stack to the next level in the CDA's software design. Let's start with yet another base class, called `BaseSensorSimTask`. This class, along with the others in this section, is located in the *./programmingtheiot/cda/sim package*. We'll use `BaseSensorSimTask` to abstract the generic sensor simulation functionality from that which is specific to each sensor simulator.

`BaseSensorSimTask` performs two key functions: it creates a `SensorData` instance, which it uses to store the latest sensor simulation data, and it provides a public interface to generate a new instance and access its data.

Here's a summary of the actions listed in PIOT-CDA-03-002 (*https://oreil.ly/mOVRM*):

- Create (or edit) the Python module named `BaseSensorSimTask` in the *./programmingtheiot/cda/sim* package and add the appropriate import statements.
- Define two class-scoped "consts" to bound the minimum and maximum value generated by the randomizer (if a random value is used for the sensor value).
- Edit the constructor so it accepts the following parameters and sets class-scoped variables for each: `name`, `typeID`, `dataSet`, `minVal`, and `maxVal`. Use the class-scoped minimum and maximum "consts" as the defaults for `minVal` and `maxVal`.

— dataSet will be an instance of SensorDataSet, which is a class defined within the SensorDataGenerator module.

— useRandomizer will be set to True if dataSet is None.

- Implement the generateTelemetry(self) -> SensorData: method—this will generate a new class-scoped SensorData instance using self.name, self.typeID, and the value extracted from self.dataSet, or a randomized value generated between self.minVal and self.maxVal if self.dataSet is None.

- Implement the getTelemetryValue(self) -> float: method to return the latest SensorData value if it exists; if not, simply invoke generateTelemetry() and then return the SensorData value.

Let's unpack these steps.

First, you'll need to create the class and add the relevant import statements. If you're using the python-components code base, this is already done for you and looks similar to the following:

```
import random

import programmingtheiot.common.ConfigConst as ConfigConst
from programmingtheiot.data.SensorData import SensorData
from programmingtheiot.cda.sim.SensorDataGenerator \
  import SensorDataSet

class BaseSensorSimTask():
  DEFAULT_MIN_VAL = ConfigConst.DEFAULT_VAL
  DEFAULT_MAX_VAL = 100.0
```

You can now create the constructor, and you'll see from the implementation how the useRandomizer flag is set:

```
def __init__(self, \
  name: str = ConfigConst.NOT_SET, \
  typeID: int = ConfigConst.DEFAULT_SENSOR_TYPE, \
  dataSet: SensorDataSet = None, \
  minVal: float = DEFAULT_MIN_VAL, \
  maxVal: float = DEFAULT_MAX_VAL):

  self.dataSet = dataSet
  self.name = name
  self.typeID = typeID
  self.dataSetIndex = 0
  self.useRandomizer = False

  self.latestSensorData = None

  if not self.dataSet:
    self.useRandomizer = True
```

```
    self.minVal = minVal
    self.maxVal = maxVal
```

If self.dataSet is None, then a random value will be generated instead (between self.minVal and self.maxVal). You'll see later how dataSet is generated and then passed into the task, but for now, just trust that it will be done a bit higher up in the stack.

Let's see how self.dataSet will be used and move on to the next method: generate Telemetry(). As indicated in the actions, this is where the SensorData instance gets created and populated with relevant data.

 As a data container, SensorData is essentially the telemetry for the sensor, since it contains the information we'll need further upstream and will eventually be converted into a format that can be transmitted via one of the protocols I'll discuss in Part III.

Here's an example implementation for generateTelemetry():

```
def generateTelemetry(self) -> SensorData:
  self.latestSensorData = \
    SensorData(typeID = self.typeID, name = self.name)

  sensorVal = ConfigConst.DEFAULT_VAL

  if self.useRandomizer:
    sensorVal = random.uniform(self.minVal, self.maxVal)
  else:
    sensorVal = \
      self.dataSet.getDataEntry(index = self.dataSetIndex)

    self.latestSensorData.setValue(sensorVal)
    self.dataSetIndex = self.dataSetIndex + 1

    lastEntryIndex = self.dataSet.getDataEntryCount() - 1

    if self.dataSetIndex >= lastEntryIndex:
      self.dataSetIndex = 0

  return self.latestSensorData
```

There's quite a bit going on here, right? As soon as this method is called, a new SensorData instance is created using self.typeID and self.name (which were set when this class was initialized) and assigned to the self.latestSensorData variable.

Then the code determines how to generate the sensor value. If the randomizer is enabled, a new value is generated as a random value between self.minVal and self.maxVal. That's pretty straightforward. But if self.dataSet is valid (not None), `self.useRandomizer` should be False, as `self.dataSet` contains all the data to be used within the simulator.

To extract it, a simple algorithm can be implemented to just grab the next element in the data set. Once the algorithm reaches the end of the data set entries, it goes back to the first index and starts all over again.

Now that the simulated sensor value is known, it can be set as the value for `self.latestSensorData`. Done.

Last, you'll need a simple method to just get that latest value—you can call this method `getTelemetryValue()`, which you may remember from the system performance module back in Chapter 2.

In this case, however, it's going to return the value stored in `self.latestSensorData` —unless it hasn't been created yet. If that's the case, the implementation can simply invoke `self.generateTelemetry()` and then return the value. Here's one way to implement this:

```python
def getTelemetryValue(self) -> float:
  if not self.latestSensorData:
    self.generateTelemetry()

  return self.latestSensorData.getValue()
```

And that's basically it for the `BaseSensorSimTask` implementation!

Now comes the easy part. In PIOT-CDA-03-003 (*https://oreil.ly/zAjaP*), the actions list three new classes to implement. The good news is that these are all subclasses of `BaseSensorSimTask`, and since this base class will do most of the heavy lifting, the subclasses each merely need to pass `name` and `typeID` into its constructor. Let's look at the actions in more detail:

- Create (or edit) `HumiditySensorSimTask`. The module and class name should be the same and derive from `BaseSensorSimTask`.

- Create (or edit) `PressureSensorSimTask`. The module and class name should be the same and derive from `BaseSensorSimTask`.

- Create (or edit) `TemperatureSensorSimTask`. The module and class name should be the same and derive from `BaseSensorSimTask`.

Take a look at the implementation of `HumiditySensorSimTask`:

```python
import programmingtheiot.common.ConfigConst as ConfigConst

from programmingtheiot.cda.sim.BaseSensorSimTask \
  import BaseSensorSimTask
from programmingtheiot.cda.sim.SensorDataGenerator \
  import SensorDataGenerator
```

```
class HumiditySensorSimTask(BaseSensorSimTask):
  def __init__(self, dataSet = None):
    super(HumiditySensorSimTask, self).__init__( \
      name = ConfigConst.HUMIDITY_SENSOR_NAME, \
      typeID = ConfigConst.HUMIDITY_SENSOR_TYPE, \
      dataSet = dataSet, \
      minVal = SensorDataGenerator.LOW_NORMAL_ENV_HUMIDITY, \
      maxVal = SensorDataGenerator.HI_NORMAL_ENV_HUMIDITY)
```

That's all there is to it! Now let's add the other two classes—PressureSensorSimTask and TemperatureSensorSimTask—but using the correct name, type ID, minVal and maxVal.

See if you can add them on your own; the guidelines are provided in PIOT-CDA-03-003 (*https://oreil.ly/zAjaP*).

Time to test these new classes. You'll see the test cases in the test path under *./programmingtheiot/part02/unit/sim*. Run all the tests in the following test case modules: HumiditySensorSimTaskTest, PressureSensorSimTaskTest, and TemperatureSensorSimTaskTest. All unit tests should pass.

Here's some sample log output from HumiditySensorSimTaskTest when running within Eclipse using PyUnit:

```
Finding files... done.
Importing test modules ... done.

2020-11-29 22:50:41,644:HumiditySensorSimTaskTest:INFO:Testing
HumiditySensorSimTask class...
2020-11-29 22:50:41,645:HumiditySensorSimTaskTest:INFO:SensorData:
name=HumiditySensor,timeStamp=20201129T22:50:41,value=40.19161945800801
2020-11-29 22:50:41,645:HumiditySensorSimTaskTest:INFO:Humidity data: 40.191619
------------------------------------------------------------------
Ran 2 tests in 0.001s

OK
```

With your sensor simulation infrastructure working, it's time to move on to simulation actuation events.

Simulating Actuators

Gathering data is pretty cool. Doing something with the data is even cooler.

Remember that actuators are responsible for triggering some kind of mechanical action. While the cooler-than-cool path forward is clearly to use the sensor data to do something tangible, like turning on the A/C or heating system, what you'll do right now is to log a message to the console indicating that the action was taken.

Before disappointment sets in, let me assure you that all the actuation functionality you're about to build can in fact be used to send real actuation events to real actuators. I'll get to this (sort of) in Chapter 4. For now, let's start building the infrastructure.

In much the same vein as the simulated sensor functionality, you'll move up from the data containers to the next level of simulated actuator functionality, beginning with PIOT-CDA-03-004 (*https://oreil.ly/RFxWX*). In this task, you'll implement `BaseActuatorSimTask`, which contains most of the functionality needed to simulate simple actuation events (that result in log messages).

`BaseActuatorSimTask` abstracts both the "activate" and "deactivate" functions of an actuator via a single call to `updateActuator(ActuatorData)`.

This is possible because `ActuatorData` contains a command parameter that can be used to instruct the actuator to turn on, turn off, rotate, and so on in conjunction with the activate and deactivate functions mentioned earlier.

Here's a summary of the actions listed in PIOT-CDA-03-004 (*https://oreil.ly/RFxWX*):

- Create (or edit) the Python module named `BaseActuatorSimTask` in the *./programmingtheiot/cda/sim* package.
- Create a constructor that includes the parameter's `name`, `typeID`, and `simpleName`, and set class-scoped variables to these values.
- Within the constructor, define a class-scoped variable to store the last executed command—you can call this `self.lastKnownCommand`.
- Create private methods to handle activation and deactivation of the actuator.
- Create a public method to accept an `ActuatorData` instance, validate the data (and type), and use the command to determine whether the activation or deactivation private method should then be invoked.

Let's take a look at each one of these steps, starting with the constructor (I'm assuming the module/class creation bit is well understood):

```
def __init__(self, \
   name: str = ConfigConst.NOT_SET, \
   typeID: int = ConfigConst.DEFAULT_ACTUATOR_TYPE, \
   simpleName: str = "Actuator"):
```

Notice the `simpleName` parameter. This isn't *really* necessary; however, it will allow you to add a customized actuator name that displays nicely on-screen. Why not just use "name" instead? You can—just remove `simpleName` as a parameter.

I left `simpleName` in because this is a simulator, and I like to have additional information within each log message for future debugging. It also shows you one other way to customize this logic. If you need to add other parameters to suit your own simulation-environment needs, feel free to do so.

Let's move on to the next two methods—these are "private," as denoted by the preceding underscore character that begins the method name. The first, _activateActuator(), is shown in all its glory as follows:

```
def _activateActuator(self, \
    val: float = ConfigConst.DEFAULT_VAL, \
    stateData: str = None) -> int:

    msg = "\n*******"
    msg = msg + "\n* O N *"
    msg = msg + "\n*******"
    msg = msg + "\n" + self.simpleName + \
        " VALUE -> " + str(val) + "\n======="

    logging.info( \
        "Simulating %s actuator ON: %s", self.name, msg)

    return 0
```

Nothing fancy: the activation functionality just logs some messages on-screen to indicate the actuator is being enabled.

Notice that the parameters are represented as a float (for the value) and a string (for the state data, if any). Neither may technically be needed—some actuators need only an ON (or OFF) to do their job. It makes sense to pass these parameters, however, since other actuators may need additional parameters as part of any actuation event.

The deactivation functionality is similar. Here's a look at the implementation:

```
def _deactivateActuator(self, \
    val: float = ConfigConst.DEFAULT_VAL, \
    stateData: str = None) -> int:

    msg = "\n*******"
    msg = msg + "\n* OFF *"
    msg = msg + "\n*******"

    logging.info( \
        "Simulating %s actuator OFF: %s", self.simpleName, msg)

    return 0
```

Almost the same, right? The difference is in the log message, where "ON" is replaced by "OFF." Interestingly, the parameters for the method call are the same. *So why does an actuator need a value and/or state data for an OFF command?*

Let's assume there's a display update associated with the "OFF" command. The message to display as part of the deactivation needs to be passed into the method. In other cases, a value may be relevant—possibly to serve as the default in case it's not preset within the actuator implementation.

What about data validation and the actual update logic? This can be contained within the updateActuator() method. This is the public interface to the actuator simulation task. It accepts a single ActuatorData parameter and returns the same (albeit a new instance of one).

You may be wondering why the activation and deactivation methods don't simply accept an ActuatorData instance as well. You can certainly change this if you'd like; however, this approach allows your base class implementation of updateActuator() to handle the generic ActuatorData parsing, so your activation and deactivation methods need only focus on processing values and taking the action. These two functions can be abstracted to subclasses at a later time, leaving the core ActuatorData processing in a single place: the base class.

Notice that the check on data is to ensure it's not "None" *and also* to confirm that typeID matches the actuator task's typeID. This should be handled for us in the class that calls this method (as you'll soon see), but it's best to validate here to ensure no error is made prior to the call.

One other type of validation you could do here (or in the activation or deactivation methods), which isn't explicitly called out, is boundary checking on the value. Since this implementation is only logging messages, it doesn't really matter. It will matter, however, if you're invoking an emulator or a real actuator. Keep that in mind. Data validation at each public interface (and also within many private functions) is critically important. It may seem like overkill, but it can mean the difference between logging a warning or an error and passing on a dangerous setting to an actuator.

In the example that follows, I'll demonstrate some *very* basic data validation within updateActuator(), including a check to ensure we're not acting on a repeated command and value; however, I strongly suggest you incorporate additional validation to accommodate your specific needs:

```
if data and self.typeID == data.getTypeID():
    statusCode = ConfigConst.DEFAULT_STATUS

    # check if the new command is repeated - if so, ignore
    curCommand = data.getCommand()
    curVal = data.getValue()

    if curCommand == self.lastKnownCommand and curVal == self.lastKnownValue:
        logging.debug( \
            "Ignoring repeated actuator command and value: %s %s", \
            str(curCommand), str(curVal))
    else:
        if curCommand == ConfigConst.COMMAND_ON:
            logging.info("Activating actuator...")
```

```
    statusCode = \
      self._activateActuator( \
        val = data.getValue(), \
        stateData = data.getStateData())

  elif curCommand == ConfigConst.COMMAND_OFF:
    logging.info("Deactivating actuator...")
    statusCode = \
      self._deactivateActuator( \
        val = data.getValue(), \
        stateData = data.getStateData())

  else:
    logging.warning( \
      "Unknown actuator command: %s", str(curCommand))
    statusCode = -1

  # update the last known actuator command
  self.lastKnownCommand = curCommand
  self.lastKnownValue = curVal

  # create the ActuatorData response from the command
  actuatorResponse = ActuatorData()
  actuatorResponse.updateData(data)
  actuatorResponse.setStatusCode(statusCode)
  actuatorResponse.setAsResponse()

  return actuatorResponse

return None
```

Let's see what we have here:

- Simple data validation: *Check.*
- Command validation: *Check.*
- Invocation of the correct actuator method: *Check.*
- Creation of a response: *Check.*

Clearly, the updateActuator() method serves as the orchestrator for all internal calls. As long as the "rules" for this orchestration and sequence of events remain the same, the base class can manage it all, even if you handle the specific activation and deactivation within a subclass.

That last step—creating a response—can take many forms. I've opted to use an Actua torData instance with a flag indicating that it's a response to an actuation command. This allows me to set the end value and resultant state data if I choose and avoids creating yet another data container class that would contain the same information as ActuatorData, but with a single Boolean flag as the delta.

OK, almost done with actuation tasks. You'll need to add just a couple more classes in, and they'll be as simple as their corresponding sensor task classes.

In PIOT-CDA-03-005 (*https://oreil.ly/jPfPb*), the actions list two new classes to implement: `HumidifierActuatorSimTask` and `HvacActuatorSimTask`. You can certainly add more classes later, but for now let's focus on these two. They are similar to their sensor simulator counterparts, and both are subclasses of a common base class named `BaseActuatorSimTask`. Like `BaseSensorSimTask`, they will do most of the heavy lifting. The two subclasses each need merely to pass their name and type ID into its constructor. Let's look at the actions in more detail:

- Create (or edit) `HumidifierActuatorSimTask`. The module and class name should be the same and derive from `BaseActuatorSimTask`.

- Create (or edit) `HvacActuatorSimTask`. The module and class name should be the same and derive from `BaseActuatorSimTask`.

Again, both implementations will be very simple. Here's the `HumidifierActuatorSim Task`:

```
import programmingtheiot.common.ConfigConst as ConfigConst

from programmingtheiot.data.ActuatorData \
    import ActuatorData
from programmingtheiot.cda.sim.BaseActuatorSimTask \
    import BaseActuatorSimTask

class HumidifierActuatorSimTask(BaseActuatorSimTask):
    def __init__(self):
        super(HumidifierActuatorSimTask, self).__init__( \
            name = ConfigConst.HUMIDIFIER_ACTUATOR_NAME, \
            typeID = ConfigConst.HUMIDIFIER_ACTUATOR_TYPE, \
            simpleName = "HUMIDIFIER")
```

Let's add the other class now—`HvacActuatorSimTask`—but using the correct name and type ID. You can add this final actuator sim task on your own, following the guidelines provided in PIOT-CDA-03-005 (*https://oreil.ly/jPfPb*).

With the actuator sim tasks implemented, let's test them out (the test cases are in the test path under *./programmingtheiot/part02/unit/sim*). Run all the tests in the test case modules `HumidifierActuatorSimTaskTest` and `HvacActuatorSimTaskTest`. All unit tests should pass.

Here's some sample log output from `HumidifierActuatorSimTaskTest` when running within Eclipse using PyUnit:

```
Finding files... done.
Importing test modules ... done.
```

```
2020-12-28 11:02:01,478:HumidifierActuatorSimTaskTest:INFO:Testing
HumidifierActuatorSimTask class...
.
.
.
2020-12-28 11:02:01,481:BaseActuatorSimTask:INFO:Activating actuator...
2020-12-28 11:02:01,481:BaseActuatorSimTask:INFO:Simulating HumidifierActuator
actuator ON:
*******
* O N *
*******
HumidifierActuator VALUE -> 18.2
=======
.
.
.
2020-12-28 11:02:01,481:BaseActuatorSimTask:INFO:Deactivating actuator...
2020-12-28 11:02:01,482:BaseActuatorSimTask:INFO:Simulating HumidifierActuator
actuator OFF:
*******
* OFF *
*******
2020-12-28 11:02:01,482:HumidifierActuatorSimTaskTest:INFO:ActuatorData: name=Not
Set,typeID=2,timeStamp=2020-12-
28T16:02:01.482102+00:00,statusCode=0,hasError=False,locationID=constraineddevice
001,elevation=0.0,latitude=0.0,longitude=0.0,command=0,stateData=None,value=21.4,
isResponse=True
------------------------------------------------------------------
Ran 1 test in 0.004s

OK
```

Obviously, these tests are very simple, as are all the simulator classes I've been discussing. Ultimately, the objective is to build a system that permits both flexibility and simplicity via a modular architecture. The abstractions you just completed are important parts of this design approach and provide the basis to support the three core principles discussed earlier: Measure, Model, and Manage, with an initial focus on measure.

 In Chapter 4, you'll build emulators that simulate sensing functionality and allow you to trigger one or more actuation events should the simulated sensors generate data that requires your device to take action. The exercises in this chapter will enable you to build additional capability into your Edge Tier environment.

With basic (and simulated) measurement capability now in place, let's take a look at the management aspects of processing this data. Eventually, much of this will be in the hands of the GDA and later as part of your cloud service infrastructure. For now, you'll build a simple test function within your CDA that looks for a simple threshold crossing and send an actuation event to the simulated actuator. Once this is functioning properly, you'll see how the infrastructure you've developed will be an important part of the next set of exercises.

First, though, let's put some basic functionality in place to use these simulators.

Connecting Simulated Sensors with the Sensor Adapter Manager

Remember the SystemPerformanceManager class you created in Chapter 2? It manages the initialization and data collection activities of the system performance tasks. You'll create similar functionality for your sensor and actuator simulators and see how each manager can also be used to control the emulator functionality you'll build in Chapter 4.

Let's start with the simulator manager first. PIOT-CDA-03-006 (*https://oreil.ly/ w2NR7*) describes the SensorAdapterManager class, which you'll eventually use to manage the initialization of all sensor tasks, simulated and emulated.

Take a look at the key activities for this module:

- Create (or rather edit) the SensorAdapterManager class in the *./src/main/python/ programmingtheiot/cda/system* package.
- Define a constructor that accepts parameters for choosing between simulated data and emulated data and poll cycle rate. Initialize a scheduler to retrieve data from the sensor tasks at the poll cycle rate interval.
- Initialize the sensor simulator (or emulator) tasks. If using simulation, create a data model for each using SensorDataGenerator (or your own model if you'd prefer).
- Add functions to start and stop the manager and trigger any necessary callbacks to an external data message listener.

On the surface, this seems relatively straightforward. There are some interesting design decisions to consider: for example, which component owns the data generation logic? I'll tackle this question when I walk through one implementation approach for the third bullet.

But first things first—let's create the SensorAdapterManager class. If you're using the sample python-components code, you'll notice it already exists, although it doesn't have much in the way of implementation detail:

```
import logging

import programmingtheiot.common.ConfigConst as ConfigConst

from programmingtheiot.common.ConfigUtil import ConfigUtil
from programmingtheiot.common.IDataMessageListener \
```

```
import IDataMessageListener

from programmingtheiot.cda.sim.SensorDataGenerator \
  import SensorDataGenerator
from programmingtheiot.cda.sim.HumiditySensorSimTask \
  import HumiditySensorSimTask
from programmingtheiot.cda.sim.TemperatureSensorSimTask \
  import TemperatureSensorSimTask
from programmingtheiot.cda.sim.PressureSensorSimTask \
  import PressureSensorSimTask

from apscheduler.schedulers.background import BackgroundScheduler

class SensorAdapterManager(object):
```

There are quite a few import statements here! Logging is an important part of both debugging and monitoring, so the Python logging infrastructure is imported, along with the utility classes ConfigConst and ConfigUtil. You can use these to incorporate configurable floor and ceiling values, as well as any simple threshold crossing parameters that are relevant for the CDA.

Other imports include the sensor simulator tasks themselves, along with the Sensor DataGenerator, which will collectively be used to generate the simulated sensor data that your CDA will utilize (and eventually send to the GDA and cloud service).

One final import is from a library called APScheduler (*https://pypi.org/project/APScheduler*), which I use in my solution set for scheduling the calls to each simulator. You could create your own scheduling mechanism, but you may find it easier to start with a library designed for this purpose.

With the imports in place and the class declared, create the SensorAdapterManager constructor and initialize the configuration properties and class-scoped variables. Let's take a look at a sample implementation:

```
def __init__(self):
  configUtil = ConfigUtil()

  self.pollRate = \
    configUtil.getInteger( \
      section = ConfigConst.CONSTRAINED_DEVICE, \
      key = ConfigConst.POLL_CYCLES_KEY, \
      defaultVal = ConfigConst.DEFAULT_POLL_CYCLES)

  self.useEmulator = \
    configUtil.getBoolean( \
      section = ConfigConst.CONSTRAINED_DEVICE, \
      key = ConfigConst.ENABLE_EMULATOR_KEY)

  self.locationID = \
    configUtil.getProperty( \
      section = ConfigConst.CONSTRAINED_DEVICE, \
```

```
        key = ConfigConst.DEVICE_LOCATION_ID_KEY, \
        defaultVal = ConfigConst.NOT_SET)

    if pollRate <= 0:
      self.pollRate = ConfigConst.DEFAULT_POLL_CYCLES

    self.scheduler = BackgroundScheduler()
    self.scheduler.add_job( \
      self.handleTelemetry, \
      'interval', \
      seconds = self.pollRate)

    self.dataMsgListener = None
```

I'll cover the first few lines of code in the next paragraph. The last line of code referencing the self.dataMsgListener instance will eventually be set to the class instance that implements IDataMessageListener. It will be used as the callback container for passing relevant messages from SensorAdapterManager to another class you'll soon create, named DeviceDataManager. For now, set it to "None"—you'll update it later in the code base.

Going back to the beginning of the constructor, notice the use of ConfigUtil, which will be the primary interface into the configuration file discussed within the introduction to this chapter. Loading data from the configuration is relatively straightforward, since ConfigUtil does all the heavy lifting. You simply need to pass in the configuration section, the name of the key, and—optionally—a default value (if the section and/or key doesn't exist).

Notice the pollRate parameter initialization code. The value is retrieved from the ConfigUtil (which pulls it from the ConfigConst.CONSTRAINED_DEVICE section). ConfigConst.DEFAULT_POLL_CYCLES will be used as the default should the key (or section) not exist.

However, that's not quite good enough: the value still requires validation to ensure the poll rate isn't a negative value, or even "0." While "–1" and "0" are valid integer values, neither is useful as a poll rate. Basic validation is paramount.

 You'll see how convenient it can be to use a configuration file to provide basic system and application settings, but it also increases the need for validation. A mistyped configuration entry can cause erroneous data, negatively affect a system's performance, or worse. Internally validating configuration settings and data values in general is critical to designing and implementing an effective system.

The next configuration parameter—enableEmulator—is a simple boolean that doesn't require much in the way of validation: it's either True or False. Until we get into Chapter 4, it will be False. Be sure to reflect this in *PiotConfig.props*, within the `ConstrainedDevice` section, as follows:

```
enableEmulator = False
```

The last configuration parameter, `locationID`, will be applied to each `SensorData` instance generated and processed within the `SensorAdapterManager`. This will be useful later on if you need to handle data from multiple devices, since it provides a convenient and user-readable way to align a `SensorData` instance to a specific device.

By default, the configuration file uses "constraineddevice001" for this value; keep it as is for now, since I'll refer to it in Part III. That said, be sure to check if it's a valid text string and set it accordingly if it can't be loaded from the configuration file.

With the poll rate and other configuration parameters set, you can now initialize the scheduler. Assuming you're following the code pattern listed previously (using APScheduler), create an instance of `BackgroundScheduler` and configure it by adding a single job that will call the soon-to-be-created `self.handleTelemetry` function with a poll rate of `self.pollRate` seconds as the interval:

```
self.scheduler = BackgroundScheduler()
self.scheduler.add_job( \
  self.handleTelemetry, 'interval', seconds = self.pollRate)
```

 In the preceding example, I'm using the interval scheduler, although the library supports other types as well. You can find additional APScheduler examples at *https://github.com/agronholm/apscheduler*.

The second step within the constructor of `SensorAdapterManager` is to initialize the sensor simulator tasks. I'll walk through the initialization for `TemperatureSensorSim Task`, and you can implement the others on your own (see PIOT-CDA-03-006 (*https://oreil.ly/w2NR7*)):

```
if not self.useEmulator:
  tempFloor = \
    configUtil.getFloat( \
      section = ConfigConst.CONSTRAINED_DEVICE, \
      key = ConfigConst.TEMP_SIM_FLOOR_KEY, \
      defaultVal = \
      SensorDataGenerator.LOW_NORMAL_INDOOR_TEMP)

  tempCeiling = \
    configUtil.getFloat( \
      section = ConfigConst.CONSTRAINED_DEVICE, \
      key = ConfigConst.TEMP_SIM_CEILING_KEY, \
      defaultVal = \
        SensorDataGenerator.HI_NORMAL_INDOOR_TEMP)
```

```
    tempData = \
      self.dataGenerator.generateDailyIndoorTemperatureDataSet( \
        minValue = tempFloor, \
        maxValue = tempCeiling, \
        useSeconds = False)

    self.tempAdapter = \
      TemperatureSensorSimTask(dataSet = tempData)
```

There's quite a bit going on in this code segment, so let's break it down.

The instance of ConfigUtil allows you to retrieve the floor and ceiling values for the humidity sensor simulation, as well as any other sensor simulation data sets. The data generator needs these to generate a reasonable range—from floor to ceiling—for each data set it produces.

Next, create an instance of SensorDataGenerator, which will be used to generate a time-based data set of humidity data with the floor and ceiling values as parameters.

Following your SensorDataGenerator instance creation code, create an instance of TemperatureSensorSimTask and pass to it a reference to the data set you just generated using SensorDataGenerator. You can also use your own or even let the simulator task generate a data set internally.

 I've chosen to generate the simulated data set within SensorAdapterManager, largely because it gives me direct control over not just one sensor simulator (or emulator) task but *all* of them. This centralized approach allows my implementation to define sensor generation logic in a single place, with one set of related dependencies (such as SensorDataGenerator). Feel free to adjust the design to meet your specific needs. This is one of many approaches that could work and yield similar results.

The final step in creating the initial version of SensorDataGenerator is to implement the remaining methods that will start and stop the manager, handle telemetry collection via the scheduler, and invoke the callback functions defined within the self.dataMsgListener instance.

Let's work backward. We'll first create a method to set the self.dataMsgListener. It will look similar to the following:

```
def setDataMessageListener( \
  self, \
  listener: IDataMessageListener):

  if listener:
    self.dataMsgListener = listener
```

That's about as easy as it gets. Notice that the listener is of type IDataMessageLis tener, which is already defined in the sample source code contained within the python-components repository. It's not *really* an interface, as you'd expect in Java—it's more of a concrete class with method declarations that simply pass. Stylistically, however, it's a good idea to think of it as an interface contract, since it will be the primary mechanism for sending data from this manager to other components within the CDA.

Next, create the handleTelemetry() function. This will be just as simple: it will delegate to another private method that will handle polling each sensor and passing its data to the self.dataMsgListener callback.

The following code sample assumes you've implemented the logic to instantiate self.humidityAdapter and self.pressureAdapter within the constructor:

```
def handleTelemetry(self):
    humidityData = self.humidityAdapter.generateTelemetry()
    pressureData = self.pressureAdapter.generateTelemetry()
    tempData     = self.tempAdapter.generateTelemetry()

    humidityData.setLocationID(self.locationID)
    pressureData.setLocationID(self.locationID)
    tempData.setLocationID(self.locationID)

    logging.info( \
      'Generated humidity data: ' + str(humidityData))
    logging.info( \
      'Generated pressure data: ' + str(pressureData))
    logging.info('Generated temp data: ' + str(tempData))

    if self.dataMsgListener:
      self.dataMsgListener.handleSensorMessage(humidityData)
      self.dataMsgListener.handleSensorMessage(pressureData)
      self.dataMsgListener.handleSensorMessage(tempData)
```

Recall the generateTelemetry() function you created within each sensor adapter task. It produces a SensorData instance that you can now modify by setting the locationID, and other properties if needed, such as longitude, latitude, and elevation.

IoT data is often time-bounded, so it's generally referred to as *time series data* (in most cases). The source of the data, including its location, should also be included. One way to capture it is via an ID value, which can either be mapped to location coordinates or embellish the location data already provided. The locationID value represents this user-friendly label and will be adequate for the tests you'll execute in this book. For additional granularity, you can store the device latitude, longitude, and elevation within the configuration file for each device application. Simply use ConfigUtil to retrieve each value as a float (which should provide sufficient coordinate detail for simple IoT environments) and then set the values within each SensorData instance using their respective setter methods.

Finally, the startManager() and stopManager() functions need to be implemented. These are very straightforward, so let's take a quick look and then move on to testing:

```
def startManager(self):
  logging.info('Started SensorAdapterManager.')

  if not self.scheduler.running:
    self.scheduler.start()
  else:
    logging.warning( \
      'SensorAdapterManager scheduler already started.')

def stopManager(self):
  logging.info('Stopped SensorAdapterManager.')

  try:
    self.scheduler.shutdown()
  except:
    logging.warning( \
      'SensorAdapterManager scheduler already stopped.')
```

Let's test your implementation to ensure it delivers the expected results. Testing the SensorAdapterManager (and the ActuatorAdapterManager, which is next) is a bit tricky, as there aren't any unit tests that provide any useful output. You'll need to test manually, using a simple test harness that's already part of the python-components code base.

You'll see the SensorAdapterManagerTest within the *./src/test/python/programmingtheiot/part02/integration/system* path. Before you run the test, make sure the enableEmulator = False key/value pair is set within the configuration file (*./config/PiotConfig.props*).

The output will be a bit lengthy, and by default, the test will take about a minute to run. Assuming you added logging in the correct places, the key things to look for are

(a) a successful start (and eventual stop) of `SensorAdapterManagerTest`, and (b) that the `SensorData` is generated from the three simulator tasks (humidity, pressure, and temperature). Let's take a look:

```
Finding files... done.
Importing test modules ... done.

2020-12-28 21:16:12,936:SensorAdapterManagerTest:INFO:Testing SensorAdapterManager
class...
2020-12-28 21:16:12,936:ConfigUtil:INFO:Loading config:
../../../../../../../config/PiotConfig.props
.
.
.
2020-12-28 21:16:13,034:SensorAdapterManager:INFO:Started SensorAdapterManager.
2020-12-28 21:16:13,036:base:INFO:Added job "SensorAdapterManager.handleTelemetry"
to job store "default"
2020-12-28 21:16:13,036:base:INFO:Scheduler started
2020-12-28 21:16:13,037:base:DEBUG:Looking for jobs to run
2020-12-28 21:16:13,037:base:DEBUG:Next wakeup is due at 2020-12-28
21:16:43.032124-05:00 (in 29.995003 seconds)
.
.
.
2020-12-28 21:17:13,037:base:INFO:Running job "SensorAdapterManager.handleTelemetry
(trigger: interval[0:00:30], next run at: 2020-12-28 21:17:43 EST)" (scheduled at
2020-12-28 21:17:13.032124-05:00)
2020-12-28 21:17:13,038:SensorAdapterManager:INFO:Generated humidity data:
name=HumiditySensor,typeID=1,timeStamp=2020-12-
29T02:17:13.037902+00:00,statusCode=0,hasError=False,locationID=constraineddevice00
1,elevation=0.0,latitude=0.0,longitude=0.0,value=35.16090174436236
2020-12-28 21:17:13,038:SensorAdapterManager:INFO:Generated pressure data:
name=PressureSensor,typeID=2,timeStamp=2020-12-
29T02:17:13.037973+00:00,statusCode=0,hasError=False,locationID=constraineddevice00
1,elevation=0.0,latitude=0.0,longitude=0.0,value=1001.786134547049
2020-12-28 21:17:13,038:SensorAdapterManager:INFO:Generated temp data:
name=TempSensor,typeID=3,timeStamp=2020-12-
29T02:17:13.038030+00:00,statusCode=0,hasError=False,locationID=constraineddevice00
1,elevation=0.0,latitude=0.0,longitude=0.0,value=20.128837377948486
.
.
.
2020-12-28 21:17:13,039:SensorAdapterManager:INFO:Stopped SensorAdapterManager.
----------------------------------------------------------------------
Ran 1 test in 60.105s

OK
```

You can run the test for much longer than 60 seconds if you'd like; however, a couple of scheduled iterations that generate `SensorData` output for each task will be sufficient for now.

Looking at the log file, the start and stop messages are logged (near the top and bottom, respectively), and the SensorData is generated and logged within SensorAdap terManager for each of the sensor tasks: humidity, pressure, and temperature.

Chapter 4 will add some additional functionality using emulator tasks. For now, let's move on to the ActuatorAdapterManager.

Connecting Simulated Actuators with the Actuator Adapter Manager

ActuatorAdapterManager, defined in PIOT-CDA-03-007 (*https://oreil.ly/Y4KYm*), has some similarities to SensorAdapterManager. Key implementation activities include the following:

- Within the constructor, set the self.useEmulator and self.locationID class-scoped variables by retrieving their values from the configuration file using Con figUtil, and define the self.dataMsgListener class-scoped variable for later use. Create an instance of each actuator simulator task—specifically, Humidifier ActuatorSimTask and HvacActuatorSimTask. (Chapter 4 will also add emulator functionality to the constructor, but that's not needed right now.)

- Create a setter for self.dataMsgListener using the same code you used for Sen sorAdapterManager. This will be needed to handle actuator command responses, which will be important when you get to Parts III and IV.

- Implement the sendActuatorCommand() function, which accepts an Actuator Data instance as a parameter, performs validation on the request, and sends it to the appropriate actuator task.

The first two activities are relatively straightforward and mimic much of what you've already implemented in SensorAdapterManager. The sendActuatorCommand() function is a bit more involved, however, so let's look at a sample implementation:

```
def sendActuatorCommand(self, data: ActuatorData) -> bool:
    if data and not data.isResponseFlagEnabled():
        if data.getLocationID() is self.locationID:
            logging.info( \
                'Processing actuator command for loc ID %s.', \
                str(data.getLocationID()))

            aType = data.getTypeID()
            responseData = None

            if aType == \
                ConfigConst.HUMIDIFIER_ACTUATOR_TYPE and self.humidifierActuator:
                responseData = self.humidifierActuator.updateActuator(data)

            elif aType == \
                ConfigConst.HVAC_ACTUATOR_TYPE and self.hvacActuator:
```

```
        responseData = self.hvacActuator.updateActuator(data)

    elif aType == \
      ConfigConst.LED_DISPLAY_ACTUATOR_TYPE and self.ledDisplayActuator:
      responseData = self.ledDisplayActuator.updateActuator(data)

    else:
      logging.warning( \
        'No valid actuator type: %s', data.getTypeID())

    if responseData:
      if self.dataMsgListener:
        self.dataMsgListener.handleActuatorCommandResponse(responseData)

      return True
  else:
    logging.warning( \
      'Invalid loc ID match: %s', str(self.locationID))
  else:
    logging.warning( \
      'Invalid actuator msg. Response or null. Ignoring.')

  return False
```

Much like SensorAdapterManager's handleTelemetry() function, there are a few things to do. Let's break down the code and ensure it aligns with the activities set forth in the previous list.

First, and perhaps most important, is parameter validation. Check if the Actuator Data instance is valid and ensure it's an incoming actuation event (that is, the isRes ponse flag is False). If for some reason a response ActuatorData is passed back into this function, log a message and immediately return False.

You'll also want to match the ActuatorData's locationID with the local self.locatio nID to ensure that any received ActuatorData is truly intended for this application and not for another one.

Proper data validation and message verification are crucial parts of an appropriate security strategy for any application that processes data from both internal components and external systems. Although these details are beyond the scope of this book, I'll tackle some very basic data validation strategies throughout. For a more thorough discussion of data and cybersecurity for applications and the IoT, see Sean Smith's book *The Internet of Risky Things* (O'Reilly).

The next validation step is to check the ActuatorData typeID against the list of known actuator simulators and, if there's a match, pass the ActuatorData instance to the appropriate actuator task. Of course, none of these steps will prevent an invalid actuator command being passed into the function, but they do serve as initial steps to mitigate the chances that an inadvertent request will be processed. Ultimately, the actuator adapter itself will need to verify that the command, value, and state data are legitimate before taking any action.

As you can see in the sample code, the typeID is used to look up preconfigured "consts" (set within ConfigConst) that use a simple integer as the lookup value to match against an existing actuator type and task instance. There are other ways to do this, each with more complexity and maintenance; this simple approach will work for our purposes.

You'll see the ActuatorAdapterManagerTest within the same path as the SensorAdapter ManagerTest (*./src/test/python/programmingtheiot/part02/integration/system*). Again, before you run the test, make sure the enableEmulator = False key/value pair is set within the configuration file (*./config/PiotConfig.props*).

The output will be a bit lengthy, and by default, the test will take about a minute to run. Assuming you added logging in the correct places, the key things to look for are (a) a successful start (and eventual stop) of SensorAdapterManagerTest, and (b) that the SensorData is generated from the three simulator tasks (humidity, pressure, and temperature). Let's take a look:

```
Finding files... done.
Importing test modules ... done.

2020-12-28 21:38:37,361:ActuatorAdapterManagerTest:INFO:Testing ActuatorAdapter
Manager class...
2020-12-28 21:38:37,361:ConfigUtil:INFO:Loading config: ../../../../../../../
config/PiotConfig.props
.
.
.
2020-12-28 21:38:37,363:ActuatorAdapterManager:INFO:Actuator command received for
location ID constraineddevice001. Processing...
.
.
.
2020-12-28 21:38:37,363:BaseActuatorSimTask:INFO:Activating actuator...
2020-12-28 21:38:37,364:BaseActuatorSimTask:INFO:Simulating HvacActuator actuator ON:
*******
* O N *
*******
HvacActuator VALUE -> 22.5
=======
2020-12-28 21:38:37,364:DefaultDataMessageListener:INFO:Actuator Command: 1
2020-12-28 21:38:37,364:ActuatorAdapterManager:INFO:Actuator command received for
location ID constraineddevice001. Processing...
2020-12-28 21:38:37,365:BaseActuatorSimTask:INFO:Deactivating actuator...
2020-12-28 21:38:37,365:BaseActuatorSimTask:INFO:Simulating HvacActuator actuator
OFF:
```

```
*******
* OFF *
*******
2020-12-28 21:38:37,365:DefaultDataMessageListener:INFO:Actuator Command: 0
------------------------------------------------------------------
Ran 2 tests in 0.004s

OK
```

Since there's no scheduled activity with this test, you can let it run its course. You'll see ON and OFF messages for all actuators that you've enabled within ActuatorAdapterManager, assuming the code was implemented correctly. (I'm showing only the HvacActuatorSimTask output here to provide some sample output for you to compare with your own.)

The next piece of the CDA puzzle is creating and integrating the DeviceDataManager, which serves as the orchestration engine. It will process and eventually transmit the sensor data generated by the CDA and manage any incoming (or internal) actuation events by sending them to the ActuatorAdapterManager.

Before we go any further, you might want to take a break. Bask in the glory of getting this far! Your sensor and actuator simulators are working, which is a big step in building your end-to-end IoT solution.

Create and Integrate the Device Data Manager

This class becomes the central focus of the CDA (there's also one within the GDA) because it handles all data collection, actuation, and redirection complexities. It's also responsible for directing the communications with the GDA, so we'll use it to facilitate data management within the CDA in many upcoming exercises.

Look back to Figure 3-3 for just a moment. Here DeviceDataManager actually *replaces* the SystemPerformanceManager and becomes the primary interface with ConstrainedDeviceApp. The SystemPerformanceManager certainly isn't going away—it's simply going to be called by DeviceDataManager instead, just like SensorAdapterManager and ActuatorAdapterManager.

This updated functionality is captured within the key actions called out in PIOT-CDA-03-008 (*https://oreil.ly/qihSP*), summarized as follows:

- Create the DeviceDataManager class, using IDataMessageListener as the base class. Import all relevant classes, including SystemPerformanceManager, SensorAdapterManager, and ActuatorAdapterManager, and instance these classes within the constructor.

- Create the startManager() and stopManager() functions. These invoke the like-named functions on SystemPerformanceManager and SensorAdapterManager.

- Implement the `IDataMessageListener`-defined methods and create separate private functions to handle the processing complexity these callback methods might require now or in future exercises.

These first two activities follow the same pattern you've grown accustomed to with `SystemPerformanceManager`, `SensorAdapterManager`, and `ActuatorAdapterManager`.

Here's a quick look at how you might want to create your constructor for `DeviceData Manager`:

```python
def __init__(self):
  self.configUtil = ConfigUtil()

  self.sysPerfMgr = SystemPerformanceManager()
  self.sysPerfMgr.setDataMessageListener(self)

  self.sensorAdapterMgr = SensorAdapterManager()
  self.sensorAdapterMgr.setDataMessageListener(self)

  self.actuatorAdapterMgr = ActuatorAdapterManager()
  self.actuatorAdapterMgr.setDataMessageListener(self)

  self.enableHandleTempChangeOnDevice = \
    self.configUtil.getBoolean( \
      section = ConfigConst.CONSTRAINED_DEVICE, \
      key = \
        ConfigConst.ENABLE_HANDLE_TEMP_CHANGE_ON_DEVICE_KEY)

  self.triggerHvacTempFloor = \
    self.configUtil.getFloat( \
      section = ConfigConst.CONSTRAINED_DEVICE, \
      key = ConfigConst.TRIGGER_HVAC_TEMP_FLOOR_KEY)

  self.triggerHvacTempCeiling = \
    self.configUtil.getFloat( \
      section = ConfigConst.CONSTRAINED_DEVICE, \
      key = ConfigConst.TRIGGER_HVAC_TEMP_CEILING_KEY)
```

Unpacking the logic a bit, you'll see the creation of the manager classes I've been discussing: `SystemPerformanceManager`, `SensorAdapterManager`, and `ActuatorAdapter Manager`. You may recall that each of these classes also implements the `setDataMessageListener(IDataMessageListener)` function, which is called here in the constructor with a reference to "self," or `DeviceDataManager`, as the `IDataMessa geListener` instance. `DeviceDataManager` becomes the message orchestration engine —it will be used to handle all callbacks from these three classes, as well as the communications infrastructure that you'll build in Part III.

Implementing `startManager()` and `stopManager()`is easier: just invoke these functions within the relevant class (`SystemPerformanceManager` and `SensorAdapterManager`), as follows:

```
def startManager(self):
  logging.info("Started DeviceDataManager.")

  self.sysPerfMgr.startManager()
  self.sensorAdapterMgr.startManager()

def stopManager(self):
  logging.info("Stopped DeviceDataManager.")

  self.sysPerfMgr.stopManager()
  self.sensorAdapterMgr.stopManager()
```

Finally, it's time to implement the `IDataMessageListener` callbacks. I'm using the word *callback* to define these functions, but they're just, well, regular functions. `SystemPerformanceManager`, `SensorAdapterManager`, and `ActuatorAdapterManager` will invoke them when they have something to pass back to `DeviceDataManager`.

`IDataMessageListener` defines the contract that `DeviceDataManager` will use in the form of these functions, and any class that has a reference to an instance of `DeviceDataManager` "knows" it can call any of those functions on the instance.

Again, in Python, the implementation I'm using is technically just a base class, not an interface per se. The Java implementation of the same name in Chapter 5 will use a real interface, so the design pattern introduced here will probably make more sense at that time.

What are these functions exactly? Each one serves its own purpose, which should be somewhat obvious from its name; however, they also serve a common goal—to move sensor or actuator data between components within the CDA and between the CDA and the GDA.

Here's the list of callback functions that you'll implement within `DeviceDataManager`, with their basic signatures defined in a language-neutral manner:

`handleActuatorCommandMessage(ActuatorData)`

Processes an incoming `ActuatorData` message and passes it to the `ActuatorAdapterManager`. This could be called internally or in response to a message received from the GDA (via the communications components, which will be explored in Part III).

`handleActuatorCommandResponse(ActuatorData)`

Processes the response to an incoming `ActuatorData` message (usually called by `ActuatorAdapterManager` in response to handling the actuator request); will also pass the response back up to the GDA.

`handleSensorMessage(SensorData)`

Processes an incoming `SensorData` message (usually called by the `SensorAdap terManager` in response to the sensor task polling scheduler). This will serve two purposes: analyzing the data to determine whether an immediate action needs to be taken (such as turning the HVAC on or off if the temperature boundary is reached), and passing the sensor data back up to the GDA.

`handleIncomingMessage(ResourceNameEnum, String)`

Processes an incoming string-based payload (which should always be in JSON format—more about this in Chapter 5). This will usually be invoked from the communications components on receipt of a message from the GDA. Once the message is validated and reconstituted into its object form, it will then be passed to the appropriate handler function—for example, `handleActuatorCommandMes sage()`. You won't do much more with this callback function until Chapter 10, when you'll see how the integration between the CDA and the GDA comes to light.

`handleSystemPerformanceMessage(SystemPerformanceData)`

Processes an incoming `SystemPerformanceData` message (usually called by the `SystemPerformanceManager` in response to the performance task polling schedu-ler.) This will also pass the data back up to the GDA.

Feel free to add other callback functions to suit your needs. The five listed here are designed to work within the context of the exercises described throughout the book, but they cer-tainly are not exhaustive or comprehensive.

Let's dig into the implementation by tackling the low-hanging fruit first. For `handleActuatorCommandResponse(ActuatorData)`, `handleIncomingMessage(Resour ceNameEnum, String)`, and `handleSystemPerformanceMessage(SystemPerformance Data)`, you can simply verify that the parameter(s) for each is valid (that is, not None) and log a debug message indicating the method was called. Until you've implemented the exercises in Part III (which will allow the CDA and GDA to communicate), there's really nothing more to be done with these callbacks.

Here are just a few shell implementation examples with embedded comments stating the work to be done. I'll leave this implementation work to you!

```
def handleActuatorCommandResponse( \
  self, data: ActuatorData) -> bool:
  # TODO: validate 'data' and log a simple message (DEBUG!)
  return True

def handleIncomingMessage( \
  self, resourceEnum: ResourceNameEnum, msg: str) -> bool:
```

```
    # TODO: validate 'data' and log a simple message (DEBUG!)
    return True

def handleSystemPerformanceMessage( \
    self, data: SystemPerformanceData) -> bool:
    # TODO: validate 'data' and log a simple message (DEBUG!)
    return True
```

Don't worry about the method signature to `handleIncomingMessage(ResourceNameE num, String)` just yet—I'll explain the `ResourceNameEnum` in more detail once you get to Chapter 5 and then again in Part III. The code that represents this class is already provided as part of the python-components repository, so you can leave it as is for now.

The remaining two callback functions play a particularly important role—one will process incoming sensor data and determine whether an actuation event needs to take place within the CDA, and the other will handle the actuation event.

Let's look at the sensor processing function first. Here's one way to implement this function. Keep in mind you'll still need to address the requirement to handle any appropriate actuation events locally:

```
def handleSensorMessage(self, data: SensorData) -> bool:
    if data:
        self._handleSensorDataAnalysis(data)

        return True
    else:
        logging.warning("Invalid sensor data. Ignoring.")

        return False
```

This function checks that data is not null and then delegates the work to a "private" method named `_handleSensorDataAnalysis(SensorData)`. (In Part III, you'll also add a method that will convert the data to JSON and send it upstream to the GDA.)

Let's look at `_handleSensorDataAnalysis(SensorData)`:

```
def _handleSensorDataAnalysis(self, data: SensorData):
    if self.handleTempChangeOnDevice and \
        data.getTypeID() == ConfigConst.TEMP_SENSOR_TYPE:

        ad = \
            ActuatorData(typeID = ConfigConst.HVAC_ACTUATOR_TYPE)

        if data.getValue() > self.triggerHvacTempCeiling:
            ad.setCommand(ActuatorData.COMMAND_ON)
            ad.setValue(self.triggerHvacTempCeiling)
        elif data.getValue() < self.triggerHvacTempFloor:
            ad.setCommand(ActuatorData.COMMAND_ON)
            ad.setValue(self.triggerHvacTempFloor)
```

```
    else:
        ad.setCommand(ActuatorData.COMMAND_OFF)

    self.handleActuatorCommandMessage(ad)
```

Remember the ConstrainedDevice section in *PiotConfig.props*? It lists a handful of parameters that set floor and ceiling values for temperature, along with a Boolean flag that indicates whether or not temperature change should be handled on the device.

These properties were loaded in the DeviceDataManager constructor and stored in the class-scoped variables self.handleTempChangeOnDevice, self.triggerHvacTemp Floor, and self.triggerHvacTempCeiling. If the sensor data value is above the ceiling or below the floor, the HVAC will be turned on via a newly instanced ActuatorData object that gets passed to the handleActuatorCommand(ActuatorData) function.

This is a *very* simple mechanism for checking if a value is above or below a particular mark and triggering an actuation event. It also assumes that the actuator itself knows whether or not to turn on the heat or the air conditioning. Not very smart, is it?

Or is it? The objective is to handle an actuation event as close as appropriate to the system that will control the actuation, while also enabling the passing of data upstream to other systems (like the GDA). This approach provides us with a solution to this challenge, if a simple and certainly improvable one.

Let's move on. With the SensorData processing logic now in place, it's time to look at that actuation processing functionality alluded to in the previous code and required as the final callback method necessary to make DeviceDataManager functional.

Here's a very simple example of the handleActuatorCommandMessage(ActuatorData) method:

```
def handleActuatorCommandMessage( \
    self, data: ActuatorData) -> bool:
    if data:
        logging.debug("Processing actuator command.")

        self.actuatorAdapterMgr.sendActuatorCommand(data)

        return True
    else:
        logging.warning("Invalid actuator command.")

        return False
```

It will handle basic data validation (checking that it's non-null, for instance), log a simple message indicating it's doing some work, and then pass the ActuatorData instance to the ActuatorAdapterManager for processing.

Since `ActuatorAdapterManager` is already written, you're basically done! But first, it's time to test things out.

Check out the `DeviceDataManagerNoCommsTest` in the *./src/test/python/program-mingtheiot/part02/integration/app* path, as explained in PIOT-CDA-03-008 (*https://oreil.ly/qihSP*). Also, you may want to change the following in the `ConstrainedDe vice` section of your *PiotConfig.props* configuration file to move things along a bit faster:

```
pollCycleSecs = 5
triggerHvacTempFloor = 19.5
triggerHvacTempCeiling = 20.2
```

Let the test run its course, examining the log output as it runs. You'll notice quite a few log messages, which you can clean up later by removing those that are unneeded —or ideally, by converting them to debug messages. More importantly, you'll see the scheduler processing system performance data as well as simulated sensor data, including temperature readings. Eventually, you should see one or more actuator messages triggered that will tell the actuator simulator to adjust the temperature.

Here's a small snippet of various log output sections depicting this process:

```
Finding files... done.
.
.
.
2020-12-29 13:43:46,960 - MainThread - root - INFO - Testing DeviceDataManager
class...
.
.
.
2020-12-29 13:43:52,048 - ThreadPoolExecutor-0_0 - root - INFO - Incoming sensor
data received (from sensor manager): name=TempSensor,typeID=3,timeStamp=2020-12-
29T18:43:52.045967+00:00,statusCode=0,hasError=False,locationID=constraineddevice00
1,elevation=0.0,latitude=0.0,longitude=0.0,value=19.924998417268583
2020-12-29 13:43:52,048 - ThreadPoolExecutor-0_0 - root - INFO - Handle temp
change: True - type ID: 3
2020-12-29 13:43:52,048 - ThreadPoolExecutor-0_0 - root - INFO - Processing
actuator command message.
2020-12-29 13:43:52,048 - ThreadPoolExecutor-0_0 - root - INFO - Actuator command
received for location ID constraineddevice001. Processing...
2020-12-29 13:43:52,049 - ThreadPoolExecutor-0_0 - root - DEBUG - New actuator
command is a repeat of current state. Ignoring: 0
.
.
.
2020-12-29 13:44:07,050 - ThreadPoolExecutor-0_0 - root - INFO - Incoming sensor
data received (from sensor manager): name=TempSensor,typeID=3,timeStamp=2020-12-
29T18:44:07.048203+00:00,statusCode=0,hasError=False,locationID=constraineddevice00
1,elevation=0.0,latitude=0.0,longitude=0.0,value=20.1185355927757
2020-12-29 13:44:07,050 - ThreadPoolExecutor-0_0 - root - INFO - Handle temp
change: True - type ID: 3
2020-12-29 13:44:07,051 - ThreadPoolExecutor-0_0 - root - INFO - Processing
```

```
actuator command message.
2020-12-29 13:44:07,051 - ThreadPoolExecutor-0_0 - root - INFO - Actuator command
received for location ID constraineddevice001. Processing...
2020-12-29 13:44:07,051 - ThreadPoolExecutor-0_0 - root - INFO - Activating
actuator...
2020-12-29 13:44:07,051 - ThreadPoolExecutor-0_0 - root - INFO - Simulating
HvacActuator actuator ON:
*******
* O N *
*******
HvacActuator VALUE -> 20.0
=======
 .
 .
 .
```

Notice that the logic implemented within DeviceDataManager processes all valid
SensorData. It sends actuation events only if the SensorData is from TemperatureSen
sorSimTask AND if the configuration has handleTempChangeOnDevice = True set.
From there, the ActuatorAdapterManager handles the actuation event and passes it
to TemperatureSensorSimTask, which ignores the command if it's a duplicate of
what's already been processed.

If your log output has similar content, congratulations! Your CDA functionality is
really coming together now, with internal message processing and actuation support.
Nicely done!

Let's connect everything. Remember ConstrainedDeviceApp? It's been a while since
you had to make any changes to its functionality. PIOT-CDA-03-009 (*https://oreil.ly/
8FxcR*) walks through the process of adding DeviceDataManager to ConstrainedDevi
ceApp.

The key steps involve replacing the calls to SystemPerformanceManager with the
same calls to DeviceDataManager. It's a quick update that finally erases the technical
debt introduced in Chapter 2 for the ConstrainedDeviceApp component.

Finally, remember to merge your Lab Module 03 branch into the primary branch as
described in PIOT-CDA-03-100 (*https://oreil.ly/pL8vQ*). Once you've completed this
step, you're officially done with this chapter's exercises!

Additional Exercises

With the right data model, you can simulate a wide range of difference sensors and
trigger appropriate actuation events based on test scenarios involving threshold
crossings within your CDA. Here are two you may want to consider implementing on
your own.

Hysteresis Management

Create an algorithm that can be used by the `SensorAdapterManager` module within the CDA to determine the temperature rise or fall trajectory and determine when, and for how long, a temperature adjustment should be actuated.

You can implement this for both temperature and humidity readings and use this algorithm to trigger actuation events for your HVAC and/or humidifier actuator simulators.

Conclusion

In this chapter, you've implemented the bulk of the CDA's core functionality—well done! You learned how to create abstractions around sensor and actuator simulators, generate time-series data related to a given sensor task, and process simple sensor threshold crossings within the `DeviceDataManager` orchestration engine, sending ON and OFF commands to the actuator simulator when appropriate.

The next chapter will expand on the simulation capabilities you've just constructed and use emulated hardware to provide a bit more realism. Chapter 5 follows with a look at data management functionality and puts in place the basis for CDA to GDA message passing using JSON translations of the sensor and actuator data you've created in this chapter.

Again, great work!

Data Emulation

Sensing and Actuation Using a Hardware Emulator

I see, hear, and smell.
Should I transmit a warning?
False alarm. Ignore.

Fundamental concepts: Design and build logical components that plug into your IoT applications and can interact with the physical world through both real and emulated sensing and actuation.

Processing sensor data from simulators and generating log output as part of an actuation event is pretty cool, but wouldn't it be even cooler to use sliders to adjust the values your sensor task is reading? Even better would be the ability to display messages on a real (or emulated) LED display when an actuation event is triggered, right?

This chapter explores how to set up, configure, and use an emulator that can provide a virtual LED display, plus temperature, pressure, humidity, and other readings.

What You'll Learn in This Chapter

Much of this chapter is dedicated to setting up and configuring the Sense-Emu emulator (*https://sense-emu.readthedocs.io/en/v1.1*), which is a virtual Sense HAT[1] device you can run on Windows, Mac, or Linux platforms (although I've found it easiest to run on Linux).

---

1 The Sense HAT is a board that can be attached to various Raspberry Pi single-board computer modules via its 40-pin GPIO interface. You can read more about the Sense HAT on the Raspberry Pi website (*https://www.raspberrypi.org/products/sense-hat*).

The Sense HAT is a board that can attach to a Raspberry Pi's 40-pin GPIO and provides a variety of sensing capabilities, including humidity, pressure, and temperature. The LED matrix displays text or graphics in multiple colors on an 8x8 grid. It also contains a built-in inertial measurement unit (IMU) and magnetometer to measure compass readings, x/y/z-axis orientation, and acceleration. The Sense-Emu emulator provides a virtual instance of the Sense HAT, which will be the focus of this chapter.

Configuring an IoT device can present you with interesting challenges, and so can installing and configuring an emulator. I'll focus on the emulator in this chapter and assume you'll be using it for future exercises, but you can certainly opt to use real hardware, such as a Raspberry Pi, to run your CDA (and GDA).[2] Should you decide to move forward with this deployment strategy, setting up your device so it can work as both a gateway device and a constrained device is a bit involved and in most cases will be specific to your device.

If you decide to set up Jenkins 2 to help with CI/CD on your local system, check out Brent Laster's book *Jenkins 2 Up & Running* (O'Reilly). If you want to run this directly on a Raspberry Pi running a Linux-based operating system (such as Raspbian), pay attention to the setup and configuration for Linux-based environments. While it is outside the scope of this book, you might want to consider this extra configuration step, as it can help with automating your development environment.

As a friendly reminder, this chapter focuses exclusively on the CDA, so the code is written in Python. As with the previous chapters, be sure to follow the steps listed in PIOT-CDA-04-000 (*https://oreil.ly/9u4ET*) and check out a new branch for this chapter.

Emulating Sensors and Actuators

Sensors read data from a system and cover a wide range of capabilities. For this next application, you'll build emulators that simulate sensing functionality and allow you to trigger one or more actuation events, should the simulated sensors generate data that requires your device to take action.

Eventually, the determination of this action will lie in the hands of the Gateway Device App and, perhaps later, the analytics component of your cloud service

---

2 If you're interested in using the Raspberry Pi, see *Raspberry Pi Cookbook*, Third Edition, by Simon Monk (O'Reilly).

infrastructure. For now, you will build a simple test function within your Constrained Device App that looks for a threshold crossing and will use that to send an actuation event to the simulated actuator. Once this is functioning properly, you'll see how the infrastructure you've developed will be an important part of the next set of exercises.

Setting Up and Configuring an Emulator

The modularity of the CDA design will allow you to add new emulator functionality without making too many changes—essentially, you'll add functionality to the Sensor AdapterManager and ActuatorAdapterManager classes to support the switch from simulation to emulation and then add in new emulator tasks for sensing and actuation.

The emulator tasks for sensing will be derived from BaseSensorSimTask, while those related to actuation will be derived from BaseActuatorSimTask. Within the manager classes, the switch between simulation and emulation will be managed within the constructor of each class.

Before I dig into the exercises and code, let's explore some of the dependencies to make the emulator functionality work properly.

The Sense-Emu Sense HAT Emulator

Building emulators can be complicated, and we're fortunate to have access to a number of different tools that support testing and emulating various hardware components useful in IoT Edge Tier processing. One such tool mentioned previously is the Sense-Emu Sense HAT emulator, which includes a graphical user interface (GUI) with levers that allow you to emulate the sensor readings from a Sense HAT card.[3]

The Sense HAT is a board that can be added to a Raspberry Pi using the 40-pin general-purpose input/output (GPIO) header. While a detailed discussion of this capability is beyond the scope of this book, a quick online search will list numerous resources with detailed descriptions of the board and its sensors, example projects, and sample code that may be useful if you plan to incorporate real hardware into your design.

Figure 4-1 is a screenshot of the Sense-Emu emulator running on my local system.

---

3 You can read more about the Sense HAT board online (*https://www.raspberrypi.org/products/sense-hat*). If you're interested in other features of the emulator, you can review the online documentation (*https://sense-emu.readthedocs.io/en/v1.0/index.html*) and check out the built-in demos located under the emulator GUI's File → "Open example" menu.

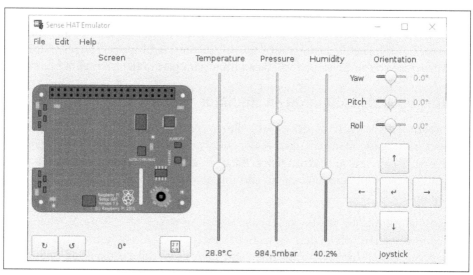

Figure 4-1. Sense-Emu Sense HAT emulator screenshot

As you can see, there are several ways to generate data within the GUI. Before taking this screenshot, I adjusted the temperature to 28.8°C, the pressure to 984.5 mbar, and humidity to 40.2%.

Once the emulator is up and running, you'll need a way to interface with it using your CDA. The Python library pisense (*https://oreil.ly/dxlHX*) supports integration with the Sense-Emu emulator and the actual Sense HAT board. You can switch between them by setting a flag within the initialization of the Sense HAT class in the pisense library.

Before we dig into the code, review PIOT-CFG-04-001 (*https://oreil.ly/arvAr*), which walks through the installation and configuration of the Sense-Emu emulator. I won't spend much time discussing it here, but there will likely be other dependencies to get the emulator working on your system. I've successfully run the Sense-Emu emulator on Windows using WSL (with a separate X11 server) and on macOS.

Last, the *PiotConfig.props* configuration file has a property under the `ConstrainedDe` `vice` section named enableEmulator. Once your emulator is set up and properly configured, and after you've completed the exercises in this section, flip the property value to "True" and you should be able to test your code against the emulator.

Let's start coding.

Programming Exercises

You'll notice a common pattern in the component relationships for the emulator functionality—it's the same as your design and implementation from Chapter 3

---

regarding the simulator functionality. This provides a great deal of flexibility for your implementation, as you'll be able to add new capabilities to your CDA that exceed the requirements specified in these exercises.

Integrating Sensing and Actuation Emulation Within Your Application Design

Figure 4-2 provides a simple design view of the CDA once these new features are incorporated.

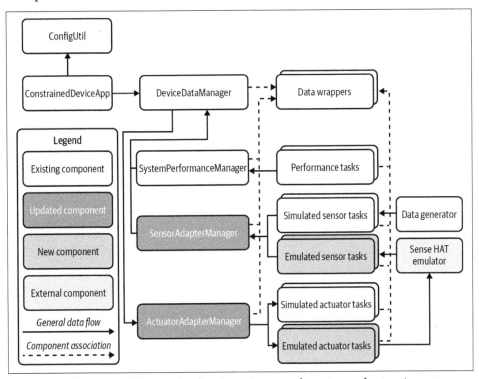

Figure 4-2. Constrained Device Application—integrated sensing and actuation app design

Notice the design looks strikingly similar to the design in Figure 3-3, where you integrated simulation functionality into your CDA. Its modularity permits adding emulator tasks with minor modifications to the manager logic.

Now let's take a look at the detailed design represented as UML. Figure 4-3 depicts one way to represent the key components of this exercise, with some of the details from the previous exercise left out for clarity.

As with the high-level design in Figure 4-2, this detailed design is similar to the UML depicted in Figure 3-4.

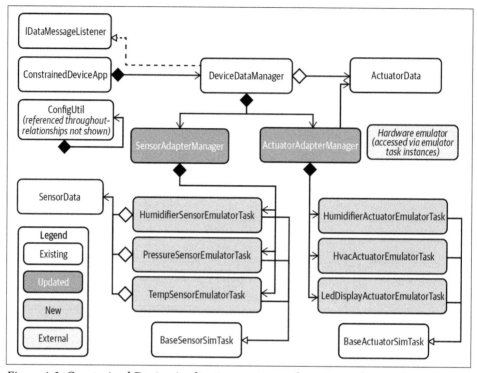

Figure 4-3. Constrained Device Application—integrated sensing and actuation app UML

Let's look at the requirements and implementation for Lab Module 04.

Emulating Sensors

Recall the two key functions that `BaseSensorSimTask` performs: it creates a `Sensor Data` instance, which it uses to store the latest sensor simulation data, and it provides a public interface to generate a new instance and access its data.

In PIOT-CDA-04-001 (*https://oreil.ly/WBcYD*), you'll create three new sensor *emulator* tasks, each of which will derive from `BaseSensorSimTask`, just as the sensor *simulator* tasks did in Chapter 3. The difference will be in the constructor and the `generateTelemetry()` method. These sensor tasks reside in the *./programmingtheiot/cda/emulated* package. Here's a summary of the actions involved:

- Create (or edit) HumiditySensorEmulatorTask, PressureSensorEmulatorTask, and TemperatureSensorEmulatorTask.

- Initialize the SenseHAT class instance using the pisense library.

- Update generateTelemetry() to retrieve data from the Sense HAT emulator.

Let's unpack these actions step by step. I'll focus on TemperatureSensorEmulator Task, since the others will look very similar.

Like the other Python modules you've edited or created, you'll need to create the class and add the relevant import statements. If you're using the python-components code base, this is already done for you and looks similar to the following:

```python
from programmingtheiot.data.SensorData import SensorData

import programmingtheiot.common.ConfigConst as ConfigConst

from programmingtheiot.common.ConfigUtil import ConfigUtil
from programmingtheiot.cda.sim.BaseSensorSimTask import BaseSensorSimTask
from programmingtheiot.cda.sim.SensorDataGenerator import SensorDataGenerator
```

The class declaration for TemperatureSensorEmulatorTask will look like this:

```python
class TemperatureSensorEmulatorTask(BaseSensorSimTask):
```

When you create the constructor, notice its similarity to the simulator tasks you've already written. The primary differences are the construction logic and the SenseHAT class instance logic from the pisense library:

```python
def __init__(self):
  super(TemperatureSensorEmulatorTask, self).__init__( \
    name = ConfigConst.TEMP_SENSOR_NAME, \
    typeID = ConfigConst.TEMP_SENSOR_TYPE)

  self.sh = SenseHAT(emulate = True)
```

 If you decide to use a real Sense HAT board and Raspberry Pi single-board computer combination, you can add another parameter to your *PiotConfig.props* within the ConstrainedDevice section indicating that hardware is (or isn't) present. If real hardware will be used in your CDA, the SenseHAT class should be initialized with emulate = False instead. If you want to dynamically switch between simulated data, emulated data, and real data (using hardware), consider using an integer value to reflect this initialization behavior in your configuration file instead.

With this complete, let's move on to the generateTelemetry() function. Here's an example you might want to use (again, for the TemperatureSensorEmulatorTask class):

```
def generateTelemetry(self) -> SensorData:
    sensorData = \
        SensorData(name = self.getName(), typeID = self.getTypeID())

    sensorVal = self.sh.environ.temperature

    sensorData.setValue(sensorVal)
    self.latestSensorData = sensorData

    return sensorData
```

It's actually a bit simpler without the simulated (or randomized) data, isn't it?

Now you can move on to the other two tasks: HumiditySensorEmulatorTask and PressureSensorEmulatorTask. Just be sure to use the correct SenseHAT function call to retrieve the appropriate value for each.

Time for the actuation emulators.

Emulating Actuators

Remember the BaseActuatorSimTask base class from Chapter 3? Like BaseSensor SimTask, it performs two primary functions—in this case, abstracting the "activate" and "deactivate" functions of an actuator, using the public method updateActua tor(ActuatorData). This will be very useful for the emulated actuator tasks, so we'll create those by deriving from BaseActuatorSimTask.

Now for the tricky part. What types of actuation events do you want to trigger? Recall our problem statement from Chapter 1:

> I want to understand the environment in my home, how it changes over time, and make adjustments to enhance comfort while saving money.

One way to interpret "comfort" is through temperature control and humidity (which plays a role in how humans feel temperature and contributes to the overall comfort and health of an indoor environment). Let's use both measurements as potential actuation triggers and name two of the actuator tasks HvacEmulatorTask and Humidi fierEmulatorTask. The HVAC will be used to control the temperature, and the humidifier will be used to adjust relative humidity.

The actuator task-naming convention drops the word "Actuator" since I think it's quite clear these devices will be turned on or off. A real-world system may also collect sensor readings from these devices. For simplicity, our virtual devices will merely accept actuation commands.

Since you'll also be using the LED matrix on the emulator, it might be helpful to dedicate an actuator to illuminating the screen, so PIOT-CDA-04-002 (*https://oreil.ly/ tN580*) also specifies an LedDisplayEmulatorTask.

Let's review the actions listed in PIOT-CDA-04-002 (*https://oreil.ly/tN580*):

- Create (or edit) HvacEmulatorTask, HumidifierEmulatorTask, and LedDisplayEmulatorTask.

- Initialize the SenseHAT instance using the pisense library.

- Update _handleActuation() to write the appropriate data to the LED display using the SenseHAT instance.

Consider that last bullet. Since the emulator doesn't actually emulate an HVAC system or a humidifier, we'll just use its LED display to notify the user that an actuation event is taking place, turning something ON or OFF. You can certainly get creative with the implementation, but for now, we'll simply scroll a message on the screen.

Here's an example of the HvacEmulatorTask, including the imports, class declaration, and constructor initialization. It looks very similar to TemperatureSensorEmulator Task, doesn't it?

```
import logging

from time import sleep

import programmingtheiot.common.ConfigConst as ConfigConst

from programmingtheiot.common.ConfigUtil import ConfigUtil
from programmingtheiot.cda.sim.BaseActuatorSimTask import BaseActuatorSimTask

from pisense import SenseHAT

class HvacEmulatorTask(BaseActuatorSimTask):
  def __init__(self):
    super(HvacEmulatorTask, self).__init__( \
      name = ConfigConst.HVAC_ACTUATOR_NAME, \
      typeID = ConfigConst.HVAC_ACTUATOR_TYPE, \
      simpleName = "HVAC")

    self.sh = SenseHAT(emulate = True)
```

Remember that the base class, `BaseActuatorSimTask`, defines two private methods named _activateActuator() and _deactivateActuator(). Both will automatically get called based on the command being sent to the updateActuator() method defined within the base class. Granted, this isn't ideal for every situation, but it will suit our needs.

Here's an example implementation for each of these methods:

```
def _activateActuator(self, \
  val: float = ConfigConst.DEFAULT_VAL, \
  stateData: str = None) -> int:

  if self.sh.screen:
    msg = self.getSimpleName() + ' ON: ' + \
    str(val) + 'C'

    self.sh.screen.scroll_text(msg)
    return 0
  else:
    logging.warning('No LED screen instance available.')
    return -1
```

The implementation looks rather similar to the simulated actuator that logged a message to the console, doesn't it?

The deactivation functionality is similar. Here's a look at the implementation:

```
def _deactivateActuator(self, \
  val: float = ConfigConst.DEFAULT_VAL, \
  stateData: str = None) -> int:

  if self.sh.screen:
    msg = self.getSimpleName() + ' OFF'
    self.sh.screen.scroll_text(msg)

    sleep(5)

    # optionally, clear the screen when done scrolling
    self.sh.screen.clear()
    return 0
  else:
    logging.warning('No LED screen instance available.')
    return -1
```

The big difference here is the sleep delay. While this is completely optional, I included it here to give the message time to scroll; however, this does interfere with the timing of the call, since it will block and hold up other CDA processing unless executed within a thread.

If you decide to pursue a multithreaded approach as part of your design, consider using a queue to store messages in case they are sent in faster than the display can process them. This brings up another interesting challenge: how can you know the rate at which to poll an emulated (or real) sensor, or how long an emulated (or real) actuation event will take?

The short answer is that you need to know the hardware specification of the sensor or actuator, the timing constraints of the device (or emulator), how often it will be invoked, and how to factor these timings into your CDA design. It can be a real problem if not managed appropriately. It's out of our scope here, but I encourage you to keep it in mind as you design your edge solution.

What, then, would be the better path forward for the deactivation functionality? If the message must have time to scroll and you know how long each character will take (let's assume it's about one half of a second, or 500 milliseconds), just calculate the length of the string to display and then multiply it by the number of seconds (or partial seconds). If, for example, the string is 20 characters, and each character takes 500 milliseconds to display and scroll, you'd need to wait for approximately 10 seconds for every character to scroll.

Perhaps a better option is to maintain a graphical 8x8 rendition with icons and/or colors indicating the state and leave it illuminated while the given state is in effect. Ah, yes—that would be an excellent supplemental exercise, wouldn't it? But I digress. Now that you know the challenge and a plausible path forward to address it, you can choose a different implementation approach!

You're almost done. There are just two more steps: integration with `SensorAdapter Manager` and integration with `ActuatorAdapterManager`.

Connecting Emulated Sensors with the Sensor Adapter Manager

This exercise, defined in PIOT-CDA-04-003 (*https://oreil.ly/ebm2P*), updates `SensorA dapterManager` by introducing the newly created emulator tasks within the constructor initialization. The design approach will let you switch easily between emulated sensor tasks and simulated sensor tasks by flipping the `enableEmulator` flag in *Piot-Config.props* from True to False.

The key actions are as follows:

- Add support for the `enableEmulator` flag from *PiotConfig.props*.
- Add the emulator sensor tasks for temperature, pressure, and humidity (and any others you wish to include).

- Use the `enableEmulator` flag to switch between using simulated sensor tasks and using emulated sensor tasks.

Since you're already familiar with the constructor of `SensorAdapterManager`, here's the code that follows immediately after declaring `self.dataMsgListener = None` (which should be the last line of code in the constructor initialization):

```
if not self.useEmulator:
  self.dataGenerator = SensorDataGenerator()

  tempFloor = \
    configUtil.getFloat( \
      section = ConfigConst.CONSTRAINED_DEVICE, \
      key = ConfigConst.TEMP_SIM_FLOOR_KEY, \
      defaultVal = SensorDataGenerator.LOW_NORMAL_INDOOR_TEMP)

  tempCeiling = \
    configUtil.getFloat( \
      section = ConfigConst.CONSTRAINED_DEVICE, \
      key = ConfigConst.TEMP_SIM_CEILING_KEY, \
      defaultVal = SensorDataGenerator.HI_NORMAL_INDOOR_TEMP)

  tempData = \
    self.dataGenerator.generateDailyIndoorTemperatureDataSet( \
      minValue = tempFloor, \
      maxValue = tempCeiling, \
      useSeconds = False)

  self.tempAdapter = \
    TemperatureSensorSimTask(dataSet = tempData)

  # TODO: add other sensor simulator tasks

else:
  # load the Temperature emulator
  tempModule = \
    import_module( \
      'programmingtheiot.cda.emulated.TemperatureSensorEmulatorTask', \
      'TemperatureSensorEmulatorTask')

  teClazz = \
    getattr(tempModule, 'TemperatureSensorEmulatorTask')

  self.tempAdapter = teClazz()

  # TODO: add other sensor emulator tasks
```

If the `self.useEmulator` flag is False, then the simulated sensor functionality will be used. The remaining code within this section is the same code you implemented in Chapter 3. But what about the else clause? Let's break it down.

The first line after the else clause is as follows:

```
tempModule = \
    import_module( \
        'programmingtheiot.cda.emulated.TemperatureSensorEmulatorTask', \
        'TemperatureSensorEmulatorTask')
```

If you've been coding in Python for a while, this may be familiar to you. The code instructs the Python interpreter to dynamically load the `TemperatureSensorEmula torTask` module (and the like-named class) using `import_module`. This simply wraps the `__import__` built-in with a slightly more user-friendly interface to perform the module load (again, only if `self.useEmulator` is True).

If you'd prefer to use the `__import__` built-in instead, you can replace the `import_module()` call with the following:

```
tempModule = \
    __import__( \

        'programmingtheiot.cda.emulated.TemperatureSens
orEmulatorTask', \

        fromlist =
['TemperatureSensorEmulatorTask']).
```

Is this dynamic module and class-loading capability strictly required for the purposes of this chapter? No, it is not. It *is*, however, a tool you can use for future integration. It serves two purposes, neither of which is needed at this time:

1. It establishes a pattern for dynamically loading modules that may not exist using a simple configuration file flag. Interesting exercise, but not critical. Yet.

2. With this pattern in place, you can implement hardware-specific code within the existing `programmingtheiot.cda.embedded` `python-components` package. This might be useful if you decide to tackle some of the optional Lab Module 04 exercises.

You can follow this same pattern to dynamically load the humidity and pressure tasks, `HumiditySensorEmulatorTask` and `PressureSensorEmulatorTask`, respectively. Be sure to add those components into your code before running the manual integration test.

Let's test things out and ensure you can flip between simulated sensing and emulated sensing. Check out the test at the end of the requirement card—you'll see the instructions are a bit more involved than in previous tests. Here's a summary:

- Make sure the `enableEmulator` flag in *PiotConfig.props* is set to True and then start the Sense-Emu emulator. From the command line, you should be able to just type `sense_emu_gui`.

- Run `SensorAdapterManagerTest` within the python-components *./src/test/python/programmingtheiot/part02/integration/system* path.

If you're running the Sense-Emu emulator under WSL and your IDE under Windows, you may find that the manual integration tests for `SensorAdapterManagerTest` generate an error. This is probably because your IDE isn't able to communicate with the X11 server. The easy (and quick) fix is simply to run your test from the command line. You can do this by navigating to the path containing `SensorAdapterManagerTest` and executing it using the following command within your virtualenv:

```
python -m unittest SensorAdapterManagerTest
```

 If you decided to set up your Python environment without using a virtualenv, make sure you're using the appropriate Python interpreter executable (such as Python 3). Also, be sure your PYTHONPATH is set within your environment. It will need to include both the *./src/main/python* and *./src/test/python* paths.

The output should include various message sequences similar to the following (depending on how long you run your tests):

```
2021-01-01 15:06:39,776:SensorAdapterManagerTest:INFO:Testing SensorAdapterManager
class...
.
.
2021-01-01 15:06:45,126:SensorAdapterManager:INFO:Generated humidity data:
name=HumiditySensor,typeID=1,timeStamp=2021-01-
01T20:06:45.125842+00:00,statusCode=0,hasError=False,locationID=constraineddevice00
1,elevation=0.0,latitude=0.0,longitude=0.0,value=0.0
2021-01-01 15:06:45,128:SensorAdapterManager:INFO:Generated pressure data:
name=PressureSensor,typeID=2,timeStamp=2021-01-
01T20:06:45.125956+00:00,statusCode=0,hasError=False,locationID=constraineddevice00
1,elevation=0.0,latitude=0.0,longitude=0.0,value=848.703369140625
2021-01-01 15:06:45,129:SensorAdapterManager:INFO:Generated temp data:
name=TempSensor,typeID=3,timeStamp=2021-01-
01T20:06:45.125996+00:00,statusCode=0,hasError=False,locationID=constraineddevice00
1,elevation=0.0,latitude=0.0,longitude=0.0,value=24.984375
.
.
2021-01-01 15:07:20,139:base:INFO:Job "SensorAdapterManager.handleTelemetry
(trigger: interval[0:00:05], next run at: 2021-01-01 15:07:25 EST)" executed
successfully
.
.
```

If this log output aligns reasonably well with your own, great! Time to move on to the actuator emulators.

Connecting Emulated Actuators with the Actuator Adapter Manager

The last formal exercise in this chapter, defined in PIOT-CDA-04-004 (*https://oreil.ly/ GrcVT*), follows the same pattern as the previous one for `ActuatorAdapterManager`:

- Add support for the `enableEmulator` flag from *PiotConfig.props*.
- Add the emulator actuator tasks for the HVAC, humidifier, and LED matrix.
- Use the `enableEmulator` flag to switch between using simulated actuator tasks and using emulated actuator tasks.

Keep in mind that the construction pattern for `ActuatorAdapterManager` will only change to support the emulator/simulator switch. Immediately after declaring `self.dataMsgListener = None` (which, again, should be the last line of code in the constructor initialization), add the following:

```
if not self.useEmulator:
  # create the humidifier actuator
  self.humidifierActuator = HumidifierActuatorSimTask()

  # create the HVAC actuator
  self.hvacActuator = HvacActuatorSimTask()
else:
  # load the HVAC emulator
  hvacModule = \
    import_module( \
      'programmingtheiot.cda.emulated.HvacEmulatorTask', \
      'HvacEmulatorTask')

  hveClazz = \
    getattr(hvacModule, 'HvacEmulatorTask')

  self.hvacActuator = hveClazz()

  # TODO: add other actuator tasks
```

Nothing new here, right? This time, you're dynamically loading the `HvacEmulator Task` but using the same logic as for the `TemperatureSensorEmulatorTask`.

Be sure to add in the `HumidifierEmulatorTask` and `LedDisplayEmulatorTask` before moving on to the manual integration tests. The same constraints hold here as for the `SensorAdapterManager` when using the Sense-Emu emulator: make sure the enable Emulator flag is True in *PiotConfig.props* and start the emulator.

As with the `SensorAdapterManagerTest`, you may want to run `ActuatorAdapterMana`
`gerTest` from within the python-components path *./src/test/python/programmingth-*
eiot/part02/integration/system/:

```
python -m unittest ActuatorAdapterManagerTest
```

For this test, be sure to also monitor the Sense-Emu GUI and observe the LED display along with the log output.

Figure 4-4 provides an example screenshot depicting the first letter of the LED "ON"
message.

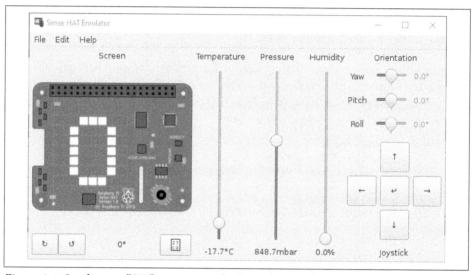

Figure 4-4. Sending an "ON" message to the Sense-Emu LED matrix

Figure 4-4 shows one small part of the scrolling text message that indicates the HVAC
is being turned "ON" (the "O" is shown). One exercise to consider is triggering two
actuation events when the temperature needs to be adjusted: one to the HVAC emulator (which can technically just log a message) and the other to the LED matrix, where
you can provide a more creative visualization of the HVAC and humidifier within the
8×8 matrix.

As for log messages, they'll look similar to the pattern expressed here:

```
2021-01-01 16:58:17,797:ActuatorAdapterManagerTest:INFO:Testing ActuatorAdapterManager
class...
    .
    .
    .
2021-01-01 16:58:25,909:ActuatorAdapterManager:INFO:Actuator command received for
location ID constraineddevice001. Processing...
2021-01-01 16:58:25,910:BaseActuatorSimTask:INFO:Deactivating actuator...
2021-01-01 16:58:36,729:DefaultDataMessageListener:INFO:Actuator Command: 0
```

```
2021-01-01 16:58:36,736:ActuatorAdapterManager:INFO:Actuator command received for
location ID constraineddevice001. Processing...
2021-01-01 16:58:36,745:BaseActuatorSimTask:INFO:Activating actuator...
2021-01-01 16:58:42,325:DefaultDataMessageListener:INFO:Actuator Command: 1
2021-01-01 16:58:42,326:ActuatorAdapterManager:INFO:Actuator command received for
location ID constraineddevice001. Processing...
2021-01-01 16:58:42,327:BaseActuatorSimTask:INFO:Deactivating actuator...
2021-01-01 16:58:51,120:DefaultDataMessageListener:INFO:Actuator Command: 0
.
.
.
```

If your tests indicate success, then it's time to celebrate. You now have not only the simulated CDA functionality working but also sensor and actuator emulation! The next chapter will look at ways to manage the data you're now generating so it can be collected, transmitted (eventually), and interpreted.

Additional Exercises

The Sense-Emu emulator's GUI allows you to adjust values via the given sliders and the joystick control. This can be a particularly useful tool for manually changing values within your emulated sensor environment to test various threshold crossing events.

Threshold Management

Create another emulator adapter that interprets the Sense-Emu GUI's joystick controls and adjusts the floor (down button) and ceiling (up button) of either your temperature or your humidity threshold crossing value.

With this in place, see if you can exercise the hysteresis management function you implemented in the additional exercise of Chapter 3 using these new threshold crossings and the simulated data values generated from SensorDataGenerator (or your own custom version).

Conclusion

In this chapter, you learned about hardware emulation and how to integrate the Sense HAT emulator into your CDA. You also learned about some of the challenges associated with triggering actuation events, and how the logic to handle such events isn't always as simple as just sending an ON or OFF command. Design-wise, you learned more about the modularity of the CDA's design and how it can help you overcome some of these challenges.

You're now ready to dive into the final chapter of Part II—Chapter 5—where you'll learn about data transformation, which will help you eventually integrate your CDA and GDA.

## CHAPTER 5

Data Management

Data Formatting and Integration

High values and low.
Make the data consistent.
Else, none may use it.

Fundamental concepts: Build two IoT performance monitoring applications—one as an IoT gateway, and the other as an IoT constrained device.

Generating telemetry within a device is one thing. Making that telemetry usable by other devices is a whole new ball game. Fortunately, there are ways to translate this raw data into a format that can address this challenge.

What You'll Learn in This Chapter

To enable the CDA and GDA to "talk" with each other, we need to have a common language and data format in place. While it would be convenient to simply send a Python object to a Java application and vice versa, that's not easily doable without using an intermediary translation first.

Data Translation and Management Concepts

With the CDA's data collection capabilities now in place, you're on track to eventually share that data with the GDA and leverage it to inform a better outcome than could likely be achieved if that data hadn't been collected (and analyzed) in the first place.

In Chapters 3 and 4, you added functionality to the CDA that allowed it to collect information from simulated (or emulated) sensors and trigger simple actuation events, including the creation of three data containers to facilitate this process: `Sensor Data`, `ActuatorData`, and `SystemPerformanceData`.

With the GDA, you can use these data containers to support more advanced management functionality. The GDA will need to interpret the CDA's data and use it to support any analytics functions you need.

We'll have to tackle two key activities to support this:

Data translation
> This entails converting (and comprehending) the data generated, and in use by, the CDA so that the GDA and relevant cloud services can process the information, regardless of how each application is implemented.

Data management
> Once the data is available and understandable, you can use it to make decisions about how to manage the environment and ultimately achieve your objective.

The programming exercises in this chapter are designed to help you work through the details of these two activities. You'll start with building translation functionality for the CDA and then move on to the GDA and build out not only data translation capabilities but also some key management functionality that we'll continue to expand on in later chapters.

Programming Exercises

You'll be developing code for both the CDA and the GDA in this chapter, so let's take a look at both designs. Figure 5-1 provides a simple design view of the CDA with the data translation and conversion logic incorporated.

Figure 5-2 depicts the GDA's design for this chapter and includes the `DataUtil`, `DeviceDataManager`, and data wrapper classes that were implemented for the CDA back in Chapter 3. There's also a `PersistenceClientAdapter` class, which will be discussed later in this chapter.

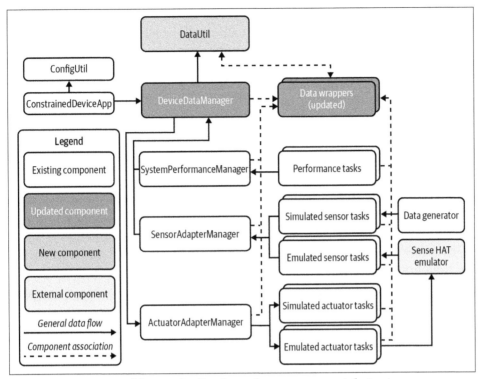

Figure 5-1. Constrained Device Application—data management design

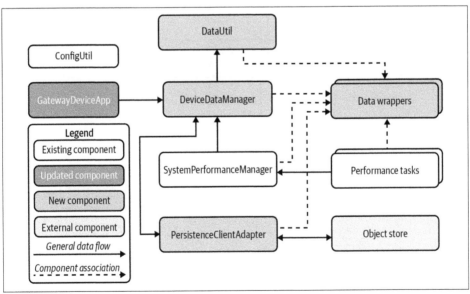

Figure 5-2. Gateway Device Application—data management design

You can see that the design concepts are nearly identical between the two applications. Each uses a `DeviceDataManager` to orchestrate the information flow within the application (which is new for the GDA in this chapter), and a new component is added—`DataUtil`—to provide a centralized data translation utility for converting the CDA's data container objects into a format that other systems can readily consume. You may have guessed by now that the data format you'll use for each translation exercise is JSON.

Let's start with the CDA, since only a few things need to be added and tested before we move on to the GDA.

Data Translation in the Constrained Device App

As you get started, be sure to check out a new branch (as explained in PIOT-CDA-05-000 (*https://oreil.ly/wZKNq*)). This will help you keep your newly added functionality separate from the code you've already implemented, tested, and merged into your primary branch.

Before digging into each exercise for the CDA, take a look at the notional UML shown in Figure 5-3 (some details have been removed for clarity).

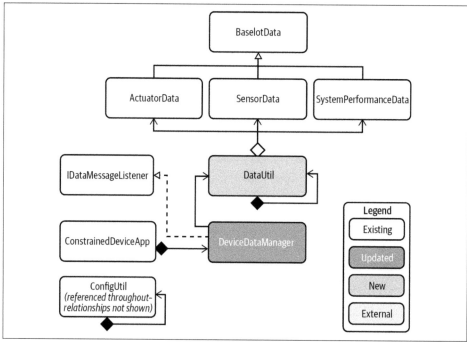

Figure 5-3. Constrained Device Application—data management UML

You can use this UML to help guide your implementation.

Now look at PIOT-CDA-05-001 (*https://oreil.ly/rXGe8*). This will be straightforward to implement. You're going to add SystemPerformanceData containers into the SystemPerformanceManager implementation you created back in Chapter 2.

Update the system performance manager

The only function that requires modification in SystemPerformanceData is handleTelemetry(). Here's the new implementation:

```
cpuUtilPct = self.cpuUtilTask.getTelemetryValue()
memUtilPct = self.memUtilTask.getTelemetryValue()

logging.debug( \
  'CPU utilization is %s percent, and memory utilization is %s percent.', \
  str(cpuUtilPct), str(memUtilPct))

sysPerfData = SystemPerformanceData()
sysPerfData.setLocationID(self.locationID)
sysPerfData.setCpuUtilization(cpuUtilPct)
sysPerfData.setMemoryUtilization(memUtilPct)

if self.dataMsgListener:
  self.dataMsgListener.handleSystemPerformanceMessage(sysPerfData)
```

It's additive in the sense that you're still retrieving the telemetry value from the CPU and memory utilization tasks, but now you're adding it into a newly instanced SystemPerformanceData. Finally, if you've set the IDataMessageListener instance, you'll pass the new SystemPerformanceData to its callback method, which is designed to handle this type of information.

The next and final CDA programming task for this chapter is outlined in PIOT-CDA-05-002 (*https://oreil.ly/a80cU*). It contains the activities you'll need to add JSON conversion functionality for your ActuatorData, SensorData, and SystemPerformanceData instances.

Add JSON translation using a data utility class

The implementation requirements for PIOT-CDA-05-002 (*https://oreil.ly/a80cU*) all center on one action:

- Create (or rather edit) the DataUtil class in the programmingtheiot.data package, and then add a function to convert each BaseIotData subclass type into JSON, and another to do the opposite.

For this exercise, I'll focus on the ActuatorData type, since implementing the other two (SensorData and SystemPerformanceData) will look nearly identical.

If you're using the sample code from python-components, you'll notice an existing DataUtil shell implementation in the programmingtheiot.data package. It relies on some of the built-in JSON translation functionality included with Python 3.

Scroll to the bottom of the sample code. There's another class contained within the DataUtil module named JsonDataEncoder. This is a very simple class that converts an object's parameters to a dictionary of key/value pairs. I'll get to this shortly, but for now, let's move on to the next action: converting ActuatorData into a JSON string.

Create a new function named ActuatorDataToJson():

```
def ActuatorDataToJson(self, data: ActuatorData = None):
    if not data:
        logging.warning('ActuatorData is null. Ignoring conversion to JSON.')
        return None

    logging.debug('Encoding ActuatorData to JSON [pre]  --> ' + \
        str(data))

    jsonData = self._generateJsonData(data)

    logging.debug('Encoding ActuatorData to JSON [post] --> ' + \
        str(jsonData))

    return jsonData
```

There's not much here, is there? That's because the heavy lifting is performed by a private function named _generateJsonData(). Let's add that implementation now (and yes, it is just one line of code):

```
def _generateJsonData(self, obj) -> str:
    return json.dumps(obj, indent = 4, cls = JsonDataEncoder)
```

But what's the purpose of the cls = JsonDataEncoder parameter? It overrides the default JSON encoder with JsonDataEncoder and tells the json.dumps() function how to extract the data from the custom BaseIotData subclasses you created in Chapter 3. Without this, the function doesn't know how to handle the conversion and will throw a TypeError exception.

Logging in Python

You've likely noticed the plethora of debug messages sprinkled throughout the code base. I find these useful for keeping tabs on the inner workings of the code even when running the unit tests. If you choose to keep these log messages in place (or even to add more), you may want to use debug or fine-grained logging so you can easily control how much is logged. This is particularly important if you reduce the polling time. You can read more about Python logging in the Python documentation (*https://oreil.ly/flwjj*).

Your code now supports `ActuatorData` to JSON conversion. Next, you'll need a way to convert a JSON representation of `ActuatorData` back into an `ActuatorData` instance. Here's a sample implementation:

```
def jsonToActuatorData(self, jsonData: str = None):
  if not jsonData:
    logging.warning('JSON data is empty or null.')
    return None

  jsonStruct = self._formatDataAndLoadDictionary(jsonData)
  ad = ActuatorData()
  self._updateIotData(jsonStruct, ad)

  return ad
```

After a simple validation check to verify the JSON string isn't null or empty, the conversion process is started. You can see the three calls:

1. Call the `_formatDataAndLoadDictionary()` function to generate a JSON structure (a dictionary of key/value pairs).

2. Create a new `ActuatorData` instance.

3. Call the `_updateIotData()` function to set the `ActuatorData` instance values with the dictionary.

You'll need to create both `_formatDataAndLoadDictionary()` and `_updateIotData()`. They will be separate functions for the same reason `_generateJsonData()` is a separate function: you'll be reusing the other functions you'll create (to convert JSON data to a `SensorData` object and to a `SystemPerformanceData` object, respectively).

Here's the sample code for both methods:

```
def _formatDataAndLoadDictionary(self, jsonData: str) -> dict:
  jsonData = \
    jsonData.replace("\'", "\"").replace( \
      'False', 'false').replace('True', 'true')

  jsonStruct = json.loads(jsonData)

  return jsonStruct

def _updateIotData(self, jsonStruct, obj):
  varStruct = vars(obj)

  for key in jsonStruct:
    if key in varStruct:
      setattr(obj, key, jsonStruct[key])
    else:
      logging.warn('JSON data key not mappable to object: %s', key)
```

The `_formatDataAndLoadDictionary()` function does two things. First, it converts any single quotes to double quotes and any boolean string representations to lowercase. This typically won't be needed for testing between the GDA and the CDA; however, it is necessary to ensure parsing accuracy by the JSON library. Second, it parses the JSON string into a dictionary of key/value pairs.

The `_updateIotData()` function accepts the JSON dictionary and the newly created `BaseIotData` subclass data container instance as parameters. It looks up the keys and values within the JSON dictionary so the value can be applied to the data container instance. It will check if the key from the JSON dictionary first exists as a variable within the data container instance: this is another validation step you should be sure to include.

With these functions now in place, you can create the `jsonToSensorData()`, `jsonTo SystemPerformanceData()`, `SensorDataToJson()`, and `SystemPerformanceDataToJ son()` functions. Each implementation will align to functions you've just created for `jsonToActuatorData()` and `ActuatorDataToJson()`, respectively. See if you can do these on your own!

 You can read more about JSON and the conversion functionality built into Python in the Python documentation (*https://oreil.ly/ g9cZt*). There's much more you can do with this module; for the CDA exercises in this chapter, you'll need to use only the `json.dumps()` and `json.loads()` functions.

Once you've completed these steps, it's time to test everything out. The `DataUtilTest` in the *./src/test/python/programmingtheiot/unit/data* path will run through a number of unit tests and let you know whether or not everything is working.

If each test passes, you should be good to go. Now you can finally get back to programming the GDA.

Data Translation in the Gateway Device App

Recall the data containers you created for the CDA in Chapter 3: `ActuatorData`, `SensorData`, and `SystemPerformanceData`. In this section, you'll build the same containers for the GDA.

Figure 5-4 depicts the notional detailed design in UML for the GDA's data management design.

You can think of this design as a cross between the CDA's design in this chapter and its design from Chapter 3. Does this design seem redundant? Why would you need to build these containers for the GDA when it's not responsible for sensing or actuation?

It's true that the GDA does not need to handle sensing and actuation in this design; it does, however, need to handle the sensing and actuation data it will receive from, and ultimately send to, the CDA. Programmatically, it will be much easier to operate on typed instances of these data containers than to parse the JSON throughout the code base. The GDA also needs to generate its own `SystemPerformanceData`, so you'll need data containers for each.

I'll briefly summarize the activities here, since each will follow the same pattern that you've implemented for the CDA. But first, be sure to check out a new branch for the GDA related to this chapter, as specified in PIOT-GDA-05-000 (*https://oreil.ly/WGpm8*).

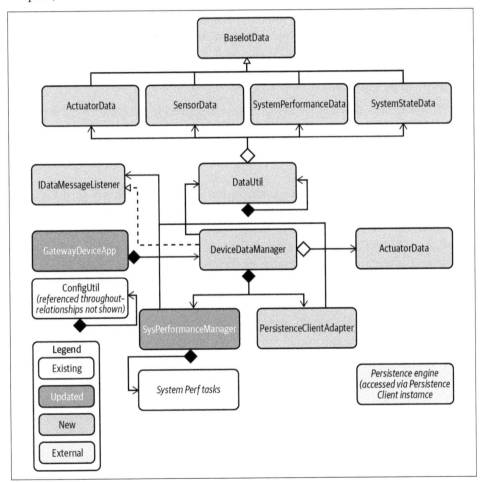

Figure 5-4. Gateway Device Application—data management UML

Implement all data container structures

Take a moment to review the content in PIOT-GDA-05-001 (*https://oreil.ly/kF4h2*), the first implementation exercise for the GDA in this chapter. It walks through the data containers described in Chapter 3 (`ActuatorData`, `SensorData`, and `SystemPer formanceData`), but in ways specific to the GDA and implemented in Java.

Let's look at the key actions this exercise entails:

- Review the existing code for `BaseIotData` (part of the java-components sample code). Feel free to create your own, but be aware that this serves as the base class for all other data containers within the GDA, much like it did for the CDA in the python-components sample code.

- Create the concrete GDA-specific implementations of the data containers you already know: `ActuatorData`, `SensorData`, and `SystemPerformanceData`. These will all derive from `BaseIotData`, so their respective implementations will be rather straightforward.

- I'll briefly walk through the same routine described in Chapter 3 with the CDA's implementation of `ActuatorData`, `SensorData`, and `SystemPerformanceData`. But first, be sure to review the sample code for `BaseIotData` provided in java-components.

The Java version of `BaseIotData` contains the same data elements as the Python version. It will set various defaults, including setting the typeID to `Config Const.DEFAULT_TYPE`, with string values either empty ("") or set to `Config Const.NOT_SET`. It also represents the timestamp String in ISO 8601 format just like its Python counterpart does: by relying on the Java class `DateTimeFormatter`, specifically the `ISO_INSTANT` constant. This means we should be able to parse the time/date string the same way with both applications, should that be necessary.

Assuming you're keeping `BaseIotData` in place, it's time to create the subclasses that will store the telemetry and command information (`SensorData` and `ActuatorData`, respectively). Both will inherit from `BaseIotData`, so you need only to add in the functionality specific to each.

The actions listed in PIOT-GDA-05-001 (*https://oreil.ly/kF4h2*) should be familiar by now, since they essentially repeat those from PIOT-CDA-03-001 (*https://oreil.ly/ HthCm*), but for the GDA. Here's the detail for `SensorData`.

Import `ConfigConst` and `java.io.Serializable` (`BaseIotData` doesn't need to be explicitly imported, as it's in the same package as `SensorData`):

```
import java.io.Serializable;
import programmingtheiot.common.ConfigConst;
```

Set the `static final serialVersionUID` (which allows you to maintain serialization compatibility across implementation updates) and the internal value. Be sure to use "value," since other systems will rely on this variable name:

```
// NOTE: Be sure to generate this yourself!
private static final long serialVersionUID = 1L;

private float value = 0.0f;

public SensorData()
{
  super();
}
```

Implement the accessor methods that will get and set the value:

```
public float getValue()
{
  return this.value;
}

public void setValue(float val)
{
  super.updateTimeStamp();

  this.value = val;
}
```

Remember that `BaseIotData` implements `updateTimeStamp()`, and it's not overridden in `SensorData`, so including the super keyword here is not necessary. It is a good practice, however. You may recall that `BaseIotData` also defines a template method named `handleUpdateData()`. It *must* be implemented by the subclass since it's declared as abstract in the base class. As with the CDA version of `SensorData`, the implementation is relatively simple.

Implement the base class template method `handleUpdateData()`:

```
protected void handleUpdateData(BaseIotData data)
{
  if (data instanceof SensorData) {
    SensorData sData = (SensorData) data;
    this.setValue(sData.getValue());
  }
}
```

There's one more action that is completely optional yet very helpful in terms of debugging: adding a `toString()` implementation. Here's how to do that:

```
public String toString()
{
  StringBuilder sb = new StringBuilder(super.toString());
```

```
    sb.append(',');
    sb.append(
      ConfigConst.VALUE_PROP).append('=').append(this.getValue());

    return sb.toString();
  }
```

Since `BaseIotData` already implements its own `toString()` version, you can leverage that within `SensorData`'s `toString()` by creating a new `StringBuilder` with the base class string representation and simply appending the unique properties of `Sensor Data`. This pattern applies to the other data containers, too! You don't have to implement, but it will make some debugging operations easier.

`ActuatorData` follows the same implementation pattern as `SensorData`, with the main differences being the addition of class-scoped variables representing the integer `command`, float-based `value`, String-based `stateData`, and boolean `isResponse`.

 The `isResponse` flag is an extra layer of protection that can help avoid resending an actuation event received by the GDA from the CDA (which I'll discuss in more detail in Part III). The logic you'll implement will manage this process so that should never occur. I mostly use it for debugging purposes in my own implementation.

Here's a quick breakdown of these activities:

- First, use the same imports that were included with `SensorData`, set the `serial VersionUID`, and create class-scoped variables for the `value`, `command`, `stateData`, and `isResponse` Boolean flag.

- Implement the accessor methods for all four class-scoped variables (`value`, `com mand`, `stateData`, and `isResponse`), and be sure to call `super.updateTimeS tamp()` whenever any of these setter methods are invoked.

- Implement the base class template method `handleUpdateData()`:

```
    protected void handleUpdateData(BaseIotData data)
    {
      if (data instanceof ActuatorData) {
        ActuatorData aData = (ActuatorData) data;
        this.setCommand(aData.getCommand());
        this.setValue(aData.getValue());
        this.setStateData(aData.getStateData());

        if (aData.isResponseFlagEnabled()) {
          this.isResponse = true;
        }
```

```
        }
    }
```

Finally, implement `SystemPerformanceData`. Like its counterparts `ActuatorData` and `SensorData`, this also derives from `BaseIotData`, except it has three class-scoped variables: CPU utilization, memory utilization, and disk utilization. (You'll see later in this chapter why disk utilization is important.)

- You'll use the same import process as with `ActuatorData` and `SensorData` but be sure to declare class-scoped variables for `cpuUtil`, `memUtil`, and `diskUtil`.

- Implement the accessor methods for all three class-scoped variables (`cpuUtil`, `memUtil`, and `diskUtil`), and remember to call `super.updateTimeStamp()` whenever any of these setter methods are invoked.

- Implement the base class template method `handleUpdateData()`:

```
protected void handleUpdateData(BaseIotData data)
{
  if (data instanceof SystemPerformanceData) {
    SystemPerformanceData sData = (SystemPerformanceData) data;

    this.setCpuUtilization(sData.getCpuUtilization());
    this.setDiskUtilization(sData.getDiskUtilization());
    this.setMemoryUtilization(sData.getMemoryUtilization());
  }
}
```

Let's run the unit tests in the java-components repository and the *./src/test/java/ programmingtheiot/part02/unit/data* path—specifically, the three test cases named for the data containers they test: *ActuatorDataTest.java*, *SensorDataTest.java*, and *SystemPerformanceDataTest.java*.

Here's some sample console output generated after running the `SystemPerformance DataTest` test case:

```
Jan 03, 2021 1:21:33 PM
programmingtheiot.part02.unit.data.SystemPerformanceDataTest testFullUpdate
INFO: Created first data obj: name=,typeID=0,timeStamp=2021-01-
03T18:21:33.036582100Z,statusCode=0,hasError=false,locationID=Not
Set,latitude=0.0,longitude=0.0,elevation=0.0,cpuUtil=0.0,diskUtil=0.0,memUtil=0.0
Jan 03, 2021 1:21:33 PM
programmingtheiot.part02.unit.data.SystemPerformanceDataTest testFullUpdate
INFO: Created second data obj: name=,typeID=0,timeStamp=2021-01-
03T18:21:33.097419200Z,statusCode=0,hasError=false,locationID=Not
Set,latitude=0.0,longitude=0.0,elevation=0.0,cpuUtil=10.0,diskUtil=10.0,memUtil=10.0
Jan 03, 2021 1:21:33 PM
programmingtheiot.part02.unit.data.SystemPerformanceDataTest testFullUpdate
INFO: Updated second data obj: name=,typeID=0,timeStamp=2021-01-
03T18:21:33.097419200Z,statusCode=0,hasError=false,locationID=Not
Set,latitude=0.0,longitude=0.0,elevation=0.0,cpuUtil=10.0,diskUtil=10.0,memUtil=10.0
```

```
Jan 03, 2021 1:21:33 PM
programmingtheiot.part02.unit.data.SystemPerformanceDataTest testDefaultValues
INFO: Created data obj: name=,typeID=0,timeStamp=2021-01-
03T18:21:33.101409500Z,statusCode=0,hasError=false,locationID=Not
Set,latitude=0.0,longitude=0.0,elevation=0.0,cpuUtil=0.0,diskUtil=0.0,memUtil=0.0
Jan 03, 2021 1:21:33 PM
programmingtheiot.part02.unit.data.SystemPerformanceDataTest testParameterUpdates
INFO: Created data obj: name=,typeID=0,timeStamp=2021-01-
03T18:21:33.103403500Z,statusCode=0,hasError=false,locationID=Not
Set,latitude=0.0,longitude=0.0,elevation=0.0,cpuUtil=10.0,diskUtil=10.0,memUtil=10.0
```

Since these are unit tests, you should see a green bar in your JUnit console for the ones that execute successfully, assuming you're running this within an IDE that supports JUnit. After successfully passing each test, you can move on to the next task within the GDA exercise set: updating SystemPerformanceManager.

Update the system performance manager

The update you'll make to the GDA's SystemPerformanceManager, described in PIOT-GDA-05-002 (*https://oreil.ly/gGAr4*), is essentially the same as what you've already done for the CDA's version. Add the class-scoped variables and functionality described in the card for PIOT-GDA-05-002 (*https://oreil.ly/gGAr4*). Implement the method handleTelemetry() as follows: create a new SystemPerformanceData instance, set the appropriate values, and then invoke the IDataMessageListener instance's callback (if not null). Here's the updated implementation for this method:

```
float cpuUtil = this.sysCpuUtilTask.getTelemetryValue();
float memUtil = this.sysMemUtilTask.getTelemetryValue();

// add diskUtil too!

_Logger.fine(
  "CPU utilization: " + cpuUtil + ", Mem utilization: " + memUtil);

SystemPerformanceData spd = new SystemPerformanceData();
spd.setLocationID(this.locationID);
spd.setCpuUtilization(cpuUtil);
spd.setMemoryUtilization(memUtil);

if (this.dataMsgListener != null) {
  this.dataMsgListener.handleSystemPerformanceMessage(
    ResourceNameEnum.GDA_SYSTEM_PERF_MSG_RESOURCE, spd);
}
```

Just remember that you'll want to create a new task to track disk utilization, much like you're already doing for CPU utilization and memory utilization.

Let's move on to the next key component in your GDA implementation journey—adding JSON conversion.

Add JSON translation using a data utility class

The implementation requirements for PIOT-GDA-05-003 (*https://oreil.ly/yDGp8*) all center on the same single action you tackled for the `DataUtil` implementation within the CDA: creating (or editing) the `DataUtil` class in the `programmingtheiot.data` package and adding the requisite public methods to convert your `BaseIotData` subclass instances into JSON and vice versa.

This time I'll focus on the `SystemPerformanceData` conversion and leave `Actuator Data` and `SensorData` to you as an implementation exercise.

Since the shell implementation of `DataUtil` already exists in java-components, you can simply edit it in place or add your own. Within the shell implementation, notice the import statement: `import com.google.gson.Gson`, provided by Google, is one of many Java-based JSON libraries. We'll use it for JSON conversion within the GDA.

Here's the sample code that will convert a `SystemPerformanceData` instance to JSON and back again:

```
public String SystemPerformanceDataToJson(
  SystemPerformanceData sysPerfData)
{
  String jsonData = null;

  if (sysPerfData != null) {
    Gson converter = new Gson();
    jsonData = converter.toJson(sysPerfData);
  }

  return jsonData;
}

public SystemPerformanceData jsonToSystemPerformanceData(String jsonData)
{
  SystemPerformanceData sysPerfData = null;

  if (jsonData != null && jsonData.trim().length() > 0) {
    Gson converter = new Gson();
    sysPerfData =
      converter.fromJson(jsonData, SystemPerformanceData.class);
  }

  return sysPerfData;
}
```

Clearly, the use of a library such as Gson can save development time. The logic to translate from `SystemPerformanceData` to JSON and back again is essentially just two lines of code. Since your CDA and GDA implementations of this class (and of the other classes, `ActuatorData` and `SensorData`) are identical (regarding their respective properties), the process is very straightforward.

The complexity arises from maintenance. Both code bases need to be maintained to ensure compatibility of type properties—if you change a parameter name in the GDA, for instance, you'll need to do the same in the CDA.

Logging in Java

A common way to track activity at runtime within a Java application is to use logging. This is not a replacement for good unit and automated testing, of course, but it can be helpful when you need to see the results of a particular call, or even the various transformation steps associated with a method call.

See if you can implement the remaining classes on your own. Just create the two methods for conversion to/from JSON for each remaining BaseIotData subclass using the pattern just shown for SystemPerformanceData.

After completing this final step, run the unit tests in DataUtilTest (it's in the *./src/ test/java/programmingtheiot/unit/data* path). It will run a bunch of unit tests that each should pass. On success, you can move on to the next exercise.

Create and integrate the device data manager

The DeviceDataManager class is the heart and soul of the GDA, much as it is for the CDA. It is, however, more involved: it orchestrates data moving from and to the CDA as well as to and from the cloud. It also plays a role in Edge Tier management: it implements the Manage functionality that lives at the edge.

The PIOT-GDA-05-004 (*https://oreil.ly/Ev9wb*) card sets the stage for all of this functionality and will take a little bit of time to get through. Here's a high-level summary of the actions you'll need to tackle within the class:

- Create (or edit) the DeviceDataManager class within the programmingth eiot.gda.app package.

- The constructor will check the configuration for the connection flags you'll use in Part III. While not critical right now, it will be good to add in the placeholders during this exercise.

- Like other management classes, this, too, will have a startManager() and stop Manager() implementation. For now, it will simply start and stop the SystemPer formanceManager, but it will soon enable or disable the various configured connections so the GDA can communicate with both the CDA and the cloud over the network.

- It will implement `IDataMessageListener`, so all method definitions in the interface class will need to be created within `DeviceDataManager` and (eventually) implemented.

- The card suggests some private methods you can create to delegate functionality that you'll likely call from one or more of the `IDataMessageListener` methods you'll implement.

`DeviceDataManager` is also the right place to handle any additional Manage-related code you want to include later. It doesn't have to provide the actual implementation of analysis algorithms, but it will serve as the gatekeeper for all message processing.

To keep things simple, you may want to consider using this class to contain all your device-specific management and message orchestration logic.

First, create (or rather edit) the `DeviceDataManager` class within the `programmingth eiot.gda.app` package and make sure it implements the `IDataMessageListener` interface. A stubbed-out version already exists within the sample java-components code you cloned in Chapter 1, with the interface implementation declared and with the import statements you'll need later. Feel free to use it as your starting point.

Create a constructor that sets class-scoped boolean values for the following configuration flags:

```
this.enableMqttClient  =
    configUtil.getBoolean(
        ConfigConst.GATEWAY_DEVICE, ConfigConst.ENABLE_MQTT_CLIENT_KEY);

this.enableCoapServer  =
    configUtil.getBoolean(
        ConfigConst.GATEWAY_DEVICE, ConfigConst.ENABLE_COAP_SERVER_KEY);

this.enableCloudClient =
    configUtil.getBoolean(
        ConfigConst.GATEWAY_DEVICE, ConfigConst.ENABLE_CLOUD_CLIENT_KEY);

this.enablePersistenceClient =
    configUtil.getBoolean(
        ConfigConst.GATEWAY_DEVICE, ConfigConst.ENABLE_PERSISTENCE_CLIENT_KEY);

initManager();
```

I'll cover the first three boolean values beginning in Part III and continuing into Part IV, and you'll get to use them as part of future updates to `DeviceDataManager` as you progress through the related exercises.

For now, create a new private method named `initManager()`. You can use this to initialize the connection objects you'll use to connect to the CDA and cloud service in Part III.

The last boolean value, however—`this.enablePersistenceClient`—will be explored as an optional activity in this chapter as an introduction to capturing and storing data locally within the GDA, so it can have a way to store state or CDA messages it may need to analyze over a period of time.

Here's an example of how you can implement the initial version of `initManager()`:

```
private void initManager()
{
  this.sysPerfMgr = new SystemPerformanceManager();
  this.sysPerfMgr.setDataMessageListener(this);

  if (this.enableMqttClient) {
    // TODO: implement this in Lab Module 7
  }

  if (this.enableCoapServer) {
    // TODO: implement this in Lab Module 8
  }

  if (this.enableCloudClient) {
    // TODO: implement this in Lab Module 10
  }

  if (this.enablePersistenceClient) {
    // TODO: implement this as an optional exercise in Lab Module 5
  }
}
```

Notice the initialization of `SystemPerformanceManager`? This is similar to the behavior you implemented in the CDA, where the `DeviceDataManager` manages the `System PerformanceManager` initialization and execution, and the application handles the start and stop of `DeviceDataManager`. I'll cover this for the GDA briefly in PIOT-GDA-05-005 (*https://oreil.ly/Ev9wb*).

The initialization of `DeviceDataManager` is almost complete. Let's move on to the start and stop methods.

Add the initial `startManager()` and `stopManager()` implementations. For now, these will be relatively simple. Eventually, you'll also use these methods to start and stop any stateful connections initialized in `initManager()` to communicate between devices and the cloud.

Here's a simple example of each method:

```
public void startManager()
{
  _Logger.info("Starting DeviceDataManager...");

  this.sysPerfMgr.startManager();
}
```

```
public void stopManager()
{
  _Logger.info("Stopping DeviceDataManager...");

  this.sysPerfMgr.stopManager();
}
```

This implementation is fairly simple, which means you can move on to the next piece: implementing the IDataMessageListener interface. In Java, an interface provides a contract that must be honored—it's just a declaration of the different methods and their respective signatures that an implementing class must, well, implement.

Here's a summary of the methods defined in the interface:

```
public boolean handleActuatorCommandResponse(
    ResourceNameEnum resourceName, ActuatorData data);

public boolean handleIncomingMessage(
    ResourceNameEnum resourceName, String msg);

public boolean handleSensorMessage(
    ResourceNameEnum resourceName, SensorData data);

public boolean handleSystemPerformanceMessage(
    ResourceNameEnum resourceName, SystemPerformanceData data);
```

Each of these will need to be implemented within DeviceDataManager. Notice that each accepts a reference to ResourceNameEnum and another parameter. The Resource NameEnum type is a Java enum that simply represents a common set of names and other related properties for passing messages between the CDA and the GDA.

 Feel free to adjust the interface and method signatures to suit your needs as you progress through the exercises in Parts III and IV. I've used these as a common way to capture the necessary parameters for the exercises in this book, but you may find an alternative signature will work more effectively with your design.

Let's look at the initial implementation of each method in turn. You'll be adding more functionality to these methods later:

handleActuatorCommandResponse(ResourceNameEnum, ActuatorData)
    This will be invoked when an ActuatorData message is received in response to an actuation event on the CDA. For this callback, simply check whether the ActuatorData reference is non-null, and then log a debug message indicating the message was received. You can also check whether the ActuatorData reference is in fact a response by calling the isResponseFlagEnabled() function. If so, check

whether the `hasError()` flag is set and log a warning message indicating an error occurred on the actuation response.

handleIncomingMessage(ResourceNameEnum, String)
This will be invoked when a message is received from the cloud service, and the String parameter will represent the data in JSON format. It will almost always be an `ActuatorData` message, so we could technically name it `handleIncomingAc` `tuatorCommand()`. For the implementation, simply log a message that the message was received if the String is non-null and not empty.

handleSensorMessage(ResourceNameEnum, SensorData)
This will be invoked when a `SensorData` message is received from the CDA. For this callback, check whether the `SensorData` reference is non-null, and then log a debug message indicating the message was received. You can also check if the `SensorData` reference has an error by checking whether the `hasError()` flag is set; if so, log a warning message.

handleSystemPerformanceMessage(ResourceNameEnum, SystemPerformanceData)
This will be invoked when a `SystemPerformanceData` message is received either internally or from the CDA. For this callback, you can implement the same logic as for `handleSensorMessage()`.

These four callback methods provide the entry point to all analysis the GDA will perform on internally generated data and on data coming in from the CDA or the cloud. You'll see in the requirements card that there are a couple of private methods defined to handle the analysis of this incoming data:

handleIncomingDataAnalysis()
This will eventually be called by `handleIncomingMessage()`, `handleSensorMessage()`, and `handleSystemPerformanceMessage()` and parameterized to meet your specific design needs. It's responsible for handling any incoming message analysis and deciding what to do. For instance, if an actuation event is received from the cloud, it must first be validated and then—if appropriate—sent on to the CDA via one of the connection paradigms I'll discuss in Part III.

handleUpstreamTransmission()
This will eventually be called by the `handleIncomingDataAnalysis()` method after data analysis is complete. Its primary responsibility is to send `SensorData` and `SystemPerformanceData` messages up to the cloud service, possibly after locally persisting the information within the GDA.

Clearly, there's much more work to be done with `DeviceDataManager`—heart and soul, as I stated earlier. But no worries! You'll get to add much more functionality as you progress through the remaining chapters.

But first, a quick dive into the optional exercises related to local data persistence.

Add local data persistence

The GDA's persistence requirements are technically optional, so you can stop here and move on to Part III if you'd like. I think you'll find this functionality useful, however, so I'll explain the exercises at a high level and leave the implementation up to you.

Since the GDA is the gateway device and provides the interface between the Edge Tier and the Cloud Tier, it can be useful for it to have some persistence ability. It should be able to at least temporarily store some state information about the Edge Tier as a whole and draw upon that state to make decisions in the future.

An example might include storing SensorData JSON data from one or more CDA implementations. Over time, the GDA can read the incoming data, detect an anomaly, and then draw upon n minutes (or hours) of locally stored data to make a decision that might shut down one of those CDA instances, instruct it to reboot, or perhaps take another action, all without having to rely on an active connection to the internet. This flexibility to act locally can prove invaluable if network connectivity is sporadic or shut down.

Additional Exercises

Your GDA now has the ability to store data locally and track your disk utilization. But what happens if your disk utilization begins to creep up to the point where you risk running out of local storage space?

Proactive Disk Utilization Management

Within the DeviceDataManager, implement the necessary functionality to monitor disk utilization on the GDA via the SystemPerformanceData messages sent by the SystemPerformanceManager. If disk utilization approaches a configured threshold (say, 50%), be sure to log a warning message.

Next, decide whether to start clearing out the older cached data entries stored in Redis (assuming you're using Redis for your object cache), or simply stop caching data entries altogether.

While neither option is ideal, it's probably better than running out of disk space and turning the GDA into a nonoperational gateway. Determine what trade-off is best and take the appropriate action, being careful not to delete needed data!

Conclusion

In this chapter, you learned about data management and transformation by converting your data objects into JSON and back again. This is a huge step forward! With this knowledge, you can add new features and data containers to support many more capabilities in the future.

It's time to learn how to connect your CDA and GDA using different messaging protocols, which I'll talk about in the introduction to Part III. From there, you'll be able to connect your systems to the cloud and complete your initial end-to-end IoT solution.

## PART III

Connecting to Other Things

Introduction

Need a connection?
Enable, then disable.
You get the message?

In Part I, I stressed that the IoT is all about integration. You set up your development environment and built your first two applications. At the end of Part I, you had your applications up and running and generating some very basic performance data, but little more.

Part II advanced the integration concept further and helped you build out a basis for connecting with the physical world. You also established more advanced data collection, transformation, and storage capabilities for your two applications, enabling your CDA and GDA to finally do something a bit more useful, although they aren't yet talking directly to each other.

Cue Part III. This is where you'll take the next step forward in your integration journey and enable your applications to talk reliably with each other.

What You'll Learn in This Section

There are purpose-built protocols for communicating between IoT devices and even many IoT-friendly cloud services, and they're in active use as of this writing. These protocols tend to fall into one of two categories: *publish/subscribe* (pub/sub) or *request/response*. These categories simply refer to the style of messaging that devices agree on in order to send or receive data over the network.

Pub/sub protocols are generally best suited for those messaging situations in which one device wants to send data to one or more unknown recipients, based on a topic name that the device and all recipients know in advance. The sending device is called the *publisher*, and the receiving device is called the *subscriber*. Pub/sub protocols typically allow multiple publishers and subscribers and include a *broker*, or server, that handles these interactions.

Request/response protocols are generally designed to support a one-to-one interaction between a device that's requesting something (such as data from a remote database) and another that's responding to the request (by reading data from a database to return it to the requester, for example). While request/response can certainly work in a true one-to-one fashion in which there's only one requester and one responder, we usually see it implemented in cases in which the responder is a server that provides many requesting clients with access to resources.

The protocols I'll discuss in the next few chapters adhere to either the pub/sub or the request/response paradigm. All function at the application layer, as defined by IETF RFC 1122 (*https://tools.ietf.org/html/rfc1122*). Figure III-1 provides an example of this,[1] including a handful of protocols you may already know and some you'll learn about in the next four chapters.

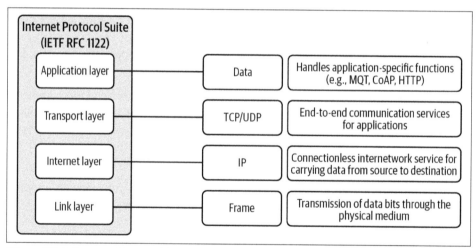

Figure III-1. Internet Protocol Suite categorization—we'll focus on the application layer in this section

---

1 R. Braden (Editor). Requirements for Internet Hosts – Communication Layers. IETF Standard RFC 1122, 1989.

You've undoubtedly heard about some of the many protocols used within the Edge Tier to communicate with sensors, actuators, and the devices that manage them. It's not in the scope of this book to work through these protocols, or even to explain them. As such, I'll focus exclusively on those that work within an IP-based environment and on the software development techniques you can employ to leverage them in your IoT solution.

Naming Conventions for Topics and Resources

Finally, these protocols all have at least one thing in common: naming conventions for topics (pub/sub) or resources (request/response). Although naming can be highly subjective, there are a few things to keep in mind to help you avoid inconsistencies and confusion for your development teams and projects. As for naming strategies, a location-based, top-down structure may work for one business, while a type-based structure may work best for another. Here are four tips for naming topics and resources, regardless of the protocol you choose:

- Topics and resources may be case sensitive. The placement of the forward slash (/) to separate different levels of naming always matters.

- Choose a top-level naming convention based on a category that represents the highest level your business needs. If that's geographic, great, but don't assume that all devices will reside in the same geographic center. As your business expands, you'll likely grow into other geographies as well. Similarly, you probably don't need to consider a topical structure that includes celestial objects, like MilkyWay/Sun/Earth/{NextSubTopic}. If you're considering deploying devices to Mars, great! However, it's probably not necessary to incorporate that into your naming strategy right now. (In 10 or 20 years, I'll probably be wrong.)

- Avoid spaces and special characters and choose a naming convention that your business and stakeholders can generally agree on. Although I use CamelCase for topic and resource names throughout the exercises in this book, you may opt for a different convention. Just be consistent and stick with the semantics and characters supported by the specification. Generally speaking, the lowest-common-denominator approach will help you avoid integration problems later. This may mean using basic ASCII lowercase characters and numbers exclusively (i.e., a–z and 0–9).

In short, like many other technical decisions, naming is about balance. I find it easiest to structure my naming strategy around categories that I'll most likely care about over the next two to five years and try not to concern myself with structures that I may care about in a decade. As you build out your infrastructure and implement the examples in each chapter, your own objectives will shape the naming conventions you ultimately settle on.

So what does this all mean for your own implementation? Basically, you'll have four types of messages to manage:

Sensor messages
These are messages sent from the sensor device upstream (from the CDA).

Actuator commands
These are messages sent from the cloud or gateway device downstream (to the CDA).

Device management status messages
These are messages that will be sent from either the CDA or the GDA upstream to either the GDA or the cloud, respectively.

Device management commands
These are messages that will be sent from either the cloud or the GDA downstream to either the GDA or the CDA, respectively.

It's easy to go overboard with naming conventions and nested subtopics, so I'll use the following relatively simple pattern for both topics and resources going forward:[2]

```
{project name}/{device name}/{message type}
```

The exercises in this part, and throughout the remainder of the book, require three categories of resource and topic names, as follows:

Sensor messages
- PIOT/ConstrainedDevice/SensorMsg

Actuator commands and responses
- PIOT/ConstrainedDevice/ActuatorCmd
- PIOT/ConstrainedDevice/ActuatorResponse

System performance messages
- PIOT/ConstrainedDevice/SystemPerfMsg
- PIOT/GatewayDevice/SystemPerfMsg

This naming approach is granular enough for the CDA and GDA integration exercises and allows for easy filtering on message type or device name. You may have another strategy that's preferable for your own environment and overall architecture.

---

2 This topic/resource naming convention will generally work well for simple testing, but in later chapters you'll see how you can adapt this to support a more detailed naming hierarchy for your own use, or to support a modified convention for integration with the cloud.

Since the message itself can contain any detail you'd like, such as the message name, type ID, or location, you can simply filter for specifics by parsing the JSON message.

 If you decide to add more device instances in your own environment, you can add another subtopic—perhaps based on region, or even on device-specific naming—or simply include the device specificity in the message itself.

As a convenience, I've defined "consts" in both python-components and java-components to represent these names. Further, I created a special "enum" class called ResourceNameEnum within the CDA and GDA source trees that uses these "consts" to represent the topic and resource names specific to each application. This "enum" class is provided to make development easier and more efficient, as the type ResourceNa meEnum can be used in place of a string-based topic or resource name throughout the code base. This allows you to add additional properties to extend its functionality without modifying interface and class signatures.

In addition to the three categories already mentioned, there are two additional categories included within ResourceNameEnum that are not needed for the exercises in this book but may be helpful for future projects:

Device management status messages
- PIOT/ConstrainedDevice/MgmtStatusMsg
- PIOT/GatewayDevice/MgmtStatusMsg

Device management commands
- PIOT/ConstrainedDevice/MgmtStatusCmd
- PIOT/GatewayDevice/MgmtStatusCmd

Feel free to use these if you'd like, or you can ignore them.

All of these topic and resource names could just as easily be loaded from the configuration file (which I'll talk about next), but I decided to include each name within the Java and Python code to simplify the exercises and avoid potential integration issues stemming from mistyped string names. Of course, this means you'll need to ensure that any changes you make in one language's ResourceNameEnum are appropriately reflected in the other.

Configuration Considerations

The sample configuration file and configuration utility (introduced in Chapter 1) has dedicated sections for each connection type. These properties can, of course, be modified to suit your needs, but it's worth calling them out here so you know what to expect when the implementation exercises begin:

```
#
# MQTT client configuration information
#
[Mqtt.GatewayService]
credFile      = ./cred/PiotMqttCred.props
certFile      = ./cert/PiotMqttLocalCertFile.pem
host          = localhost
port          = 1883
securePort    = 1884
defaultQoS    = 0
keepAlive     = 30
enableCrypt   = False
```

The host key refers to the network address of the server for that particular protocol. You can change this from localhost to a different server name; however, keep in mind that it's your responsibility to ensure the data you send to any server is not sensitive in any way (or that it's appropriately protected and encrypted), because it's no longer under your control once it leaves your computer. The examples in this section will reference local servers running on your local system to get you started.

Implementing Exercises and Validation

For each protocol that I'll discuss, it's important to validate that your code is passing the correct messages. After each key step in the implementation process, I'll pause briefly and ask you to run some tests with a protocol analyzer, such as Wireshark (*https://gitlab.com/wireshark/wireshark*). This will help with your testing and overall understanding of the protocol.

There are other protocol analyzers available, too! Choose one you're comfortable with. All of the related examples and screenshots I'll show use Wireshark (v3.2.6 or higher).

Wireshark is an open source protocol analyzer that runs as an application on your computer and supports the IoT protocols that I'll discuss throughout this section. For installation instructions, see the Wireshark website (*https://www.wireshark.org*).

Security Considerations

Since we're dealing with application-layer protocols that work on top of the transport layer, encrypting the connections can be handled at the transport layer. TCP/IP connections can use Transport Layer Security (*https://tools.ietf.org/html/rfc8446*) (TLS); UDP/IP connections can use Datagram Transport Layer Security (*https://tools.ietf.org/html/rfc6347*) (DTLS). Once data traversing the connection "pipe" is encrypted, you can consider authentication (verifying who's who) and authorization (allowing or disallowing access to certain things).

At the end of each chapter in this section, I discuss protocol encryption support and provide some additional references for you to consider in your own implementations. I then suggest exercises for you to implement and integrate into your environment. For initial testing and validation, you'll be communicating with a local server on your local system and analyzing the network traffic using a protocol analyzer such as Wireshark to see the packet detail, so all examples will use unencrypted connections.

In determining an appropriate architecture, implementation, and deployment approach for any IoT ecosystem, security must be front and center. Your security strategy will largely depend on legal, technical, data management, and business requirements that will vary, so I won't provide guidance on this subject other than to point out what I believe to be rather obvious steps: use encryption, ensure you have an appropriate authentication and authorization strategy, and validate all inputs, outputs, and data at each logical layer.

## CHAPTER 6

MQTT Integration—Overview and Python Client

Build a Publish/Subscribe Client in Python Using MQTT

Did you even hear?
I have nothing in return.
Finally—an ACK!

Fundamental concepts: Overview of publish/subscribe messaging at the application layer; features of MQTT; implementation strategies and exercises specific to the Constrained Device App written in Python.

Messaging between devices and systems is a key concept in facilitating robust and meaningful data integration across the Internet of Things. It also poses a variety of challenges for the architect and developer that go beyond just "making it work." With IP-based transport protocols (such as TCP and UDP), we're generally interested in packet reliability, latency, loss, speed, efficiency, and of course security (to name just a few areas of concern).

At the application layer, our concerns with protocol choice become more nuanced. What problem is the business trying to solve? Does it just want to send data sets reliably between two or more systems, or does it need a way to stream video from remote devices? While these are two basic examples and could both technically use the same underlying transport protocol(s), they have very different application-layer protocol needs.

In addition to business needs, you'll also need to consider the implementation challenges associated with the messaging protocols you plan to use.

Publish/subscribe (or *pub/sub*) is a term that captures the type of messaging between one application or system and another. One will publish a message to a destination using a specific name, which is usually called a *topic*. The other will subscribe to the destination system using the same topic name as the publisher. Whenever the publisher sends a message, the subscriber is notified and forwarded that message. This process is handled by a broker application that can support multiple publishers and subscribers and that may reside on the same system or on another system that's accessible to each system and application.

There are quite a few pub/sub protocols, but in this chapter, I'll focus on the Message Queuing Telemetry Transport (MQTT) protocol.[1]

What You'll Learn in This Chapter

After working through this content and the code examples and exercises, you'll understand the principles behind publish/subscribe protocols and how to use these protocols in your own software applications. Specifically, you'll learn how pub/sub works, why it's useful, and how to write client software that can interact with a pub/sub broker (the server) to support your application's needs. You'll also learn how to incorporate Quality of Service (QoS) in your message distribution strategy.

The exercises in this chapter are specific to the Constrained Device Application written in Python.

About MQTT

The first version of the MQTT messaging protocol was written by Dr. Andy Stanford-Clark and Arlen Nipper in 1999.[2] Originally designed to monitor oil pipelines, it's now widely used as a messaging protocol across a range of industries for exchanging IoT messages between devices on internal networks and those communicating with IoT-centric cloud services.

The nonprofit consortium Organization for the Advancement of Structured Information Standards (OASIS) standardized version 3.1.1 (*https://oreil.ly/PkprZ*) of the MQTT protocol specification in 2013, and the International Standards Organization (ISO) ratified it (*https://oreil.ly/PQwqs*) in 2016.

As of this writing, the latest version of the specification is version 5.0, which introduces many new features to the protocol, including the ability to support request/

---

1 See the MQTT website (*https://mqtt.org*) for more details on the protocol and links to official version specifications.

2 The MQTT FAQ page (*https://mqtt.org/faq*) provides a brief history of MQTT and other information about the protocol.

response interactions.[3] There's also an extremely lightweight version of MQTT called MQTT-SN (*https://oreil.ly/9QwVP*) that's designed for wireless networks and constrained devices.

For this chapter and the remainder of the book, I'll refer to MQTT version 3.1.1, as it's currently the most widely used version across available commercial cloud services using the protocol.

Connecting to a Broker

Before any messages can be sent or received, each client must first connect to the broker (server) over TCP/IP, with Transport Layer Security (TLS) enabled if encrypted connections are important.

> MQTT does not specify encryption—only topic-level authentication, which will be discussed later. To enable encryption, TLS can be configured with many broker implementations, and it is supported by many MQTT client library implementations.

Once a connection is established, the client can send messages to or receive messages from other clients that are also connected to the broker. A pub/sub system permits a many-to-many relationship scheme between clients via the message broker (the MQTT server). Some MQTT brokers offer high availability by permitting multiple broker instances to share state information. For our purposes, we'll assume that a single broker instance is being utilized, but with two or more clients.

Figure 6-1 depicts the connections between two clients and an MQTT broker, with Client A as the publisher and Client B as the subscriber.

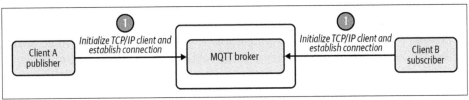

Figure 6-1. Connection between two clients and an MQTT broker

As implied, the order of the connections to the MQTT broker from Client A and Client B doesn't matter to the broker. Of course, if Client B connects *after* Client A starts publishing messages, it won't receive any messages sent prior to connecting!

---

3 See Section 4.10 of MQTT version 5.0 (*https://oreil.ly/yfRBK*).

Message Passing

Messages are passed between clients using topics. Simply put, a topic is a name that's used to identify a place on the server to temporarily store and distribute messages. Topics in MQTT are case sensitive, meaning that the topic names *MyTopic* and *mytopic* are completely different. MQTT supports hierarchical topic names, allowing you to create subtopics and sub-subtopics simply by separating each topic name with a "/" character to represent parent → child → grandchild → relationships (such as *MyTopic/Category/Data*). Topics can also contain *wildcards*, which any subscriber can use to filter topics and receive only those messages that map to a specific naming convention or even all subtopics for a specific topic.

Example 1: Client A (the CDA) wants to send, or publish, messages to any interested listener, or subscriber, on topic *PIOT/ConstrainedDevice*. Assuming Client A doesn't specify any authentication requirement for *PIOT/ConstrainedDevice*, any subscriber that knows the name of this topic and has a connection to the same broker that Client A is connected to can subscribe and receive those messages.

Example 2: Client A (again, the CDA) wants to send messages to any interested subscriber on the following topics:

- *PIOT/ConstrainedDevice/SensorMsg*
- *PIOT/ConstrainedDevice/MgmtStatusMsg*

Client B (the GDA) wants to receive all messages from Client A, so—assuming there are no authentication requirements for any of the topics Client A is publishing to, and Client A and Client B are both connected to the same broker—Client B will now need to subscribe to *PIOT/ConstrainedDevice* (since Client A may publish messages to this top-level topic), *PIOT/ConstrainedDevice/SensorMsg*, and *PIOT/ConstrainedDevice/MgmtStatusMsg*.

Wildcards are a powerful and convenient way to subscribe to complex topic hierarchies. The "#" character allows access to all subtopics from that point on (such as *PIOT/#*). The "+" character provides access to a single level in the hierarchy (e.g., *PIOT/+/MgmtStatusMsg*).

Using the "#" wildcard, you can make your programming work easier. Instead of subscribing to the three subtopics separately, simply subscribe to *PIOT/ConstrainedDevice/#*. Only subscribers can use wildcards.

Be aware that overusing wildcards when subscribing to MQTT topics can potentially be problematic—the subscriber must be prepared for an influx of unnecessary messages that will need to be processed, and it also places additional load on the broker. Thus it should be used only when needed.

Figure 6-2 depicts this entire process, including the connection sequence of Client A and Client B to the MQTT broker. Note the numbering of each step—Client A doesn't need to wait for Client B to subscribe, although it's implied in this example.

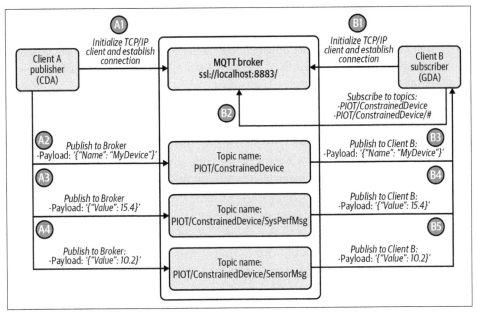

Figure 6-2. Example of a publish/subscribe interaction using MQTT

There are many strategies for defining topic structures for pub/sub environments. While a location-based, top-down structure may work for one business, a type-based structure may work best for another. In addition to the naming convention hints mentioned in the introduction for this section, here are a few specific considerations for naming MQTT topics:

- MQTT topics are case sensitive. The topic *PIOT/ConstrainedDevice* is NOT the same as *piot/constraineddevice*.
- There's no need to start your topic with a "/"; doing so only adds confusion, since it is likely to be treated as the second level by your broker implementation. Consider starting all topics with the name only.
- Although powerful, wildcards are your frenemies. They can be super helpful in that your subscribers can collect vast amounts of data without knowing every single subtopic ever devised. But this does, of course, come with a cost: more data to parse, more load on the network and broker, and more information that you

may never care about. It's all about trade-offs. Use wildcards wisely, and remember that with great power… (you get the point).[4]

Control Packets and the Structure of an MQTT Message

Every MQTT message is packaged within a *Control Packet*.[5] A Control Packet can be thought of as the envelope containing all the context and data for an MQTT message. To minimize the space required for a message, Control Packets have at least one and no more than three components:

Fixed header (required: 2 to 5 bytes in length)[6]
> All Control Packets have a fixed header, where the first byte includes four bits representing the type, with the remaining four bits reserved for other flags (depending on the specific Control Packet type). Bytes two through five represent the size of the Control Packet, which can be up to 256 MB in length.[7]

Variable header (optional: 2+ bytes)[8]
> Most Control Packets have a variable header, which contains the protocol type and protocol level, connection flags, and any authentication credentials. Connection flags are simply on/off bits that indicate what other items may be included in the payload, such as authentication, QoS, and Wills (more on each of these in the next section).

Payload (optional: 0+ bytes)[9]
> Some Control Packets have a payload. The payload may contain message data or connection-specific data (like authentication credentials), as alluded to in the previous bullet describing connection flags within the variable header.

The Control Packet type represents the type of message that's being sent—either from a client to the server or vice versa—and what, if anything, will be contained in the variable header and payload (as well as how the payload will be constructed). As a 4-bit field, there's room for up to 16 different types, although MQTT v3.1.1 specifies only 14 types, with 2 reserved and unused.

---

4 There's a great deal of discussion on how and when the words "power" and "responsibility" were first linked. An interesting exploration of this topic can be found on the website Quote Investigator (*https://oreil.ly/upXh1*).

5 Andrew Banks and Rahul Gupta, MQTT Version 3.1.1 (*https://oreil.ly/LsCKn*). OASIS Standard, 2014. Section 2.

6 See Section 2.2 of MQTT version 3.1.1.

7 See Section 2.2.3 of MQTT version 3.1.1.

8 See Section 2.3 of MQTT version 3.1.1.

9 See Section 2.4 of MQTT version 3.1.1.

MQTT v5.0 uses one of these two reserved Control Packet types, leaving only one remaining as reserved. This new Control Packet—AUTH—allows the client and server to support a protracted authentication model, such as challenge and response.[10]

Here's a brief summary of the different Control Packet types you'll encounter when using MQTT:[11]

CONNECT (client to server)
This is the first Control Packet sent from the client to server after establishing a connection.

CONNACK (server to client)
This is the first Control Packet sent from the server to the client when acknowledging the CONNECT Control Packet.

PUBLISH (client to server, or server to client)
This is sent from the publishing client to the server, or from the server to the subscribing client, to transmit a message.

PUBACK (client to server, or server to client)
This is sent from the server to the publishing client, or from the subscribing client to the publishing server, when QoS 1 is set. For more information on MQTT v3.1.1 QoS levels and their meaning, see the next section on QoS.

PUBREC (client to server, or server to client)
This is sent from the server to the publishing client, or from the subscribing client to the publishing server, when QoS 2 is set.

PUBREL (client to server, or server to client)
This is sent in response to a PUBREC Control Packet when QoS 2 is set.

PUBCOMP (client to server, or server to client)
This is sent in response to a PUBREL Control Packet when QoS 2 is set.

SUBSCRIBE (client to server)
This is sent from the client to the server when requesting a subscription to one or more topics.

SUBACK (server to client)
This is sent from the server to the subscribing client in response to a SUBSCRIBE Control Packet.

---

10 See Section 3.15 of MQTT version 5.0 (*https://oreil.ly/yfRBK*).

11 See Section 3 of MQTT version 3.1.1 (*https://oreil.ly/LsCKn*).

UNSUBSCRIBE (client to server)

This is sent from the client to the server when unsubscribing from one or more topics.

UNSUBACK (server to client)

This is sent from the server to the unsubscribing client in response to an UNSUBSCRIBE Control Packet.

PINGREQ (client to server)

This is sent from the client to the server for Keep Alive processing. I'll discuss this further in the next section.

PINGRESP (server to client)

This is sent from the server to the client in response to a PINGREQ Control Packet.

DISCONNECT (client to server)

This is sent from the client to the server to indicate a clean disconnect from the server.

MQTT also provides support for message delivery behavior through different QoS levels. Version 3.1.1 of the specification supports three QoS levels, as follows:[12]

QoS 0: Fire and forget

A message is sent from the sender to the receiver once at most, and no attempt is made by the sender to retry.

QoS 1: At least once

A message is sent from the sender to the receiver at least once. The sender will retry until the receiver sends it a PUBACK Control Packet; hence, there is the possibility of duplicate messages being sent to the receiver by the sender.

QoS 2: At most once

A message is sent from the sender to the receiver exactly once. At the MQTT protocol level, a series of Control Packets are exchanged between the sender and receiver to assure delivery without duplicates. Once a message is published, the receiver must send a PUBREC Control Packet, after which the sender will send the PUBREL Control Packet, followed by the receiver's PUBCOMP Control Packet being sent back to the sender.

QoS relationships are between a single sender and a receiver. When a client sends a message to the server, it does at a QoS level specific to that connection. Likewise, a client that subscribes to a given topic does so with a desired QoS level pertaining to

---

12 See Section 4.3 of MQTT version 3.1.1 (*https://oreil.ly/LsCKn*).

their unique connection to the server. This will make more sense after implementing the publish and subscribe functionality in the next section.

 Depending on the MQTT client and/or server implementation you're working with, you may find that adherence to QoS levels varies. Check the documentation for the given implementation to see where it may diverge from the specification regarding QoS behavior.

Finally, there's the Retain flag, which can be set as part of any PUBLISH message. This tells the server to store the message and its QoS level so it can be sent to a future subscriber for the same topic in which it was originally published.[13]

You'll almost always use an MQTT client library, such as Eclipse Paho (*https:// www.eclipse.org/paho*), to connect to an MQTT broker. This will help to mask much of the complexity of creating and handling the different Control Packets and their respective options. Although the protocol specifics are abstracted, you'll want to choose your QoS levels carefully, as each QoS level will come with its own benefits and potential costs.

 Performance considerations related to QoS levels are important, and I expect to dig into those in further detail with a later release.

The next section walks through the process of adding MQTT to your CDA and GDA. The exercises walk you through some basic MQTT integration logic and will help you get a better understanding of how some of these Control Packets look when using a protocol analyzer such as Wireshark.

Adding MQTT to Your Applications

Let's recall our overall design plan. We have two device types that we'd like to connect: a constrained device and a gateway device. Each is running a dedicated application— a Constrained Device App and a Gateway Device App, respectively. To keep things simple, we'll continue with our implementation approach in Python (Constrained Device App) and Java (Gateway Device App) and use the Eclipse Paho MQTT client for each. For now, let's just run both applications on our workstation—we'll integrate them into our systems architecture soon enough.

---

13 See Section 4 of MQTT version 3.1.1 (*https://oreil.ly/LsCKn*).

Figure 6-3 depicts a systems view of these relationships. Notice the broker is a separate application, or service, and is not implemented within either of our applications; it stands alone and can even be deployed to a different, dedicated device if desired. For our purposes, we'll simply run it alongside the other applications on our workstation. We'll use the Mosquitto[14] MQTT Broker for this and all other MQTT examples that run on our local network.

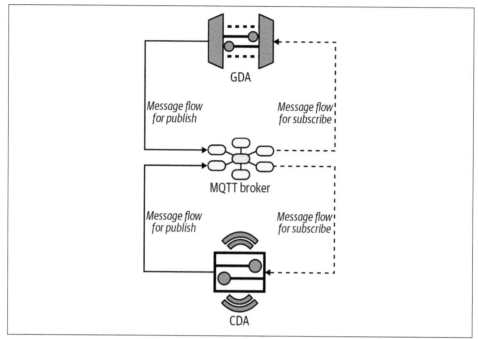

Figure 6-3. Systems view of pub/sub message flow between two applications

MQTT has a lot of qualities and features that are important to cover for both your CDA and your GDA. The next section digs into the broker setup, which your CDA and GDA will rely on, followed by some additional specifics on the protocol itself. I'll first walk you through a client implementation in Python within the CDA and discuss the protocol idiosyncrasies along the way, and then I'll move more quickly through the Java implementation within the GDA.

---

14 Roger A. Light, "Mosquitto: Server and Client Implementation of the MQTT Protocol" (*https://doi.org/ 10.21105/joss.00265*), *Journal of Open Source Software* 2, no. 13 (2017): 265.

Installing and Configuring an MQTT Broker

To test and validate our client MQTT code, we'll need a server to talk to. Mosquitto (*https://mosquitto.org/download*) is an open source broker that can be installed on Windows, Mac, or Linux. For the MQTT exercises in this chapter, I'm using Mosquitto version 1.4.8. Remember, the broker is the MQTT server, so I'll use the terms *broker* and *server* interchangeably when discussing MQTT and other pub/sub protocols.

For now, you can just use the default Mosquitto broker configuration (*https://oreil.ly/JDYac*), so you don't need to provide your own. Once it's installed, start it up and watch the log file to ensure it's running.

> If you decide to modify the default configuration file, be sure to first back up the original in case you need to return to it later.

Running Mosquitto within a bash terminal will generate output similar to the following after startup:

```
1597076291: mosquitto version 1.4.8 (build date Tue, 18 Jun 2019 11:59:34 -0300)
starting
1597076291: Using default config.
1597076291: Opening ipv4 listen socket on port 1883.
1597076291: Opening ipv6 listen socket on port 1883.
```

Programming Exercises

This is where the fun begins with MQTT—I'll walk you through the details of integrating your CDA with an MQTT broker so they can communicate. Let's take a look at the overall design of the approach, shown in Figure 6-4.

Notice that there is one new component that will need to be implemented (plus two related interfaces that are already created for you), along with a reference to the MQTT broker (shown in gray).

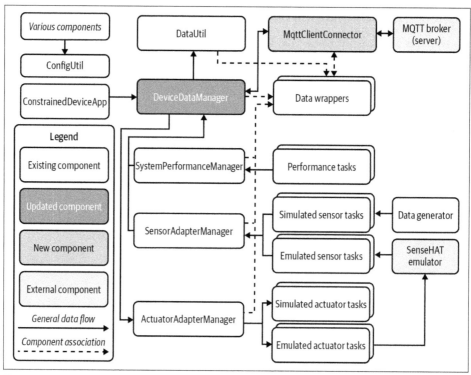

Figure 6-4. Constrained Device Application design with integrated MQTT client

Figure 6-5 depicts the notional UML for this design, with a focus on the relationship between `DeviceDataManager` and `MqttClientConnector`, along with a few other components for context.

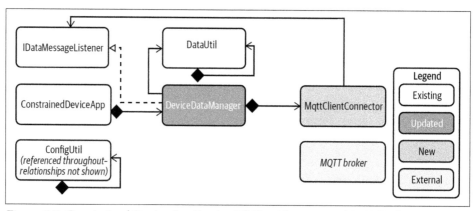

Figure 6-5. Constrained Device Application UML with integrated MQTT client

Let's look at the client connector and the two interfaces you'll be working with:

- MqttClientConnector: A simple adaptor that delegates the calls made to it to the underlying MQTT client instance (implemented using the *delegation* design pattern[15]).

- IDeviceMessageListener: A simple interface that defines callbacks for handling various message types.

- IPubSubClient: A simple interface that defines the accessor methods for any pub/sub client connector (such as MqttClientConnector).

As I mentioned previously, you need to implement only the first one—MqttClient Connector. I've provided sample implementations of the two interfaces, IDeviceMes sageListener and IPubSubClient, for you to use as is or to modify to your liking.

 As of this writing, Python doesn't have a formal interface specification, unlike Java or C++. There are a few ways to implement interface functionality in Python, but to keep things simple, I'm going to define both IDeviceMessageListener and IPubSubClient as simple informal interfaces—basically, as classes that have empty implementations that can be defined by the implementing class. Feel free to use an alternative approach, such as a metaclass or base class definition.

Let's get started with the MqttClientConnector. This adaptor, which acts as a delegate to the paho-mqtt client (*https://pypi.org/project/paho-mqtt*) that connects to the MQTT broker, should allow you to swap out MQTT client implementations if you want to experiment with others or perhaps even build your own implementation.

The first step, of course, is to review the information in the Programming the IoT project board under Chapter 6—MQTT Client (CDA) (*https://oreil.ly/xzM76*) and check out a new branch for this chapter (PIOT-CDA-06-000 (*https://oreil.ly/VqYd7*)).

 You may recall that paho-mqtt was one of the libraries you imported when setting up your virtualenv environment and used pip to install *basic_imports.txt*. This library gives you the ability to connect to an MQTT server to publish messages and subscribe for updates from a topic. You can read all about its features online (*https://pypi.org/project/paho-mqtt*).

---

15 Erich Gamma et al., *Design Patterns: Elements of Reusable Object-Oriented Software* (Boston: Addison-Wesley, 1994).

Create the MQTT Connector Abstraction Module

As is our typical pattern, you may want to create your own issue and simply map it to the one I've already created. Let's review PIOT-CDA-06-001 (*https://oreil.ly/MVr81*) in more detail. I'll walk through the specifics, as this one is a bit involved.

The actions are summarized as follows:

- Navigate to the *programmingtheiot/cda/connection* package in the sample code.
- Within the `MqttClientConnector`, make sure the following import statements exist at the beginning of the module:

```
import paho.mqtt.client as mqttClient

from programmingtheiot.common import ConfigUtil
from programmingtheiot.common import ConfigConst
from programmingtheiot.common import IDataMessageListener

from programmingtheiot.cda.connection import IPubSubClient
```

- Create a constructor that initializes the MQTT client properties. You can keep the clientID empty or null for now, but be sure to retrieve the MQTT host, port, and keepAlive values from the configuration file and store them in locally scoped variables (you'll need them when you establish the connection in the next action step). The code will look similar to the following:

```
self.config = ConfigUtil()

self.dataMsgListener = None

self.host = \
  self.config.getProperty( \
    ConfigConst.MQTT_CLOUD_SECTION, \
    ConfigConst.HOST_KEY, \
    ConfigConst.DEFAULT_HOST)

self.port = \
  self.config.getInteger( \
    ConfigConst.MQTT_CLOUD_SECTION, \
    ConfigConst.PORT_KEY, \
    ConfigConst.DEFAULT_MQTT_PORT)

self.keepAlive = \
  self.config.getInteger( \
    ConfigConst.MQTT_CLOUD_SECTION, \
    ConfigConst.KEEP_ALIVE_KEY, \
    ConfigConst.DEFAULT_KEEP_ALIVE)

logging.info('\tMQTT Broker Host: ' + self.host)
```

```
logging.info('\tMQTT Broker Port: ' + str(self.port))
logging.info('\tMQTT Keep Alive:  ' + str(self.keepAlive))
```

NOTE: The clientID must be unique if you plan to use multiple clients with your local broker, as you'll need to ensure the clientID doesn't conflict with any other name being used.

- Add the connectClient() method, add the logic to create an instance of the client if needed, and then connect to the broker, if not already connected, and log an info message indicating the connector was started. Your code should look similar to the following:

```
if not self.mqttClient:
    self.mqttClient = \
      mqttClient.Client( \
        client_id = self.clientID, clean_session = True)
    self.mqttClient.on_connect = self.onConnect
    self.mqttClient.on_disconnect = self.onDisconnect
    self.mqttClient.on_message = self.onMessage
    self.mqttClient.on_publish = self.onPublish
    self.mqttClient.on_subscribe = self.onSubscribe

if not self.mqttClient.is_connected():
    self.mqttClient.connect(self.host, self.port, self.keepAlive)
    self.mqttClient.loop_start()
    return True
else:
    logging.warn( \
      'MQTT client already connected. Ignoring connect.')
    return False
```

- Add the disconnectClient() method, add the logic to disconnect from the broker if currently connected, and log an info message indicating the connector was stopped. Be sure to stop the network loop, as indicated in the following sample code:

```
if self.mqttClient.is_connected():
    self.mqttClient.loop_stop()
    self.mqttClient.disconnect()
```

- Implement the remaining three methods from the IPubSubClient interface: publishMessage(), subscribeToTopic(), and setDataMessageListener(). For now, just log a message indicating they were called, and return False. A follow-up task will address their implementation details.

- Add a setter for the IDataMessageListener instance. You'll use this for passing incoming MQTT messages to the DeviceDataManager a bit later in Part III.

I've created a bunch of tests for you to use; be sure to review the code and the instructions under the Test section, especially since you'll need to ensure your MQTT broker is up and running first!

OK, now that you've written the code and verified it works, let's unpack some of the complexities this task introduces.

In the action step called "Create a constructor that initializes the MQTT client properties," most of the code is simply pulling (and checking) the MQTT client initialization parameters from the configuration. Keep these configuration parameters in mind, as you'll need them for the next key action: *Add the connectClient() method*.

The content of `connectClient()` is pretty simple. Basically, you need to first check whether the client's been created—if not, create it. Then check whether the client is already connected, and if it isn't, connect to the MQTT server.

This should be reasonably self-explanatory, except perhaps for that last line of code: `self.mqttClient.loop_start()`. Why is this necessary? The documentation for the paho-mqtt client network loop (*https://oreil.ly/1FSQ5*) tells us that this is one of a handful of methods within the client class that processes network events. This is necessary to ensure that all incoming and outgoing messages are processed.

If you want more control over this process, you can call one of the other loop methods manually, although for our purposes, the `loop_start()` method will suffice.

The `loop_start()` runs as a background thread and won't block your main application thread, allowing you to perform other tasks. It also provides another benefit—it will attempt to reconnect to the server automatically if the client disconnects from the broker without sending an explicit disconnect request. This is tremendously useful, as your connection uses a stateful TCP/IP connection with MQTT at the application layer. If that connection fails (which I've certainly experienced on a few occasions), you'll probably want this connection to be reestablished without your having to write a ton of retry logic yourself.

Before we go any further, let's create the disconnect logic. Look at the *Add the disconnectClient() method* action step. Note that the `loop_stop()` method is called to tell the background network data processing thread to quit. Although the `disconnect()` method on your client instance will close the connection, you should call this method to ensure the network loop thread is properly stopped if you followed the example and called `loop_start()` after `connect()`.

Finally, create the setter function for the `IDataMessageListener` callback implementation. This will look identical to the same setter functionality you implemented in other classes, such as the `SystemPerformanceManager`.

You now have an MQTT client that will connect to the MQTT server and then disconnect on demand using the configuration parameters you've specified in your *PiotConfig.props* file. Granted, this doesn't do much that's functionally interesting in terms of building your solution. It does, however, trigger a number of Control Packets that you can observe in Wireshark or another protocol analyzer of your choosing.

Testing and validating the connection

Let's run a quick test and see what Control Packets get generated. If you're using Wireshark, launch it now. Make sure it can listen for packets on your loopback adapter, and start listening for packets. Start the Mosquitto broker as well.

Now, in the `MqttClientConnectorTest` unit test, uncomment the `testConnectAnd Disconnect()` test method, and run the test—it will take about 35 seconds to execute (assuming keepAlive property in the *PiotConfig.props* configuration file is set to 30).

In Wireshark, click on the "Protocol" tab and scroll until you see the first of what should be five MQTT packets, as shown in Table 6-1.

Table 6-1. MQTT CONNECT and DISCONNECT Control Packet Sequence as shown in Wireshark

No.	Time	Source	Destination	Protocol	Length	Info
6158	259.168438	::1	::1	MQTT	109	Connect Command
6160	259.171805	::1	::1	MQTT	68	Connect Ack
6712	289.185977	::1	::1	MQTT	66	Ping Request
6714	289.186184	::1	::1	MQTT	66	Ping Response
6814	294.169673	::1	::1	MQTT	66	Disconnect Req

Notice that there are five Control Packets exchanged between the client and the server: CONNECT, CONNACK, PINGREQ, PINGRESP, and DISCONNECT.

If you click on each one of these, you'll notice that the largest in terms of bytes is the CONNECT Control Packet (78 bytes total, with 12 bytes specific to the MQTT Control Packet). The other packets represent, in order, the following Control Packets: CONNACK (4 bytes), PINGREQ (2 bytes), PINGRESP (2 bytes), and DISCONNECT (2 bytes).

I've set up an MQTT-specific filter within Wireshark to display only the packets I care about, which is why Table 6-1 is showing only MQTT protocol packets and nothing else.

Let's look more closely at the CONNECT Control Packet, as it has some properties that will be helpful to more fully understand. The following text output shows a detailed expansion of the MQTT portion of this packet in Wireshark:

```
MQ Telemetry Transport Protocol, Connect Command
    Header Flags: 0x10, Message Type: Connect Command
    0001 .... = Message Type: Connect Command (1)
    .... 0000 = Reserved: 0
    Msg Len: 12
    Protocol Name Length: 4
    Protocol Name: MQTT
    Version: MQTT v3.1.1 (4)
    Connect Flags: 0x02, QoS Level: At most once delivery (Fire and Forget), Clean
Session Flag
        0... .... = User Name Flag: Not set
        .0.. .... = Password Flag: Not set
        ..0. .... = Will Retain: Not set
        ...0 0... = QoS Level: At most once delivery (Fire and Forget) (0)
        .... .0.. = Will Flag: Not set
        .... ..1. = Clean Session Flag: Set
        .... ...0 = (Reserved): Not set
    Keep Alive: 30
    Client ID Length: 0
    Client ID:
```

Notice the Connect Flags listed from top to bottom: User Name Flag, Password Flag, Will Retain, QoS Level, Will Flag, and Clean Session Flag.

User Name and Password.   These allow for basic user/password authentication of connecting clients by the server. If these flags are set, the payload must contain this information. As per the MQTT v3.1.1 specification, you can have a username without a password but not the other way around. You can read about the details of the payload structure of the CONNECT Control Packet pertaining to username and password in the specification.[16] Additional security topics can be found in the MQTT v3.1.1 specification (*https://oreil.ly/LsCKn*) under the Security section.

Will Retain, QoS Level, and Will Flag.   A will in MQTT is just a message that the client can set on the server that will be sent out to other connected clients on its behalf if it gets disconnected without sending a DISCONNECT, among other reasons documented in the specification. The QoS and Retain flags relate to how the will message

---

16 See Section 3.1.3 of MQTT version 3.1.1 (*https://oreil.ly/LsCKn*).

will be published. I'll discuss both QoS and Retain in a bit more detail in "Add Publish, Subscribe, and Unsubscribe Functionality" on page 192.

You can see the Keep Alive is set to 30 (seconds), which is expected, since that's the value pulled from the configuration file. This simply tells the server to expect a message from the client every 30 seconds—if not a published message, it will be a PINGREQ. The server will disconnect the client if one is not received within a certain amount of time after the Keep Alive period.

Finally, there's the Client ID—currently set to nothing (as it's 0 bytes in length). This is kind of interesting, since the MQTT broker has logged what looks like a client ID, as shown in the following log output:

```
1597319136: mosquitto version 1.4.8 (build date Tue, 18 Jun 2019 11:59:34 -0300)
starting
1597319136: Using default config.
1597319136: Opening ipv4 listen socket on port 1883.
1597319136: Opening ipv6 listen socket on port 1883.
1597319155: New connection from ::1 on port 1883.
1597319155: New client connected from ::1 as 05c3d124-0286-4447-a4c0-7d4e07005441
(c1, k30).
1597319190: Client 05c3d124-0286-4447-a4c0-7d4e07005441 disconnected.
```

In the PIOT-CDA-06-001 (*https://oreil.ly/MVr81*) task, I didn't specify a client ID, and in my sample code, I didn't set one. Notice that one has been created for the client session within the broker—specifically, 05c3d124-0286-4447-a4c0-7d4e07005441. This is for the broker to handle the client connection on its end and will be valid only while the client is connected.

If you look at both the paho-mqtt source code documentation (*https://pypi.org/project/paho-mqtt*) and the MQTT protocol specification (*https://oreil.ly/LsCKn*) pertaining to client IDs, this all makes sense. The Paho library tells us how it will handle zero-length client IDs for each version of MQTT (v3.1.1 is the default): that is, a zero-length client ID will be sent to the broker. The MQTT v3.1.1 specification also makes it clear how it will handle this situation: one will be generated by the broker. The one caveat is that a client connection with NO client ID must NOT set Clean Session to "False"—it MUST be established as a new clean session (which is the default).

You can easily test this yourself by setting the clean_session = False parameter when you create the MQTT client instance without a valid client ID. You'll see that the Paho library will throw an exception and fail to create the client instance. Unless this exception is handled, it will result in your CDA being terminated.

If an MQTT v3.1.1 broker were to receive a CONNECT request with no client ID but with the Clean Session flag set to "False," the spec would state that it must return an error and close the connection. The Paho library catches this for us and throws the exception straightaway.

So, in short, these examples are all fine:

- ```
  self.mqttClient = \
      mqttClient.Client( \
          client_id = "MyValidClientID", clean_session = False)
  ```
- ```
  self.mqttClient = \
      mqttClient.Client( \
          client_id = "MyValidClientID", clean_session = True)
  ```
- `self.mqttClient = mqttClient.Client(clean_session = True)`
- `self.mqttClient = mqttClient.Client()`

But these are NOT:

- ```
  self.mqttClient = \
      mqttClient.Client(client_id = "", clean_session = False)
  ```
- `self.mqttClient = mqttClient.Client(clean_session = False)`

Make sense? Let's rerun this test, but add in your own client ID this time. It's super easy—you just need to set it as the client_id parameter when you create the MQTT client instance in the MqttClientConnector constructor. For example:

```
if not clientID:
    clientID = 'myMqttClientID'

self.mqttClient = \
  mqttClient.Client(client_id = clientID, clean_session = False)
```

Save the updates and then run the MqttClientConnectorTest again. You'll see something similar to the following in your server's log file:

```
1597321903: mosquitto version 1.4.8 (build date Tue, 18 Jun 2019 11:59:34 -0300)
starting
1597321903: Using default config.
1597321903: Opening ipv4 listen socket on port 1883.
1597321903: Opening ipv6 listen socket on port 1883.
1597321915: New connection from ::1 on port 1883.
1597321915: New client connected from ::1 as myMqttClientID (c1, k30).
1597321950: Client myMqttClientID disconnected.
```
```

Let's look at the Wireshark output and see how the CONNECT Control Packet has changed in the MQTT portion of the packet:

```
MQ Telemetry Transport Protocol, Connect Command
    Header Flags: 0x10, Message Type: Connect Command
    0001 .... = Message Type: Connect Command (1)
    .... 0000 = Reserved: 0
    Msg Len: 41
    Protocol Name Length: 4
    Protocol Name: MQTT
    Version: MQTT v3.1.1 (4)
    Connect Flags: 0x02, QoS Level: At most once delivery (Fire and Forget), Clean
Session Flag
        0... .... = User Name Flag: Not set
        .0.. .... = Password Flag: Not set
        ..0. .... = Will Retain: Not set
        ...0 0... = QoS Level: At most once delivery (Fire and Forget) (0)
        .... .0.. = Will Flag: Not set
        .... ..1. = Clean Session Flag: Set
        .... ...0 = (Reserved): Not set
    Keep Alive: 30
    Client ID Length: 29
    Client ID: CDAMqttClientConnectorTest001
```

This time, the MQTT packet length is 41 bytes, since the client ID "CDAMqttClient ConnectorTest001" is 29 bytes and is the only thing that has changed from the previous CONNECT Control Packet (which was only 12 bytes in length).

 An additional and important note on the use of client IDs: if you attempt to connect to the broker with two (or more) different clients that each use the same client ID, the MQTT v3.1.1 specification states that the server must disconnect the earlier connection. Recall that the loop_start() call in the paho-mqtt library will attempt to automatically reconnect the client to the server if the connection fails. Under these circumstances, if you have two (or more) clients attempting to connect (or automatically reconnect) to the broker using the same client ID, a race condition will ensue, with the broker dropping the earlier connection in favor of the more recent one, in perpetuity. The moral of the story is: don't reuse client IDs across multiple clients.

If you're using a clean session with each new connection, using a custom client ID doesn't really help, so you shouldn't set it if you're not going to take advantage of the reliability features from storing previous connection state with the broker. This will help avoid some of the issues I just warned about.

Now that your CDA is connected to the server, how will it get notified when a message is received from a topic it's subscribed to?

Dealing with callbacks

The Paho library provides several *callback functions*, or methods that get invoked when an event is triggered (such as when a message is received by the client). Callbacks are a common way to handle asynchronous (or even synchronous) events. It's kind of like registering your phone number for a callback from customer service instead of waiting on the phone for someone to pick up. You can do other things until the phone rings and they're ready to handle your request. There's really no magic here, although it sometimes seems like magic when it's set up properly.

The paho-mqtt library defines a number of empty callbacks that represent the signature of the method but don't actually do anything (yet). Since they're definitions only, they're designed so you can swap them out with your own method implementations.

In Python, this is easy to do—you just create your own method (named however you wish) with the same signature as the empty callback method and assign that to the empty callback referenced within your paho-mqtt client instance.

 You can review all the callbacks defined by the paho-mqtt library, along with their associated (and well-written) documentation (*https://oreil.ly/dJ8tR*), within the client code itself. The documentation is, I believe, relatively self-explanatory, so I'll discuss only the specific callbacks and associated parameters that will be useful for your CDA implementation.

For the purposes of your CDA implementation, the callbacks you'll need to implement are as follows (there are more, of course, but these are most important for the current task at hand):

- on_connect()
- on_disconnect()
- on_message()
- on_publish()
- on_subscribe()

That was a lot to digest. Now you should be familiar with how MQTT works in general, and with some of the complexities a library helps to abstract, making your development tasks much easier.

Some of this complexity does require additional development work, including the callback implementations, so let's dig into that now.

Add Callbacks to Support MQTT Events

This is where, once implemented, you'll see the fruits of your effort realized. You can create your own task to link to PIOT-CDA-06-002 (*https://oreil.ly/ZFPcr*), of course. Here are the steps you'll take to implement the callback functions:

- Update the `onConnect()` callback method to handle connection notification events. For now, just log a message indicating the client has successfully connected. Use the following signature:

  ```
  def onConnect(self, client, userdata, flags, rc):
  ```

- Update the `onDisconnect()` callback method to handle connection notification events. For now, just log a message indicating the client has successfully connected. Use the following signature:

  ```
  def onDisconnect(self, client, userdata, rc):
  ```

- Update the `onMessage()` callback method, which is perhaps most important—this will be called whenever a message is received on the topic for which your client has subscribed; you can add a log message for now, although eventually this will invoke another callback on the `IDataMessageListener` instance. Use the following signature:

  ```
  def onMessage(self, client, userdata, msg):
  ```

  NOTE: The `onMessage()` callback parameter named "msg" will be of type `MQTTMessage`, which will contain all the context—including the byte[] payload—of the message received from the broker.

- Update the `onPublish()` callback to handle message publish notification events. For now, just log a message with the MID, or message ID. Use the following signature:

  ```
  def onPublish(self, client, userdata, mid):
  ```

- Update the `onSubscribe()` callback to handle topic subscription notification events. For now, just log a message with the MID. Use the following signature:

  ```
  def onSubscribe(self, client, userdata, mid, granted_qos):
  ```

- Back in the `connectClient()` method, add the callback assignments *before* the connection call is issued to the broker, as follows:

  ```
  self.mqttClient.on_connect = self.onConnect
  self.mqttClient.on_disconnect = self.onDisconnect
  self.mqttClient.on_message = self.onMessage
  self.mqttClient.on_publish = self.onPublish
  self.mqttClient.on_subscribe = self.onSubscribe
  ```

Although this looks like a lot of work, it should be relatively quick, since you'll just log messages indicating something happened after the callbacks were invoked.

To test this, you can uncomment the `testPublishAndSubscribe()` test case, and run the `MqttClientConnectorTest` unit test. The connect/disconnect and publish/subscribe test cases should now succeed.

Before moving on to publishing messages and subscribing to topics, let's look back for just a moment. Notice the signatures for these callback functions—the connect and disconnect callbacks have an "rc" parameter, which represents the result code. You can use this to determine if there is an error condition associated with the connect or disconnect and take appropriate action. Another important parameter—"mid"—is used in the publish and subscribe callbacks to represent the message ID. This is particularly useful if you need to track a specific publish or subscribe event for a given topic. Specifics for these and the other callback parameters can be found in the Paho client documentation (*https://oreil.ly/r1vHn*).

Once the callbacks are all implemented, it's time to run another test. This time, you'll want to observe the log messages that are generated by your `onConnect()` and `onDis connect()` callbacks. For now, if these callbacks are triggered and your log messages look correct, the tests pass.

With your callback infrastructure now in place, it's time to get to publishing and subscribing.

Add Publish, Subscribe, and Unsubscribe Functionality

The core of any pub/sub protocol is, of course, publishing messages and subscribing to topics (to receive messages published by other clients). I've already mentioned how QoS works with MQTT, so let's get to writing code that can take advantage of the core capabilities of this protocol.

The requirements to support pub/sub within your `MqttClientConnector` are located in PIOT-CDA-06-003 (*https://oreil.ly/5CgvN*). Here's a summary of the steps:

- Update the `publishMessage()` method to handle all publish functionality. It will accept the topic name, message content, and requested QoS level for parameters. It must validate the topic name and QoS level. If the topic is invalid, return False. If the QoS level is < 0 or > 2, set it to `ConfigConst.DEFAULT_QOS`, which must be defined as a class-scoped "constant." If the publish is valid and the call to the MQTT client is successful, return True.

- Update the `subscribeToTopic()` and `unsubscribeFromTopic()` methods to handle all subscribe/unsubscribe functionality. The subscribe function will accept the topic name and requested QoS level for parameters. It must validate the topic name and QoS level. If the topic is invalid, return False. If the QoS level is < 0 or

> 2, set it to ConfigConst.DEFAULT_QOS, which must be defined as a class-scoped "constant." If the subscription is valid and the call to the MQTT client is successful, return True.

Let's take a look at the implementation for all of these methods, starting with publish Message():

```
def publishMessage( \
  self, resource: ResourceNameEnum = None, \
  msg: str = None, \
  qos: int = ConfigConst.DEFAULT_QOS) -> bool:

  if qos < 0 or qos > 2:
    qos = ConfigConst.DEFAULT_QOS

  if resource:
    msgInfo = \
      self.mqttClient.publish( \
        topic = resource.value, payload = msg, qos = qos)

    # this will block and wait for the publish to complete
    msgInfo.wait_for_publish()

    return True

  return False
```

The function wait_for_publish() will block until the publish event is complete. You can read more about this in the Paho documentation (*https://oreil.ly/LQJaH*).

Moving on to the subscribe/unsubscribe functionality, you'll notice a similar method signature for subscribe, with unsubscribe requiring only the topic name:

```
def subscribeToTopic( \
  self, resource: ResourceNameEnum = None, \
  callback = None, \
  qos: int = ConfigConst.DEFAULT_QOS) -> bool:

  if qos < 0 or qos > 2:
    qos = ConfigConst.DEFAULT_QOS

  if resource:
    logging.info('Subscribing to topic %s', resource.value)

    self.mqttClient.subscribe(resource.value, qos)

    return True

  return False

def unsubscribeFromTopic(self, resource: ResourceNameEnum):
  if resource:
```

```
logging.info('Unsubscribing from topic %s', resource.value)
self.mqttClient.unsubscribe(resource.value)
return True

    return False
```

 For both the publish and the subscribe functionality, your callbacks will be notified when the server receives and acknowledges the events, so the boolean return to each method is just an indicator that the call itself succeeded. You'll need to track the MID within the callbacks if you want to be assured of successful message delivery or topic subscription to the broker.

A final note on topic subscriptions: you can define a unique callback method per subscription topic, which you won't need until Chapter 10, so I'll cover this advanced capability at that time.

Time to test things out. Let's observe the integration tests with Wireshark running. Fire up Wireshark and run the integration test named MqttClientConnectorTest.

If everything is implemented correctly, you'll see log output that aligns closely with that specified in the test instructions.

Table 6-2 shows the protocol analyzer output from running this new test.

Table 6-2. MQTT PUBLISH and SUBSCRIBE Control Packet Sequence using QoS 2 as shown in Wireshark

No.	Time	Source	Destination	Protocol	Length	Info
90	3.614652	::1	::1	MQTT	107	Connect Command
93	3.615603	::1	::1	MQTT	117	Subscribe Request (id=1) [PIOT/ ConstrainedDevice/MgmtStatusMsg]
96	3.619205	::1	::1	MQTT	68	Connect Ack
98	3.619368	::1	::1	MQTT	69	Subscribe Ack (id=1)
248	8.615582	::1	::1	MQTT	154	Publish Message (id=2) [PIOT/ ConstrainedDevice/MgmtStatusMsg]
250	8.61579	::1	::1	MQTT	68	Publish Received (id=2)
254	8.61614	::1	::1	MQTT	68	Publish Release (id=2)
256	8.616308	::1	::1	MQTT	68	Publish Complete (id=2)
348	13.615976	::1	::1	MQTT	116	Unsubscribe Request (id=3)
350	13.616152	::1	::1	MQTT	68	Unsubscribe Ack (id=3)
1522	43.630572	::1	::1	MQTT	66	Ping Request
1524	43.630766	::1	::1	MQTT	66	Ping Response
1623	48.6168	::1	::1	MQTT	66	Disconnect Req

Notice the additional Control Packets! Since I'm monitoring the loopback adapter on my PC, I'm actually seeing the client publishing a message to the server and the server publishing that same message back to my client, since my client has subscribed to the same topic that it's publishing to. To make the table cleaner, I've removed these duplicate Control Packet types.

If you add them up, you'll notice that there are (drumroll)...13.

Wait, what? There are supposed to be 14, right? Correct—we're missing one: PUBACK, which we'll see only when using QoS 1. This is because the test uses QoS 2 for the publish and subscribe calls.

If I rerun the same test using QoS 1, you'll see that the PUBREL and PUBCOMP have been replaced with a single PUBACK.

Table 6-3 shows us the change reflected in Wireshark's capture.

Table 6-3. MQTT publish and subscribe Control Packet Sequence using QoS 1 as shown in Wireshark

No.	Time	Source	Destination	Protocol	Length	Info
689	19.684216	::1	::1	MQTT	107	Connect Command
693	19.685325	::1	::1	MQTT	117	Subscribe Request (id=1) [PIOT/ConstrainedDevice/MgmtStatusMsg]
695	19.68849	::1	::1	MQTT	68	Connect Ack
697	19.689293	::1	::1	MQTT	69	Subscribe Ack (id=1)
786	24.686409	::1	::1	MQTT	154	Publish Message (id=2) [PIOT/ConstrainedDevice/MgmtStatusMsg]
788	24.686661	::1	::1	MQTT	68	Publish Ack (id=2)
955	29.68658	::1	::1	MQTT	116	Unsubscribe Request (id=3)
957	29.686801	::1	::1	MQTT	68	Unsubscribe Ack (id=3)
1763	59.703109	::1	::1	MQTT	66	Ping Request
1765	59.703298	::1	::1	MQTT	66	Ping Response
1837	64.688483	::1	::1	MQTT	66	Disconnect Req

The PUBACK now shows up. So we have 14 Control Packets in total, but you need to run separate tests using two different QoS levels to see them all.

Finally, let's look at two details—one for SUBSCRIBE and the other for PUBLISH:

```
MQ Telemetry Transport Protocol, Subscribe Request
    Header Flags: 0x82, Message Type: Subscribe Request
    1000 .... = Message Type: Subscribe Request (8)
    .... 0010 = Reserved: 2
    Msg Len: 51
    Message Identifier: 1
    Topic Length: 46
```

```
Topic: PIOT/ConstrainedDevice/MgmtStatusMsg
Requested QoS: At least once delivery (Acknowledged deliver) (1)
```

In the SUBSCRIBE Control Packet detail shown in the preceding protocol analyzer output, the topic name of *PIOT/ConstrainedDevice/MgmtStatusMsg* is included in the request, as well as the *requested* QoS. This simply means that the client is asking the server to deliver messages on the specified topic at the maximum QoS level of 2, although the server may not be able to do so:

```
MQ Telemetry Transport Protocol, Publish Message
    Header Flags: 0x32, Message Type: Publish Message, QoS Level: At least once
    delivery (Acknowledged deliver)
    0011 .... = Message Type: Publish Message (3)
    .... 0... = DUP Flag: Not set
    .... .01. = QoS Level: At least once delivery (Acknowledged deliver) (1)
    .... ...0 = Retain: Not set
    Msg Len: 88
    Topic Length: 46
    Topic: PIOT/ConstrainedDevice/MgmtStatusMsg
    Message Identifier: 1
    Message: 544553543a205468697320697320746865204344412066d65…
```

In the PUBLISH Control Packet detail shown in this protocol analyzer output, the topic name of *PIOT/ConstrainedDevice/MgmtStatusMsg* is once again included in the request, as well as the specific QoS level (2). As this is a publish message, and I've included the actual payload, it's shown encoded within the message, bringing the total bytes for this particular message to 88 (as shown in the `Msg Len` property).

The following protocol analyzer output shows the full content of the message, including the payload, which you can make out as "TEST: This is the CDA message payload":

```
0000   32 58 00 2e 50 72 6f 67 72 61 6d 6d 69 6e 67 49   2X..ProgrammingI
0010   6f 54 2f 43 6f 6e 73 74 72 61 69 6e 65 64 44 65   oT/ConstrainedDe
0020   76 69 63 65 2f 4d 67 6d 74 53 74 61 74 75 73 4d   vice/MgmtStatusM
0030   73 67 00 01 54 45 53 54 3a 20 54 68 69 73 20 69   sg..TEST: This i
0040   73 20 74 68 65 20 43 44 41 20 6d 65 73 73 61 67   s the CDA messag
0050   65 20 70 61 79 6c 6f 61 64 2e                     e payload.
```

That was definitely a lift, but it was well worth it, since you should now have a good handle on how MQTT works. But we're not quite done—you still need to integrate this functionality within the rest of the CDA and then make sure everything is working properly.

Integrate the MQTT Connector into Your CDA

The final CDA exercise for this chapter is generally straightforward but involves a few steps:

- Add/manage the `MqttClientConnector` instance within `DeviceDataManager`.
- Subscribe/unsubcribe to actuator commands when the `DeviceDataManager` starts/stops, respectively.

Take a look at PIOT-CDA-06-004 (*https://oreil.ly/d7L0e*)—it walks through the steps to accomplish this.

You'll need to initialize the `MqttClientConnector` in the constructor, start it up within the `startManager()` function and subscribe to the appropriate topic(s), and then stop the client and unsubscribe when `stopManager()` is called.

Here's some example code you can use within the constructor:

```
enableMqttClient = \
  configUtil.getBoolean( \
    section = ConfigConst.CONSTRAINED_DEVICE, \
    key = ConfigConst.ENABLE_MQTT_CLIENT_KEY)

self.mqttClient = None

if enableMqttClient:
  self.mqttClient = MqttClientConnector()
  self.mqttClient.setDataMessageListener(self)
```

And finally, the updated start/stop logic for `DeviceDataManager`:

```
# use within the startManager() function
if self.mqttClient:
  self.mqttClient.connectClient()
  self.mqttClient.subscribeToTopic( \
    resource = ResourceNameEnum.CDA_ACTUATOR_CMD_RESOURCE, qos = 1)

# use within the stopManager() function
if self.mqttClient:
  self.mqttClient.disconnectClient()
  self.mqttClient.unsubscribeFromTopic( \
    resource = ResourceNameEnum.CDA_ACTUATOR_CMD_RESOURCE)
```

Notice I'm using qos = 1 in the subscription call. Feel free to use 0 or 2—all three levels are supported by the Mosquitto broker, although some broker instances—particularly those that are hosted within some cloud services—may not be.

Also, check out the resource = ResourceNameEnum.CDA_ACTUATOR_CMD_RESOURCE parameter. I created ResourceNameEnum in both the python-components package and the java-components package to normalize resource and topic names between both applications. There are certainly other ways to manage this; I simply chose this path. You can update the method definitions for publish, subscribe, and unsubscribe to simply accept strings if you'd like.

With these updates in place, you're ready to test out your code. The *./src/test/python/ programmingtheiot/part03/integration/app* path contains a test case class named Data-DeviceManagerTestWithComms you can use to run a few simple tests to verify that your MQTT connection (still) works and that your newly added publish and subscribe functionality works as planned.

You may want to make a temporary edit to DeviceDataManager and simply comment out the startup of SystemPerformanceManager and SensorAdapterManager within its startManager() function for this one test (then uncomment them after testing). This will make your search through the log messages a bit easier.

The output you'll see in the console depends on the log messages you've decided to include, of course, but might look similar to the following:

```
Finding files... done.
.
.
.
2021-01-04 23:12:04,193 - MainThread - root - INFO - Testing DeviceDataManager class...
.
.
.
2021-01-04 23:12:04,277 - MainThread - root - INFO - Started DeviceDataManager.
2021-01-04 23:12:04,277 - MainThread - root - INFO - Using auto-generated
client ID: None
2021-01-04 23:12:04,277 - MainThread - root - INFO -        MQTT Broker Host: localhost
2021-01-04 23:12:04,277 - MainThread - root - INFO -        MQTT Broker Port: 1883
2021-01-04 23:12:04,277 - MainThread - root - INFO -        MQTT Keep Alive:  30
2021-01-04 23:12:04,278 - MainThread - root - INFO - Attempting to connect to MQTT
broker: localhost
2021-01-04 23:12:04,279 - Thread-2  - root - INFO - [Callback] Connected to MQTT
broker. Result code:
0
2021-01-04 23:12:04,279 - MainThread - root - INFO - Created DataUtil instance.
2021-01-04 23:12:04,279 - MainThread - root - DEBUG - Encoding ActuatorData to JSON
[pre] -->
name=Not Set,typeID=0,timeStamp=2021-01-
05T04:12:04.279662+00:00,statusCode=0,hasError=False,locationID=constraineddevice00
1,elevation=0.0,latitude=0.0,longitude=0.0,command=1,stateData=None,value=0.0,isRes
ponse=False
2021-01-04 23:12:04,279 - MainThread - root - INFO - Encoding ActuatorData to JSON
[post] --> {
    "timeStamp": "2021-01-05T04:12:04.279662+00:00",
    "hasError": false,
    "name": "Not Set",
    "typeID": 0,
    "statusCode": 0,
    "latitude": 0.0,
    "longitude": 0.0,
    "elevation": 0.0,
    "locationID": "constraineddevice001",
```

```
        "isResponse": false,
        "command": 1,
        "stateData": null,
        "value": 0.0
}
2021-01-04 23:12:04,280 - Thread-2    - root - INFO - [Callback] Subscribed MID: 1
2021-01-04 23:12:04,280 - Thread-2    - root - INFO - [Callback] Actuator command
message received. Topic: PIOT/ConstrainedDevice/ActuatorCmd.
2021-01-04 23:12:14,280 - MainThread - root - INFO - Disconnecting from MQTT
broker: localhost
2021-01-04 23:12:14,281 - Thread-2    - root - INFO - [Callback] Disconnected from
MQTT broker. Result
code: 0
2021-01-04 23:12:14,281 - MainThread - root - INFO - Stopped DeviceDataManager.
2021-01-04 23:12:14,282 - MainThread - root - INFO - Stopped
SystemPerformanceManager.
2021-01-04 23:12:14,282 - MainThread - root - INFO - SystemPerformanceManager
scheduler already stopped. Ignoring.
2021-01-04 23:12:14,282 - MainThread - root - INFO - Stopped SensorAdapterManager.
2021-01-04 23:12:14,282 - MainThread - root - INFO - SensorAdapterManager scheduler
already stopped.
Ignoring.
-------------------------------------------------------------------
Ran 3 tests in 10.090s

OK (skipped=2)
```

The log output I care about (mostly) is the following:

```
2021-01-04 23:12:04,280 - Thread-2    - root - INFO - [Callback] Actuator command
message received. Topic: PIOT/ConstrainedDevice/ActuatorCmd.
```

If you also received something similar, great! Your CDA is now well on its way to being a valuable member of your Edge Tier design.

What About Security?

MQTT supports username and password authentication, and—while not explicitly specified—can (and should) be used over an encrypted network connection. I'll talk more about enabling TLS to encrypt your MQTT connection in Chapter 10. Username authentication over an encrypted MQTT connection will be part of one of the exercises in Chapter 11.

Additional Exercises

I mentioned you can implement subscription callback logic later in Chapter 10, but why not now? If you'd like, you can read through Chapter 10 now and see if you can implement the CDA's MqttClientConnector callback subscriber functionality at this time. One option is to create a dictionary of resource names to callback functions that can be used to support this capability. See if you can make this work on your own.

Conclusion

As always, remember to commit your code and merge your Lab Module 06 branch into the primary branch as specified in PIOT-CDA-06-100 (*https://oreil.ly/roZJx*). Once you've done that, let's recap what you learned. In this chapter, you learned about the MQTT protocol, and how to use the paho-mqtt Python library to connect to an MQTT broker using a new class abstraction named `MqttClientConnector`.

Your CDA is now connection-enabled—congratulations! Now let's move on to Chapter 7 and add MQTT support to your GDA.

MQTT Integration–Java Client

Build a Publish/Subscribe Client in Java Using MQTT

Wash, rinse, and repeat.
What purpose does it now serve?
Practice makes perfect!

Fundamental concepts: Continued work with the MQTT pub/sub protocol; implementation strategies and exercises specific to the Gateway Device App written in Java; integration strategies using MQTT to communicate between the Constrained Device App and the Gateway Device App.

This chapter continues with the patterns established in Chapter 6, but with a focus on building your MQTT client connection logic within the GDA. This will eventually be used to support integration between the CDA and the GDA and will also lay the groundwork for the GDA to communicate with one or more cloud services using MQTT.

What You'll Learn in This Chapter

You'll continue digging into MQTT fundamentals, but this time you'll focus on building out your GDA functionality via integration with an open source MQTT library. Not only will this allow you to test your gateway and eventually integrate with remote cloud services that implement the MQTT protocol via a hosted broker, but it will also enable you to talk to the CDA in a reliable manner.

You'll see how MQTT can be used to push updates to one or more devices (such as your CDA) via a gateway (your GDA) and learn how to do so using an open source MQTT Java client library.

Programming Exercises

The steps you need to take to integrate MQTT with your GDA are nearly identical to those you just implemented for your CDA, allowing the GDA and the MQTT broker to communicate. Figure 7-1 depicts the components specific to the GDA.

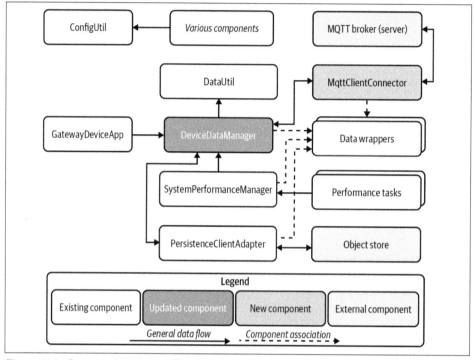

Figure 7-1. Gateway Device Application design with integrated MQTT client

As with the CDA design, there are four new components, only one of which you need to implement: MqttClientConnector. The others are provided for you from the java-components source code you've already downloaded.

Figure 7-2 depicts the notional UML for this design. In a similar fashion to the CDA, the diagram focuses on the relationship between DeviceDataManager and MqttClientConnector; a few of the other GDA components are shown to provide context.

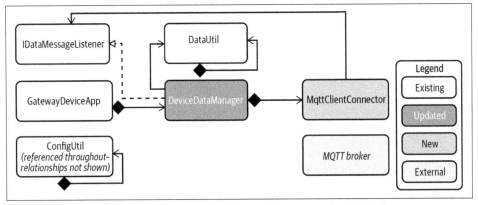

Figure 7-2. Gateway Device Application UML with integrated MQTT client

The MqttClientConnector will also provide an adapter to the Eclipse Paho Java client (*https://oreil.ly/FH1GO*), which is referenced in the *pom.xml* that's part of java-components and should be available for your client adapter to import. Because I've included this reference in the *pom.xml* that's part of java-components, you shouldn't have anything left to do to gain access to the client library.

OK, let's get started on the GDA's MQTT client implementation. The first step is, of course, to review the information in the Programming the IoT project board under Chapter 7–MQTT Client Integration (*https://oreil.ly/UZbJu*) and check out a new branch for this chapter (PIOT-GDA-07-000 (*https://oreil.ly/t7i2K*)).

Create the MQTT Connector Abstraction Module

Review the card named PIOT-GDA-07-001 (*https://oreil.ly/mgdk7*). This will focus on getting your GDA's version of MqttClientConnector working—again, with the Paho Java client.

Here are the basic steps. Be sure to review the code samples in PIOT-GDA-07-001 (*https://oreil.ly/mgdk7*) for additional details.

- Ensure the following import statements exist in the class:

```
import java.util.Properties;
import java.util.logging.Level;
import java.util.logging.Logger;

import org.eclipse.paho.client.mqttv3.IMqttDeliveryToken;
import org.eclipse.paho.client.mqttv3.MqttCallbackExtended;
import org.eclipse.paho.client.mqttv3.MqttClient;
import org.eclipse.paho.client.mqttv3.MqttConnectOptions;
import org.eclipse.paho.client.mqttv3.MqttException;
import org.eclipse.paho.client.mqttv3.MqttMessage;
```

```
import org.eclipse.paho.client.mqttv3.MqttPersistenceException;
import org.eclipse.paho.client.mqttv3.MqttSecurityException;
import org.eclipse.paho.client.mqttv3.persist.MemoryPersistence;

import programmingtheiot.common.ConfigConst;
import programmingtheiot.common.ConfigUtil;
import programmingtheiot.common.IDataMessageListener;
import programmingtheiot.common.ResourceNameEnum;
```

- Create class-scoped declarations for the variables described in the PIOT-GDA-07-001 (*https://oreil.ly/mgdk7*) card, including `MqttClient` and `IDataMessageListener`. For now, just set these and the other class-scoped variables to the defaults described within the card.

- Edit the no-arg constructor and initialize the class-scoped properties the MQTT client will eventually need when a connection is made. Retrieve the host, port, and keepAlive values from the configuration file using `ConfigUtil`. Use the following code sample to guide your implementation:

```
public MqttClientConnector()
{
  super();

  ConfigUtil configUtil = ConfigUtil.getInstance();

  this.host =
    configUtil.getProperty(
      ConfigConst.MQTT_GATEWAY_SERVICE,
      ConfigConst.HOST_KEY,
      ConfigConst.DEFAULT_HOST);

  this.port =
    configUtil.getInteger(
      ConfigConst.MQTT_GATEWAY_SERVICE,
      ConfigConst.PORT_KEY,
      ConfigConst.DEFAULT_MQTT_PORT);

  this.brokerKeepAlive =
    configUtil.getInteger(
      ConfigConst.MQTT_GATEWAY_SERVICE,
      ConfigConst.KEEP_ALIVE_KEY,
      ConfigConst.DEFAULT_KEEP_ALIVE);

  // NOTE: clientID should be customized in a later exercise
  this.clientID = MqttClient.generateClientId();
  this.persistence = new MemoryPersistence();
  this.connOpts = new MqttConnectOptions();

  this.connOpts.setKeepAliveInterval(this.brokerKeepAlive);
  this.connOpts.setCleanSession(false);
```

```
this.connOpts.setAutomaticReconnect(true);

    // NOTE: URL does not have a protocol handler for "tcp",
    // so construct the URL manually
    this.brokerAddr = this.protocol + "://" + this.host + ":" + this.port;
}
```

NOTE: Before moving on, there are two important implementation constructs to keep in mind: (1) the clientID must be set before initializing the MQTT client—the example above uses a randomly generated ID, although this can (and should) be specific to your GDA instance, and (2) the examples in this chapter use the synchronous MQTT client, although you'll likely need to use the asynchronous MQTT client for future integration testing. Both updates are described in PIOT-GDA-10-001 (*https://oreil.ly/EAjey*) and PIOT-GDA-10-002 (*https://oreil.ly/pRCcj*).

- Update the connectClient() method, add the logic to connect to the broker if not already connected, and log an info message indicating the connector was started. The key lines of code include the following; however, be sure to enclose within a try/catch and handle an MqttException, logging a message with the exception stack trace on error:

```
@Override
public boolean connectClient()
{
  try {
    if (this.mqttClient == null) {
      this.mqttClient =
        new MqttClient(
          this.brokerAddr, this.clientID, this.persistence);
      this.mqttClient.setCallback(this);
    }

    if (! this.mqttClient.isConnected()) {
      _Logger.info(
        "MQTT client connecting to broker: " + this.brokerAddr);
      this.mqttClient.connect(this.connOpts);
      return true;
    } else {
      _Logger.warning(
        "MQTT client already connected to broker: " + this.brokerAddr);
    }
  } catch (MqttException e) {
    // TODO: handle this exception
    _Logger.log(
      Level.SEVERE, "Failed to connect MQTT client to broker.", e);
  }
```

```
    return false;
  }
```

- Update the `disconnectClient()` method, add the logic to disconnect from the broker if currently connected, and log an info message indicating the connector was stopped. See the card for details on the implementation.

- Implement the remaining three methods from the `IPubSubClient` interface: `publishMessage()`, `subscribeToTopic()`, and `setDataMessageListener()`. For now, just log a message indicating they were called, and return False. A follow-up task will address their implementation details.

- Implement the required callback methods from `MqttCallbackExtended`. For now, just log a message indicating they were called. A follow-up task will address their implementation details.

- Create a setter for the `IDataMessageListener`—this will allow you to pass incoming MQTT messages back to the `DeviceDataManager` implementation, which implements this interface.

Be sure to review the implementation samples shown in the Kanban card for PIOT-GDA-07-001 (*https://oreil.ly/mgdk7*) for details on the above instructions. Once completed, and after your MQTT broker is operational and started, you can test your initial implementationby running the `MqttClientConnectorTest` integration tests. For now, only one should pass (the connect and disconnect test case).

As with the CDA implementation, it makes sense to look at some of the details for the GDA implementation. As you read through the issue, I'm sure you've noticed that the Java-specific implementation of the paho-mqtt client introduces some differences from the Python implementation. In terms of constructing the client and issuing a simple CONNECT message, there are three differences to keep in mind:

1. A client ID is required. You can use the static `MqttClient.generateClientId()` method or create your own. The rules about client IDs are the same as those I mentioned previously, so be sure each client uses a unique client ID.

2. Persistence is required for reliable messaging. If you want to use QoS levels 1 or 2 on the client side, you'll need to specify an implementation of `MqttClientPersis tence`. This can be file-based or in-memory, using default implementations of each. For now, you can use `MemoryPersistence`, although keep in mind that any internal state will be lost if the client restarts.

3. Connection options are contained within a class instance called `MqttConnectOp tions`. This is used to store the keepAlive value, Clean Session Flag, and, perhaps most importantly, the automatic reconnect flag.

In the constructor for your `MqttClientConnector`, you should create (or generate) the client ID, `MqttClientPersistence` instance (using either `MemoryPersistence` or `MqttDefaultFilePersistence`), and `MqttConnectOptions`, for use later when the `connectClient()` method is called.

Let's quickly tackle that last bullet next: create the setter method for the `IDataMessage Listener` callback implementation. Functionally, this is the same as the like-named setter within the CDA's MQTT client adapter and will look identical to the same setter functionality you implemented in Chapters 2 and 5.

Moving on to the `connectClient()`, you'll see one significant difference from the Python implementation—no network loop. This is because the client library implements this functionality for you, so there's no need to explicitly call it on your own.

Finally, the `disconnectClient()` is very straightforward. I didn't include any sample code, as it's only three lines of code (two if you want to be a bit clever): first, check whether the client exists, then see if it's connected, and if so, call the `disconnect()` method. Easy.

Testing and validating the connection

Let's run a quick test and see what Control Packets get generated. If you're using Wireshark, launch it now. Make sure it can listen for packets on your loopback adapter and then start listening for packets. Start the Mosquitto broker as well.

In the `MqttClientConnectorTest` test case, uncomment the `testConnectAndDiscon nect()` test method, and run the test—just like the CDA version of this test, it will take about 35 seconds to execute.

Table 7-1 depicts the Wireshark output you can expect to see after successfully running the `testConnectAndDisconnect()` integration test.

Table 7-1. MQTT CONNECT and DISCONNECT Control Packet Sequence as shown in Wireshark

No.	Time	Source	Destination	Protocol	Length	Info
31342	667.426633	127.0.0.1	127.0.0.1	MQTT	77	Connect Command
31344	667.428227	127.0.0.1	127.0.0.1	MQTT	48	Connect Ack
31944	697.430629	127.0.0.1	127.0.0.1	MQTT	46	Ping Request
31946	697.430955	127.0.0.1	127.0.0.1	MQTT	46	Ping Response
32042	702.438447	127.0.0.1	127.0.0.1	MQTT	46	Disconnect Req

Besides the loopback address (127.0.0.1) in the source and destination, the output is essentially the same as that shown in Table 6-1. All five expected Control Packets are shown: CONNECT, CONNACK, PINGREQ, PINGRESP, and DISCONNECT.

The main difference is seen in the packet detail for CONNECT, as shown below:

```
MQ Telemetry Transport Protocol, Connect Command
    Header Flags: 0x10, Message Type: Connect Command
        0001 .... = Message Type: Connect Command (1)
        .... 0000 = Reserved: 0
    Msg Len: 31
    Protocol Name Length: 4
    Protocol Name: MQTT
    Version: MQTT v3.1.1 (4)
    Connect Flags: 0x00, QoS Level: At most once delivery (Fire and Forget)
        0... .... = User Name Flag: Not set
        .0.. .... = Password Flag: Not set
        ..0. .... = Will Retain: Not set
        ...0 0... = QoS Level: At most once delivery (Fire and Forget) (0)
        .... .0.. = Will Flag: Not set
        .... ..0. = Clean Session Flag: Not set
        .... ...0 = (Reserved): Not set
    Keep Alive: 30
    Client ID Length: 19
    Client ID: paho226689729099300
```

Notice that the Client ID is set (paho226689729099300), which also lines up with what we should expect, since I explicitly set it with my Java client using the MqttClient.generateClientId() method.

Add Callbacks to Support MQTT Events

The Paho Java library also provides a number of callback definitions, but as of this writing, they're different from those in the Python library. Using the MqttCallbackEx tended interface, you have four to implement: connectComplete(), connection Lost(), deliveryComplete(), and—perhaps most useful for the purposes of the GDA—messageArrived().

The requirements for this activity can be found in PIOT-GDA-07-002 (*https://oreil.ly/ CR2bw*). Here's a brief summary of the implementation details:

- Add the connectComplete() and connectionLost() callback methods to handle connection notification events. For now, just log a message indicating the client has successfully connected. Use the following signatures:

  ```
  public void connectComplete(boolean reconnect, String serverURI);
  public void connectionLost(Throwable t);
  ```

- Add the deliveryComplete() callback method to handle publish notification events. For now, just log a message indicating the client has successfully published a message. Use the following signature:

  ```
  public void deliveryComplete(IMqttDeliveryToken token);
  ```

- Add the `messageArrived()` callback method, which is perhaps most important—this will be called whenever a message is received on the topic for which your client has subscribed; you can add a log message for now, although eventually this will invoke another callback on the `IDataMessageListener` instance. Use the following signature:

  ```
  public void messageArrived(String topic, MqttMessage message);
  ```

  NOTE: The `messageArrived()` callback parameter named "message" (of type `MqttMessage`) will contain all the context—including the `byte[]` payload—of the message received from the broker.

- Back in the `connectClient()` method, make sure you set the callback reference to "this," which is the `MqttClientConnector`, since it implements `MqttCallback Extended`:

  ```
  this.mqttClient.setCallback(this);
  ```

Testing will be similar to that for the CDA. Start up your MQTT broker if it's not already running, enable the `testConnectAndDisconnectCallbacks()` test case, and run the `MqttClientConnectorTest` unit test as described in the Tests section of PIOT-GDA-07-002 (*https://oreil.ly/CR2bw*). All test cases should succeed.

In Java, you'll need to implement the method signatures as defined, since you're implementing an interface contract. That said, you can name the parameters whatever you want.

Once the callbacks are all implemented, run the integration test as described in the "Tests" section of the issue. Make sure the callbacks get triggered and verify with the test case that all is well.

You can review all the callbacks defined by the Paho Java library, along with their associated (and well-written) Javadoc documentation (*https://oreil.ly/Cl9h2*).

Add Publish, Subscribe, and Unsubscribe Functionality

You already know about QoS levels and have some experience using the pub/sub features of MQTT with your CDA, so let's get right into the related GDA code.

Take a look at the requirements described in PIOT-GDA-07-003 (*https://oreil.ly/RO5Sg*), and implement the following:

- Update the `publishMessage()` method to handle all publish functionality. It will accept the topic name, message content, and requested QoS level for parameters. The topic name and QoS validation rules from the CDA apply here as well, of course.

- Update the `subscribeToTopic()` and `unsubscribeFromTopic()` methods to handle all subscribe and unsubscribe functionality. Remember to validate all parameters!

Let's take a look at the sample implementation for all these methods, starting with `publishMessage()` (and yes, I added `isConnected()` as a convenience):

```
public boolean isConnected()
{
  return (this.mqttClient != null && this.mqttClient.isConnected());
}

@Override
public boolean publishMessage(
  ResourceNameEnum topicName, String msg, int qos)
{
  // TODO: determine how verbose your logging should be,
  // especially if this method is called often
  if (topicName == null) {
    _Logger.warning(
      "Resource is null. Unable to publish message: " +
      this.brokerAddr);
    return false;
  }

  if (msg == null || msg.length() == 0) {
    _Logger.warning(
      "Message is null or empty. Unable to publish message: " +
      this.brokerAddr);
    return false;
  }

  if (qos < 0 || qos > 2) {
    qos = ConfigConst.DEFAULT_QOS;
  }

  try {
    byte[] payload = msg.getBytes();
    MqttMessage mqttMsg = new MqttMessage(payload);
    mqttMsg.setQos(qos);
    this.mqttClient.publish(topicName.getResourceName(), mqttMsg);
    return true;
  } catch (Exception e) {
    _Logger.log(
      Level.SEVERE,
      "Failed to publish message to topic: " + topicName, e);
```

```
  }

  return false;
}
```

Moving on to the subscribe/unsubscribe functionality, you'll notice these follow the same pattern as their CDA counterpart:

```
@Override
public boolean subscribeToTopic(ResourceNameEnum topicName, int qos)
{
  if (topicName == null) {
    _Logger.warning(
      "Resource is null. Unable to subscribe to topic: " +
      this.brokerAddr);

    return false;
  }

  if (qos < 0 || qos > 2) {
    _Logger.warning("Invalid QoS. Using default. QoS requested: " + qos);
    qos = ConfigConst.DEFAULT_QOS;
  }

  try {
    this.mqttClient.subscribe(topicName.getResourceName(), qos);

    _Logger.info(
      "Successfully subscribed to topic: " + topicName.getResourceName());

    return true;
  } catch (Exception e) {
    _Logger.log(
      Level.SEVERE, "Failed to subscribe to topic: " + topicName, e);
  }

  return false;
}

@Override
public boolean unsubscribeFromTopic(ResourceNameEnum topicName)
{
  if (topicName == null) {
    _Logger.warning(
      "Resource is null. Unable to unsubscribe from topic: " +
      this.brokerAddr);

    return false;
  }

  try {
    this.mqttClient.unsubscribe(topicName.getResourceName());
```

```
  _Logger.info(
    "Successfully unsubscribed from topic: " +
    topicName.getResourceName());

  return true;
} catch (Exception e) {
  _Logger.log(
    Level.SEVERE, "Failed to unsubscribe from topic: " + topicName, e);
}

  return false;
}
```

A final note on topic subscriptions: as with the Python MQTT client, you can also define unique callbacks per subscription topic. It's a bit more involved in Java, as you need to implement a separate callback interface for each. I'll discuss this further in Chapter 10, as you won't need this capability for any of the exercises in this chapter.

Time to test things out. Let's observe the integration tests with Wireshark running. Fire up Wireshark and run the integration test named MqttClientConnectorTest.

Following the testing patterns with the previous GDA requirements, make sure your MQTT broker is running, and uncomment the testPublishAndSubscribe() unit test in the MqttClientConnectorTest test case. As with the other MQTT tests you've already run, this should run without any errors.

Now for some real fun—let's compare this output with that from the CDA. Make sure Wireshark is running along with your MQTT broker, and let's execute this test again. You may want to execute only testPublishAndSubscribe() to avoid any extra noise in your protocol analyzer output.

While the test executes, look at Wireshark and examine the output. It should look similar to the content shown in Table 7-2.

Table 7-2. MQTT PUBLISH and SUBSCRIBE Control Packet Sequence using QoS 2 as shown in Wireshark

No.	Time	Source	Destination	Protocol	Length	Info
75	5.168764	127.0.0.1	127.0.0.1	MQTT	77	Connect Command
77	5.170104	127.0.0.1	127.0.0.1	MQTT	48	Connect Ack
79	5.176926	127.0.0.1	127.0.0.1	MQTT	93	Subscribe Request (id=1) [PIOT/GatewayDevice/MgmtStatusMsg]
81	5.177121	127.0.0.1	127.0.0.1	MQTT	49	Subscribe Ack (id=1)
225	10.180238	127.0.0.1	127.0.0.1	MQTT	130	Publish Message (id=2) [PIOT/GatewayDevice/MgmtStatusMsg]
227	10.18053	127.0.0.1	127.0.0.1	MQTT	48	Publish Received (id=2)
229	10.181193	127.0.0.1	127.0.0.1	MQTT	48	Publish Release (id=2)

No.	Time	Source	Destination	Protocol	Length	Info
231	10.181389	127.0.0.1	127.0.0.1	MQTT	48	Publish Complete (id=2)
303	15.183483	127.0.0.1	127.0.0.1	MQTT	92	Unsubscribe Request (id=3)
305	15.183721	127.0.0.1	127.0.0.1	MQTT	48	Unsubscribe Ack (id=3)
1087	45.185789	127.0.0.1	127.0.0.1	MQTT	46	Ping Request
1089	45.186054	127.0.0.1	127.0.0.1	MQTT	46	Ping Response
1191	50.189787	127.0.0.1	127.0.0.1	MQTT	46	Disconnect Req

As expected, there are 13 Control Packets—everything except PUBACK, as this test was run with QoS 2 enabled.

Table 7-3 shows us the same test run, but with QoS 1 enabled instead. Lo and behold, there's our missing PUBACK.

Table 7-3. MQTT publish and subscribe Control Packet Sequence using QoS 1 as shown in Wireshark

No.	Time	Source	Destination	Protocol	Length	Info
163	5.919503	127.0.0.1	127.0.0.1	MQTT	77	Connect Command
165	5.920732	127.0.0.1	127.0.0.1	MQTT	48	Connect Ack
167	5.928247	127.0.0.1	127.0.0.1	MQTT	93	Subscribe Request (id=1) [PIOT/GatewayDevice/MgmtStatusMsg]
169	5.928458	127.0.0.1	127.0.0.1	MQTT	49	Subscribe Ack (id=1)
348	10.93348	127.0.0.1	127.0.0.1	MQTT	130	Publish Message (id=2) [PIOT/GatewayDevice/MgmtStatusMsg]
350	10.933754	127.0.0.1	127.0.0.1	MQTT	48	Publish Ack (id=2)
405	15.936125	127.0.0.1	127.0.0.1	MQTT	92	Unsubscribe Request (id=3)
407	15.936365	127.0.0.1	127.0.0.1	MQTT	48	Unsubscribe Ack (id=3)
1773	45.938298	127.0.0.1	127.0.0.1	MQTT	46	Ping Request
1775	45.938511	127.0.0.1	127.0.0.1	MQTT	46	Ping Response
1969	50.939777	127.0.0.1	127.0.0.1	MQTT	46	Disconnect Req

So we have reasonable confidence that our two MQTT client applications—one for the CDA and the other for the GDA—are behaving as expected. Let's do one more quick comparison, though.

Recall the PUBLISH payload content that followed the QoS 1 run depicted in Table 6-3. Here it is one more time:

```
0000   32 58 00 2e 50 72 6f 67 72 61 6d 6d 69 6e 67 49   2X..ProgrammingI
0010   6f 54 2f 43 6f 6e 73 74 72 61 69 6e 65 64 44 65   oT/ConstrainedDe
0020   76 69 63 65 2f 4d 67 6d 74 53 74 61 74 75 73 4d   vice/MgmtStatusM
0030   73 67 00 01 54 45 53 54 3a 20 54 68 69 73 20 69   sg..TEST: This i
```

```
0040   73 20 74 68 65 20 43 44 41 20 6d 65 73 73 61 67      s the CDA messag
0050   65 20 70 61 79 6c 6f 61 64 2e                        e payload.
```

For comparison purposes, I published the same message again, but with a slightly dif-ferent topic name and message. Here it is:

```
0000   32 54 00 2a 50 72 6f 67 72 61 6d 6d 69 6e 67 49      2T.*ProgrammingI
0010   6f 54 2f 47 61 74 65 77 61 79 44 65 76 69 63 65      oT/GatewayDevice
0020   2f 4d 67 6d 74 53 74 61 74 75 73 4d 73 67 00 02      /MgmtStatusMsg..
0030   54 45 53 54 3a 20 54 68 69 73 20 69 73 20 74 68      TEST: This is th
0040   65 20 47 44 41 20 6d 65 73 73 61 67 65 20 70 61      e GDA message pa
0050   79 6c 6f 61 64 2e                                    yload.
```

Besides the topic name and the payload content, they're nearly the same. Take a quick look at the third and fourth byte in both (in bold)—for the CDA test it was "00 2e" and for the GDA test it was "00 2a." This happens to be the 2-byte representation of the topic length. The CDA's topic was 46 bytes, and the GDA's topic was 42 bytes.

Again, this is validation that we have protocol compatibility between the two clients. This is good, since we're going to see if we can get them to talk with each other.

Integrate the MQTT Connector into Your GDA

The final GDA exercise for this chapter is generally straightforward but involves a few steps:

- Add and manage the `MqttClientConnector` instance within `DeviceDataManager`.
- Subscribe/unsubscribe to actuator commands when the `DeviceDataManager` starts/stops, respectively.

Take a look at PIOT-GDA-07-004 (*https://oreil.ly/mJQHX*)—this activity follows a similar path to the MQTT Connector integration logic for the CDA but includes additional work, since the GDA serves as the orchestration engine for *all* Edge Tier messages.

This means the initialization logic is a bit more involved. Let's take a look at one way you can pull this off, using the following class-scoped member declarations and con-structor implementation as a guide:

```
private boolean enableMqttClient = true;
private boolean enableCoapServer = false;
private boolean enableCloudClient = false;
private boolean enableSmtpClient = false;
private boolean enablePersistenceClient = false;

private SystemPerformanceManager sysPerfMgr = null;

private IPubSubClient mqttClient = null;
private ICloudClient cloudClient = null;
```

```
private IPersistenceClient persistenceClient = null;
private IRequestResponseClient smtpClient = null;
private CoapServerGateway coapServer = null;

public DeviceDataManager()
{
  super();

  ConfigUtil configUtil = ConfigUtil.getInstance();

  this.enableMqttClient = configUtil.getBoolean(
    ConfigConst.GATEWAY_DEVICE,
    ConfigConst.ENABLE_MQTT_CLIENT_KEY);

  this.enableCoapServer = configUtil.getBoolean(
    ConfigConst.GATEWAY_DEVICE,
    ConfigConst.ENABLE_COAP_SERVER_KEY);

  this.enableCloudClient = configUtil.getBoolean(
    ConfigConst.GATEWAY_DEVICE,
    ConfigConst.ENABLE_CLOUD_CLIENT_KEY);

  this.enablePersistenceClient = configUtil.getBoolean(
    ConfigConst.GATEWAY_DEVICE,
    ConfigConst.ENABLE_PERSISTENCE_CLIENT_KEY);

  initManager();
}
```

The class-scoped declarations are self-explanatory—they simply declare variables that will hold boolean values that indicate whether or not a particular connection is enabled, and of course the references to those connection implementations (e.g., IPub SubClient, which will be the MqttClientConnector instance).

The constructor also looks relatively straightforward, as it pulls these connection enablement flags from the configuration file.

But then it invokes initManager(). Let's take a look at that implementation:

```
private void initManager()
{
  this.sysPerfMgr = new SystemPerformanceManager();
  this.sysPerfMgr.setDataMessageListener(this);

  if (this.enableMqttClient) {
    this.mqttClient = new MqttClientConnector();
    this.mqttClient.setDataMessageListener(this);
  }

  // TODO: put other connection initializers here
}
```

We'll get to the connector initializations for the other protocols and cloud client later in Parts III and IV, so let's just focus on the two of importance: SystemPerformance Manager and MqttClientConnector.

With the connection classes instanced, you can add them into the DeviceDataManager's startManager() and stopManager() methods. As part of this process, you can also subscribe to/unsubscribe from any relevant topics the GDA will be interested in, including sensor data, system performance data, and actuator command responses coming from the CDA.

 You can add other subscriptions as well, of course, including for those topics that might be hosted in the cloud—more on that in Chapter 11.

Here's some sample code for the start sequence:

```
public void startManager()
{
  _Logger.info("Starting DeviceDataManager...");

  this.sysPerfMgr.startManager();

  if (this.enableMqttClient) {
    try {
      int qos = ConfigConst.DEFAULT_QOS;

      if (this.mqttClient.connectClient()) {
        this.mqttClient.subscribeToTopic(
          ResourceNameEnum.CDA_ACTUATOR_RESPONSE_RESOURCE, qos);

        this.mqttClient.subscribeToTopic(
          ResourceNameEnum.CDA_SENSOR_MSG_RESOURCE, qos);

        this.mqttClient.subscribeToTopic(
          ResourceNameEnum.CDA_SYSTEM_PERF_MSG_RESOURCE, qos);

        _Logger.info("MQTT client connection started.");
      } else {
        _Logger.warning("MQTT client connection start failed.");
      }
    } catch (Exception e) {
      _Logger.warning("Failed to start MQTT client.");
    }
  }
}
```

Lastly, you can implement the stop functionality using code similar to the following:

The unsubscribe is necessary only if your GDA will be starting and stopping the DeviceDataManager more than once during its runtime.

```
public void stopManager()
{
  _Logger.info("Stopping DeviceDataManager...");

  this.sysPerfMgr.stopManager();

  if (this.enableMqttClient) {
    try {
      if (this.mqttClient.disconnectClient()) {
        this.mqttClient.unsubscribeFromTopic(
          ResourceNameEnum.CDA_ACTUATOR_RESPONSE_RESOURCE);

        this.mqttClient.unsubscribeFromTopic (
          ResourceNameEnum.CDA_SENSOR_MSG_RESOURCE);

        this.mqttClient.unsubscribeFromTopic (
          ResourceNameEnum.CDA_SYSTEM_PERF_MSG_RESOURCE);

        _Logger.info("Stopped MQTT client.");
      } else {
        _Logger.warning("Failed to stop MQTT client.");
      }
    } catch (Exception e) {
      _Logger.warning("Failed to stop MQTT client.");
    }
  }
}
```

Before moving onto testing, be sure to check the updates in the Kanban board (*https://oreil.ly/programming-iot-kanban*) for all of these exercises, but specifically for PIOT-GDA-07-004 (*https://oreil.ly/mJQHX*). I've shown a relatively simple approach for abstracting the MQTT client functionality in this chapter, which is sufficient to move forward with basic integration testing. A more advanced approach is introduced in Chapter 10, which will enable more advanced integration capabilities, but will also require updates to some of your code.

Ready to test everything? The DeviceDataManagerWithCommsTest contains the manual integration tests to check this functionality. It's located in the *./programmingtheiot/part03/integration/app* path. testStartAndStopManagerWithMqtt is the specific test you'll want to run.

As with the CDA, you may want to make a temporary edit to DeviceDataManager and simply comment out the startup of SystemPerformanceManager within its startManager() function for this one test (then uncomment them after testing).

Your log output may vary, of course, but should be of similar form and function to the following:

```
Jan 07, 2021 9:26:54 PM programmingtheiot.gda.connection.MqttClientConnector
initCredentialConnectionParameters
INFO: Checking if credentials file exists and us loadable...
Jan 07, 2021 9:26:54 PM programmingtheiot.common.ConfigUtil getCredentials
.
.
.
Jan 07, 2021 9:26:54 PM programmingtheiot.gda.app.DeviceDataManager startManager
INFO: Starting DeviceDataManager...
Jan 07, 2021 9:26:54 PM programmingtheiot.gda.connection.MqttClientConnector
connectClient
programmingtheiot.gda.connection.MqttClientConnector connectClient
INFO: Using client ID for broker connection: paho97098106156000
Jan 07, 2021 9:26:55 PM programmingtheiot.gda.connection.MqttClientConnector
connectClient
INFO: Attempting to connect to broker: tcp://localhost:1883
Jan 07, 2021 9:26:55 PM programmingtheiot.gda.connection.MqttClientConnector
connectClient
INFO: Connected to broker: tcp://localhost:1883
Jan 07, 2021 9:26:55 PM programmingtheiot.gda.connection.MqttClientConnector
connectComplete
INFO: MQTT connection successful (is reconnect = false). Broker:
  tcp://localhost:1883
Jan 07, 2021 9:26:55 PM programmingtheiot.gda.app.DeviceDataManager
startManager
INFO: MQTT client connection established.
.
.
.
Jan 07, 2021 9:26:55 PM programmingtheiot.gda.connection.MqttClientConnector
subscribeToTopic
INFO: Subscribing to topic: PIOT/ConstrainedDevice/SensorMsg
Jan 07, 2021 9:26:55 PM programmingtheiot.gda.connection.MqttClientConnector
publishMessage
INFO: Publishing message to topic: PIOT/ConstrainedDevice/SensorMsg
Jan 07, 2021 9:26:55 PM programmingtheiot.gda.connection.MqttClientConnector
messageArrived
INFO: MQTT message received.
    Topic: PIOT/ConstrainedDevice/SensorMsg
    Timestamp: 1610072815718
    Payload: {"value":0.0,"name":"Some Sensor","timeStamp":"2021-01-
08T02:26:55.651361600Z","statusCode":0,"typeID":0,"loca
tionID":"constraineddevice001","latitude":0.0,"longitude":0.0,"elevation":0.0,
"timeStampMillis":1610072815651}
.
.
.
Jan 07, 2021 9:27:55 PM programmingtheiot.gda.connection.MqttClientConnector
disconnectClient
```

```
INFO: Disconnecting from broker...
Jan 07, 2021 9:27:55 PM programmingtheiot.gda.connection.MqttClientConnector
disconnectClient
INFO: Disconnected from broker: tcp://localhost:1883
Jan 07, 2021 9:27:55 PM programmingtheiot.gda.app.DeviceDataManager stopManager
INFO: Stopping DeviceDataManager...
Jan 07, 2021 9:27:55 PM programmingtheiot.gda.connection.MqttClientConnector
disconnectClient
INFO: Disconnecting from broker...
Jan 07, 2021 9:27:55 PM programmingtheiot.gda.connection.MqttClientConnector
disconnectClient
INFO: Disconnected from broker: tcp://localhost:1883
Jan 07, 2021 9:27:55 PM programmingtheiot.gda.app.DeviceDataManager stopManager
INFO: Disconnected MQTT client.
```

My own solution includes a number of additional log messages, which I've omitted
here for brevity. The point is that the following were successful, as indicated by
receipt of the message on the subscription topic:

- Connection to the MQTT broker succeeded

- Subscription, publish, and receipt of message to/on the topic PIOT/Constrained-
  Device/SensorMsg succeeded

- Disconnect from the MQTT broker succeeded

This functionality serves as the core MQTT integration logic the GDA will need not
only to communicate with the CDA but also to process relevant messages and take
action as appropriate. This is certainly a well-earned milestone!

What About Security and Overall System Performance?

Chapter 10 brings these concepts together in one place since the concepts apply to
both the CDA and the GDA. I'll explore some security aspects of MQTT as well as
the performance implications of different QoS levels in the related exercises for the
chapter.

Additional Exercises

At this point in your IoT programming journey, you may be thinking about some
Edge Tier projects you can implement using the knowledge you've acquired. Here are
two simple exercises to get you started.

Subscriber Callbacks

The additional exercise described in Chapter 6 mentions the use of subscriber callbacks for your CDA. These are relatively straightforward to implement in Python,
since you just need to add a method that can handle incoming messages for a given

topic. In Java, it's a bit more involved, as you need to define a callback class to handle this. Although I'll cover this in Chapter 10, you may want to briefly skip ahead and read through that chapter's section describing the IMqttMessageListener interface to see how you might tackle this functionality now.[1]

CDA to GDA Integration

I'm sure you're wondering why we don't tackle CDA to GDA integration using MQTT at this point, especially since you finally have your MQTT clients up and running with both applications. The exercises in Chapter 10 work through many different integration scenarios, so you can skip ahead and work through those MQTT-specific exercises now if you'd like!

The next two chapters work through another messaging protocol that adheres to the request/response paradigm, and so Chapter 10 will consider ways you might want to use pub/sub, request/response, or perhaps even both to address your Edge Tier integration objectives.

Conclusion

Remember to merge all your changes back into the primary branch by following the instructions in PIOT-GDA-07-100 (*https://oreil.ly/XxsEb*)!

In this chapter, you've learned about the MQTT protocol and how it works. You integrated an open source MQTT client (Eclipse Paho) using both Python and Java with your CDA and GDA, respectively, and ran a bunch of tests to prove protocol compatibility between the two, wrapping up with an integration test that passed a message back and forth.

---

1 For more information on IMqttMessageListener, see the online documentation (*https://oreil.ly/XK5Lz*).

CoAP Server Implementation

Building a Request/Response Server Using CoAP

What is your response?
I made my request again.
Finally confirmed!

Fundamental concepts: Overview of request/response messaging at the application layer; features of CoAP; creating a CoAP server in Java for your GDA.

In Chapters 6 and 7, we explored IoT messaging basics using the MQTT protocol for pub/sub communications. In this chapter, we'll explore IoT messaging using request/response protocols, specifically the Constrained Application Protocol (CoAP), which has similarities to Hypertext Transfer Protocol (HTTP) but was designed for light-weight communications between devices.

Like *pub/sub*, *request/response* is a term that captures a type of messaging interaction between two systems. This can be thought of as a peer-to-peer protocol, in which a client sends an action request to a server for a specific resource, which the server can accept or reject. A *resource* is just something that the server manages. This could be a static file (like a simple web page, video clip, or image), a database or other enterprise system, or one part of a more dynamic interaction that involves multiple requests and responses. In each case, the response includes some indication of the action the server took (or didn't take) in the form of a response code.

Much like talking to an MQTT server, CoAP requires knowledge of the server's address and the port. Once you identify the target server and port, the resource name will follow similar naming conventions to those of pub/sub topics.

If you're familiar with Representational State Transfer (REST), you'll recognize the four different actions (referred to as *methods*) a client can request: GET, PUT, POST, and DELETE. I'll discuss each of these as you progress through the chapter.

What You'll Learn in This Chapter

After working through this content and the code examples and exercises, you'll understand the principles behind request/response protocols and how to use these protocols in your own IoT environment. Specifically, you'll learn how request/response works, why it's useful, and how to write a simple CoAP server to support your application's needs.

About CoAP

The CoAP IETF specification, RFC 7252 (*https://tools.ietf.org/html/rfc7252*), was designed as a machine-to-machine (M2M) protocol for use with low-power devices running over a UDP/IP datagram socket connection. You can think of it as a light-weight HTTP, since it doesn't require the same overhead as a typical HTTP connection that uses TCP/IP sockets. The IETF CoRE working group began work on the CoAP specification in 2010, and the IETF adopted it as a standard in 2014.

Client to Server Connections

Although there is a current specification for CoAP over TCP/IP (RFC 8323 (*https://tools.ietf.org/html/rfc8323*)), RFC 7252 specifies a CoAP implementation that relies on UDP/IP datagram sockets, with Datagram Transport Layer Security (DTLS) enabled if encrypted connections are required.

There are four security modes defined in the CoAP specification:

- *NoSec:* No encryption
- *PreSharedKey:* DTLS is enabled with a list of preshared keys
- *RawPublicKey:* DTLS is enabled with an asymmetric key pair without a certificate
- *Certificate:* DTLS is enabled with an asymmetric key pair with an X.509 certificate[1]

Typical CoAP clients simply set the target URL (protocol, host, port, and resource URI) and open and close the UDP connection for each request/response. CoAP supports asynchronous message exchanges, using both confirmed (CON) and

---

1 Zach Shelby, Klaus Hartke, and Carsten Bormann, *The Constrained Application Protocol (CoAP)* (*https://tools.ietf.org/html/rfc7252*), IETF Proposed Standard RFC 7252 (2014), 68.

nonconfirmed (NON) message exchanges. CON messages are managed through a stop-and-wait message retransmission capability with an exponential backoff to provide a reliability mechanism.

Both CON and NON messages benefit from duplicate detection to avoid duplicates. The client implementations we'll work with set CON and NON flags through a simple boolean parameter in the method request.

Figure 8-1 depicts a simple request interaction between a single CoAP client and the server.

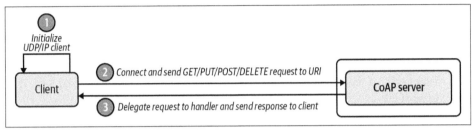

Figure 8-1. Connection between a single client and a CoAP server

As shown, the client application creates a CoAP client module and then uses it to issue a GET, POST, PUT, or DELETE request to the server, which responds in kind.

Request Methods

Although RESTful protocols may provide additional method options (such as PATCH or FETCH), IETF RFC 7252 specifies only GET, POST, PUT and DELETE,[2] so I'll focus on those methods in this chapter.

Here's a quick rundown of the behaviors you can expect from a compliant server when issuing a request with any of these method options in your own client application:

GET
> This is the data retrieval method, which asks the server to "get" the data associated with a given resource. This method is specified as "safe," meaning it doesn't incur a change on the server and is idempotent. What does this mean, exactly? Irrespective of how many times the request is invoked (that is, how many times the request is sent to the server), the server will simply respond with the existing data associated with the request. In other words, the server won't change the data based on the request.

---

2 Shelby, Hartke, and Bormann, *CoAP*, 47–48.

POST

> This method is sent to represent a creation request and is expected to result in the server creating the specified resource with the given content. The specification allows a POST to succeed and *not* create a new resource but instead trigger an update or a delete on the given resource. As should be obvious, a POST method request is not "safe": it will incur a change on the server, and it is not idempotent. If a POST is issued over and over again, the client should expect to find, on success, that the POST caused the requisite change on the server with *each* request.

PUT

> This method is sent to represent an update request but can also trigger a creation action on the server if the resource to be updated doesn't already exist. The context of the message represents the updated content for the named resource. This means that it isn't "safe," as it will incur a change on the server, but it is idempotent.

DELETE

> This method is designed to delete a resource on the server. On success, the client can expect the requested resource to be deleted from the server. As such, it isn't "safe," but it is idempotent. Once a resource is deleted, issuing a DELETE request against the deleted resource repeatedly should have no effect on the server.

Message Passing

Datagram messages are passed from the client to the server as request messages targeting a specific named resource, with the server returning a response message (assuming it's up, running, and capable of sending a response). Message passing is asynchronous in CoAP. However, the client library used by the client application may mask this, or at least provide the option of sending what appears to be a synchronous request to the server, returning only after a response has been received.

In CoAP, a resource is a hierarchical name to a server-based, well, *resource*, much like you'd see in an HTTP URL. The naming convention of the client request conforms to the URI generic syntax (*https://tools.ietf.org/html/rfc3986*), so resource names in CoAP are only case sensitive following the port in the URL (for example, *coap://lcoalhost:5683/resourceName*), similar to MQTT topics.

As implied, CoAP supports hierarchical resource names, where you can create child resources from a parent resource simply by separating each resource entry with a forward slash (/) character to represent this relationship (as in *SomeCategory/SomeDevice/SomeMessageType/SomeElement*, for example, or perhaps just *SomeCategory/SomeDevice/SomeMessageType*).

While the URI generic syntax supports a limited number of special characters, don't confuse that with wildcard support. CoAP does *not* specify wildcards, in kind with the URI generic syntax specification, so don't try to use them in your CoAP resource naming scheme!

Let's look at two simple examples.

Example 1: One client updates the server using PUT, while another retrieves it using GET.

Client A will write new data to a single resource on a given CoAP server. Let's name this resource as follows: PIOT/ConstrainedDevice/SensorMsg.

The client will create a URI that represents the resource. The URI will include the requisite access and location information, such as the protocol, host, port, and path (e.g., *coap://localhost:5683/PIOT/ConstrainedDevice/SensorMsg*). Then it will issue a PUT method request with the payload data. Once the data is successfully received and processed (that is, stored locally) by the server, any authorized client can retrieve this information using the GET method issued to the same resource.

Example 2: One client updates the server using PUT, while another is notified of these updates using OBSERVE (a specialized GET).

Client A will perform the same task as described in Example 1, but Client B will be notified of updates to this data and sent the updated information after it's successfully processed by the server. Let's use the same resource name: PIOT/ConstrainedDevice/SensorMsg.

To retrieve the data Client A wrote to the resource, Client B has two choices:

- Poll the server at regular intervals using a GET request for each of the preceding resources.
- Observe (via a specialized GET request) and be notified when a resource is updated and simply process the data as it's available.

For the first option, Client B simply needs to issue the GET request for the resource whenever it wants to check for updates. This process is pretty straightforward but can be inconvenient for the client, since it doesn't really know when the data is updated. It simply requests whatever happens to be the current information at its configured poll interval.

The second option is perhaps a better path forward. While the CoAP specification doesn't define an observe method directly, it can be added, since the protocol is designed to be extensible (in this case, via IETF RFC 7641 (*https://tools.ietf.org/html/rfc7641*)). This allows the client to send the server a specialized GET request, or an

OBSERVE, which instructs the server to push new information for the requested resource whenever it's available. This can be convenient since the client no longer has to manage this process itself (although it certainly needs to process the notifications).

Figure 8-2 depicts a simple CoAP request/response process, including the connection sequence of Client A and Client B to the CoAP server.

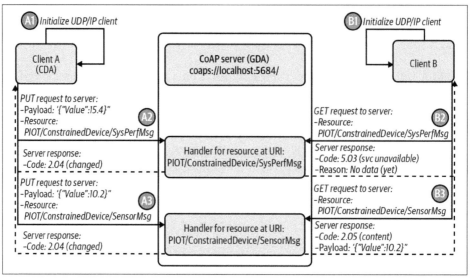

Figure 8-2. Two clients communicating via a CoAP server

Note the numbering of each step in Figure 8-2. Client A doesn't know or care about Client B. Nor does the server, for that matter. Client B and Client A are simply individual peer-to-peer connections to the same server, each issuing its respective requests for specific resources.

Figure 8-3 depicts a more involved CoAP request/response process using the observer pattern. Look at step B3— notice that it's now followed by two additional steps (B4 and B5). This is because Client B is telling the CoAP server it wants to *observe* the PIOT/ConstrainedDevice/SensorMsg resource and receive updates without asking again.

As with Figure 8-2, Figure 8-3 shows how each client connects and issues its own request method to achieve its desired outcome using PUT and GET initially, and then PUT and OBSERVE.

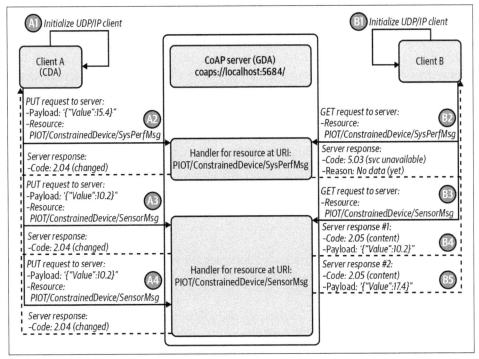

Figure 8-3. Two clients communicating via a CoAP server with OBSERVE enabled

There are many strategies for defining resource names for use in request/response environments. The MQTT topic–naming tips in Chapter 6 mostly apply to CoAP resource names as well.

 In addition to the CoAP URI scheme description from the specification,[3] you may also want to review the URI naming syntax specified in IETF RFC 3986 (*https://tools.ietf.org/html/rfc3986*) to ensure the resource names you create follow convention.

Unlike MQTT topic names, however, the leading "/" is always assumed and therefore is not needed when creating the resource name without the preceding URL protocol, host, and port information. In fact, depending on the library, the forward slash, if it exists, may need to be stripped from the beginning.

---

3 Shelby, Hartke, and Bormann, *CoAP*, 59–63.

Datagram Packets and the Structure of a CoAP Message

Like MQTT Control Packets, CoAP messages follow a compact binary format that contains a required header and other optional sections, including a payload. The format is defined such that each message can fit within a UDP datagram, up to its maximum packet size, including UDP/IP overhead. CoAP messages will always have a fixed header and up to three additional (but optional) components, as follows:

Fixed header (required: 4 bytes long)[4]

All messages have a fixed header, which represents:

- the version (currently always set to 01 binary)

- the message type (0: Confirmable, 1: Nonconfirmable, 2: Acknowledgment, or 3: Reset)

- the token length

- the request or response code (documented as "c.dd," such as "0.01," which represents a GET request, or "4.04," which represents a "not found" response)

- the message ID (used for message deduplication and for mapping Confirmable and Nonconfirmable messages)

Token (optional: 0...8 bytes)[5]

Although technically optional, the messages you'll create and process will include a token (which the library will include). This is necessary for mapping responses to their respective requests.

Options (optional: 0+ bytes) [6]

This field allows us to set various options, as specified by the CoAP Option Numbers Registry,[7] each of which has its own semantics (meaning, format, length of the value, and so on). One such option is "Content-Formats,"[8] which has its own registry and allows you to set an internet media type, which in turn dictates the format of the payload.

---

4 Shelby, Hartke, and Bormann, *CoAP*, 15–17.

5 Shelby, Hartke, and Bormann, *CoAP*, 16.

6 Shelby, Hartke, and Bormann, *CoAP*, 17–20.

7 Shelby, Hartke, and Bormann, *CoAP*, 89–91.

8 Shelby, Hartke, and Bormann, *CoAP*, 81–93.

Payload (optional: 0+ bytes)[9]

> If there is a payload included in the message, it will be preceded by a payload marker of 1 byte, set to 0xFF, immediately following any of the previous components. Note that the specification states that a payload market followed by a zero-length payload must be processed as an error.

Fortunately, the CoAP libraries we'll use hide much of this complexity. We can just focus on setting the flags that we care about and/or that must be customized. For example, we'll want to set the CON flag to enable message confirmation, ensuring we'll receive an acknowledgment that the message was processed.

As you've likely already noticed, the IETF RFC 7252 specification (*https://tools.ietf.org/html/rfc7252*) discusses the specifics associated with each message in significant detail. I'll discuss those relevant to the upcoming exercise and the context of the software we're going to start writing.

Regarding the implementation, I'll walk through the creation of two simple CoAP servers: one hosted within the GDA that will use the Eclipse Californium (*https://github.com/eclipse/californium*) CoAP Java library, and the other hosted within the CDA that will use either the aiocoap[10] CoAP Python library or the CoAPthon3[11] Python library. These open source libraries include test code and client libraries that I'll revisit in Chapter 9 when you build your corresponding CoAP client in either Java or Python.

Putting It All Together

What we'll do here is much like the design from Chapter 6 that uses MQTT. Here, instead of MQTT as the communications protocol connecting both applications, you'll use CoAP in a request/response setting.

A request is made for a resource, such as *PIOT/ConstrainedDevice/SensorMsg/TempSensor*, and must be interpreted by the server according to the specific type of request (e.g., GET, PUT, POST, or DELETE). So how are these resources managed within the CoAP server?

A CoAP server manages resources using *resource handlers* for each resource, where the resource handler will implement the supported request method(s)—that is, GET, PUT, POST, and/or DELETE (there are others as well, although this section will

---

9 Shelby, Hartke, and Bormann, *CoAP*, 17.

10 Amsüss, Christian and Wasilak, Maciej, "aiocoap: Python CoAP Library." Energy Harvesting Solutions, 2013–. *http://github.com/chrysn/aiocoap*.

11 Giacomo Tanganelli, Carlo Vallati, and Enzo Mingozzi, "CoAPthon: Easy Development of CoAP-Based IoT Applications with Python" (*https://doi.org/10.1109/WF-IoT.2015.7389028*), *2015 IEEE 2nd World Forum on Internet of Things (WF-IoT)* (Milan: IEEE, 2015), 63–68.

discuss only GET and PUT). You can think of a resource handler as a delegate of sorts —that is, a component to which the server passes an incoming request for further processing.

Each resource handler has a name and is actually part of a tree structure once added to the server. Recall the "/" separator from one of the previous examples: *PIOT/ ConstrainedDevice/SensorMsg*. In this case, there's only three levels, with the final level named "SensorMsg." This may be fine for some applications, but let's say you want to access a specific sensor. You can either replace "SensorMsg" with the sensor name (e.g., "TempSensor") or use "SensorMsg" as a category and add the sensor name to the end (e.g., *PIOT/ConstrainedDevice/SensorMsg/TempSensor*).

The specific naming approach will depend on your implementation. You'll see where this differential comes into play during the implementation exercise: resource names within the GDA's CoAP server may not require the additional granularity, whereas those within the CDA's CoAP server probably will.

Let's take a look at how this tree structure works with the last example: *PIOT/ ConstrainedDevice/SensorMsg/TempSensor*. Each level is separated by the "/" character, so there are actually four levels, with the fourth and final level, named "TempSensor," responsible for handling any request that's issued to the server for *PIOT/ ConstrainedDevice/SensorMsg/TempSensor*. Yet the others need to be in place for the invocation chain to succeed, which means each level must have a resource handler.

It's probably easiest to think of this as a tree structure, as shown in Figure 8-4.

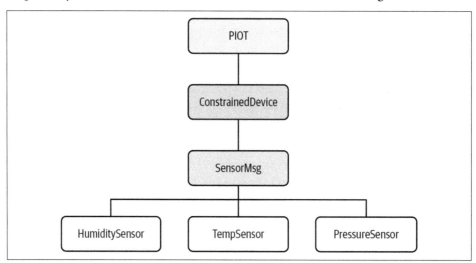

Figure 8-4. CoAP resource handler tree structure example

I've included a couple more leaf nodes to showcase the relationship between Temp-Sensor and SensorMsg, namely HumiditySensor and PressureSensor, but I'll focus only on TempSensor for now.

To make the TempSensor resource available via the server, the chain of resources must exist and must be named appropriately within the server as well. Depending on the library being used, the creation of this tree structure can be somewhat manually intensive. The good news is that the only real functionality required is for the resource handler representing the leaf nodes—again, our focus is on TempSensor. The SensorMsg, ConstrainedDevice, and PIOT resource handlers are basically empty implementations. In fact, the default implementation of a resource handler can simply return an error code or no data if the requester decides it wants to issue a GET against, say, *PIOT/ConstrainedDevice*.

Now that you have a handle on, well, resource handlers, you'll need to consider the server's design, and where within the Edge Tier it will be instanced. As a lightweight request/response protocol, you can choose whether to implement the CoAP server within the CDA or within the GDA.

Implement the server within the GDA
> The CDA will issue PUT requests to the GDA to submit the latest sensor readings and GET requests (via asynchronous resource observations or a scheduled poll) to retrieve actuator command updates.

Implement the server within the CDA
> The GDA will issue GET requests to the CDA (via asynchronous resource observations or a scheduled poll) to retrieve the latest sensor readings and PUT requests to update actuator values.

For example, the GET handler for a given resource must, in fact, retrieve a resource—or at least try to do so—and must be both safe and idempotent. We can technically run our GDA on a different system, but we'll continue to run both applications within our local network.

Figures 8-5 and 8-6 depict a logical view of this updated relationship, where the GDA is the CoAP server (Figure 8-5) or the CDA is the CoAP server (Figure 8-6). Notice that, in each case, the server is now integrated as part of the application and is not a separate process. This provides tremendous flexibility in handling requests but also introduces further complexity and implementation responsibilities on the part of the CDA or GDA application.

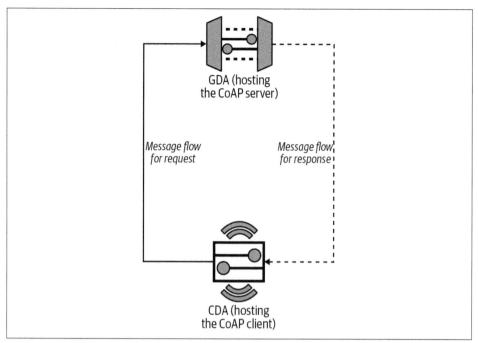

Figure 8-5. Notional interaction between a CoAP client (CDA) and a CoAP server (GDA)

 Building an effective server is a complicated business, even when using well-known specifications and existing open source libraries. This chapter will address some of the basics to help you get your CoAP server up and running, but it won't delve into all the nuances and edge cases a server must typically address, such as authentication, authorization, validation, and encryption. Chapter 10 will dig into some of these topics; however, it's your responsibility to ensure you're addressing the security and access requirements for your environment.

Of course, knowing the lightweight nature of CoAP, it's natural to ask: *why not build the server into the CDA instead?* You can! In fact, considering the protocol's support for GET and PUT specifically, there's natural alignment with sensor data retrieval (GET) and actuator command signaling (PUT).

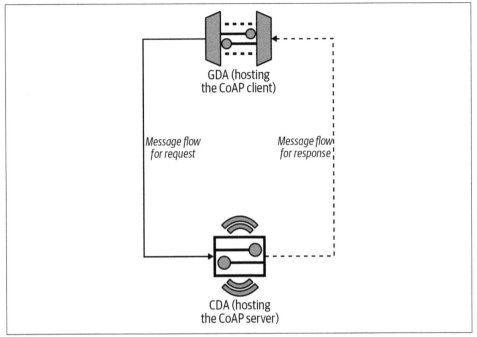

Figure 8-6. Notional interaction between a CoAP client (GDA) and a CoAP server (CDA)

It's your decision, and you can certainly go down this design path. The examples I'll provide in this chapter, and the requirements specified in the Kanban board, explore both approaches. Which one to choose? As with most things, it depends.

Hosting the CoAP server within the CDA allows you to use a resource naming convention that maps directly to each device and sensor/actuator hosted on that device. Since CoAP supports observability, you can configure the CoAP client (in this case, the GDA) to observe one or more resources on the CDA, and the CDA will notify the client whenever the resource is updated. Further, any actuation event can be triggered via a PUT or a POST. Your CDA will also have to manage incoming connections and decide how to throttle requests, which introduces additional technical and security challenges.

If you choose to host your CoAP server within the GDA, you may find this provides some additional flexibility in resource naming, where a more generic resource name can be used, and the payload content can be parsed to determine device or sensor specificity. It also permits the CDA—as the client—to determine when it should send sensor data to the GDA, which can be beneficial if the CDA's updates are sporadic and don't warrant the overhead of observation from a separate client. Finally, hosting the server within the GDA allows it to be implemented as an event aggregator, that is, as a central clearing house of sorts for incoming CoAP (and perhaps MQTT) messages—it simply awaits messages to be sent, slightly reducing its complexity.

 It goes without saying that any connected system—especially one that hosts a server that permits one or more connections—introduces additional networking and security complexities that are outside the scope of this book.

The series of cards (*https://oreil.ly/f9RLv*) related to this chapter provide some exercises you can implement that relate to creating a CoAP server in both the GDA and the CDA. However, the CoAP examples throughout this book (and specifically those in Chapters 8, 9, and Chapter 10, "Edge Integration") focus on the GDA as the CoAP server and on the CDA as the CoAP client.

Now, let's dig into the CoAP server programming exercises and build out this functionality.

Programming Exercises

Figure 8-7 provides a notional design diagram representing the GDA with a built-in CoAP server, with Figure 8-8 depicting the same but with the CDA providing the built-in CoAP server. Notice that the pattern for both is similar to what you've already seen (and implemented) with MQTT, except this time you'll be implementing a server within the GDA and CDA and using *resource handlers* to process the incoming requests.

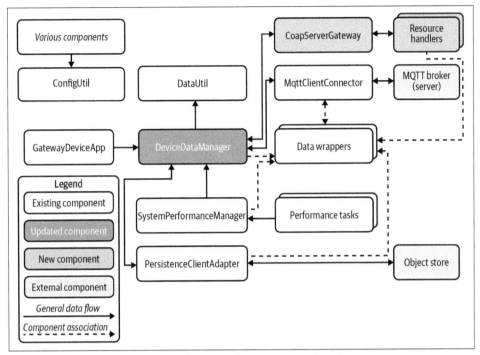

Figure 8-7. Gateway Device App design with an integrated CoAP server

If you choose to implement the CDA CoAP server exercises, Figure 8-8 depicts an example design, which looks strikingly similar to the GDA's design.

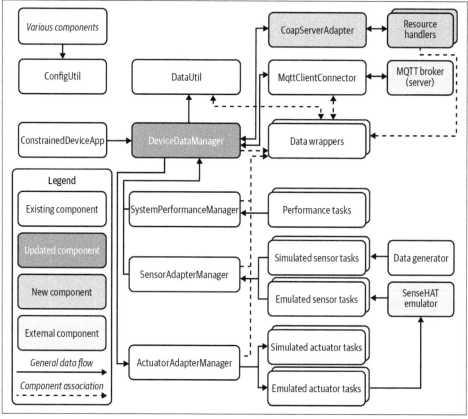

Figure 8-8. Constrained Device App design with an integrated CoAP server

While the core design and implementation principles are very similar between the GDA and the CDA, each depends on different open source libraries and will certainly have different detailed implementations. Again, the focus on this chapter will be on the GDA, with brief callouts to supplemental exercises pertaining to the CDA.

Add CoAP Server Functionality to the Gateway Device Application

Ensure your Java project has the Eclipse Californium CoAP libraries installed. If you followed the system configuration instructions and configured your *pom.xml* accordingly, this should already be available to your development environment or can be accessed via this book's java-components sample code repository referenced in Chapter 1.

Before you start developing your server, it's helpful to have access to some tools that you can use for testing. PIOT-CFG-08-001 (*https://oreil.ly/J4Hpb*) provides some very basic instructions on installing and using the Eclipse Foundation Californium (Cf) Tools project (*https://github.com/eclipse/californium.tools*).

As with each preceding chapter, be sure to follow the instructions listed in PIOT-GDA-08-000 (*https://oreil.ly/K7Vqr*) so you're starting with a new branch for this set of exercises.

Create the CoAP server abstraction and integrate it with DeviceDataManager

The first exercise, PIOT-GDA-08-001 (*https://oreil.ly/XhA67*), walks through the basic server implementation. It won't add all the features you'll need just yet but will get your server container in place so that it can create and manage the resource handlers that will come next.

The key design principle with the server for both the GDA and the CDA is centered on adaptation—the implementation for your server provides an adapter to an existing CoAP library, but with an API that's suited for the purposes of this exercise and future exercises. The goal is to enable the server to abstract the library functionality without reinventing the wheel. We're very fortunate to have access to excellent open source libraries that solve many implementation and integration challenges, so you can keep the server implementation relatively simple and still avoid unnecessary imports throughout the rest of your code.

 As a reminder, if you're using the sample code, you won't have to create a server adapter class—it already exists but has no real implementation. This will be the case for other components within this exercise as well.

The description of PIOT-GDA-08-001 (*https://oreil.ly/XhA67*) is self-explanatory, so let's take a look at the actions. Here's a summary of the implementation details specified within the card:

- Create (or edit) the `CoapServerGateway` class, add the relevant class-scoped variables, and create the initialization logic.
- Create accessor methods—start with the setter for `IDataMessageListener`.
- Add resource handler registration functionality.
- Integrate `CoapServerGateway` with `DeviceDataManager`.

While these appear very simple on the surface, there's some nuance to each action that is worthy of further exploration. Let's break things down.

The first is straightforward, of course—create your adapter class named `CoapServer Gateway` within the `programmingtheiot.gda.connection` package following the instructions listed in the card. The only implementation decision is to either inherit from CoapServer (provided by the californium-core package) or instance it within the class. I'd suggest the latter option, as it will allow you to fully control your adapter interface and simply delegate to the server instance.

As part of your adapter implementation, you'll need (at least) two class-scoped variables: one to reference CoapServer (assuming you're using an adapter pattern and not deriving from the class) and the other to reference IDataMessageListener. The former will reference the californium-core server instance, while the latter will be an instance of your DeviceDataManager. Recall that DeviceDataManager is the orchestration "engine" for all of your GDA functionality and will be passed into some of your resource handlers as the callback that will handle incoming SensorData and SystemPerformanceData messages from the CDA.

When you create your constructor, decide whether you want to pass in a reference to IDataMessageListener when CoapServerGateway is instantiated, and identify any other parameters that might be useful. For this exercise, you won't need any extras, but feel free to update your design to meet your specific needs.

As for accessor methods, you can create a setter for IDataMessageListener. If you pass the reference into the constructor, this isn't really needed; however, it's good to have it in place in case you decide to change your instancing strategy later.

Add a resource handler registration method. While this will be public facing, it will generally be used internally only. That's because the server should have enough knowledge about its environment to know which resource handlers need to be instanced and when. Of course, this can be managed externally as well—for instance, via the DeviceDataManager. This method design gives you the option of doing either (or both). Here's one example signature to consider:

```
public void addResource(
  ResourceNameEnum name, String endName, Resource resource)
{
    // TODO: implement this
}
```

ResourceNameEnum contains predefined resource (or topic) names that you can use throughout this project. These predefined names may not be granular enough to support all users of the server. To maintain some flexibility with naming granularity, the preceding signature example includes the endName parameter, which can simply be appended to the ResourceNameEnum name (preceded by a forward slash, of course) to provide that detail. If the parameter is null or empty, you can simply ignore it.

Hardcoding names is rarely a good idea; however, every device within the Edge Tier that may want to communicate with your CoAP GDA server will have to know the resource it's interested in using. Using a common naming strategy across all resources is critical to supporting this objective, which is one of the reasons Resour ceNameEnum exists in both the GDA and the CDA source tree. As shown in the addResource() signature, you can add an endName, but then your CDA instances will also need to know about it— either dynamically through discovery or by using a preconfigured naming convention. Otherwise, the resource won't be found, and your server will not provide much value.

There's not much left to your server adapter. The penultimate step is to initialize the CoapServer, which is essentially one line of code. However, I'd suggest you create a private initServer() method to be invoked by the constructor (as shown in PIOT-GDA-08-001 (*https://oreil.ly/XhA67*)) —you can also use it to handle the creation of all relevant resource handlers.

For now, it will consist of only a few lines of code; however, once the resource handler classes are defined, it will require more work. Also, in Chapter 10, I'll briefly delve into DTLS, which provides encryption support for CoAP messaging, although it's outside the scope for this book.

The last steps for this module are simply to add the startServer() and stop Server() methods. These are very simple and just delegate to the start() and stop() methods already implemented by CoapServer. You can choose to handle exceptions that may get thrown, as well as handle any additional logic you decide to add later.

Finally, review the last few steps of this card, in which you integrate CoapServerGate way into DeviceDataManager. You can add a new flag to the *PiotConfig.props* file under the GatewayDevice section called "enableCoapServer = True" and parse it within the DeviceDataManager constructor to determine whether CoapServerGate way should be initialized and started or stopped via the startManager() and stopMan ager() methods.

There are no tests for this exercise since there's not much to test at this point. Before moving on to the next step, however, it may help to review a detailed design diagram —in UML—for the current state of the GDA. Figure 8-9 depicts the notional UML for the functionality that will be included in this chapter.

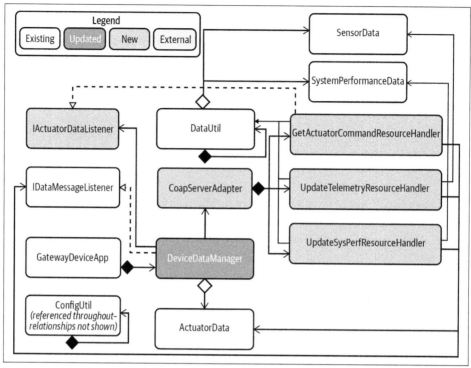

Figure 8-9. Gateway Device App UML with an integrated CoAP server

I've highlighted the new or modified components according to the legend provided in the diagram and removed many of the other components that you implemented in previous exercises. There are five new components, one of which you've just implemented (CoapServerGateway). Three are resource handlers, and the last one is an interface.

You'll implement two resource handlers in the next exercise, and the last resource handler (along with its interface) in the exercise that follows. While there is a semblance of complexity in this design, if you trace it through, you'll see how CoAP messages will flow through the application.

Notice that the two "Update" resource handlers (which you'll implement next) are responsible for receiving SensorData and SystemPerformanceData. These will arrive in JSON format (remember Chapter 5?) from the CDA and will need to be validated and instanced as their associated data containers. Once this is complete, each handler needs a way to send the newly instanced data container to the orchestration manager —that is, the instance of IDataMessageListener (which will be DeviceDataManager).

Once DeviceDataManager has the information, it can then decide what to do next: store the information locally (again, from Chapter 5), send it up to the cloud for storage and processing (which I'll discuss in Chapter 11), or determine whether an action should be taken.

That last decision—whether to trigger an action—is why the "Get" resource handler exists. It implements the `IActuatorDataListener` interface, which `DeviceDataMan ager` will reference. This allows `DeviceDataManager` to pass an `ActuatorData` message to the resource handler. Implementation details aside, the CDA will be asking this resource for actuation commands, essentially completing our circle of Edge Tier life.

Ready to move on? Let's create all the resource handlers described in PIOT-GDA-08-002 (*https://oreil.ly/zdCae*) and PIOT-GDA-08-003 (*https://oreil.ly/cZBvw*).

Create resource handlers to support data update requests

Recall that resource handlers provide the implementation of the GET, PUT, POST, and DELETE requests for a named resource. In this exercise, you'll be implementing the PUT request only (you can certainly implement the others if you'd like, although this exercise will focus on the PUT method, as the others aren't relevant for the work I'm about to discuss).

Since the GDA is hosting the CoAP server, the CDA needs a way to send in its `Sensor Data` and `SystemPerformanceData` updates. As such, your CoAP server will need resource handlers that can provide this capability—one to process `SensorData` updates, and the other to process `SystemPerformanceData` updates.

PIOT-GDA-08-002 (*https://oreil.ly/zdCae*) explains the requirements for each resource handler—`UpdateSystemPerformanceResourceHandler` and `UpdateTeleme tryResourceHandler` (or simply `UpdateSensorDataResourceHandler`, if you'd prefer); you'll see that their implementations are nearly identical, with only very minor differences. The java-components source repository includes a class named `Generi cCoapResourceHandler` within the *programmingtheiot.cda.connection.handlers* package. You can use this as a template for your two new resource handlers.

Take a look at PIOT-GDA-08-002 (*https://oreil.ly/zdCae*) in detail. The key activities include the following:

- Make sure each resource handler is derived from `CoapResource`.
- The constructor should accept a reference to `ResourceNameEnum` (be sure to store this in a class-scoped variable—it will be needed when valid PUT requests are processed).
- Include a setter for `IDataMessageListener`—or, more conveniently, include a parameter in the constructor to set an `IDataMessageListener` reference (be sure to store the reference in a class-scoped variable).

- Add the PUT handler functionality.

The last bullet, where you add the PUT functionality, is where much of the interesting work occurs. Let's review one implementation solution (which is the handlePUT() implementation for UpdateSystemPerformanceResourceHandler):

```java
@Override
public void handlePUT(CoapExchange context)
{
  ResponseCode code = ResponseCode.NOT_ACCEPTABLE;

  context.accept();

  if (this.dataMsgListener != null) {
    try {
      String jsonData = new String(context.getRequestPayload());

      SystemPerformanceData sysPerfData =
        DataUtil.getInstance().jsonToSystemPerformanceData(jsonData);

      // TODO: Choose the following (but keep it idempotent!)
      //   1) Check MID to see if it's repeated for some reason
      //      - optional, as the underlying lib should handle this
      //   2) Cache the previous update - is the PAYLOAD repeated?
      //   2) Delegate the data check to this.dataMsgListener

      this.dataMsgListener.handleSystemPerformanceMessage(
        ResourceNameEnum.CDA_SYSTEM_PERF_MSG_RESOURCE, sysPerfData);

      code = ResponseCode.CHANGED;
    } catch (Exception e) {
      _Logger.warning(
        "Failed to handle PUT request. Message: " +
        e.getMessage());

      code = ResponseCode.BAD_REQUEST;
    }
  } else {
    _Logger.info(
      "No callback listener for request. Ignoring PUT.");

    code = ResponseCode.CONTINUE;
  }

  String msg =
    "Update system perf data request handled: " + super.getName();

  context.respond(code, msg);
}
```

Your implementation of handlePUT() needs to override the base class implementation, which will return an unimplemented response back to the requester, hence the @Override annotation. You'll also need to ensure you've imported the classes for SystemPerformanceData, DataUtil, and ResourceNameEnum.

Within the method, you'll need to accept the message (via context.accept()), parse the CoapExchange message—which contains everything you need to know about the CoAP request that the server handed off to this method—and then decide what to do with it.

Data and request validation is critically important within an IoT environment, and there are excellent books that delve into this topic in much more detail than I can.

The CoapExchange parameter (named "context") contains the payload, which should carry the JSON data representing either a SystemPerformanceData or a SensorData message. You won't know until you parse it, because there's really nothing preventing the client from sending something completely different, like a plain-text message that says "hey, how are you?"

One way to do this is to wrap the data conversion within a try/catch block. The conversion itself will be handled by DataUtil (which you implemented in Chapter 5). On success, you'll end up with your data container instance—a reference to either SystemPerformanceData (UpdateSystemPerformanceResourceHandler) or Sensor Data (UpdateTelemetryResourceHandler).

This next step is important: what will you do with the converted data? Recall that PUT requests must be idempotent, which means the same request issued with the same data should NOT change the internal state of the object (as the request would technically be adding a new one, not updating an existing one). First, is the request itself repeated? Deduplication is part of the spec, so we shouldn't have to concern ourselves with a duplicate request. But what if the client sends the same thing as a separate request? One solution is to compare the incoming data with the previously cached data's timestamp to avoid storing redundant copies of data that may negatively impact your downstream analysis.

 All of this validation begs the question: Should you implement a PUT or a POST? They result in similar status code responses, so for the purposes of this exercise, either can be used. I've opted to use the PUT request, although you may find POST is more appropriate for your needs.

Depending on your decision logic, some of this validation process may be best delegated to the IDataMessageListener callback; however, bear in mind that the client is expecting a valid response code that represents the action the server did or didn't take. So if the validation is delegated, you'll need to also handle any return value from the IDataMessageListener callback and use that to inform which response code is set.

 The callbacks defined in IDataMessageListener and implemented in DeviceDataManager—handleSystemPerformanceMessage() and handleSensorMessage()—require the ResourceNameEnum for internal routing, so you need to keep a reference to the ResourceNameEnum that was used as part of the name for the resource handler.

If the conversion fails or throws an exception, decide whether logging an error message makes sense (for debugging, yes, but recognize that a flood of bad requests can quickly fill your local log file storage), and set the response code to Response Code.BAD_REQUEST (or similar).

On success, simply call the respond() method on the context, passing in the response code and the response payload, which can technically be anything you'd like, although IETF RFC 7252 (*https://tools.ietf.org/html/rfc7252*) does provide some guidance, depending on the request method chosen. For instance, if you choose to implement POST, and the result is the creation of a new resource (which PUT also supports), the server should return the new URI for that resource.[12]

Does this mean you need to change your design? Nope. Recall that the resource names (and, once registered with the CoAP server, their respective URIs) are predefined as part of the server initialization process.

To test this new functionality, you can follow the instructions specified in the Tests section of PIOT-GDA-08-002 (*https://oreil.ly/zdCae*). This will show you one option for creating your own integration test to verify your PUT logic works as expected.

If you'd like to add even more logic to your CoAP server and handlers, see "Additional Exercises" at the end of this chapter for further ideas on enhanced CoAP server functionality.

Create resource handlers to support data retrieval requests

In the previous exercise, you learned how to create data ingest points for the CDA to pass its generated data to the GDA using CoAP resource handlers specific to each data type—SensorData and SystemPerformanceData. In this exercise, you'll build a resource handler that allows the CDA to retrieve ActuatorData (in JSON format) from the GDA.

---

12 Shelby, Hartke, and Bormann, *CoAP* (*https://tools.ietf.org/html/rfc7252*), 47.

PIOT-GDA-08-003 (*https://oreil.ly/cZBvw*) specifies the requirements for this handler; you can model it after the GenericCoapResourceHandler class in the pro grammingtheiot.gda.connection.handlers package and name it GetActuatorCom mandResourceHandler, which will look similar to the previous handler implementations. The main differences are as follows:

- It will implement the IActuatorDataListener interface (which is provided in the java-components repository within the programmingtheiot.common package).

- It will need to store a class-scoped reference to an ActuatorData instance, which will be set by the onActuatorDataUpdate() method defined in IActuatorData Listener.

- It will support observability, meaning the client (CDA) can register for updates to the resource and be notified when an actuator command is available. You'll need to call super.setObservable(true) in the constructor.

- It will implement GET only.

First, let's take a look at one way to implement the IActuatorDataListener interface. It defines a single method that will be used by the DeviceDataManager to notify the resource handler when a new ActuatorData message is available:

```
public boolean onActuatorDataUpdate(ActuatorData data)
{
  if (data != null) {
    if (this.actuatorData == null) {
      this.actuatorData = new ActuatorData();
    }

    this.actuatorData.updateData(data);

    // notify all connected clients
    super.changed();

    _Logger.fine(
      "Actuator data updated for URI: " + super.getURI() +
      ": Data value = " + this.actuatorData.getValue());

    return true;
  }

  return false;
}
```

Why? Recall that DeviceDataManager is essentially the glue that holds all of the GDA's workflows together. Since it will potentially receive and disseminate actuation commands (generated internally or via the Cloud Tier), it will also need a way to pass these commands back to the CDA. This mechanism can be partly implemented through the onActuatorDataUpdate() method just described.

Since this method will be invoked by the DeviceDataManager instance, its interface will need to be properly defined and exposed by its implementing resource handler (via IActuatorDataListener, which the resource handler implements, and DeviceDataManager references). The IDataMessageListener interface, which DeviceDataManager implements, defines a method which CoapServerGateway will use to pass the IActuatorDataListener instance (the resource handler) to DeviceDataManager, thereby completing the callback handshake workflow circuit. You'll see in the next exercise how to implement this within CoapServerGateway.

Once the handshake process is implemented, the actual data processing logic is relatively straight-forward—the data is first validated, then copied into the existing (or newly created) class-scoped instance of ActuatorData, and finally passed back to the client via a call to the changed() method (which notifies all observing clients). Since changed() is implemented by the super class, there's nothing left to do except log a debug message and return the status.

Although this one method handles some of the key requirements for this exercise, we're not yet done. Let's implement the GET request next. Here's one way to do this:

```
@Override
public void handleGET(CoapExchange context)
{
  String      jsonData = "";
  ResponseCode code    = ResponseCode.NOT_ACCEPTABLE;

  context.accept();

  // TODO: validate the request

  try {
    jsonData =
      DataUtil.getInstance().actuatorDataToJson(
        this.actuatorData);
    code = ResponseCode.CONTENT;
  } catch (Exception e) {
    _Logger.warning(
      "Failed to handle PUT request. Message: " + e.getMessage());

    code = ResponseCode.INTERNAL_SERVER_ERROR;
  }

  context.respond(code, jsonData);
}
```

This implementation looks very similar to the handlePUT() method from the previous exercise; the main difference is the payload and response code (Response Code.CONTENT, if successful).

You can (and should) add further validation of the request as well. While I've implemented only one actuation handler, you can create unique handlers for each type of actuation if they require special handling on the server side. For the purposes of this exercise, one handler type is actually sufficient, as the CDA will only need to register for actuation events for temperature adjustment.

While the coding for this handler is relatively simple, the complexity associated with this handler and the others is really in the sequencing of instance creation and registration with the DeviceDataManager. With all handlers now implemented, let's move on and explore how this sequencing will occur.

Create the resource handlers within the Gateway Device App CoAP server

The final exercise for the GDA in this chapter, described in PIOT-GDA-08-004 (*https://oreil.ly/yUsv6*), involves updates to two classes: CoapServerGateway and DeviceDataManager, with the latter being very minor, so we'll start there.

The first category of actions in the card is simply to implement the setActuatorData Listener(String name, IActuatorDataListener listener) method within DeviceDataManager. This requires a class-scoped variable of type IActuatorDataListener to be declared within DeviceDataManager. Once this is created, simply set it to the listener parameter.

If you plan to create multiple IActuatorDataListener instances (via two or more resource handlers that operate on ActuatorData GET requests), you may want to use the name parameter as a key and store each instance in a Map. This isn't necessary for the purposes of this exercise, but it may be helpful for your own implementation.

The next and last category of actions is to complete the CoapServerGateway implementation, which involves creating and registering the resource handlers that you created earlier.

PIOT-GDA-08-004 (*https://oreil.ly/yUsv6*) breaks this down into a number of steps that can be summarized as follows:

- Create all required handler instances within the initServer() method, and call it either from the startServer() method (before actually starting the CoAP server) or from the constructor.
- Implement the addResource() method, which will perform simple parameter validation and then delegate its work to another method responsible for creating the resource hierarchy.

- Implement the resource hierarchy method that will process each resource instance, expanding its name into the appropriate hierarchy of generic resources, with the actual resource at the very end of the hierarchy, and finally, adding the top-level resource to the server's root resource.

One way to understand how the resource handler chain will be created is to use a simple coding example:

```
CoapResource top =
    new CoapResource("PIOT").add(
        new CoapResource("ConstrainedDevice").add(
            new UpdateSystemPerformanceResourceHandler(
                "SystemPerfMsg")));

this.coapServer.add(top);
```

You can use this approach for all your resource handlers, of course—it's certainly the most straightforward! The other approach is to parse the string representing the resource name (e.g., *PIOT/ConstrainedDevice/SystemPerfMsg*) and create the resource chain dynamically. While the code will not be nearly as clean or as easy to follow as the preceding snippet, it does provide tremendous flexibility, as you can add more resource names to `ResourceNameEnum` to suit your project needs.

Notice that each level contains only one hierarchy level and name, with the final level containing the specific resource handler designated to handle the required work. Hence, "SystemPerfMsg" is the name for the resource handler `UpdateSystemPerfor manceResourceHandler`, which implements the logic to add a new `SystemPerforman ceData` data object to the server.

Let's assume the latter path is best and work through that implementation. First, you'll need to create all the handler instances, and register the `GetActuatorComman dResourceHandler` with the `DeviceDataManager`. The `initServer()` method will handle this and will call `addResource()` whenever a resource has been instanced.

Here's a slightly trimmed down version of `initServer()`, which should provide enough detail on how each resource handler type is created and registered; feel free to add the others on your own (e.g., `UpdateTelemetryResourceHandler`, and any other custom resource handlers you implement). An updated version of this can be found in PIOT-GDA-08-004 (*https://oreil.ly/yUsv6*):

```
private void initServer()
{
  this.coapServer = new CoapServer();

  GetActuatorCommandResourceHandler getActuatorCmdResourceHandler=
    new GetActuatorCommandResourceHandler(
      ResourceNameEnum.CDA_ACTUATOR_CMD_RESOURCE);
```

```
  if (this.dataMsgListener != null) {
    this.dataMsgListener.setActuatorDataListener(
      null, // not needed for now
      getActuatorCmdResourceHandler);
  }

  addResource(
    ResourceNameEnum.CDA_ACTUATOR_CMD_RESOURCE,
    null, // not needed for now
    getActuatorCmdResourceHandler);

  // TODO: implement the telemetry resource handler(s)

  UpdateSystemPerformanceResourceHandler
    updateSysPerfResourceHandler =
      new UpdateSystemPerformanceResourceHandler(
        ResourceNameEnum.CDA_SYSTEM_PERF_MSG_RESOURCE,
        this.dataMsgListener);

  addResource(
    ResourceNameEnum.CDA_SYSTEM_PERF_MSG_RESOURCE,
    null, // not needed for now
    updateSystemPerformanceResourceHandler);
}
```

The `addResource()` implementation is just the public-facing interface to the server for adding new resources and provides some basic validation of the parameter values. It delegates the resource hierarchy creation logic as follows:

```
public void addResource(
  ResourceNameEnum resourceType,
  String endName,
  Resource resource)
{
  // TODO: while not needed for this exercise, you may want to
  // include the endName parameter as part of this resource
  // chain creation process

  if (resourceType != null && resource != null) {
    // break out the hierarchy of names and build the resource
    // handler generation(s) as needed, checking if any parent
    // already exists - and if so, add to the existing resource
    createAndAddResourceChain(resourceType, resource);
  }
}
```

And finally, we come to the resource chain hierarchy creation method, of which only the signature is shown (due to the length of the method):

```
createAndAddResourceChain(
  ResourceNameEnum resource, Resource resource)
```

A full sample implementation is posted within the card—just scroll down to the resource tree creation action in PIOT-GDA-08-004 (*https://oreil.ly/yUsv6*).

Finally, your GDA CoAP server is nearing completion! Run the tests at the end of the card as indicated, and you should see log output similar to that posted in the card. Here's a small sample of the end of the log file my test generated:

```
Feb 22, 2021 6:54:57 PM
programmingtheiot.part03.integration.connection.CoapServerGatewayTest
testRunSimpleCoapServerGatewayIntegration
INFO:  --> WebLink: /PIOT/ConstrainedDevice/ActuatorCmd. Attributes:
org.eclipse.californium.core.server.resources.ResourceAttributes@32eebfca
Feb 22, 2021 6:54:57 PM
programmingtheiot.part03.integration.connection.CoapServerGatewayTest
testRunSimpleCoapServerGatewayIntegration
INFO:  --> WebLink: /PIOT/ConstrainedDevice/SensorMsg. Attributes:
org.eclipse.californium.core.server.resources.ResourceAttributes@4e718207
Feb 22, 2021 6:54:57 PM
programmingtheiot.part03.integration.connection.CoapServerGatewayTest
testRunSimpleCoapServerGatewayIntegration
INFO:  --> WebLink: /PIOT/ConstrainedDevice/SystemPerfMsg. Attributes:
org.eclipse.californium.core.server.resources.ResourceAttributes@1d371b2d
Feb 22, 2021 6:56:57 PM org.eclipse.californium.core.CoapServer stop
INFO: Stopping server
Feb 22, 2021 6:56:57 PM org.eclipse.californium.core.network.CoapEndpoint stop
INFO: Stopping endpoint at address 0.0.0.0/0.0.0.0:5683
```

With your CoAP server functionality in place, your GDA now supports two different IoT protocols—MQTT and CoAP. Congratulations! Be sure to commit and merge your code as indicated in PIOT-GDA-08-100 (*https://oreil.ly/JN5bT*).

If you'd like to add CoAP server functionality to your CDA, read on for a brief introduction to adding this capability. Otherwise, feel free to move on to Chapter 9, where I'll discuss integrating a CoAP client into your CDA so it can interact with your GDA server.

Add CoAP Server Functionality to the Constrained Device Application (Optional)

While incorporating a CoAP server within your CDA lies generally outside the scope of this book, you can do so either by building your own CoAP library by implementing the IETF RFC 7252 specification (*https://tools.ietf.org/html/rfc7252*) or by using an existing open source library. The examples I discuss in the programming exercises for this chapter (*https://oreil.ly/f9RLv*) focus on two open source libraries: aiocoap,[13] which relies upon asyncio, and CoAPthon3.[14]

The library you choose is up to you, of course, and all the Chapter 8 numbered cards provide some simple integration examples for the two I mentioned.

If you followed the system configuration instructions and configured your Python development environment accordingly, you should already have both libraries available. PIOT-CFG-08-002 (*https://oreil.ly/XitVV*) provides additional documentation links that may be helpful. I found that a thorough review of the online documentation and open source code repositories was useful in my own study.

Much like with the GDA's CoAP server implementation, a CDA CoAP server will need to do the following:

- Create the CoAP server abstraction (PIOT-CDA-08-001 (*https://oreil.ly/K3u9T*)).
- Create the resource handler(s) to support data update requests (PIOT-CDA-08-002 (*https://oreil.ly/r5Xz5*)).
- Create the resource handler(s) to support data retrieval requests (PIOT-CDA-08-003 (*https://oreil.ly/R1Mzf*)).
- Create and manage the resource handlers within the CDA's CoAP server abstraction (PIOT-CDA-08-004 (*https://oreil.ly/6cgje*)).

If you decide to go down this path, be sure to follow the instructions listed in PIOT-CDA-08-000 (*https://oreil.ly/j93KW*) before implementing your server.

A brief summary of the Constrained Device Application's CoAP server abstraction

As with the GDA's implementation, PIOT-CDA-08-001 (*https://oreil.ly/K3u9T*) walks through the basic server implementation, which includes details on how to manage the start and stop process using both referenced open source libraries.

As with the GDA's first exercise in this chapter, there are no existing tests specific to this exercise since there's not much to test at this point. However, you may want to create your own test, just to verify that the server can start and, perhaps after a minute or so, stop cleanly.

Before moving into a review of the remaining steps, it's helpful to review a notional UML design diagram to depict the design differences with the GDA (as shown in Figure 8-10).

---

13 Amsüss, Christian and Wasilak, Maciej, "aiocoap: Python CoAP Library" (*http://github.com/chrysn/aiocoap*).

14 Tanganelli, Vallati, and Mingozzi, "CoAPthon" (*https://doi.org/10.1109/WF-IoT.2015.7389028*).

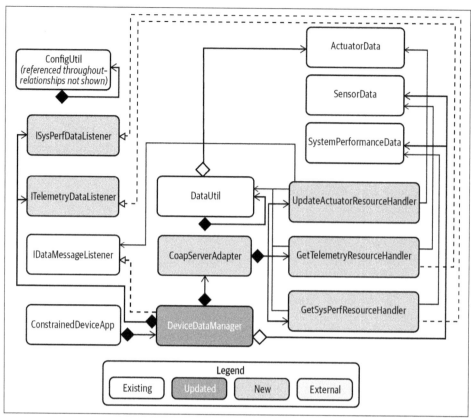

Figure 8-10. Constrained Device App UML with an integrated CoAP server

The modified component is the same as with the GDA—DeviceDataManager. The new functionality is slightly different, aside from the CoapServerAdapter. You've probably noticed the name change from the GDA—this is to avoid any potential confusion from naming a CDA component as a "gateway."

The main difference, however, is with the resource handler names and implementations. The GDA's CoAP server and associated resource handlers are designed to manage incoming SensorData and SystemPerformanceData PUT updates from the CDA, and ActuatorData GET requests from the CDA. The CDA's CoAP server does the opposite—it will need to permit SensorData and SystemPerformanceData GET requests from the GDA, and incoming ActuatorData PUT updates from the GDA.

The single "Update" resource handler (UpdateActuatorResourceHandler) is responsible for receiving an ActuatorData message. This will arrive in JSON format (see Chapter 5)—this time from the GDA—and of course must be validated and instanced as its associated data containers.

Let me again stress the importance of building a secure resource handler and server in general, especially when dealing with incoming actuation events. While doing so is outside the scope of this book, you will need to ensure that the incoming connection is secure, the request is authenticated and authorized, and the data is valid and appropriate.

Once incoming data validation and conversion is complete, the handler will need a way to send the newly instanced data container to the orchestration manager—that is, the instance of IDataMessageListener (which will be DeviceDataManager). Once DeviceDataManager has the information, it can then decide what to do next: pass it to the ActuatorAdapterManager (which should perform additional validation), or log the message if DeviceDataManager determines the data shouldn't be processed.

The "Get" resource handlers exist to provide access to SensorData and SystemPerformanceData instances generated by the CDA. These can also be implemented to support observability, which allows the GDA to simply request updates from each resource when available (or it can poll the resources at regular intervals itself[15]). The GetTelemetryResourceHandler will implement (or rather inherit from) the ITelemetryDataListener class, and the GetSystemPerformanceResourceHandler will derive from the ISystemPerformanceDataListener class.

Both handlers will need to be referenced with the DeviceDataManager class. IDataMessageListener provides an interface for setting these references: setSystemPerformanceDataListener and setTelemetryDataListener, respectively.

The implementation within DeviceDataManager should account for multiple ITelemetryDataListener instances, although there will be only one ISystemPerformanceDataListener instance within the CDA.

I've shortened the names for some components in the UML for rendering purposes. For example, ISystemPerformanceDataListener is shown as ISysPerfDataListener.

The online exercises provide further detail on implementation options, of course, and are regularly reviewed and updated (as needed), so be sure to check back for updates. If you choose to implement the CDA exercises, be sure to commit and merge your

---

15 Depending on your deployment approach, polling may or may not be a good idea, as it can be difficult to manage and hard to scale.

branches back into the primary branch by following the instructions in PIOT-GDA-08-100 (*https://oreil.ly/JN5bT*).

If you've worked through all the exercises in Chapter 8—congratulations! At this point, you should technically have a functioning CoAP server within (at least) the GDA, and possibly within the CDA as well.

Additional Exercises

There's no end to the new capabilities you may want to add to your CoAP servers. Here are just three.

Add More Resource Handlers

This is relatively straightforward, since you now have practice implementing a few resource handlers in both Java and Python. See if you can identify others that might be relevant to your needs and add them to your server. Write a custom resource handler for each and test it out using the command-line client discussed in PIOT-CFG-08-001 (*https://oreil.ly/J4Hpb*).

Add a Custom Discovery Service

CoAP supports resource discovery via the issuance of a specially formatted GET request. You can create your own using a separate resource name and resource handler. The resource handler queries the server for all existing resource names and returns a custom JSON response with the resource names and other relevant metadata that a client may need to issue requests (assuming you trust the clients issuing the request in the first place).

Add Dynamic Resource Creation

You may recall the brief discussion in the previous section on PUT versus POST and the integration of a CoAP server within the GDA. For this exercise, add POST functionality to your `SensorData` and `SystemPerformanceData` resource handler, and see if you can dynamically create a new resource handler instance and register it with the same naming prefix as the existing one (e.g., *PIOT/ConstrainedDevice/SensorMsg*), but appended with the name of the sensor itself (e.g., *PIOT/ConstrainedDevice/SensorMsg/TempSensor*). Once this is complete, return the new URI to the client. In Chapter 9, you'll implement a CoAP client, which you may want to use to verify this new (but again, optional) feature.

Conclusion

In this chapter, you learned about the CoAP protocol and how you can implement a CoAP server within your Gateway Device Application. Optionally, you learned about some of the design considerations for implementing a CoAP server within your Constrained Device Application and may have even implemented the server in both applications. This chapter provided the groundwork for communicating between both applications using CoAP. To complete this circle, you'll need a CoAP client, of course, which will be discussed in Chapter 9.

CoAP Client Integration

Building a Request/Response Client Using CoAP

Request is received.
Send the notification.
Who is listening?

Fundamental concepts: Create a CoAP client in Python for your CDA to communicate with the GDA's CoAP server.

This chapter continues our exploration of CoAP with a discussion of the client implementation—specifically, within the CDA, with some guidance on building a CoAP client within your GDA as well.

What You'll Learn in This Chapter

Chapter 8 discussed the basics of CoAP and developing a server hosted within the GDA, with an optional set of exercises enabling a CoAP server within the CDA. This chapter focuses on building a CoAP client that will be part of the CDA, with optional exercises enabling the GDA to support a CoAP client. If you implement the exercises in this chapter, you'll learn how to integrate CoAP client functionality into your CDA (and optionally into your GDA) so it can communicate with the GDA's CoAP server.

Design Concepts

Let's quickly review the two client connection examples discussed in Chapter 8, with some minor modifications to each example. We'll discuss them in more detail in this chapter—that is, the CDA as the CoAP client and the GDA as the CoAP server.

Example A-1: The CDA writes telemetry updates to the GDA's CoAP server.

1. The CDA will write new data to a single resource hosted within the GDA's CoAP server. This resource's name will be PIOT/ConstrainedDevice/SensorMsg.

2. The CDA will connect to the resource at *coap://localhost:5683/PIOT/Constrained-Device/SensorMsg* hosted by the GDA and issue a PUT request with a Sensor Data instance converted to JSON as its payload.

3. On success, the server will respond with a response code indicating the resource was CREATED or CHANGED. On failure, the client will need to handle the exception or unsuccessful response code and react accordingly.

Example A-2: The CDA observes actuator commands on the GDA's CoAP server.

1. The CDA will monitor an existing resource for updates via an OBSERVE request (which is essentially a slightly modified GET). The resource's name will be PIOT/ConstrainedDevice/ActuatorCmd.

2. The CDA will connect to the resource at *coap://localhost:5683/PIOT/Constrained-Device/ActuatorCmd* and issue an OBSERVE request.

3. The GDA will respond whenever it has an ActuatorData instance—in the form of a JSON payload—that needs to be sent to the CDA. If no update is available, neither application takes any action.

The GDA hosts both resources and is already designed to support these request types —PUT for Example A-1 and OBSERVE (GET) for Example A-2.

What if we want to switch roles and have the CDA host our resources while the GDA issues the requests? As discussed in Chapter 8, this is certainly feasible, and you may have opted to build a CoAP server as part of your CDA when you worked through the optional exercises.

Let's examine two similar examples, but with the CDA acting as the server and the GDA as the client.

Example B-1: The GDA writes actuator commands to the CDA's CoAP server.

1. The GDA will write new data to a single resource hosted within the CDA's CoAP server. This resource's name will be *PIOT/ConstrainedDevice/ActuatorCmd*.

2. The GDA will connect to the resource at *coap://localhost:5683/PIOT/Constrained-Device/ActuatorCmd* hosted by the CDA and issue a PUT request with an `Actua torData` instance converted to JSON as its payload.

3. On success, the server will respond with a response code indicating the resource was CREATED or CHANGED. On failure, the client will need to handle the exception or unsuccessful response code and react accordingly.

Example B-2: The GDA observes telemetry updates on the CDA's CoAP server.

1. The GDA will monitor an existing resource for updates via an OBSERVE request (which is essentially a slightly modified GET). The resource's name will be PIOT/ConstrainedDevice/SensorMsg/TempSensor.

2. The GDA will connect to the resource at *coap://localhost:5683/PIOT/Constrained-Device/SensorMsg/TempSensor* hosted by the CDA and issue an OBSERVE request.

3. The CDA will respond whenever it has a `SensorData` instance—in the form of a JSON payload—that needs to be sent to the GDA. If no update is available, no action is taken by either application.

Figures 9-1 (CDA CoAP client) and 9-2 (GDA CoAP client) provide a high-level design view of each application.

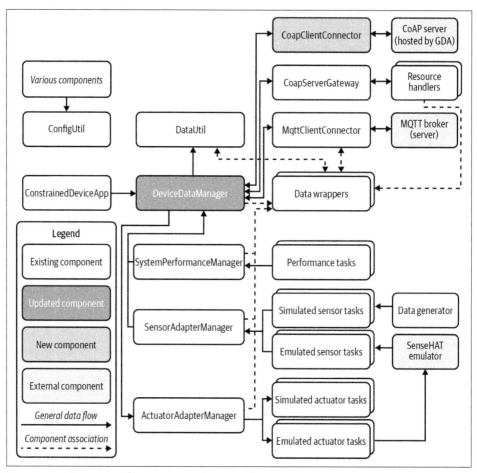

Figure 9-1. Constrained Device App design with an integrated CoAP client

Both diagrams depict the use of `CoapClientConnector` to talk to the CoAP server—in Figure 9-1, the CDA is the client and the GDA is the server, while Figure 9-2 depicts the opposite arrangement.

Since this chapter is about building a CoAP client within the CDA, Figure 9-1 will be central to the exercises in the next section.

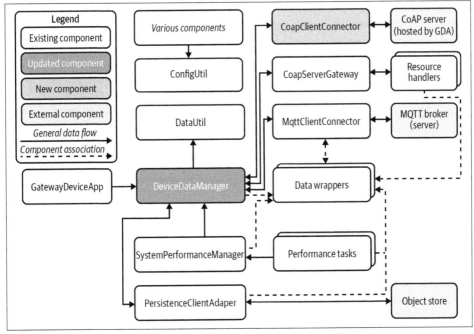

Figure 9-2. Gateway Device App design with an integrated CoAP client

Before jumping into the programming exercises, it will be helpful to review the series of cards related to this chapter (*https://oreil.ly/MQriR*), which provide some exercises you can implement related to creating a CoAP server in both the GDA and the CDA. However, the CoAP examples throughout this book (particularly in Chapters 8, 9, and 10) focus on the GDA as the CoAP server and the CDA as the CoAP client.

Now, let's dig into the CoAP server programming exercises and build out this functionality.

Programming Exercises

The programming exercises in this section concentrate on integration CoAP client capabilities within the CDA—in particular the client adapter, or the implementation of GET, PUT, POST, DELETE, and OBSERVE request method types as part of the client adapter.

The integration tests, which you'll execute manually, will attempt to connect from your CDA's CoAP client to your GDA's CoAP server. To do this, you'll probably want to run your GDA as an application within a separate console. This will allow you to click on the various Python unit tests and execute them individually within your IDE while the GDA is running. And yes, I've provided a few simple command-line instructions you can execute within your console to handle this.

Before running each integration test, you may want to fire up your protocol analyzer as well, since I'll show some examples of CoAP messages passed between the CoAP client you'll implement and the server you implemented within Chapter 8.

 Recall the development environment setup instructions back in Chapter 1, which suggest using Linux as your operating environment. Most of my own unit and integration testing is done in Linux (WSL, specifically). Depending on the library you choose for implementing your CDA's CoAP client, you will need to be aware of any potential low-level Python-specific networking calls that rely on OS-specific bindings.

Add CoAP Client Functionality to the Constrained Device Application

The CDA-specific examples I discuss in the programming exercises for this chapter (*https://oreil.ly/MQriR*) leverage two different CoAP libraries: aiocoap,[1] which relies on asyncio, and CoAPthon3.[2] If you implemented the CDA CoAP server exercises in Chapter 8, at least one of these will be familiar. The examples I discuss in this section use aiocoap[3] and Python's asyncio module.

As with each preceding chapter, be sure to follow the instructions listed in PIOT-CDA-09-000 (*https://oreil.ly/tLpdp*) so you're starting with a new branch for this set of exercises.

Create the CoAP client abstraction and integrate it with DeviceDataManager

The first exercise, PIOT-CDA-09-001 (*https://oreil.ly/LruRw*), walks through the basic client implementation. This will primarily initialize the client using the configuration properties in *PiotConfig.props*, so it will be important to ensure the configuration file has the correct settings in place.

Here's a sample section from the python-components configuration file (*PiotConfig.props*):

```
[Coap.GatewayService]
credFile     = ./cred/PiotCoapCred.props
certFile     = ./cert/PiotCoapLocalCertFile.pem
host         = localhost
port         = 5683
```

1 Amsüss, Christian and Wasilak, Maciej, "aiocoap: Python CoAP Library." Energy Harvesting Solutions, 2013–. *http://github.com/chrysn/aiocoap*.

2 Giacomo Tanganelli, Carlo Vallati, and Enzo Mingozzi, "CoAPthon: Easy Development of CoAP-Based IoT Applications with Python" (*https://doi.org/10.1109/WF-IoT.2015.7389028*), *2015 IEEE 2nd World Forum on Internet of Things (WF-IoT)* (Milan: IEEE, 2015).

3 Be sure to review the aiocoap FAQ (*https://oreil.ly/zTFVA*) before beginning any of these exercises.

```
securePort    = 5684
enableAuth    = False
enableCrypt   = False
```

For the time being, only the host and port properties are relevant. Assuming your CoAP server (GDA) is running on the same system as your CDA, you can leave these configuration properties as they are. For these exercises, I'd suggest you do run both your GDA and your CDA on the same system. This will make debugging more convenient and help limit other potential connectivity issues that are unrelated to the software implementation.

Before implementing the CoapClientConnector, let's take a look at the UML design for the CDA's end state, once the CoAP client functionality is integrated. Figure 9-3 depicts a notional UML design that includes the key components most relevant to this chapter's exercises (many other components have been removed for clarity).

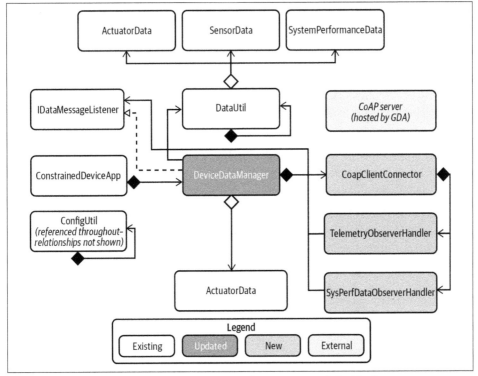

Figure 9-3. Constrained Device App UML with an integrated CoAP client

DeviceDataManager will get some updates (eventually), while the main component for this entire chapter is CoapClientConnector. This means that each exercise will add a bit more functionality to CoapClientConnector. This also means that as you go you'll have the opportunity to test each feature—that is, GET, PUT, POST, DELETE, and OBSERVE—using your updated `CoapClientConnector` and existing GDA CoAP server.

PIOT-GDA-09-001 (*https://oreil.ly/40MeX*) focuses on initializing the CoAP client instance and adding some helper methods to make it easier to process GET, PUT, POST, DELETE, and OBSERVE requests. The key activities include:

- Creating (or editing) the `CoapClientConnector` class
- Adding the relevant class-scoped variables
- Creating the initialization logic—it's already stubbed out within the `python-components` sample source repository
- Adding the resource name creation function—this is boilerplate code that creates the URI you'll use for each request

As always, there are some nuances, especially since the sample code and library (aio-coap)[4] both use asyncio.

 I've only successfully tested the next set of CDA exercises—beginning with PIOT-CDA-09-001 (*https://oreil.ly/LruRw*)—within a Linux operating environment.

The first step—creating the class and initializing all relevant local variables—can be implemented a few ways. Review the card for important details on the requisite import statements and class declaration.

Regardless of which CoAP library you choose (the card gives you a choice), the constructor initialization logic will be similar to the following (again, see PIOT-CDA-09-001 (*https://oreil.ly/LruRw*) for any relevant updates):

```
def __init__(self, dataMsgListener: IDataMessageListener = None):
  self.config = ConfigUtil()
  self.dataMsgListener = dataMsgListener
  self.enableConfirmedMsgs = False
  self.coapClient = None

  self.observeRequests = { }

  self.host    = \
    self.config.getProperty( \
      ConfigConst.COAP_GATEWAY_SERVICE, \
      ConfigConst.HOST_KEY, \
```

---

4 Amsüss, Christian and Wasilak, Maciej, "aiocoap: Python CoAP Library" (*http://github.com/chrysn/aiocoap*).

```
      ConfigConst.DEFAULT_HOST)

  self.port    = \
    self.config.getInteger( \
      ConfigConst.COAP_GATEWAY_SERVICE, \
      ConfigConst.PORT_KEY, \
      ConfigConst.DEFAULT_COAP_PORT)

  self.uriPath = \
    "coap://" + self.host + ":" + str(self.port) + "/"

  logging.info('\tHost:Port: %s:%s', self.host, str(self.port))

  # hostname check is optional - but be sure to call self._initClient()
  try:
    tmpHost = socket.gethostbyname(self.host)

    if tmpHost:
      self.host = tmpHost
      self._initClient()
    else:
      logging.error("Can't resolve host: " + self.host)
  except socket.gaierror:
    logging.info("Failed to resolve host: " + self.host)
```

The basic initialization pattern is probably familiar by now. The constructor is parameterized and accepts an IDataMessageListener reference. (This can also be set via a separate setter method, such as the MqttClientConnector class from Chapter 6.)

Next is initializing class-scoped variables and loading configuration parameters. This includes declaring self.coapClient, which will be set to the appropriate reference via a call to self._initClient(), and retrieving the CoAP host and port parameters from the configuration file.

The final step is simply to check whether the CoAP host is reachable via the network (or, as is likely for this exercise, the loopback adapter) and then to instance the CoAP client.

With the constructor complete, you can now implement the _initClient() method. If you're using aiocoap[5] and asyncio, here's one way to pull this off:

```
def _initClient(self):
  asyncio.get_event_loop().run_until_complete( \
    self._initClientContext())

async def _initClientContext(self):
  try:
    logging.info( \
```

---

5 Amsüss, Christian and Wasilak, Maciej, "aiocoap: Python CoAP Library" (*http://github.com/chrysn/aiocoap*).

```
            "Creating CoAP client for URI path: " + self.uriPath)

        self.coapClient = await Context.create_client_context()

        logging.info( \
          "Client context created. Will invoke resources at: " + \
            self.uriPath)
    except Exception as e:
        # obviously, this is a critical failure - you may want to
        # handle this differently
        logging.error( \
          "Failed to create CoAP client to URI path: " + self.uriPath)
        traceback.print_exception(type(e), e, e.__traceback__)
```

 If you're not already familiar with Python's asyncio module (*https:// oreil.ly/SoyHb*), you should review the documentation thoroughly, as well as the developer's guide (*https://oreil.ly/ZUviy*). The asyncio module is a very powerful concurrency feature and is important to understand for these exercises.

In the preceding example, the _initClient() method is retrieving the asyncio event loop and passing in the _initClientContext() coroutine to be run until complete (defined as such by async preceding the method declaration).

Within _initClientContext(), an aiocoap[6] Context is used to create the client "context," which is referred to simply as self.coapClient throughout the CoapClientCon nector class. On success, this new context provides access to the underlying CoAP infrastructure via methods that allow you to send GET, PUT, POST, DELETE, and OBSERVE requests to a CoAP server.

The final step is to create a simple helper method that will create a resource URI from a set of given parameters. You'll need to generate this for each request prior to sending, since the request APIs you'll create in the following exercises allow the caller to specify a different ResourceNameEnum each time.

Here's one implementation approach to consider:

```
def _createResourcePath( \
  self, resource: ResourceNameEnum = None, name: str = None):

  resourcePath = ""
  hasResource = False

  if resource:
    resourcePath = resourcePath + resource.value
```

---

6 Amsüss, Christian and Wasilak, Maciej, "aiocoap: Python CoAP Library" (*http://github.com/chrysn/aiocoap*).

```
        hasResource = True

    if name:
        if hasResource:
            resourcePath = resourcePath + '/'

        resourcePath = resourcePath + name

    return self.uriPath + resourcePath
```

You'll reuse this method often, so feel free to make modifications as you see fit. Just be sure to return the full URI, including the protocol, host, port, and resource path.

Finally, review the last few steps of this card, which integrate `CoapClientConnector` into `DeviceDataManager`. This pattern should be familiar by now, since it's the same process you followed for integrating the `MqttClientConnector`, so simply follow the listed steps in PIOT-CDA-09-001 (*https://oreil.ly/LruRw*).

With the basic shell of the `CoapClientConnector` in place, let's move on to the request method implementation exercises, starting with GET.

Add the GET request method implementation

You may recall the brief discussion on CoAP CON (confirmed) and NON (nonconfirmed) messages near the beginning of Chapter 8. CON requests trigger an acknowledgment (ACK) from the server to the client for a request, and again from the client to the server when a response is received.

 It's easy to enable a request to be either CON or NON. You can choose to set this by default or enable it through the request methods you'll adapt. The examples I provide all include a boolean parameter as part of each method's signature (required for the integration test cases that have already been written), so you may want to leave it as it is. Feel free to edit this out across the board if you'd prefer; just keep in mind that there likely will be times you'll want to issue either a NON or a CON request, depending on the problem you're looking to solve.

Let's quickly review the requirements for PIOT-CDA-09-002 (*https://oreil.ly/jzcrL*)— the GET request—in which you'll add support for GET CON and NON requests. Notice the method signature:

```
sendGetRequest( \
    self, \
    resource: ResourceNameEnum = None, \
    name: str = None, \
    enableCON: bool = False, \
    timeout: int = IRequestResponseClient.DEFAULT_TIMEOUT) -> bool:
```

The parameters are clear enough. The `resource` parameter represents the `Resource NameEnum` that will be used to construct the URI, a name that, if non-null, can be appended to `resource`. The `enableCON` parameter—set to "False" by default—provides a means to set a request as either NON or CON. A `timeout` value is provided in case the underlying infrastructure supports this, or in case you want to implement your own (you can ignore it for this exercise).

Finally, the return will be a Boolean. While Python doesn't enforce this, the annotation provided is helpful to understanding the intent. This means that there must be a callback within the `CoapClientConnector` to handle the requested data. Enter the `IDataMessageListener` instance (set during construction). The complexity with this method, like others that expect a meaningful server response, is mostly in parsing that response and passing it along to the appropriate callback function. Fortunately, our case will be straightforward, since this client will generally send GET requests for `ActuatorData` commands from the GDA. This means, of course, that the response payload, on success, should be an `ActuatorData` instance in JSON format.

Let's look at one implementation approach:

```
sendGetRequest( \
  self, \
  resource: ResourceNameEnum = None, \
  name: str = None, \
  enableCON: bool = False, \
  timeout: int = IRequestResponseClient.DEFAULT_TIMEOUT) -> bool:

if resource or name:
  resourcePath = self._createResourcePath(resource, name)

  logging.debug("Issuing GET to path: " + resourcePath)

  asyncio.get_event_loop().run_until_complete( \
    self._handleGetRequest( \
      resourcePath = resourcePath, enableCON = enableCON))
else:
  logging.warning( \
    "Can't issue GET - no path or path list provided.")
```

Notice the call to `self._createResourcePath()`, which will generate the URI to use in the upcoming GET request. This is followed by a call to yet another method—a coroutine—that can be executed within the event loop. This applies the same technique used to create the client context: the coroutine is invoked within the event loop, and the caller simply waits for it to complete, effectively executing this as a blocking call.

You may choose to alter this implementation approach and return control to the main thread immediately. If so, you need to devise an alternative approach for handling the async response to the request.

Here's one way to implement the coroutine:

```
async def _handleGetRequest( \
  self, resourcePath: str = None, enableCON: bool = False):

  try:
    msgType = NON

    if enableCON:
      msgType = CON

    msg = \
      Message( \
        mtype = msgType, code = Code.GET, uri = resourcePath)

    req = self.coapClient.request(msg)
    responseData = await req.response

    self._onGetResponse(responseData)

  except Exception as e:
    # TODO: for debugging, you may want to optionally include
    # the stack trace, as shown
    logging.warning( \
      "Failed to process GET request for path: " + resourcePath)
    traceback.print_exception(type(e), e, e.__traceback__)
```

Notice the check of enableCON—if True, the msgType is set to CON, or else it defaults to NON. Following this test is a three-step process:

1. *Create the message:* This will include the message type (CON or NON), the request method code (GET), and the URI (resourcePath).

2. *Create and send the request:* This will be a Future that represents the client context and the request message.

3. *Wait for and handle the response:* The response will contain the payload and other relevant information sent from the server in response to the request, which will then be handled by the method _onGetResponse(), described in PIOT-CDA-09-002 (*https://oreil.ly/jzcrL*).

Shall we kick the tires? Check out the test instructions embedded near the end of the card. They suggest creating your own CoAP GET test cases: one for CON and the other for NON. You can place the code for the three steps just listed, plus the two test cases for PUT, POST, and DELETE, within the same test class. However, it may be easier to create separate test classes, as you'll be able to execute one at a time without telling the interpreter to skip over any other tests in the same class (since some functionality won't be implemented yet and the tests will fail).

Once these new test cases are created, I'd suggest running your GDA CoAP server as a stand-alone application. Just be sure to update the GatewayDeviceApp so it doesn't force an exit after *n* seconds.

 The default main() method implementation for the GatewayDevice ceApp in the java-components repository will run for some number of minutes before automatically exiting. You can easily change this by modifying the code within the main() method, but again, this is up to you.

Before recompiling and starting your GDA, be sure to set its configuration to enable the CoAP server. In the *java-components/config/PiotConfig.props* file, simply set all the other connectors to "False" and set enableCoapServer to "True":

```
[GatewayDevice]
# …
enableMqttClient          = False
enableCoapServer          = True
enableCoapClient          = False
enableCloudClient         = False
enableSmtpClient          = False
# …
```

Assuming you have Maven installed and accessible from your console, you can run the GDA by opening a console, navigating to the java-components (or piot-java-components) directory, and typing in the following:

```
cd piot-java-components
mvn install -DskipTests
java -jar target/gateway-device-app-0.0.1-jar-with-dependencies.jar
```

With your GDA running, you can test your new CoAP client GET functionality and analyze the request and response data using a protocol analyzer such as Wireshark (discussed in Chapters 6 and 7).

 You can filter on CoAP messages within Wireshark by using "coap" as the filter string.

While the test executes, look at Wireshark and examine the output. It should look similar to the content shown in Table 9-1.

Table 9-1. CoAP GET nonconfirmed (NON) request as shown in Wireshark

No.	Time	Source	Destination	Protocol	Length	Info
179	3.633710	::1	::1	CoAP	104	NON, MID:46636, GET, TKN:08 88, coap://localhost/PIOT/ConstrainedDevice/ActuatorCmd
180	3.715214	::1	::1	CoAP	328	NON, MID:19866, 2.05 Content, TKN:08 88, coap://localhost/PIOT/ConstrainedDevice/ActuatorCmd (text/plain)

As expected, there are two packets—the request from the client to the server, followed by the response from the server to the client.

Here's the payload of the response:

```
0000   18 00 00 00 60 0d 12 de 01 1c 11 80 00 00 00 00   ....`..........
0010   00 00 00 00 00 00 00 00 00 00 00 01 00 00 00 00   ................
0020   00 00 00 00 00 00 00 00 00 00 00 01 16 33 dd fe   .............3..
0030   01 1c d2 43 52 45 4d 9a 08 88 c0 ff 7b 22 63 6f   ...CREM.....{"co
0040   6d 6d 61 6e 64 22 3a 30 2c 22 76 61 6c 75 65 22   mmand":0,"value"
0050   3a 30 2e 30 2c 22 69 73 52 65 73 70 6f 6e 73 65   :0.0,"isResponse
0060   22 3a 66 61 6c 73 65 2c 22 73 74 61 74 65 44 61   ":false,"stateDa
0070   74 61 22 3a 22 54 45 53 54 49 4e 47 20 50 55 52   ta":"TESTING PUR
0080   50 4f 53 45 53 20 4f 4e 4c 59 21 22 2c 22 6e 61   POSES ONLY!","na
0090   6d 65 22 3a 22 4e 6f 74 20 53 65 74 22 2c 22 74   me":"Not Set","t
00a0   69 6d 65 53 74 61 6d 70 22 3a 22 32 30 32 31 2d   imeStamp":"2021-
00b0   30 32 2d 32 36 54 30 34 3a 31 39 3a 32 37 2e 37   02-26T04:19:27.7
00c0   35 32 38 34 38 5a 22 2c 22 73 74 61 74 75 73 43   52848Z","statusC
00d0   6f 64 65 22 3a 30 2c 22 74 79 70 65 49 44 22 3a   ode":0,"typeID":
00e0   30 2c 22 6c 6f 63 61 74 69 6f 6e 49 44 22 3a 22   0,"locationID":"
00f0   4e 6f 74 20 53 65 74 22 2c 22 6c 61 74 69 74 75   Not Set","latitu
0100   64 65 22 3a 30 2e 30 2c 22 6c 6f 6e 67 69 74 75   de":0.0,"longitu
0110   64 65 22 3a 30 2e 30 2c 22 65 6c 65 76 61 74 69   de":0.0,"elevati
0120   6f 6e 22 3a 30 2e 30 2c 22 74 69 6d 65 53 74 61   on":0.0,"timeSta
0130   6d 70 4d 69 6c 6c 69 73 22 3a 31 36 31 34 33 31   mpMillis":161431
0140   33 31 36 37 37 35 32 7d                           3167752}
```

Although the formatting doesn't make for easy reading, it's very clearly a JSON-formatted representation of an ActuatorData instance. It's also very kind of the server to let us know that this ActuatorData instance is for "TESTING PURPOSES ONLY!"

For final verification, I added some additional debug messages to my CDA's CoAP client. Here's a sample of the log output:

```
2021-02-25 23:24:11,530:DataUtil:INFO:Created DataUtil instance.
2021-02-25 23:24:11,530:DataUtil:DEBUG:Converting JSON to ActuatorData [pre]  -->
```

```
{'command': 0, 'value': 0.0, 'isResponse': False, 'stateData': 'TESTING PURPOSES
ONLY!', 'name': 'Not Set', 'timeStamp': '2021-02-26T04:24:11.526788Z',
'statusCode': 0, 'typeID': 0, 'locationID': 'Not Set', 'latitude': 0.0,
'longitude': 0.0, 'elevation': 0.0, 'timeStampMillis': 1614313451526}
2021-02-25 23:24:11,530:DataUtil:WARNING:JSON data contains key not mappable to
object: timeStampMillis
2021-02-25 23:24:11,530:DataUtil:DEBUG:Converted JSON to ActuatorData [post] -->
name=Not Set,typeID=0,timeStamp=2021-02
-26T04:24:11.526788Z,statusCode=0,hasError=False,locationID=Not
Set,elevation=0.0,latitude=0.0,longitude=0.0,command=0,stateData=TESTING PURPOSES
ONLY!,value=0.0,isResponse=False
2021-02-25 23:24:11,530:DefaultDataMessageListener:INFO:Actuator Command Msg: 0
```

 You may have noticed the one warning message indicating the time
StampMillis key isn't mappable to an object; this is by design. I
include the timeStampMillis variable in the Java BaseIotData
class, but not in the Python version. My DataUtil implementation
picks this up and logs a warning indicating the delta, although it
doesn't fundamentally change the content, as the timestamp is
already embedded.

So far, so good. Let's run the test once more—but this time, execute the Confirmed
GET request. Be sure to launch Wireshark before running the test. Your test results
should look similar to those depicted in Table 9-2.

Table 9-2. CoAP GET Confirmed (CON) request as shown in Wireshark

No.	Time	Source	Destination	Protocol	Length	Info
10251	287.435938	::1	::1	CoAP	104	CON, MID:41837, GET, TKN:bd 54, coap://localhost/PIOT/Constrained Device/ActuatorCmd
10252	287.438018	::1	::1	CoAP	56	ACK, MID:41837, Empty Message
10253	287.440199	::1	::1	CoAP	328	CON, MID:19229, 2.05 Content, TKN:bd 54, coap://localhost/PIOT/ ConstrainedDevice/ActuatorCmd (text/plain)
10254	287.441059	::1	::1	CoAP	56	ACK, MID:19229, Empty Message

Notice that there are now four packets shown in Table 9-2—the request from the client to the server, followed by an ACK from the server; and the response from the
server to the client, followed by an ACK from the client. Each ACK includes the same
MID, or message ID, from the preceding request or response.

After checking the Wireshark output, the payload content is an ActuatorData
instance in JSON format, which looks identical to the previous example (except for
the timestamp, of course).

Getting information is good, right? How about giving information? Let's implement the PUT request method next.

Add the PUT request method implementation

The requirements for PIOT-CDA-09-003 (*https://oreil.ly/fY10w*)—the PUT request—will be very similar to those for the GET request, except that this request will allow your client to send a payload to the server. This means that the method signature needs to include a payload parameter. To keep things simple, I'd suggest interpreting this as a string, as it's going to be converted to a byte array before sending upstream.

Here's the method signature, along with a sample implementation:

```
sendPutRequest( \
  self, \
  resource: ResourceNameEnum = None, \
  name: str = None, \
  payload: str = None, \
  enableCON: bool = False, \
  timeout: int = IRequestResponseClient.DEFAULT_TIMEOUT) -> bool:

  if resource or name:
    resourcePath = self._createResourcePath(resource, name)

    logging.debug("Issuing PUT to path: " + resourcePath)

    asyncio.get_event_loop().run_until_complete( \
      self._handlePutRequest( \
        resourcePath = resourcePath, \
        payload = payload, \
        enableCON = enableCON))
  else:
    logging.warning( \
      "Can't issue PUT - no path or path list provided.")
```

Here again is a call to a coroutine (although this one also accepts a payload parameter, which is of course necessary if you're going to be sending the server some data). Here's one way to implement it:

```
async def _handlePutRequest( \
  self, \
  resourcePath: str = None, \
  payload: str = None, \
  enableCON: bool = False):

  try:
    msgType = NON

    if enableCON:
      msgType = CON
```

```
payloadBytes = b''

# decide which encoding to use - this can also
# be loaded from the configuration file but must
# also align to the server
if payload:
  payloadBytes = payload.encode('utf-8')

msg = \
  Message( \
    mtype = msgType, payload = payloadBytes, \
    code = Code.PUT, uri = resourcePath)

req = self.coapClient.request(msg)
responseData = await req.response

# TODO: see card for implementation details
self._onPutResponse(responseData)

except Exception as e:
  # TODO: for debugging, you may want to optionally include
  # the stack trace, as shown
  logging.warning( \
    "Failed to process PUT request for path: " + resourcePath)
  traceback.print_exception(type(e), e, e.__traceback__)
```

The process is very similar to the one used for sending a GET request; the only difference is the inclusion of a payload. This adds one additional step—converting the payload string to bytes with an appropriate encoding scheme.

The encoding you choose needs to support the character set used within the string being sent, of course. Let's assume for our purposes that UTF-8 encoding is sufficient.

With the payload now converted to bytes, you can set the related payload parameter within the message object, create and send the request, then wait for and handle the response via the _onPutResponse() method (see PIOT-CDA-09-003 (*https://oreil.ly/ fY10w*) for implementation details).

Time to test out your new PUT functionality. Make sure the GDA is running, and that you've added the requisite PUT tests for CON and NON within your test suite (just follow the same pattern as with your GET tests). You can create an empty SensorData message for this exercise within the test case, convert it to JSON using DataUtil, and send it on its way.

Let's use Wireshark again to review the messaging sequence, starting with NON requests. It should look similar to the content shown in Table 9-3.

Table 9-3. CoAP PUT nonconfirmed (NON) request as shown in Wireshark

No.	Time	Source	Destination	Protocol	Length	Info
4516	125.290961	::1	::1	CoAP	367	NON, MID:15734, PUT, TKN:93 c0, coap://localhost/PIOT/ConstrainedDevice/SensorMsg
4537	125.370967	::1	::1	CoAP	103	NON, MID:50505, 2.04 Changed, TKN: 93 c0, coap://localhost/PIOT/ConstrainedDevice/SensorMsg (text/plain)

As expected, there are two packets—the request from the client to the server, followed by the response from the server to the client. This time, the server responded with the expected Changed response code (this is good).

Here's the payload of the response:

```
0000   18 00 00 00 60 0d 38 e7 00 3b 11 80 00 00 00 00   ....`.8..;......
0010   00 00 00 00 00 00 00 00 00 00 00 01 00 00 00 00   ................
0020   00 00 00 00 00 00 00 00 00 00 00 01 16 33 cd 74   .............3.t
0030   00 3b e3 c9 52 44 c5 49 93 c0 c0 ff 55 70 64 61   .;..RD.I....Upda
0040   74 65 20 74 65 6c 65 6d 65 74 72 79 20 72 65 71   te telemetry req
0050   75 65 73 74 20 68 61 6e 64 6c 65 64 3a 20 53 65   uest handled: Se
0060   6e 73 6f 72 4d 73 67                              nsorMsg
```

This time, the payload response is a simple text message: "Update telemetry request handled: SensorMsg." For now, this is fine (and it is what I coded in my GDA resource handler), although it would be better to use a JSON-formatted message that's easier for the CDA to interpret. This is an opportunity! Feel free to add another response-specific data type—derived from BaseIotData if you wish—and incorporate the JSON conversion logic within DataUtil in both the GDA and the CDA.

Once again, for final verification, here's a sample of the CDA's log output:

```
2021-02-26 00:17:13,090:CoapAsyncClientConnector:DEBUG:Path:     ('PIOT',
'ConstrainedDevice', 'SensorMsg')
2021-02-26 00:17:13,090:CoapAsyncClientConnector:DEBUG:Query:    ()
2021-02-26 00:17:13,090:CoapAsyncClientConnector:DEBUG:Options: ()
2021-02-26 00:17:13,090:CoapAsyncClientConnector:DEBUG:Response code: 2.04 Changed
2021-02-26 00:17:13,090:CoapAsyncClientConnector:DEBUG:Request code:  PUT
2021-02-26 00:17:13,090:CoapAsyncClientConnector:DEBUG:Token:    b'\x93\xc0'
2021-02-26 00:17:13,090:CoapAsyncClientConnector:DEBUG:MID:      50505
2021-02-26 00:17:13,090:CoapAsyncClientConnector:DEBUG:Host:     localhost
2021-02-26 00:17:13,090:CoapAsyncClientConnector:DEBUG:Payload: b'Update telemetry
request handled: SensorMsg'
2021-02-26 00:17:13,090:CoapAsyncClientConnector:INFO:SUCCESS: Changed
2021-02-26 00:17:13,090:CoapAsyncClientConnector:INFO:Response valid for this
device. Processing...
2021-02-26 00:17:13,090:CoapAsyncClientConnector:INFO:PUT response received.
```

Seems we're on a roll, so let's keep going—this time, send a Confirmed PUT request. Again, be sure to launch Wireshark and filter on "coap." Your results should look similar to those depicted in Table 9-4.

Table 9-4. CoAP PUT confirmed (CON) request as shown in Wireshark

No.	Time	Source	Destination	Protocol	Length	Info
37571	1068.829198	::1	::1	CoAP	367	CON, MID:41213, PUT, TKN:1e 0c, coap://localhost/PIOT/Constrained Device/SensorMsg
37572	1068.901062	::1	::1	CoAP	56	ACK, MID:41213, Empty Message
37573	1068.903746	::1	::1	CoAP	103	CON, MID:21527, 2.04 Changed, TKN:1e 0c, coap://localhost/PIOT/ConstrainedDevice/SensorMsg (text/plain)
37574	1068.905111	::1	::1	CoAP	56	ACK, MID:21527, Empty Message

Notice there are now four packets: the request from the client to the server, followed by an ACK from the server; and the response from the server to the client, followed by an ACK from the client. Each ACK includes the same message ID (MID) as the preceding request or response.

The Wireshark output shows that the payload content is an `ActuatorData` instance in JSON format, which looks identical to the previous example.

I also checked the GDA log file, which included this in the output:

```
INFO: Sensor data message received. Pushing upstream:
PIOT/ConstrainedDevice/SensorMsg. Message: name=,typeID=0,timeStamp=2021-02-
26T05:32:56.543297+00:00,statusCode=0,hasError=false,locationID=constraineddevice00
1,latitude=0.0,longitude=0.0,elevation=0.0,value=0.0
```

The GDA handled the PUT request from the CDA, converted the JSON payload to a `SensorData` instance, passed the data to the `DeviceDataManager`, and then logged a message indicating it's going to send the data upstream (to the cloud—eventually).

This is good news indeed. The glue that connects the CDA and GDA to each other via CoAP is holding, and the GDA is doing its job by (or at least telling me it's planning on) sending the `SensorData` onward to the cloud. Your CDA CoAP client is nearly complete.

There are the other two request types, POST and DELETE, which are described in PIOT-CDA-09-004 (*https://oreil.ly/8Nh5T*) and PIOT-CDA-09-005 (*https://oreil.ly/MynSb*). The pattern for POST will be nearly identical to PUT, and DELETE will be nearly identical to GET. Due to their similarities, I'll skip over these remaining types. Feel free to take some time and work on those two exercises.

This leaves us with the OBSERVE functionality. This requires a bit more work. It's no harder to implement than a PUT (there's really just one additional parameter in the request), but it does need to be managed. A method that supports the observation start process should also have an observation stop, right?

Add the OBSERVE (GET) request method implementation

Since OBSERVE is essentially a special type of GET request, there will be some implementation similarities. However, as discussed in PIOT-CDA-09-006 (*https://oreil.ly/L5ZoU*), OBSERVE will require some additional work. Here's the breakdown of activities:

- Send the initial GET request with the OBSERVE flag enabled and register that request resource within the client.
- After receiving the initial response, send another request that waits for updates from the server.
- When a stop observation request is received, look up the initial request resource and cancel the appropriate observation (or assume there's only one observer per client and avoid this registration complexity altogether).

Depending on the CoAP library you decide to use, there may be other steps involved to support OBSERVE. Be sure to review the instructions in PIOT-CDA-09-006 (*https://oreil.ly/L5ZoU*) for further details, along with future implementation updates.

Here are the start and stop method signatures, along with their notional implementations:

```
def startObserver( \
  self, \
  resource: ResourceNameEnum = None, \
  name: str = None) -> bool:

  if resource or name:
    resourcePath = self._createResourcePath(resource, name)

    if resourcePath in self.observeRequests:
      logging.warning( \
        "Already observing resource %s. Ignoring start observe request.", \
        resourcePath)
      return

    asyncio.get_event_loop().run_until_complete( \
      asyncio.ensure_future( \
        self._handleStartObserveRequest(resourcePath)))
  else:
    logging.warning( \
      "Can't issue OBSERVE - GET - no path or provided.")
```

```
def stopObserver( \
  self, \
  resource: ResourceNameEnum = None, \
  name: str = None) -> bool:

  if resource or name:
    resourcePath = self._createResourcePath(resource, name)

    if not resourcePath in self.observeRequests:
      logging.warning( \
        "Resource %s not being observed. Ignoring stop observe request.", \
        resourcePath)
      return

    resourcePath = self._createResourcePath(resource, name)

    asyncio.get_event_loop().run_until_complete( \
      self._handleStopObserveRequest(resourcePath))
  else:
    logging.warning( \
      "Can't cancel OBSERVE - GET - no path provided.")
```

Nothing new here—both the startObserver() and stopObserver() methods do some preprocessing and then simply delegate to their respective coroutines. Let's look at each in turn:

```
async def _handleStartObserveRequest( \
  self, \
  resourcePath: str = None):

  msg = Message(code = Code.GET, uri = resourcePath, observe = 0)
  req = self.coapClient.request(msg)

  self.observeRequests[resourcePath] = req

  try:
    # send the initial request
    responseData = await req.response

    # TODO: validate response first
    self._onGetResponse(responseData)

    # wait for each observed update
    async for responseData in req.observation:
      # TODO: validate response first, then see card for details
      self._onGetResponse(responseData)

      req.observation.cancel()
      break

  except Exception as e:
```

```
# TODO: log warning and possibly stack trace,
# then be sure to stop observing...
logging.warning( \
  "Failed to execute OBSERVE - GET. Recovering...")
traceback.print_exception(type(e), e, e.__traceback__)
```

Notice that the message object is created with the `observe = 0` parameter. This will tell the server that it should register this client's context and request for future notifications. The first request, then, sets the stage for this observation interaction between the client and the server. The next, which follows the "wait for each observed update" comment, will wait for notifications from the server until explicitly told to cancel observing.

Which brings us to the stop observation coroutine, shown next:

```
async def _handleStopObserveRequest( \
  self, \
  resourcePath: str = None, \
  ignoreErr: bool = False):

  if resourcePath in self.observeRequests:
    logging.info('Handle stop observe invoked: ' + resourcePath)

    try:
      observeRequest = self.observeRequests[resourcePath]
      observeRequest.observation.cancel()
    except Exception as e:
      if not ignoreErr:
        logging.warning( \
          "Failed to cancel OBSERVE - GET: " + resourcePath)

    try:
      del self.observeRequests[resourcePath]
    except Exception as e:
      if not ignoreErr:
        logging.warning( \
          "Failed to remove observable from list: " + \
          resourcePath)

  else:
    logging.warning( \
      'Resource not currently under observation. Ignoring: ' + \
      resourcePath)
```

Now that the observe functionality is complete, you'll need a resource to observe. It needs to be updated regularly in order to test whether the observation functionality is working. Table 9-5 shows the initial GET (CON) request (and ACK) to establish the OBSERVE interaction, followed by four NON responses with content.

Table 9-5. CoAP OBSERVE (CON first, then NON) request as shown in Wireshark

No.	Time	Source	Destination	Protocol	Length	Info
248	6.724864	::1	::1	CoAP	108	CON, MID:37992, GET, TKN:95 08, coap://localhost/PIOT/ConstrainedDevice/TestUpdateMsg
249	6.808216	::1	::1	CoAP	313	ACK, MID:37992, 2.05 Content, TKN: 95 08, coap://localhost/PIOT/ConstrainedDevice/TestUpdateMsg (text/plain)
466	12.692861	::1	::1	CoAP	313	NON, MID:17749, 2.05 Content, TKN: 95 08, coap://localhost/PIOT/ConstrainedDevice/TestUpdateMsg (text/plain)
850	22.692874	::1	::1	CoAP	313	NON, MID:17750, 2.05 Content, TKN: 95 08, coap://localhost/PIOT/ConstrainedDevice/TestUpdateMsg (text/plain)
1179	32.692583	::1	::1	CoAP	313	NON, MID:17751, 2.05 Content, TKN: 95 08, coap://localhost/PIOT/ConstrainedDevice/TestUpdateMsg (text/plain)

You've probably noticed the resource URI: *coap://localhost/PIOT/ConstrainedDevice/TestUpdateMsg*. To support this new resource, I created a new `ResourceNameEnum` entry specifically for this purpose. I also built a custom resource handler that creates a thread that updates an `ActuatorData` instance every 10 seconds. Feel free to do the same within your own development environment.

Another observation from the output in Table 9-5 is that the first GET request is a CON message, while the server to client notifications are NON messages. The custom resource handler explicitly sets the response message type to NON, although it could just as easily be set to CON.

 It's very important to ensure that your OBSERVE client explicitly cancels the observation request when complete. Otherwise, the server may continue to try to connect to the client and send it an update. Of course, the connection will fail if the client is no longer listening, but the server may continue trying to send updates in perpetuity. Be sure to handle these exceptional cases at both ends of the connection.

At this point, congratulations are certainly in order. With the completion of the CDA's CoAP client, you now can now pass messages between your GDA and your CDA using either MQTT or CoAP. This is a major milestone! If you're interested in branching out further, you can also add a CoAP client to your GDA. I'll briefly discuss this next, although it's not required for the remaining exercises in the book.

Add CoAP Client Functionality to the Gateway Device App (Optional)

You can optionally incorporate a CoAP client within your GDA. The Californium CoAP library provides both server and client libraries, so adding CoAP client support to the GDA is relatively straightforward. It follows the same design pattern as CDA's CoAP client approach and is also documented within the PIOT-GDA-09 cards (*https://oreil.ly/MQriR*).

If you decide to go down this path, be sure to follow the instructions listed in PIOT-GDA-09-000 (*https://oreil.ly/2GV4p*) before implementing your server.

A brief summary of the Gateway Device Application's CoAP client abstraction

As with the CDA's implementation, PIOT-GDA-09-001 (*https://oreil.ly/40MeX*) walks through the basic CoAP client abstraction for the GDA. Figure 9-4 depicts the associated detailed UML design, which introduces a couple of additional classes—response handlers, to be specific—that implement a simple interface used for handling callbacks when an observe response is received asynchronously from the server.

The online exercises provide further detail on implementation options and are regularly reviewed and updated. If you choose to implement the GDA exercises, be sure to commit and merge your branches back into the primary branch by following the instructions in PIOT-GDA-09-100 (*https://oreil.ly/sJtZB*).

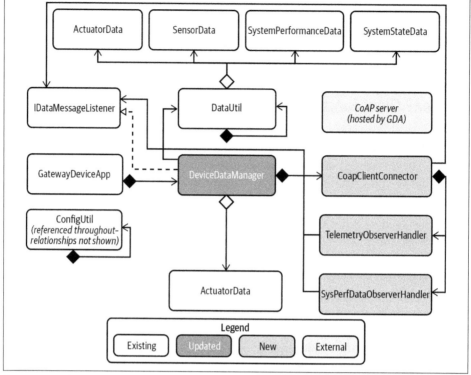

Figure 9-4. Gateway Device App UML with an integrated CoAP client

Additional Exercises

There's no end to the new capabilities you can add to your CoAP servers. Here are two more you might want to consider.

Add a Robust OBSERVE Cancel Feature

I've mentioned the importance of incorporating a robust OBSERVE cancellation feature within your CoAP client. This is to ensure that the CoAP server will stop sending observation updates to a registered CoAP observer client, should that client either fail without sending the cancellation or simply forget to implement the cancellation request. Ideally, this will be handled at both the client and the server, so the server will decide to simply remove the client registration if the client is no longer reachable after a period of time.

Add Support for DELETE and POST

The exercises in this book don't require support for resource deletion, and you can use PUT to address resource updates. What would it look like to incorporate DELETE support for a resource? How about POST? See if you can identify some use cases that may benefit from each, and then implement these request methods within your CoAP server's resource handlers and CoAP client on your own.

Conclusion

In this chapter, you learned about the CoAP protocol and how you can implement a CoAP client within your Constrained Device Application. You also learned about (and optionally tried out) some of the design differences between a CDA CoAP client and a GDA CoAP client. This chapter continued building on your CoAP knowledge framework, which began in Chapter 8 with a CoAP server and completes now with your CoAP client. You're now ready to tackle Edge Tier integration, which follows in Chapter 10.

Edge Integration

Integration at the Edge Using MQTT and CoAP

The request has failed.
Fall back and try another.
Now, fire and forget.

> **Fundamental concepts**: Connect your Constrained Device App and Gateway Device App using the CoAP and MQTT protocols to send data and trigger actuation events.

At this point, you're probably anxious to pass messages between your CDA and your GDA. This chapter is all about connecting these two applications in a meaningful way, using both CoAP and MQTT.

What You'll Learn in This Chapter

Edge integration is one of the more challenging aspects of designing and implementing an IoT ecosystem, since it often involves multiple protocols, security constraints, data formatting idiosyncrasies, and much more. While I won't tackle all of these concerns, all of your work leading up to this point has been to prepare for this moment: the integration of your Edge Tier applications—the CDA and the GDA.

In this chapter, you'll learn how to finally integrate your two applications using both CoAP (which you started digging into in Chapters 8 and 9) and MQTT (which you learned about in Chapters 6 and 7).

Most of the attention in this chapter will be on testing your connection layers (for example, `MqttClientConnector` with your locally running MQTT broker, and your GDA's `CoapServerGateway` with your CDA's `CoapClientConnector`).

You'll also learn some basic encryption concepts, including how to use TLS to encrypt the connection between your two MQTT clients and your locally running MQTT broker. I'll briefly introduce DTLS encryption between your CoAP server and your client as well, although the exercises will focus on the former.

Design Concepts

Security is a critical component of any IoT ecosystem, and this chapter will just barely scratch its surface. One of its key concepts is enabling encrypted MQTT connections between your CDA and GDA devices. This sets the stage for future encrypted MQTT connections between your GDA and the cloud.

 As of this writing, the latest proposed TLS standard is v1.3, specified by the IETF RFC 8446 (*https://tools.ietf.org/html/rfc8446*).

This chapter will help you configure your MQTT communications to use Transport Layer Security (TLS) to encrypt the messaging traffic between your CDA and your GDA. With connection encryption enabled, you'll be able to pass messages between your CDA and your GDA securely and act on the data your application receives, whether that's an actuation command received by the CDA from the GDA or telemetry that the CDA sends to the GDA for processing and interpretation.

Since the encryption requirements are a bit more involved, I'll spend a bit more time discussing them and leave most of the internal business logic (interpreting data and deciding what to do with it) for homework.

The exercises in this chapter actually span configuration, programming, and integration testing, so I renamed that section "Functional Exercises." Before digging into these exercises, however, let's briefly review your forthcoming updates to the CDA and GDA.

You'll add features to both applications that will enable them to pass messages to each other and make reasonably intelligent decisions regarding any appropriate actions. (You implemented some of this in Chapter 9 using CoAP; this chapter completes the Edge Tier integration circle.)

Design-wise, nothing here is new—only modified. The MQTT client connector class for each application will be slightly modified to support TLS-encrypted connections with the broker, and the DeviceDataManager will incorporate some additional intelligence to process those messages that each application instance needs to act on.

As with all preceding chapters, be sure to check out a new branch for both your CDA and your GDA, as explained in PIOT-CDA-10-000 (*https://oreil.ly/aqfBX*) and PIOT-GDA-10-000 (*https://oreil.ly/j8Fsc*).

Let's get started.

Security Exercises

This section centers on security and encryption—specifically, on configuring TLS within your MQTT communications environment. I'll point you to a Kanban board exercise that will help you configure your MQTT broker to support TLS, and then I'll walk through two programming exercises, one for the GDA and the other for the CDA, that enable TLS within your `MqttClientConnector`.

Adding TLS Support to Your MQTT Broker

Enabling TLS (via port 8883) on the Mosquitto broker is documented on the Mosquitto website (*https://mosquitto.org*). I've written a brief summary in PIOT-CFG-10-001 (*https://oreil.ly/ydh35*) with links to the documentation and specific instructions related to the development environment you've been working in. Be sure to review these important configuration instructions before moving on.

 PIOT-CFG-10-001 (*https://oreil.ly/ydh35*) points out the importance of keeping private keys safe and secure, and I want to shout that again here. Even though you're likely generating only test keys, be sure to keep them in a safe place.

Be sure to run the tests described at the end of the exercise to verify that TLS is enabled and functioning.

Incidentally, you can also enable preshared key (PSK) encryption and authorization using a client-specific key. Further discussion is outside the scope of this chapter, but you may want to consider enabling PSK in your environment as a further verification step for all clients connecting into your MQTT broker.

Add Security Features to Your Gateway Device App MQTT Client Connector

With your Mosquitto instance now TLS-enabled, it's time to do the same with your Gateway Device Application's MQTT client connector.

You can refer to the Appendix for the notional UML representation of the GDA, although there's really nothing new with the design, aside from tweaks to the `MqttClientConnector`.

PIOT-GDA-10-001 (*https://oreil.ly/EAjey*) walks through this setup and explains how you can use the java-components module `SimpleCertManagementUtil` (located in the `programmingtheiot.common` package) to load an X.509 certificate at runtime from within your `MqttClientConnector` class.

Take a look at the key actions:

- Import the required dependencies.
- Add a private method to load credentials from a separate file (referenced by the configuration file).
- Add a private method to handle SSL socket factory initialization.
- Initialize the MQTT client connection with encryption enabled.

The code samples within PIOT-GDA-10-001 (*https://oreil.ly/EAjey*) walk through the specified actions in detail. To summarize, most of the code updates involve moving some configuration logic to a new private method, checking the configuration to see if the `enableCrypt` flag is True in the `Mqtt.GatewayService` section, and then loading the appropriate certificate(s). As with all the other exercises in this book, be sure to read the instructions in this card thoroughly as well as the MQTT broker configuration information in PIOT-CFG-10-001 (*https://oreil.ly/ydh35*) before you start coding.

After adding the appropriate import statements and declaring some new class-scoped variables in `MqttClientConnector`, the first functional implementation action in PIOT-GDA-10-001 (*https://oreil.ly/EAjey*) is to create the private method `initCreden` `tialConnectionParameters(String configSectionName)`.

This method provides a relatively simple way to load key/value auth pairs (user and password, for instance) from a separate file that is referenced by *PiotConfig.props* but is not part of the code repository.

`ConfigUtil` already supports this feature, so you just need to use it or load your credentials using your own method.

 The `Properties` object loaded by `ConfigUtil` will contain any credentials specified in `credFile` from the referenced section of your *PiotConfig.props*. This is to help prevent you (if not stop you) from making inadvertent credential commits to git, which is generally a bad idea. Also, keep in mind that any credentials stored within the `Properties` object returned by this method will remain in memory until the `Properties` object is properly garbage collected.

Here's one way to implement this method:

```
private void initCredentialConnectionParameters(
  String configSectionName)
{
  ConfigUtil configUtil = ConfigUtil.getInstance();

  try {
    _Logger.info(
      "Checking if credentials file exists...");

    Properties props =
      configUtil.getCredentials(configSectionName);

    if (props != null) {
      this.connOpts.setUserName(
        props.getProperty(
          ConfigConst.USER_NAME_TOKEN_KEY, ""));

      this.connOpts.setPassword(
        props.getProperty(
          ConfigConst.USER_AUTH_TOKEN_KEY,
          "").toCharArray());

      _Logger.info("Credentials now set.");
    } else {
      _Logger.warning("No credentials are set.");
    }
  } catch (Exception e) {
    _Logger.log(
      Level.WARNING,
        "Credential file non-existent. Disabling auth.");
  }
}
```

The next privately-scoped method you'll create within MqttClientConnector is named initSecureConnectionParameters(String configSectionName). The parameter allows you to specify the section name to be used for loading the MQTT-specific configuration properties. For the exercises in this book, the value will be either Mqtt.GatewayService or Cloud.GatewayService.

Why? This will allow you to use the same code for encrypting your connection to your local MQTT broker and one of the cloud service MQTT brokers I'll discuss in Chapter 11—all by simply loading different configuration values from another configuration file section.

Here's the code sample:

```
private void initSecureConnectionParameters(
  String configSectionName)
{
  ConfigUtil configUtil = ConfigUtil.getInstance();
```

```
try {
  _Logger.info("Configuring TLS...");

  if (this.pemFileName != null) {
    File file = new File(this.pemFileName);

    if (file.exists()) {
      _Logger.info(
        "PEM file valid. Using secure connection: " +
        this.pemFileName);
    } else {
      this.enableEncryption = false;

      _Logger.log(
        Level.WARNING,
        "PEM file invalid. Using insecure connection: " +
        pemFileName, new Exception());

      return;
    }
  }

  SSLSocketFactory sslFactory =
    SimpleCertManagementUtil.getInstance()
      .loadCertificate(this.pemFileName);

  this.connOpts.setSocketFactory(sslFactory);

  // override current config parameters
  this.port =
    configUtil.getInteger(
      configSectionName,
      ConfigConst.SECURE_PORT_KEY,
      ConfigConst.DEFAULT_MQTT_SECURE_PORT);

  this.protocol = ConfigConst.DEFAULT_MQTT_SECURE_PROTOCOL;

  _Logger.info("TLS enabled.");
} catch (Exception e) {
  _Logger.log(
    Level.SEVERE,
    "Failed to init MQTT TLS. Using insecure connection.", e);

  this.enableEncryption = false;
}
}
```

Most of this code is built to handle exceptions and fall back to an unencrypted
MQTT connection if the certificate (PEM) file can't be found or it fails to load from
within the SimpleCertManagementUtil class.

You can change this, of course. In some cases, if the connection can't be secured, it may be best (or even required) that you shut down the application or disable the MQTT connection. For local loopback adapter testing on your own protected system, this may not be as much of an issue. How you handle this is up to you.

If all goes well, you'll be the proud new owner of an SSLSocketFactory instance, returned by the utility class. Once this is in hand, simply tell the Paho library to use it as the socket factory:

```
this.connOpts.setSocketFactory(sslFactory);
```

That's it. Just one line of code. There are still a couple things remaining, however.

Since the MQTT broker will, by default, use TCP port 1883 for unencrypted connections and TCP port 8883 for encrypted connections, the logic needs to set the proper port based on the success of the certificate load. It also needs to change the protocol from "tcp" to "ssl." You may recall that the protocol and port are class-scoped variables, which will be used when the connection is established.

The next step is to call this method. There are two ways to do this. The first is from within the constructor, after the MqttConnectOptions() class is instanced and stored within the this.connOpts class-scoped variable. The second is by migrating all of the initialization code to a new private method named initClientParameters(String configSectionName).

The instructions in PIOT-GDA-10-001 (*https://oreil.ly/EAjey*) provide details on the initClientParameters() implementation, followed by a minor update to the no-arg constructor, which will pass the configuration section name. This will be useful later when you may want the GDA to manage two MQTT client instances—one to talk with the local broker, and one to talk with another broker hosted in the Cloud Tier.

You'll notice the sample code for this method also attempts to load the clientID from the configuration file. I suggest you consider this approach, or something similar to ensure a GDA-specific clientID, as it will help ensure it remains consistent from each test run to the next. Once this is in place, you can also experiment with setting the useCleanSession flag to true, either by loading it from the configuration file or setting it within your class instance.

After loading the configuration parameters, including the configuration file's clientID, the next key requirement in this method is to check if the configuration specifies that the MQTT connection should be encrypted. Here's the code to perform this work:

```
this.enableEncryption =
  configUtil.getBoolean(
    configSectionName, ConfigConst.ENABLE_CRYPT_KEY);

// if encryption is enabled, try to load and apply the cert(s)
```

```
if (this.enableEncryption) {
  initSecureConnectionParameters(configSectionName);
}
```

My implementation stores the `enableEncryption` flag in a class-scoped variable for convenience. You may choose to enable encryption by default, in which case this check is moot.

With this work complete, you're actually ready to run some basic integration tests between the GDA and the MQTT broker with TLS enabled. The requirements card technically allows you to skip this in favor of completing the next two GDA-specific assignments. It would be better to try it out before moving on, though, so start up your MQTT broker, making sure that TLS is enabled. You might also want to start up your protocol analyzer and filter on TLS packets for your loopback adapter.

Copy the CA certificate you generated in PIOT-CFG-10-001 (*https://oreil.ly/ydh35*) to the "cert" or another directory you want to reference. (Make sure it's *not* part of your Git repository—notice the example path is */someNonGitPath*, which should be changed appropriately.) Then update *PiotConfig.props* as follows:

```
[Mqtt.GatewayService]
certFile      = /someNonGitPath/cert/server.crt
host          = localhost
port          = 1883
securePort    = 8883
defaultQoS    = 0
keepAlive     = 60
enableAuth    = False
enableCrypt   = True
```

There are only two tests to run at this point—connectAndDisconnect() and testPublishAndSubscribe(). Both are simple test cases within the MqttClientConnectorTest test class, which already exists in the `java-components` sample source code as part of the `programmingtheiot.part03.integration.connection` package.

You can highlight each test individually and execute the tests one at a time within Eclipse. Although my solution implementation and yours will likely be different, here's a small output sample from running the testPublishAndSubscribe() test:

```
Feb 27, 2021 8:37:34 PM programmingtheiot.gda.connection.MqttClientConnector
initSecureConnectionParameters
INFO: Configuring TLS...
Feb 27, 2021 8:37:34 PM programmingtheiot.gda.connection.MqttClientConnector
initSecureConnectionParameters
INFO: PEM file valid. Using secure connection: ./cert/server.crt
.
.
.
Feb 27, 2021 8:37:40 PM programmingtheiot.gda.connection.MqttClientConnector
messageArrived
INFO: MQTT message received.
```

```
Topic: PIOT/GatewayDevice/MgmtStatusMsg
Timestamp: 1614476260345
Payload: TEST: This is the GDA message payload 3.
.
.
.
Feb 27, 2021 8:39:10 PM programmingtheiot.gda.connection.MqttClientConnector
disconnectClient
INFO: Disconnecting from broker...
Feb 27, 2021 8:39:10 PM programmingtheiot.gda.connection.MqttClientConnector
disconnectClient
INFO: Disconnected from broker: ssl://localhost:8883
During the test execution, I also captured some output from the Mosquitto broker,
which accepted the connection:
1614476254: New connection from 127.0.0.1 on port 8883.
1614476255: New client connected from 127.0.0.1 as paho300417207003000 (p2, c1, k60).
1614476325: Saving in-memory database to /var/lib/mosquitto/mosquitto.db.
1614476350: Client paho300417207003000 disconnected.
```

Table 10-1 shows the initial output from Wireshark. It shows that I am indeed communicating via TLS (v1.3) between the GDA's MQTT client and the Mosquitto MQTT broker.

Table 10-1. TLS v1.3 handshake snapshot between the GDA's MQTT client and the MQTT broker

No.	Time	Source	Destination	Protocol	Length	Info
447	13.477683	127.0.0.1	127.0.0.1	TLSv1.3	441	Client Hello
449	13.479117	127.0.0.1	127.0.0.1	TLSv1.3	2393	Server Hello, Change Cipher Spec...
451	13.491547	127.0.0.1	127.0.0.1	TLSv1.3	50	Change Cipher Spec
453	13.543462	127.0.0.1	127.0.0.1	TLSv1.3	134	Application Data
455	13.543740	127.0.0.1	127.0.0.1	TLSv1.3	299	Application Data
457	13.543842	127.0.0.1	127.0.0.1	TLSv1.3	299	Application Data

Now let's tackle this same challenge for the CDA.

Add Security Features to Your Constrained Device App MQTT Client Connector

Recall that PIOT-GDA-10-001 (*https://oreil.ly/EAjey*) walks through the GDA's MQTT encryption setup and explains how you can use the java-components module SimpleCertManagementUtil (located in the programmingtheiot.common package) to load an X.509 certificate at runtime from within your MqttClientConnector class.

While the principles are essentially the same for the CDA, the implementation is different—and a bit more straightforward. The Appendix provides a notional UML representation for the CDA. Again, the only change for this part of Chapter 10 is with the MqttClientConnector.

Since MQTT supports a username and password (or just a username without a password), you can add the same credential load feature you recently implemented for your GDA as part of your CDA. (It's not required for the exercises in this book, so I excluded it as a requirement.) The ConfigUtil class in python-components supports a similar credential properties load feature as the GDA's version of ConfigUtil, defined by the method def getCredentials(self, section: str) -> dict. Feel free to try it out if you'd like.

Take a look at the key actions:

- Import the requisite dependencies.
- Check the configuration file for the enableCrypt flag and the certificate file.
- Initialize the MQTT client connection with encryption enabled.

There's only one import statement to add:

```
import ssl
```

Checking the configuration is also straightforward. You can do it within the constructor:

```
self.enableEncryption = \
  self.config.getBoolean( \
    ConfigConst.MQTT_GATEWAY_SERVICE,
      ConfigConst.ENABLE_CRYPT_KEY)

self.pemFileName = \
  self.config.getProperty( \
    ConfigConst.MQTT_GATEWAY_SERVICE,
      ConfigConst.CERT_FILE_KEY)
```

Finally, enabling TLS on the Paho connection is essentially one line of code, wrapped in a try/except block. Within the connectClient() method, and *before* you call self.mqttClient.connect(), add the following:

```
try:
  if self.enableEncryption:
    logging.info("Enabling TLS encryption...")

    self.port = \
      self.config.getInteger( \
        ConfigConst.MQTT_GATEWAY_SERVICE,
        ConfigConst.SECURE_PORT_KEY,
        ConfigConst.DEFAULT_MQTT_SECURE_PORT)

    self.mqttClient.tls_set( \
      self.pemFileName, tls_version = ssl.PROTOCOL_TLSv1_2)
```

```
except:
  logging.warn( \
    "Failed to enable TLS. Using unencrypted connection.")
```

Notice the protocol version—TLS v1.2. As of this writing, this is the latest supported TLS version within Python 3.9.

That's basically it. Let's give a go and run one of the tests within the `MqttClientCon nectorTest` test case, named `testActuatorCmdPubSub()`.

Be sure to update the CDA's *PiotConfig.props* to set the secure MQTT port to 8883 and point to the proper file location for the certFile. Make sure your MQTT broker is still running and configured to use TLS and run the test.

Your CDA log output will probably include messages similar to the following:

```
Finding files... done.
Importing test modules ... done.

2021-02-27 21:27:07,812:MqttClientConnectorTest:INFO:Testing MqttClientConnector
class...
 .
 .
 .
2021-02-27 21:27:07,816:MqttClientConnector:INFO:Attempting to connect to MQTT
broker: localhost
2021-02-27 21:27:07,817:MqttClientConnector:INFO:Enabling TLS encryption...
2021-02-27 21:27:07,834:MqttClientConnector:INFO:[Callback] Connected to MQTT
broker. Result code: 0
2021-02-27 21:27:07,834:MqttClientConnector:INFO:Subscribing to topic
PIOT/ConstrainedDevice/ActuatorCmd
2021-02-27 21:27:07,835:MqttClientConnector:INFO:[Callback] Subscribed MID: 1
2021-02-27 21:27:12,834:MqttClientConnector:INFO:[Callback] Actuator command
message received. Topic: PIOT/ConstrainedDe
vice/ActuatorCmd.
2021-02-27 21:27:12,834:MqttClientConnector:INFO:ActuatorData JSON: {
    "timeStamp": "2021-02-28T02:27:07.816353+00:00",
    "hasError": false,
    "name": "Not Set",
    "typeID": 0,
    "statusCode": 0,
    "latitude": 0.0,
    "longitude": 0.0,
    "elevation": 0.0,
    "locationID": "constraineddevice001",
    "isResponse": false,
    "command": 7,
    "value": 0.0,
    "stateData": "Not Set"
}
 .
 .
 .
```

```
.
2021-02-27 21:28:17,835:MqttClientConnector:INFO:[Callback] Disconnected from MQTT
broker. Result code: 0
Ran 5 tests in 70.025s
```

```
OK (skipped=4)
```

The Mosquitto log indicates the connection was accepted:

```
1614479212: New connection from 127.0.0.1 on port 8883.
1614479212: New client connected from 127.0.0.1 as … (p2, c1, k60).
1614479227: New connection from ::1 on port 8883.
1614479227: New client connected from ::1 as constraineddevice001 (p2, c1, k60).
1614479297: Client constraineddevice001 disconnected.
```

Since we're using TLS v1.2, the Protocol is different than the GDA's, as shown in Table 10-2.

Table 10-2. TLS v1.2 handshake snapshot between the CDA's MQTT client and the MQTT broker

No.	Time	Source	Destination	Protocol	Length	Info
173	3.550736	::1	::1	TLSv1.2	276	Client Hello
177	3.558601	::1	::1	TLSv1.2	2254	Server Hello, Certificate, Server Key…
179	3.559846	::1	::1	TLSv1.2	157	Client Key Exchange, Change Cipher Spec…
181	3.560315	::1	::1	TLSv1.2	306	New Session Ticket, Change Cipher Spec…
185	3.560937	::1	::1	TLSv1.2	127	Application Data
187	3.562012	::1	::1	TLSv1.2	97	Application Data

Now for the real fun. Each of the two MqttClientConnectorTest classes you ran—one for the GDA and the other for the CDA—includes a "testIntegrateWith…" test case. You can use these test cases to kick the tires on this fancy new TLS-encrypted MQTT connection. There's still some implementation work remaining within both the CDA and the GDA, so the tests won't do anything interesting, but they will give you a taste of how both applications can connect and exchange messages.

The other implementation exercises in this chapter focus on building out business logic, which the Kanban cards walk through in detail. I'll touch briefly on each one but will leave the implementation exercises to you.

Functional Exercises

The remaining CDA and GDA exercises center mostly on the DeviceDataManager within each application. They afford you a great deal of flexibility in how you tackle them. The Kanban cards provide some guidance, but you're welcome to tweak the logic to meet your needs. This work will set you up for the remaining exercises in the book, when you connect into the cloud and handle actuation events from a simple analytics function hosted in the cloud service you select.

Let's look at the Gateway Device App (GDA) exercises first.

Adding Business Logic to the Gateway Device App

PIOT-GDA-10-002 (*https://oreil.ly/pRCcj*) requires a few more modifications to the GDA's MqttClientConnector. This functionality changes from synchronous broker interactions to asynchronous (via a couple small code changes) and introduce new logic to handle incoming CDA messages on subscribed topics for SystemPerforman ceData and SensorData.

The first action involves changing from the synchronous MQTT client to the asynchronous client. This is relatively straight forward and only requires changing two lines of code - the MQTT client declaration and instantiation. See the code suggestions at the beginning of PIOT-GDA-10-002 (*https://oreil.ly/pRCcj*) for details.

The next action centers on updating the subscriber functionality. Perhaps the easiest way forward is to receive the message, check the topic it was received on, and identify the appropriate DataUtil method to call and convert the JSON payload into the correct data container (such as SystemPerformanceData or SensorData).

An alternative is to implement the IMqttMessageListener interface and register the instance as a callback for messages on a given topic. This provides a cleaner abstraction and also allows you to separate the logic, placing it in a new class that can live outside MqttClientConnector or simply be implemented as an inner class.

Here's one implementation approach that uses the IMqttMessageListener interface:

```
private class ActuatorResponseMessageListener
  implements IMqttMessageListener
{
  private ResourceNameEnum resource = null;
  private IDataMessageListener dataMsgListener = null;

  ActuatorResponseMessageListener(
    ResourceNameEnum resource,
    IDataMessageListener dataMsgListener)
  {
    this.resource = resource;
    this.dataMsgListener = dataMsgListener;
  }

  @Override
  public void messageArrived(
    String topic, MqttMessage message)
```

```
    throws Exception
  {
    try {
      ActuatorData actuatorData =
        DataUtil.getInstance().jsonToActuatorData(
          new String(message.getPayload()));

      if (this.dataMsgListener != null) {
        this.dataMsgListener.handleActuatorCommandResponse(
          resource, actuatorData);
      }
    } catch (Exception e) {
      _Logger.warning(
        "Failed to create  ActuatorData from payload.");
    }
  }
}
```

You can now add `IMqttMessageListener` as the callback reference for your actuation event subscriptions. What better place to handle this than in the `connectComplete()` callback? After all, it gets called once the GDA's MQTT connection to the MQTT broker is, well, complete!

Here's one approach you might consider:

```
@Override
public void connectComplete(
  boolean reconnect, String serverURI)
{
  _Logger.info(
    "MQTT connection successful (is reconnect = " +
    reconnect + "). Broker: " + serverURI);

  int qos = 1; // TODO: read this from the config file

  try {
    this.mqttClient.subscribe(
      ResourceNameEnum.CDA_ACTUATOR_RESPONSE_RESOURCE
        .getResourceName(),
      qos,
      new ActuatorResponseMessageListener(
        ResourceNameEnum.CDA_ACTUATOR_RESPONSE_RESOURCE,
        this.dataMsgListener));
  } catch (MqttException e) {
    _Logger.warning(
      "Failed to subscribe to CDA actuator topic.");
  }
}
```

Whether you choose this or the generic-message-handler approach, they ultimately do the same thing—handle the incoming message, convert the JSON to the appropriate data container, and then send it to the appropriate `IDataMessageListener` method (implemented by `DeviceDataManager`).

This brings us to the next activity—implementing PIOT-GDA-10-003 (*https://oreil.ly/9brY9*). This requirements card picks up where the previous card left off: by interpreting the incoming data from the `MqttClientConnector` within the `DeviceDataManager` and doing something useful with it.

Again, the implementation details are up to you. One option is to store the data temporarily and then (once you've implemented the exercises in Chapter 11) blast it up to the cloud. The other is to analyze the data and determine if an actuation event might be appropriate (which is what the card suggests). For instance, if the incoming `SensorData` indicates an anomaly within the CDA, it may make sense to track it for a few more messages and then generate an `ActuatorData` for the related actuator (such as the HVAC) and enable or disable the system. Suggested implementation details are included within the card.

With these exercises complete, you can now move on to the CDA.

Adding Business Logic to the Constrained Device App

PIOT-CDA-10-002 (*https://oreil.ly/ZBQ35*) focuses on the `DeviceDataManager` and on interpreting `ActuatorData` commands received via the GDA. Regardless of where the `ActuatorData` is sourced, the CDA needs to interpret the message and decide if it should be passed on to the `ActuatorAdapterManager` (which already contains the necessary logic to pass an actuation event to the appropriate actuator instance). The logic you implement here can be a simple pass-through, or you can introduce some additional analysis to decide if you want to stop it in its tracks and take some other course of action (such as reading another sensor value to determine whether you really want to trigger the requested actuation).

The Kanban card leaves much on the table. It introduces a few lines of code for you to use as they are or as a basis for adding more functionality.

Of course, you'll need to receive actuation events if you're going to act on them, which is the focus of PIOT-CDA-10-003 (*https://oreil.ly/xbAg1*). This card introduces callback handler logic to the CDA's `MqttClientConnector` that's similar to what you implemented within the GDA, except this implementation is concerned only with processing incoming `ActuatorData` messages.

The card suggests one approach for handling this. Recall the `onConnect()` callback method from Chapter 6. The underlying MQTT client infrastructure invokes it when the MQTT client connection succeeds. At this point, and assuming it's successful, the CDA knows it's connected to the MQTT broker. Since it also knows it's interested in receiving actuator events, you can subscribe to those events within this method.

But it gets better. You can specify a callback function for a specific topic that will get called whenever a message is published to said topic. The card provides the details, with only a dozen lines of code or so between the subscription and the callback.

Here's the subscription and callback registration code:

```
self.mqttClient.subscribe( \
  topic = \
    ResourceNameEnum.CDA_ACTUATOR_CMD_RESOURCE.value, \
  qos = 1)

self.mqttClient.message_callback_add( \
  sub = ResourceNameEnum.CDA_ACTUATOR_CMD_RESOURCE.value, \
  callback = self.onActuatorCommandMessage)
```

These two calls go hand in hand. The first is the subscription, which is required to let the broker know you're interested in receiving messages on a given topic. The second is the callback to be invoked when a topic's message is published and received by your client.

I set the default QoS to 1 in this example. However, it would be better to pull this from the configuration file so you can easily adjust it and other configuration parameters from a single source (like *PiotConfig.props*). You can place this within your onConnect() callback.

Last, the callback needs to consider the incoming message payload (which will be a byte array) and transform that to an ActuatorData instance. That instance can then be passed along to the appropriate IDataMessageListener callback function (again, implemented by DeviceDataManager).

Here's one implementation approach:

```
def onActuatorCommandMessage(self, client, userdata, msg):
  logging.info( \
    "[Callback] Actuator command received. Topic: %s.", \
    msg.topic)

  if self.dataMsgListener:
    try:
      # assumes all data is encoded using UTF-8
      actuatorData = \
        DataUtil().jsonToActuatorData( \
          msg.payload.decode('utf-8'))

      self.dataMsgListener.handleActuatorCommandMessage( \
        actuatorData)
    except:
      logging.exception( \
        "Failed to convert payload to ActuatorData: ")
```

Notice the "decode" call: it requires an encoding scheme to properly convert the data into a string that can be parsed by DataUtil. You can handle this within DataUtil and check if the parameter to jsonToActuatorData() is a byte array or not, or you can handle it here, as I have. Either way, you'll need to ensure the string data is consistently encoded throughout your system. I'm using UTF-8, which is a relatively transferable encoding scheme.

Before wrapping up PIOT-CDA-10-003 (*https://oreil.ly/xbAg1*), be sure to review the card's commentary on a potential deadlock condition that could arise under certain scenarios. Compare the card's given scenario with your own anticipated use case. If they're similar, and you're encountering a deadlock condition during testing, do tread carefully, as adding your own multithreading logic can introduce a multitude of new complexities, debugging challenges, and other potential headaches if not carefully thought out and properly implemented.

The final exercise for the CDA, PIOT-CDA-10-004 (*https://oreil.ly/Z4M8d*), is similar to the final exercise in this chapter for the GDA, except it handles SensorData and SystemPerformanceData. It will publish it to the appropriate MQTT topic for the GDA to retrieve or else PUT it in a CoAP request to the GDA for further processing.

Performance Testing Exercises

You've likely noticed a number of "INT"-related integration tasks within this chapter in the Programming the IoT Kanban board. While all deal with various integration-related tasks, there are two that you should execute within your local environment (only). This will give you a better sense of how QoS levels in MQTT, confirmed messages in CoAP, and TLS-enabled MQTT connections can affect system performance.

PIOT-INT-10-001 (*https://oreil.ly/uamea*) (MQTT) and PIOT-INT-10-002 (*https://oreil.ly/uoVhA*) (CoAP) walk through a few simple performance tests to see how the reliability features of each protocol affect messaging performance between applications.

Be sure to run each test ONLY on your local system.

Here are some questions to ponder while you're executing these tests:

- How does the QoS level impact the timing of messages processed by the CDA or GDA using MQTT?

- What happens when you run the same QoS test with TLS enabled?

- What performance gain is achieved from using NON requests in CoAP?

Let's take a look at some data pertaining to the first two questions. Table 10-3 depicts the results of one test I ran to answer both.

Table 10-3. MQTT message performance example with and without TLS using QoS 0, 1, and 2

Java client to local MQTT broker				
QoS level	TLS enabled (Y/N)	Message count	Payload size (bytes)	Elapsed time (sec)
0 1 2	N N N	10000 10000 10000	264 264 264	1.973 2.385 3.747
0 1 2	Y Y Y	10000 10000 10000	264 264 264	2.120 2.729 4.822

The values in Table 10-3 were generated while running my MQTT client and broker on the same system (via the loopback network adapter). In this example, I ran my GDA instance under WSL (Ubuntu 20.04LTS) with OpenJDK 14.0.2. The GDA's MqttClientConnector delegated its MQTT calls to the Java Paho library. Notice the time delta between QoS 0 and QoS 2 messages (and also when using TLS or unencrypted).

In some cases, QoS 2 may be unnecessary; in others, it may absolutely be needed to meet a message delivery robustness requirement. Ultimately, you'll need to examine your requirements and determine which QoS is most appropriate for your needs.

Table 10-4 exercises a similar test for CoAP but compares confirmed (CON) and nonconfirmed (NON) request types using GET and PUT only. I've kept my server implementation and handlers for each request type as simple as possible—that is, no server-based logging, with the GET request creating a new ActuatorData instance with a fixed payload with each invocation. In this example, I ran my GDA instance under the same operating environment as before, with my CoapServerGateway delegating its CoAP calls to Eclipse Californium. My CDA also ran under WSL with Python 3.9.1, with its CoapClientConnector delegating its CoAP calls to aiocoap.[1]

Table 10-4. CoAP message performance example using CON and NON requests

Python client to Java server (local)				
Request type	ACK type	Message count	Payload size (bytes)	Elapsed time (sec)
GET GET	CON NON	10000 10000	264 264	13.708 12.095
PUT PUT	CON NON	10000 10000	264 264	12.227 10.149

Performance testing is highly system (and implementation) specific, so your own tests will probably yield very different results. Irrespective of your system configura-

---

1 Amsüss, Christian and Wasilak, Maciej, "aiocoap: Python CoAP Library." Energy Harvesting Solutions, 2013–. *http://github.com/chrysn/aiocoap.*

tion, you'll likely experience some kind of performance hit when introducing reliable message delivery with either protocol.

See if you can generate your own performance data using similar parameters on your local system for both protocols. What did you observe? Did the results inform your thinking on how you might design your IoT edge integration solution?

Additional Exercises

This chapter is chock-full of opportunity. I've given you quite a few additional exercises to test integration and try out new message interpretation paradigms. My guess is you already have some in mind.

You may want to start your own Kanban board and add cards to capture some of these integration exercises. I believe you'll find the process to be both tedious and incredibly rewarding. You'll have a growing tally of use cases and "out of the box" tests that you can apply to IoT challenges you're facing now or in the future. Feel free to use the empty requirement template I introduced back in Chapter 1.

To get you started, here's one you may want to tackle.

Add DTLS Support to Your CoAP Client and Server

There are two optional exercises that very briefly touch on DTLS support for your CDA's `CoapClientConnector` and GDA's `CoapServerGateway` modules. Check out PIOT-CDA-10-005 (*https://oreil.ly/NEbJ8*) (related to the CDA) and PIOT-GDA-10-004 (*https://oreil.ly/1FUUB*) (related to the GDA) to learn more, and see if you can incorporate DTLS support between your own CoAP server and the CoAP client.

These optional exercises, along with others that may be added in the future, will continue to evolve to support new learning opportunities. Be sure to monitor updates to the Programming the IoT Kanban board (*https://oreil.ly/programming-iot-kanban*) for updates.

Conclusion

This wraps up Part III, "Connecting to Other Things". If you've implemented the exercises, you should now have an Edge Tier design and implementation that allow messaging and actionable notifications between your CDA and your GDA. You should also have the ability to enable TLS-based encryption if you're using MQTT. This means you can add MQTT authentication and authorization and have some confidence that this sensitive information will be encrypted on your network.

Your GDA is almost ready to connect to a cloud service that supports MQTT and TLS encryption. Be sure to commit and merge your CDA and GDA branches back into the primary branch by following the instructions in PIOT-GDA-10-100 (*https://oreil.ly/MARAg*).

On to Part IV and the final two chapters of the book.

Connecting to the Cloud

Introduction

Blue skies, no limits.
How oddly trite a statement.
There is sky...with clouds.

So far, you've learned how to pull your Edge Tier together, and you've added some useful capabilities to your GDA and CDA applications. Your system can collect data from simulated and emulated sensors, process it within the Edge Tier, and trigger actuation events based on preconfigured floor and ceiling limits.

Of course, this doesn't make your system part of the IoT, since you haven't yet connected it to the internet—at least not yet!

What You'll Learn in This Section

Chapter 11 digs into the internet connectivity aspect of the IoT by walking through some exercises to connect your GDA into one or more IoT-enabled cloud services using the MQTT protocol. There are certainly other ways to do this—many cloud services provide numerous mechanisms for connecting gateway devices into their platform. To keep things simple and largely platform agnostic, though, I'll focus the exercises on MQTT connectivity only.

Finally, in Chapter 12, I'll discuss a few IoT-specific use cases that you can implement on your own. These will help you apply the concepts and principles from earlier chapters to new IoT problem areas and build solutions.

While cloud computing is a complex topic, I think you'll soon see how straightforward the process of connecting to the cloud can be. And once your code is functioning in the cloud, the sky is the limit for what you can do next.

Integrating with Various Cloud Services

Using MQTT to Connect to Various Cloud Platforms

Free thought and action.
Select a wise path forward
And make your future.

> **Fundamental concepts**: Learn how to use MQTT to integrate your GDA with various IoT-enabled cloud services.

More cloud services are now supporting the IoT, which opens numerous doors for cloud integration. There are many excellent books and online training guides that explore those services in detail, but it's not possible to cover them all meaningfully here. Instead, this chapter will cover the basics of using MQTT to connect into a small handful of these services. It focuses on connectivity, not on analytics or cloud-specific services.

Why the limited focus?

Connecting different types of systems together is hard and often complex. This is particularly true when integrating the Cloud Tier and Edge Tier within an IoT environment. Once you've successfully (and securely[1]) established this connection and are properly managing your devices, the challenges are mostly centered on data management, event management, and analytics, which are common to non-IoT systems as well.

---

1 As securely as reasonable and appropriate, although we all know that the most secure computer system is one that's locked up, disconnected from the internet, and never powered on.

If you're interested in further study on IoT security and various IoT-enabled cloud services, you might find these two other O'Reilly books useful: *The Internet of Risky Things* by Sean Smith, and *Scalable Architecture for the Internet of Things* by Dejan Mijic, Draško Draškovic, and Ervin Varga.

What You'll Learn in This Chapter

How exactly do you connect your GDA to the cloud? Depending on the service you're using, you may have multiple options: an API embedded within a cloud-service provider library that uses HTTP/S, MQTT over WebSockets, MQTT directly, TCP/IP sockets, and so forth.

The protocol you choose will depend on your objectives and network configuration: that is, your firewall rules and other internet connectivity constraints. This chapter, as noted, will focus on using MQTT. All of the IoT-enabled cloud services I'll discuss support MQTT (as of this writing, version 3.1.1).

I'll show you one way to create a simple cloud connection abstraction layer that uses MQTT over TLS to connect your GDA to various cloud services. I'll also introduce a simple high-level design for Functions-as-a-Service (FaaS) that can reside within your selected cloud service and help manage data coming from your GDA and actions (actuation events) that will be sent back.

Design Concepts

At this point, your Edge Tier design is mostly complete. All it lacks is that final connector abstraction to provide access to the virtually unlimited scalability of the cloud.

Figure 11-1 depicts this missing link: CloudClientConnector. Notice the implied relationship with MqttClientConnector? We'll leverage this relationship to facilitate GDA-to-cloud connectivity using MQTT.

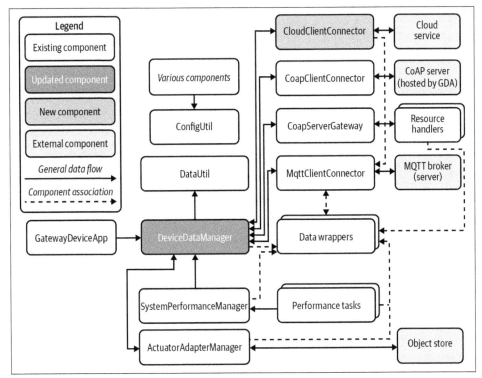

Figure 11-1. Notional design for the Gateway Device Application

There's always some nuance in a design, of course, and the GDA updates for this chapter are no different. Figure 11-2 sheds light on these nuances and provides a detailed view of the design for your GDA. (I have removed many of the existing components for clarity.)

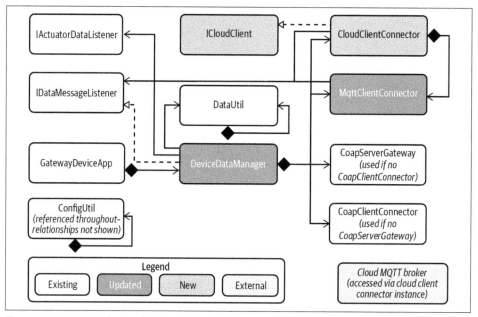

Figure 11-2. UML design for the Gateway Device Application

Notice the addition of two new components: ICloudClient and CloudClientConnector. ICloudClient provides a contractual interface definition for CloudClientConnector, which you may find useful as we explore connectivity with different cloud service providers (CSPs). It will be the primary interface to the cloud used by Device DataManager (not explicitly shown in Figure 11-2, but part of the upcoming implementation detail).

You can use this abstraction to create custom implementations of CloudClientConnector for each cloud service without affecting the core design of the GDA or the work you need to do within DeviceDataManager.

The primary example in this chapter doesn't utilize a CSP-specific API, only MQTT. That's why CloudClientConnector creates and manages an instance of MqttClientConnector. You'll delegate the communications work to it for the primary exercise. The optional exercises will connect into other cloud services and may require you to create a custom CloudClientConnector implementation for each.

Some CSPs require only a server certificate(s) to enable TLS, along with a client auth credential for connectivity. Others may require both client and server certificates to encrypt the connection and authorize the client.

Programming Exercises

In this section, I'll first cover the basic plumbing to update your GDA design by implementing the components in Figure 11-2. I'll then cover some CSP integration specifics.

 As of this writing, the CSP-specific exercises work as described; however, CSPs may introduce changes that render some or all of these exercises moot. Be sure to check each provider's website and integration instructions regularly for changes that may impact your implementation.

These exercises are centered on the GDA, so you won't have to implement anything within your CDA. Be sure to quickly review PIOT-GDA-11-000 (*https://oreil.ly/QWnmN*) and check out a new GDA branch for this chapter so you can easily track (and then merge) your cloud-integration-specific changes.

Add the Cloud Client and Other Related Components

The implementation for the GDA starts with PIOT-GDA-11-001 (*https://oreil.ly/qv4x3*), where you'll make minor adjustments to your MqttClientConnector. (They should remind you of the updates you made to this module back in Chapter 10 when you implemented PIOT-GDA-10-001 (*https://oreil.ly/EAjey*).) These adjustments let you leverage MqttClientConnector from your soon-to-be-implemented Cloud ClientConnector.

First, you'll add a new constructor that lets you choose between the Cloud.Gateway Service and Mqtt.GatewayService configuration file sections.

Then you'll add protected methods for publish and subscribe/unsubscribe that accept the topic name parameter as a String and the payload as a byte[].

Update the MQTT client connector implementation

Let's take a look at one way to implement the constructor update requirements:

```
public MqttClientConnector()
{
  this(false);
}

public MqttClientConnector(boolean useCloudGatewayConfig)
{
  super();

  this.useCloudGatewayConfig = useCloudGatewayConfig;
```

```
if (useCloudGatewayConfig) {
  initClientParameters(ConfigConst.CLOUD_GATEWAY_SERVICE);
} else {
  initClientParameters(ConfigConst.MQTT_GATEWAY_SERVICE);
}
}
```

You may have already migrated the initialization functionality to `initClientParame ters(String)`, so this update should be a breeze. If not, no worries! Simply review PIOT-GDA-10-001 (*https://oreil.ly/EAjey*) and introduce those changes now.

The next set of methods might seem like a reimplementation of the public `publish Message()`, `subscribeToTopic()`, and `unsubscribeFromTopic()` methods. Fortunately, they're not! You can delegate the publish, subscribe, and unsubscribe calls to the new, protected methods that use similar names. `CloudClientConnector`, which you'll implement next, will invoke these directly. Protected methods in Java can be accessed by classes in the same package, so while the `IPubSubClient` interface won't define them, `CloudClientConnector` can use them by leveraging all of the awesomeness your existing `MqttClientConnector` provides.

Here's what their signatures will look like:

```
protected boolean publishMessage(
  String topic, byte[] payload, int qos)
{
  // TODO: implement this and return true on success
  return false;
}

protected boolean subscribeToTopic(String topic, int qos)
{
  // TODO: implement this and return true on success
  return false;
}

protected boolean unsubscribeFromTopic(String topic)
{
  // TODO: implement this and return true on success
  return false;
}
```

You can easily implement these methods using the logic you've already implemented for their public counterparts.

For publish, you will probably want to move the functionality to this new protected method so it can be reused as is. For subscribe and unsubscribe, your implementation may vary depending on how you've implemented callback listeners for subscription events.

You can change these signatures, but since `CloudClientConnector` will also use them, I suggest keeping them as simple as possible.

Add the Cloud Client Connector implementation

The `CloudClientConnector` provides the requisite functionality to communicate with one or more cloud services by abstracting some configuration logic and adjusting topic names so they're compatible with the CSP's topic naming constructs.

It then delegates all of the MQTT-specific functionality to `MqttClientConnector`, meaning your initial implementation of `CloudClientConnector` will be relatively basic.

PIOT-GDA-11-002 (*https://oreil.ly/eZ1EQ*) defines the requirements for `ICloud Client`, which is essentially implemented for you within the card. This is the interface `DeviceDataManager` will use after creating the instance of `CloudClientConnector`.

You may have noticed that none of the methods specifies a QoS level. The primary reason is that most CSPs permit only two QoS levels for MQTT messaging—"0" (fire and forget) and "1" (at least once). With limited QoS levels and the probability of setting a single level for your application, this is well suited as a configuration parameter.

> QoS "0" messaging may be fine internally, since you typically have more control over the networking environment and the traffic traversing the network. However, you may want to specify QoS "1" for cloud integration and just deal with any potential duplicate messages.

If you choose to use dynamic QoS levels (for example, switching between "0" and "1" depending on the message type), you can adjust these interfaces.

PIOT-GDA-11-003 (*https://oreil.ly/g41Ze*) specifies the initial implementation for `CloudClientConnector`, which will create and manage the instance of `MqttClientConnector`. It will subsequently be instanced by `DeviceDataManager`, which will access its functionality via the `ICloudClient` public method signatures.

This card has three key requirements:

- Implement the interfaces defined in `ICloudClient`.
- Add the logic necessary to use `MqttClientConnector` as the connector to the CSP's MQTT broker.
- Integrate `CloudClientConnector` with `DeviceDataManager`.

Let's stub out the interface defined in ICloudClient first. This requires the "imple ments ICloudClient" statement in the class declaration and concrete implementations of the following method interfaces:

```
public boolean connectClient();

public boolean disconnectClient();

public boolean sendEdgeDataToCloud(
   ResourceNameEnum resource, SensorData data);

public boolean sendEdgeDataToCloud(
   ResourceNameEnum resource, SystemPerformanceData data);

public boolean subscribeToCloudEvents(ResourceNameEnum resource);

public boolean unsubscribeFromCloudEvents(
   ResourceNameEnum resource);

public boolean setDataMessageListener(
   IDataMessageListener listener);
```

The connectClient() and disconnectClient() methods can simply delegate directly to the MqttClientConnector. You should do the same with setDataMessage Listener() as well, although you may decide to also keep a reference to IDataMessa geListener internally for other functionality you might decide to implement later.

The subscribeToCloudEvents() and unsubscribeFromCloudEvents() implementations can also be delegated directly to the MqttClientConnector instance by creating the appropriate topic name from the ResourceNameEnum and then calling the protected subscribeToTopic() and unsubscribeFromTopic() methods.

Last but not least, the sendEdgeDataToCloud() methods will need to convert their respective data objects to JSON and then invoke the protected publishMessage() method on the MqttClientConnector instance.

I'll walk through an example of sendEdgeDataToCloud() later in this section.

The first step, however, is to create an instance of the MqttClientConnector and then properly configure it.

In CloudClientConnector, create a class-scoped reference to MqttClientConnector —this time using the class type, not the interface. You'll need to reference the protected methods it declares as part of your ICloudClient implementation.

Create an instance of MqttClientConnector in the constructor, passing in "true" to the overloaded constructor and storing the reference in your class-scoped variable.

Because `MqttClientConnector` will now use the `Cloud.GatewayService` section of the configuration, it can also load a PEM file that holds the CSP's root certificates. After Chapter 10's work, you should have a functioning `MqttClientConnector` that works over TLS connections.

You'll probably need a couple additional properties that can also be loaded from the configuration file. Here are two that you'll need later:

API key or user credential
> Remember the work you did to integrate this with your `MqttClientConnector` in Chapter 10? You can load credentials via the *PiotConfig.props* file indirectly because it references a separate credential file that will never be stored in your repository and that looks for the `userToken` and `authToken` key.

Topic prefix or base name
> Each CSP discussed in this chapter uses its own topic prefix to identify API version, region, service type, and so on. This can be extracted a number of different ways, but I'll show only one.
>
> *PiotConfig.props* defines the "baseTopic" property that can store this value.

 As a reminder, do NOT use *PiotConfig.props* to store any auth credentials or secrets. Store them in the credential file instead—and remember NOT to commit that to your repository.

Out of these two steps, `MqttClientConnector` won't handle dynamic topic creation based on a customized scheme (e.g., one that requires prepending a base topic name) —you'll have to handle this in `CloudClientConnector`.

Every call to publish or subscribe will require this custom topic. An easy solution is to create a new method—a protected one would be ideal, as you will see in the next section—that accepts a `ResourceNameEnum` and then prepends the base topic name and any other cloud-specific topic information.

Here's what it might look like:

```
private String createTopicName(ResourceNameEnum resource)
{
  return (
    this.topicPrefix + resource.getDeviceName() +
    "/" + resource.getResourceType()).toLowerCase();
}
```

And finally, here's how you can invoke it using the `ICloudClient`-specific publish methods:

```
@Override
public boolean sendEdgeDataToCloud(
  ResourceNameEnum resource, SensorData data)
{
  if (resource != null && data != null) {
    String topicName = createTopicName(resource);

    try {
      String payload =
        DataUtil.getInstance().sensorDataToJson(data);

      _Logger.finest(
        "Publishing payload value(s) to cloud: " + topicName);

      // TODO: retrieve QoS level from config and set
      // as a class-scoped variable: this.qosLevel
      this.mqttClient.publishMessage(
        topicName, payload.getBytes(), this.qosLevel);

      return true;
    } catch (Exception e) {
      _Logger.warning(
        "Failed to publish message to cloud: " + topicName);
    }
  }

  return false;
}
```

Follow the instructions at the end of the card to integrate `CloudClientConnector` with `DeviceDataManager`. It follows the same pattern you've used previously for MQTT and CoAP.

Your GDA now has what it needs to connect into the cloud.

You'll eventually modify your `CloudClientConnector` to meet your CSP's specific integration requirements. The next section discusses an optional design consideration to make this easier, though it does require some additional plumbing.

Another design consideration (optional—sort of)

As you build out your cloud connectivity abstraction layer using `CloudClientConnector`, you may be wondering how you could experiment with multiple cloud services without redesigning your GDA or maintaining multiple versions of `CloudClientConnector`.

If you're feeling ambitious, you can create yet another layer of abstractions using the notional detailed design specified in Figure 11-3. However, you may want to hold off until you've successfully tested your first cloud integration using `CloudClientConnector` as it is.

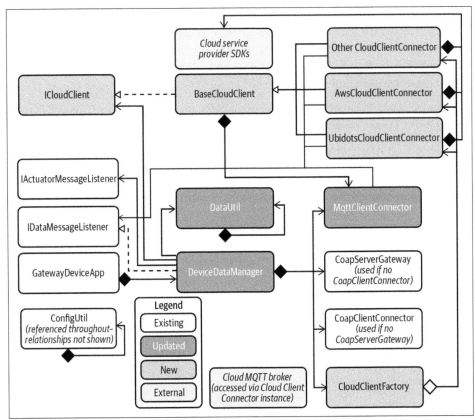

Figure 11-3. Notional detailed design with multiple cloud client abstractions (optional)

Here's where another design pattern comes into play—*Factory*.[2] A Factory pattern provides a generic interface for creating complex objects that provide specific implementations of a given interface.

To get more specific, the Factory (named CloudClientFactory) provides a method to create (or retrieve) an instance of a complex type that implements a given interface (such as ICloudClient). The caller doesn't know about the implementation details and doesn't care. It just wants access to the functionality specified by the interface.

By generalizing the public interface to CloudClientConnector and abstracting the core functionality within a new class—BaseCloudClient—you can effectively create a custom cloud integration layer for each CSP.

---

2 Erich Gamma et al., *Design Patterns: Elements of Reusable Object-Oriented Software* (Boston: Addison-Wesley, 1994).

Notice the divergence from the design depicted in Figure 11-2. The core design actually remains the same. Adding the `BaseCloudClient` provides an opportunity to incorporate the `MqttClientConnector` directly in the base class, should it provide sufficient capabilities for securely connecting with your selected CSP, all while remaining generically implemented.

Optionally, each `ICloudClient` implementation can leverage the CSP's SDK and bypass `MqttClientConnector` completely.

This design approach provides tremendous flexibility in how you create your cloud integration logic. It also allows the end user of the cloud client—`DeviceDataManager` —to focus on its job: orchestrating all of the messages that traverse the edge and flow to and from the cloud.

It can be helpful to consider how the cloud-based design of your ecosystem may be affected. Figure 11-4 depicts a notional and very simplistic microservices design supporting data ingestion, processing, and event generation, depending on the CSP you select.

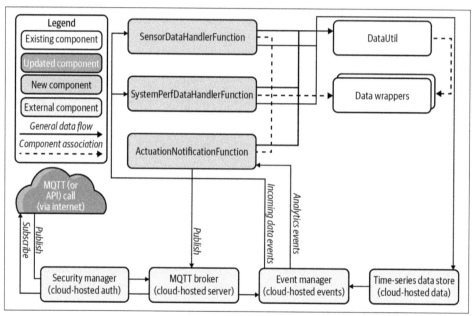

Figure 11-4. Notional design for the cloud services functions (optional)

The notional high-level designs depicted in Figures 11-3 and 11-4 serve as mostly optional design constructs to consider for experimentation purposes.

Integrating with an IoT Cloud Service Provider (CSP)

The number of IoT-enabled CSPs continues to grow, and the services being offered—both in the cloud and at the edge—are expanding rapidly. New service offerings are regularly added, including advanced gateway applications and ML-based Edge Tier inference capabilities.

The GDA functionality you've already developed, including the recent `ICloudClient` abstraction, can be used as part of your integration logic to communicate with some of these services using MQTT over TLS.

In the following list are a few CSPs that support MQTT as of this writing:

- AWS IoT Core (*https://aws.amazon.com/iot-core*)
- Azure IoT Hub (*https://azure.microsoft.com/en-us/services/iot-hub*)
- Google Cloud IoT (*https://cloud.google.com/solutions/iot*)
- IoT on IBM Cloud (*https://www.ibm.com/cloud/internet-of-things*)
- Ubidots (*https://www.ubidots.com*)

You'll find that each CSP may implement the MQTT specification a little differently. You can usually find a link to a CSP's MQTT documentation, where an explanation is provided on where the CSP's MQTT broker is aligned to the spec and where it differs. Be sure to review this information before settling on MQTT as your cloud connection paradigm.

This is not an exhaustive accounting—just a handful of CSPs that, as of this writing, support the MQTT protocol. The list should be helpful if you'd like to use your GDA (with additional modifications) to connect into one or more of these services.

If you're interested in a self-hosted and open source IoT platform that leverages a microservices design and incorporates multiprotocol support, you may also want to look into the Mainflux IoT Platform (*https://www.mainflux.com*).

Each CSP works differently, but you can probably expect most to do the following:

- Create an account.

- Generate and register the appropriate credentials (auth token and/or PKI [public key infrastructure] for your device).

- Provision one or more virtual devices (manually or automatically) and create the appropriate security policies for access.

- Configure your data processing logic (manually or using the CSP's services).

- Create any requisite event-triggering rules to invoke other services or publish messages back to your GDA.

- Create a dashboard to graphically monitor (and manually act on) your device's telemetry.

While I won't go into significant detail on any of these CSPs' IoT solutions, I'll briefly cover two very simple MQTT-based connectivity examples using Ubidots and AWS IoT Core.

Ubidots Connectivity Overview Using MQTT

Ubidots is an IoT CSP that supports device integration with your edge system using several protocols, including MQTT over TLS. This is the service provider I discuss in my Connected Devices class because it provides a way for students to integrate their GDA with the cloud without having to deploy any custom code.

As of this writing, Ubidots supports two types of accounts: industrial (with a brief free trial period) and STEM (for educational use only and with limited features).

The Ubidots dashboard provides a number of widgets, along with a drag-and-drop web-based interface for integrating them with a data stream coming from your GDA.

Figure 11-5 depicts a dashboard I created to track system performance across three different IoT gateways deployed in my home, along with a few basic environmental measures collected from one of those gateway devices connected to a Sense HAT module.

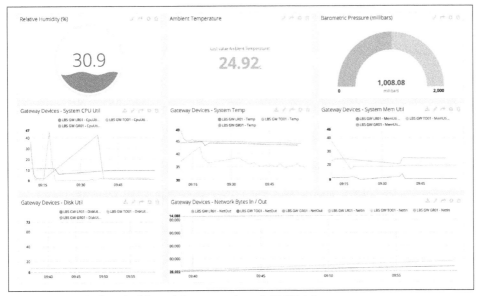

Figure 11-5. Ubidots dashboard depicting three IoT GDA instances

Neat, huh? So how does it work? Be sure you've reviewed PIOT-CFG-11-001 (*https://oreil.ly/3cgBP*), and then let's talk devices and telemetry.

Data sources and variables

In a nutshell: devices are data sources, and data sources have variables. Variables represent time-series data, or dots, that are collected and can be represented within a dashboard environment like the one I created in Figure 11-5.

Now, there needs to be some kind of tie-in with your physical device and the sensor or system performance data it's generating, right? Indeed, there is! Using MQTT topics, each device (or data source) has its own topic name and ID. Variables have their own topic names and IDs, each one mapped to a data source.

Topic names

Let's look at an example. The notional topic name "mydevice/myvariable" represents portions of an MQTT topic representing a data source (mydevice) and dot (myvariable). This topic will always be preceded by the Ubidots API topic structure.

At the time of this writing, the Ubidots MQTT topic structure begins with "/v1.6/devices/," and is followed by the device label and, optionally, the variable label. Using the notional topic name mentioned previously, this means the topic for "myvariable" would be "/v1.6/devices/mydevice/myvariable." You can read more about Ubidots MQTT topic names online (*https://oreil.ly/sKpHX*).

Auth tokens

Ubidots provides an administrative console and an API you can use to generate authentication tokens. You can read more about this process online (*https://oreil.ly/Pg9Br*).

The token you generate will be used as the username in your MQTT message. Remember way back in Chapter 6, when you learned that MQTT supports usernames and passwords? You finally get to use that feature of the protocol!

 Be sure to keep in mind the API token usage instructions (*https://oreil.ly/Pg9Br*). And always keep your API token, and any other generated tokens, safe and private. Treat them the same as you would any other highly sensitive information!

Connecting to the MQTT service using TLS

Once you've generated a new token, you can add it to your credential file as the value for the userAuth key and, if needed, update your *PiotConfig.props* Cloud.GatewayService section with credFile = *{your credential file}*.

With the updates you introduced to your MqttClientConnector in Chapter 10 to support credential loading from a separate file, *PiotConfig.props* and your credential file should be set up properly. If so, the value should be loaded and set as the username for all MQTT requests.

To use TLS (and I strongly recommend that you do), you'll need the Ubidots PEM certificate. The SimpleCertManagementUtil class (discussed in Chapter 10) should be integrated with your MqttClientConnector. As long as you specify the PEM filename properly within the Cloud.GatewayService section as the value for certFile and you've set the enableCrypt flag in the configuration file to "true," MqttClientConnector should load it automatically.

 Never connect your IoT device to a cloud service (or any external system over an unsecured network) without enabling encryption and strong authentication measures. Choose security over convenience. You can read more about how this works in the Ubidots MQTT documentation (*https://oreil.ly/XGqff*).

For clients that have a high keepAlive value, watch for autodisconnects. The current documentation states that a PINGREQ Control Packet must be received at least every 180 minutes, or else the broker will disconnect the client.

Creating data sources and variables

The admin console makes it very easy to create new data sources and associated variables. You can also publish a message to a data source topic using the appropriate JSON content.

This latter approach can be very convenient if you don't want to track data sources and variable names in two different places. The Ubidots send data documentation (*https://oreil.ly/YYyJY*) explains the JSON structure in detail.

Figure 11-6 shows a way to create new data sources and variables. I've used it to create my own (hence the name "LBS IoT Gateway").

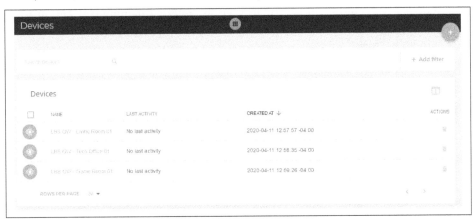

Figure 11-6. Ubidots dashboard for creating new devices

(Hmm..."No last activity." Looks like I need to update my auth key)

Publishing messages

If you're using MQTT, there are two ways to publish messages to your data source: use JSON or just use the raw value. I'll focus on JSON, as the message format is similar to that which your `DataUtil` will generate. This is where you may have to make some adjustments to your code in `CloudClientConnector`.

My own solution for generating consistent Ubidots topic names involves the following implementation of `CloudClientConnector`'s `createTopicName()` method:

```
protected String createTopicName(
    ResourceNameEnum resource, String itemName)
{
    // e.g., /v1.6/devices/constraineddevice/sensormsg-tempsensor
    StringBuilder buf = new StringBuilder(this.topicPrefix);

    buf.append(
        resource.getDeviceName().toLowerCase()).append('/');
```

```
    buf.append(
      resource.getResourceType().toLowerCase()).append('-');

    buf.append(itemName);

    return buf.toString();
  }
```

How does this work? It will generate the following String representation:

/v1.6/devices/{device name}/{telemetry type}-{item name}

The approach I've chosen allows me to keep my internal naming convention while supporting a more granular naming convention and adapting to the Ubidots convention with little effort.

Each time I publish a message, I invoke `createTopicName()` to generate the topic name and then delegate nearly everything else to the `MqttClientConnector`. I've also created a separate private method named `publishMessageToCloud()`, which is invoked by the public `sendEdgeDataToCloud()` method. Here's how they work in tandem, along with `createTopicName()`, to align with the Ubidots MQTT topic naming convention:

```
@Override
public boolean sendEdgeDataToCloud(
  ResourceNameEnum resource, SensorData data)
{
  if (resource != null && data != null) {
    String payload =
      DataUtil.getInstance().sensorDataToJson(data);

    return this.publishMessageToCloud(
      resource, data.getName(), payload);
  }

  return false;


private boolean publishMessageToCloud(
  ResourceNameEnum resource, String itemName, String payload)
{
  String topicName = createTopicName(resource, itemName);

  try {
    _Logger.finest(
      "Publishing payload value(s) to Ubidots: " + topicName);

    return this.mqttClient.publishMessage(
      topicName, payload.getBytes(), 1);
  } catch (Exception e) {
```

```
    _Logger.warning(
        "Failed to publish message to Ubidots: " + topicName);
    }

    return false;
}
```

As you can see, the `itemName` is just the `SensorData` name, which in this case is set all the way down in the CDA!

Incidentally, you can also add features to `DataUtil` to customize the payload to be specific to the JSON formatting rules of Ubidots or any other CSP. It's just another method, and you can invoke it from within `CloudClientConnector` to avoid propagating a different format throughout your code base.

Subscribing to events

Topic subscription messages follow a similar paradigm to publishing—identify the topic (data source and variable) from which you'd like to receive updates and issue the subscribe request.

The same adjustment you made to `CloudClientConnector` for publishing should carry over here, provided you invoke the `createTopicName()` method to generate your topic string. Just keep in mind that you'll have to parse whatever data you're sent.

Triggering actions

How about triggering an actuation event from the cloud? You can use the Ubidots interface to create a rule for publishing a dynamically generated (or existing) value to an existing variable and add a subscription for that variable within your `CloudClient Connector`.

Figure 11-7 represents a screenshot for a temperature event.

Figure 11-7. Creating an event trigger in Ubidots

I created this event to send a text message to my phone if the inside temperature of my house drops below a certain threshold or rises above another threshold for a certain period of time.

When I first created this event, I inadvertently set the floor and ceiling temperatures very close together, so I was getting text message alerts multiple times a day. Not quite what I was looking for. I adjusted the range so I would receive an event only when I had left a window open too long during the winter.

Further information

If you'd like to dig further into the details of the Ubidots MQTT-specific connections, be sure to review the Ubidots MQTT broker article (*https://oreil.ly/sKpHX*).

Also, Ubidots supports API authentication using HTTP or HTTPS. If this is important for your implementation, you can read more about this functionality in the Ubidots API authentication article (*https://oreil.ly/Pg9Br*).

AWS IoT Core Connectivity Overview Using MQTT

Amazon Web Services (AWS) is likely a familiar name. AWS provides a number of IoT services and capabilities that allow you to manage your devices and handle their data across a wide range of scalable services and tools.

Within the Edge Tier, you can use AWS IoT Greengrass (*https://aws.amazon.com/greengrass*) to pull in some cloud-based functionality to process data streams, whether connected to AWS or temporarily disconnected from the cloud.

As of this writing, AWS provides a variety of free-tier services that support IoT telemetry processing; many others offer free trials.

 It's very important to review the available service offerings and associated costs of the CSP you select before committing to a particular design and usage pattern. The free trial period, along with some free-tier services, can be a great way to familiarize yourself with these offerings; however, be aware that some of these services will incur costs (which may be significant) following the trial period or if your usage exceeds that allowed by the free tier. Most CSPs, including AWS, offer online tools that let you calculate your planned usage and estimate your projected costs.

The first step in connecting your GDA into AWS is to create an AWS account (if you haven't created one already). Then navigate to your AWS console, which as of this writing can be accessed from your web browser (*https://console.aws.amazon.com*).

I recommend reviewing the AWS IoT quick start tutorial (*https://oreil.ly/nsD6s*) first. For a more detailed hands-on tutorial, you may also want to review the AWS IoT Core hands-on tutorial (*https://oreil.ly/3nOC8*). As always, these details may change with time.

Provisioning a new device

In AWS, you can onboard a single device or multiple devices at once. Each device provisioned through the onboarding process will have a *device shadow*: an associated JSON file representing its most recent state. You can use the shadow to update the device state, whether or not it's currently connected to AWS. I'll briefly walk through the setup process for a single device: your GDA.[3]

From the AWS Console, find the Services drop-down and select "Internet of Things – IoT Core." On the left navigation pane, click Onboard → "Get started" and then "Onboard a device" → "Get started." Select "Get started" again, and then choose your operating environment and language (specifically, Java).

The next window will ask you to name your device; I've chosen "PiotGDA01" for my device's name. This will also generate your shadow.

Figure 11-8 shows a portion of a screen similar to the one you'll see after clicking "Next step."

At this point, I have a thing registered and named "PiotGDA01," along with a policy and a connection kit automatically generated by AWS. I'll use the policy to set access permissions within AWS, and the connection kit to retrieve the PKI infrastructure my GDA will need to securely connect into AWS IoT Core.

---

3 You may also want to review Chapter 2 of Dejan Mijic, Draško Draškovic, and Ervin Varga, *Scalable Architecture for the Internet of Things* (O'Reilly).

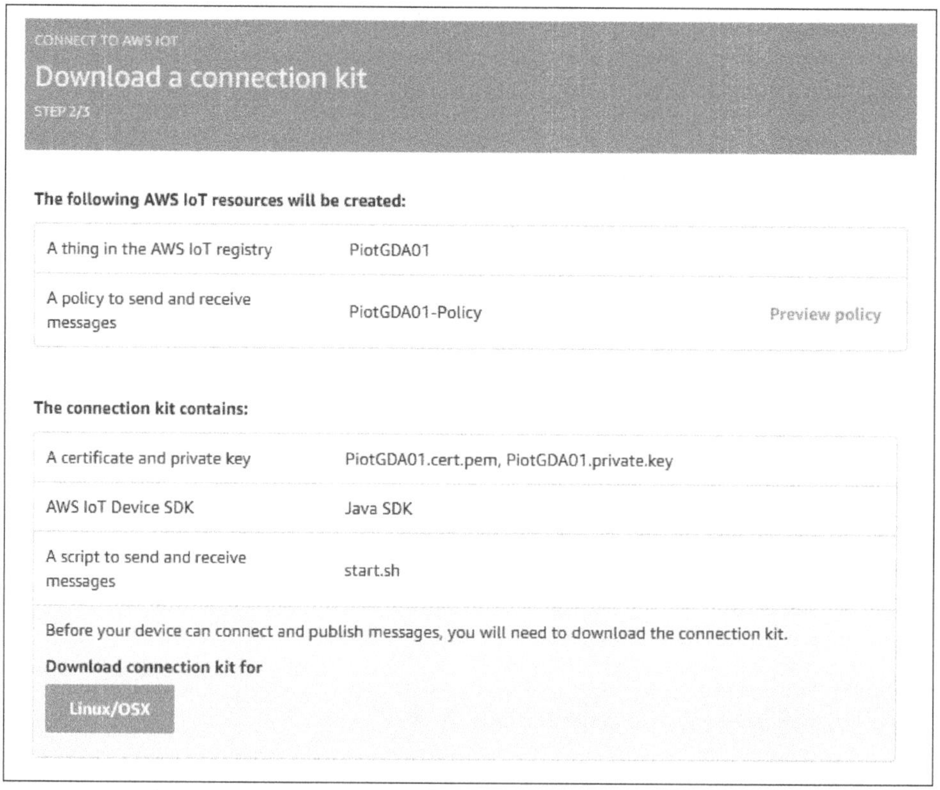

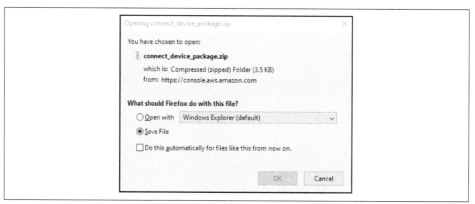

Figure 11-8. Thing successfully created; just need to download the connection kit

Figure 11-9 shows the dialog box that you'll see after clicking on the operating system button (in my case, it's Linux/OSX).

Figure 11-9. Downloading the connection kit, along with your PKI

This file is super important—not only does it contain a shell script you can execute to retrieve the SDK, but it also contains your PKI, which includes your private key. Be sure to keep this safe and secure at all times!

Once this is downloaded, click "Next step." The next page provides instructions for executing the shell script, which will download the AWS root CA, along with the AWS Java SDK, its dependencies, and some examples you can use to get started.

If all goes well, the script will also execute a simple publish/subscribe application to verify connectivity with AWS IoT Core. When I ran this on my own system (under WSL), the application generated the following log output (only partially represented here):

```
Cert file:../PiotGDA01.cert.pem Private key: ../PiotGDA01.private.key
Mar 07, 2021 8:27:47 PM com.amazonaws.services.iot.client.core.AwsIotConnection
onConnectionSuccess
INFO: Connection successfully established
Mar 07, 2021 8:27:47 PM com.amazonaws.services.iot.client.core.AbstractAwsIotClient
onConnectionSuccess
INFO: Client connection active: sdk-java
1615166867709: >>> hello from blocking publisher - 1
1615166867709: >>> hello from non-blocking publisher - 1
1615166867750: <<< hello from blocking publisher - 1
1615166867766: <<< hello from non-blocking publisher - 1
1615166868710: >>> hello from non-blocking publisher - 2
1615166868711: >>> hello from blocking publisher - 2
1615166868742: <<< hello from non-blocking publisher - 2
1615166868768: <<< hello from blocking publisher - 2
```

I ran this test for a bit longer than the log indicates, so you'll see in Figure 11-10 the AWS IoT Monitor depicting the total messages published, along with the single successful connection.

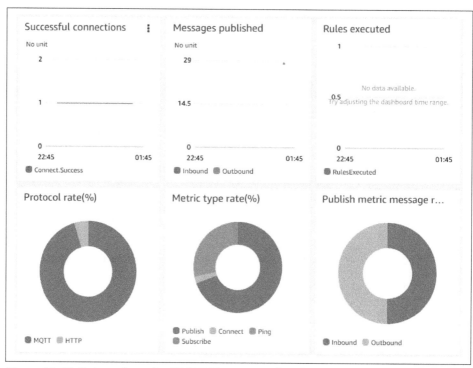

Figure 11-10. Snippet from the AWS IoT monitor after the initial connectivity test

Of course, the real fun begins after you've incorporated similar connection and messaging functionality into your GDA. But let's first discuss topic names, certificates, and keys.

Topic names

Since you'll connect into your AWS IoT environment using a client endpoint name, you can use the same topic names you're already using within your Edge Tier. (You can read more about topic names within AWS in the developer guide (*https://oreil.ly/CO9dJ*).) Two of the topic names I'll use in this section are:

PIOT/ConstrainedDevice/SensorMsg

PIOT/ConstrainedDevice/ActuatorCmd

 The resource and topic naming convention for this book uses CamelNotation, which is supported by the MQTT specification and can work well for disambiguation. You may want to alter this to align with your CSP's best practices.

Authentication and authorization

Your GDA will be able to connect to and interact with IoT Core only if it is authenticated and your requests— including to connect—are authorized.

In this section, I'll briefly describe authentication using the X.509 certificates you already downloaded as part of the connection kit. Authorization is handled via one or more policies that you specify and attach to your device shadow within AWS. For more information on AWS IoT security, including client and server authentication, see the developer guide (*https://oreil.ly/TXZGJ*).

Policies are an important part of your configuration. A policy can provide or limit access to certain resources and activities, so it's important to ensure proper setup. AWS should have generated a default policy based on your device name (e.g., PiotGDA01-Policy) and attached your device certificate.

This default policy permits publish, subscribe, and connect messages for a default list of test resources. Your GDA and its client ID will need permission to connect, publish, and subscribe, so you'll need to edit the policy to include this information. Any topic to which your GDA will either publish or subscribe will need to be listed as a permitted resource in the policy as well.

Editing the policy is straightforward. Within the IoT console, on the left side of the screen, expand Secure and click Policies. You should see your device name with "-Policy" appended. Click the policy name and scroll through to see where the topic names and client IDs are listed. You can simply choose to "Edit policy document" and add the new planned topics as resources (they'll map to ResourceNameEnum) and the client ID you plan to use for your GDA at the end of the document in the iot:Con nect section.

Here's an example (sensitive info replaced with "XXXXX" and test policies removed):

```
{
  "Version": "2012-10-17",
  "Statement": [
    {
      "Effect": "Allow",
      "Action": [
        "iot:Publish",
        "iot:Receive"
      ],
      "Resource": [
        "arn:aws:iot:XXXXX:XXXXX:topic/PIOT/GatewayDevice/SystemPerfMsg",
        "arn:aws:iot: XXXXX:XXXXX:topic/PIOT/GatewayDevice/SensorMsg",
        "arn:aws:iot: XXXXX:XXXXX:topic/PIOT/ConstrainedDevice/SystemPerfMsg",
        "arn:aws:iot: XXXXX:XXXXX:topic/PIOT/ConstrainedDevice/SensorMsg"
      ]
    },
    {
```

```
      "Effect": "Allow",
      "Action": [
        "iot:Subscribe"
      ],
      "Resource": [
        "arn:aws:iot: XXXXX:XXXXX:topicfilter/PIOT/ConstrainedDevice/ActuatorCmd"
      ]
    },
    {
      "Effect": "Allow",
      "Action": [
        "iot:Connect"
      ],
      "Resource": [
        "arn:aws:iot: XXXXX:XXXXX:client/gatewaydevice001"
      ]
    }
  ]
}
```

Notice that the publish section of the policy has two actions—`iot:Publish` and `iot:Receive`—whereas the subscribe section has just one—`iot:Subscribe`.

The connect section specifies the `iot:Connect` action, which will need to identify your device's client ID to permit connection events. These updates will be important —they define whether your GDA will be able to effectively integrate with IoT Core. For example, your GDA (named `gatewaydevice001`, as shown in the preceding example) won't be permitted to connect to IoT Core using MQTT unless you've defined a policy that permits this behavior.

When your edits are complete, save the policy. Time to write some code.

 As of this writing, each policy can maintain only five versions, so if you find you're unable to save your edits, you may have reached this limit. Simply click Versions and, if appropriate, delete those you are certain you no longer need. Then set the default for the version you want to use.

Connecting to the MQTT service using TLS

When you downloaded the connectivity kit for your language (Java) and platform, the zip file included your public certificate and PKI pair (private key and public key). The public certificate is used to prove your ownership of the public key, which the server will use to decrypt the data you send as encrypted locally by your private key. All are important in ensuring trusted and secure communications with an endpoint.

I've written some detailed requirements and related instructions to help you build out your remaining GDA infrastructure within the Kanban board. Be sure to review PIOT-GDA-11-005 (*https://oreil.ly/DRACO*) and PIOT-GDA-11-006 (*https://oreil.ly/*

Goctq) for the plumbing, and PIOT-GDA-11-007 (*https://oreil.ly/JC81s*) for the AWS-specific connectivity requirements and instructions.

Once you've completed these tasks, you can update your *PiotConfig.props* with the following:

```
[Cloud.GatewayService]
cloudServiceName = AWS

[Cloud.GatewayService.AWS]
certFile        = ./cert/PiotGDA01.cert.pem
privateKeyFile  = ./cert/PiotGDA01.private.key
cloudServiceName = AWS
securePort      = 8883
defaultQoS      = 0
keepAlive       = 60
clientEndpoint  = <client>.iot.<region>.amazonaws.com
```

With the introduction of `CloudClientFactory`, which you can use for any of your cloud client connection abstractions, the `Cloud.GatewayService` section now has only one entry: `cloudServiceName`. This tells the Factory which class to instantiate. The CSP-specific `ICloudClient` implementation will use the appropriate configuration section name to retrieve the parameters it needs to initialize the connection (for instance, the AWS `ICloudClient` instance will retrieve its properties from `Cloud.GatewayService.AWS`).

The `CloudClientFactoryTest` test class provided within the `programmingth eiot.part04.integration.connection` package provides a very simple set of calls to kick the tires on the connection logic and log a bunch of messages that should help with debugging.

In my own implementation, I added some additional log messages to verify message conversion. I also sent a `SensorData` instance to the actuator listener just to see if it was received (it was). Of course, this means I'll need to do more validation within my topic listener!

Your log output may look similar or not. Here's a quick sample of the log output from my own test:

```
Mar 08, 2021 1:14:36 PM programmingtheiot.gda.connection.CloudClientFactory
createCloudClient
INFO: Attempting to instance cloud client using cloud service name: AWS
Mar 08, 2021 1:14:36 PM programmingtheiot.gda.connection.AwsCloudClientConnector
initMqttClient
INFO: Initializing AWS MQTT client...
Cert file:./cert/PiotGDA01.cert.pem Private key: ./cert/PiotGDA01.private.key
.
.

.
Mar 08, 2021 1:14:37 PM com.amazonaws.services.iot.client.core.AbstractAwsIotClient
```

```
onConnectionSuccess
INFO: Client connection active: gatewaydevice001
Mar 08, 2021 1:14:42 PM programmingtheiot.gda.connection.AwsCloudClientConnector
subscribeToCloudEvents
INFO: Successfully subscribed to topic: PIOT/ConstrainedDevice/ActuatorCmd
.
.
.
Mar 08, 2021 1:14:42 PM programmingtheiot.common.DefaultDataMessageListener
handleActuatorCommandResponse
INFO: Topic: PIOT/ConstrainedDevice/ActuatorCmd, Message:
name=,typeID=0,timeStamp=2021-03-08T18:14:42.385353700Z,status
Code=0,hasError=false,locationID=Not
Set,latitude=0.0,longitude=0.0,elevation=0.0,command=0,isResponse=false,value=0.0
Mar 08, 2021 1:14:47 PM com.amazonaws.services.iot.client.core.AwsIotConnection
onConnectionClosed
INFO: Connection permanently closed
Mar 08, 2021 1:14:47 PM com.amazonaws.services.iot.client.core.AbstractAwsIotClient
onConnectionClosed
INFO: Client connection closed: gatewaydevice001
```

If I refresh the AWS IoT Monitor, Figure 11-11 shows the results (after many, many test runs).

This is the proof you need to verify that your GDA has connected and can publish messages and receive notifications on subscriptions. Now to actually do something with all of this information: let's build out a simple Lambda function to handle these events.

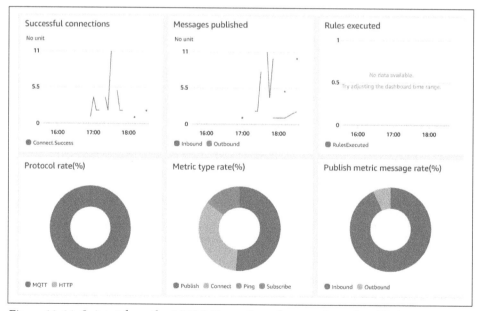

Figure 11-11. Snippet from the AWS IoT monitor after running a few GDA integration tests

Creating a function to handle incoming messages

Going back to Figure 11-4 ("Notional design for the cloud services functions"), I've highlighted a few simple functions that can be implemented within an environment like AWS. Functions such as these (implemented using AWS Lambda) can be used to provide custom handling for incoming messages from the MQTT broker hosted within AWS IoT Core.

To create an AWS Lambda, select the Services drop-down from the top of your management console. Click Lambda under the "Compute" section and then click "Create function" in the next window (or select one you've already created if you have a Lambda ready to go).

You can use the built-in code editor ("Author from scratch") or an existing template. I've chosen "Author from scratch" in the example that follows. Give your function a name (such as `PiotHandleSensorData`) and select the runtime you'd like to use (such as Python 3.7). I'm using the default execution role for my implementation.

Click "Create function" to complete the creation process.

From this point on, you can use the embedded code editor to write your function or develop it within your IDE. If you choose to use your IDE, you'll need to generate a zip file with the files and directory structure for each module dependency that is not part of Python 3.7 and upload it to your function.

If you choose "Author from Scratch" in Python and use the IDE within your local environment, you can use Maven to generate your zip file. If you're developing your function in Python and using your python-components repository, I've described one way to do this in PIOT-CFG-11-002 (*https://oreil.ly/5E3re*).

Figure 11-12 depicts a screen similar to the one you'll likely see.

Figure 11-12. Snippet from the AWS Lambda function overview screen for PiotHandle SensorData

Some of the code is already generated; you can change it to support your specific needs. The default module name is *lambda_function.py*, and the invoked function name is `lambda_handler(event, context):`. Feel free to leave these, since the Lambda function will be invoked from within your soon-to-be rules environment using the name you gave it.

For convenience, I've renamed the module *SensorDataHandlerFunction.py* and changed the function name to `handleSensorData(event, context):`. To rename yours, you'll need to scroll down to "Runtime settings" and edit the Handler, which defaults to `lambda_function.lambda_handler`.

Figure 11-13 provides a snippet from the Lambda editor screen. You can see that the Handler info is now `SensorDataHandlerFunction.handleSensorData`.

Figure 11-13. Creating a Lambda function using the web-based code editor

For all of this to work, the Lambda function will need to be deployed and have a policy attached permitting access to DynamoDB. You can configure this using the Identity and Access Manager (IAM): select IAM from the Services drop-down menu.

AWS provides numerous prebuilt policies that you can use to support this type of activity. To learn more about policy management and IAM in general, please see the AWS IAM documentation (*https://oreil.ly/Nf7BE*).

With your policy attached and the Lambda deployed, you can create and execute a test to verify that it functions properly. Click on the Test drop-down and click "Configure test event." Select a test template (like hello-world), provide a name, and drop in some sample JSON as the input.

Figure 11-14 shows a snippet from the "Configure test event" pop-up window.

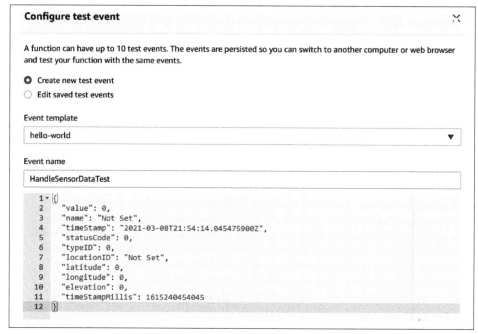

Figure 11-14. Creating a Lambda test event

You may need to click the "Format JSON" button before creating the test; otherwise you may get an error.

With your Lambda created, an appropriate policy attached, and a test in place, you can deploy the function and invoke it when data arrives within IoT Core.

Triggering actions

You can create a rule within the AWS IoT console based on a simple query statement (using SQL). Once the rule is defined, it will "fire" whenever there's an event that aligns with the specified SQL.

Let's say you want to fire a rule whenever a new SensorData instance (in JSON) is received. In the AWS IoT console, navigate to Act on the left side of the interface and click Rules. Give it a name, such as StoreSensorData, along with a description, and then choose the SQL version you'd like to use from the drop-down.

In the terminal-like window below the SQL version selector, type in the SQL command. In this case, you might type:

```
SELECT * FROM 'PIOT/ConstrainedDevice/SensorMsg'
```

That's it! The screenshot in Figure 11-15 provides a bit more clarity.

Rule query statement

Indicate the source of the messages you want to process with this rule.

Using SQL version

2016-03-23 ▾

Rule query statement

SELECT <Attribute> FROM <Topic Filter> WHERE <Condition>. For example: SELECT temperature FROM 'iot/topic' WHERE temperature > 50.
To learn more, see AWS IoT SQL Reference.

```
1  SELECT * FROM 'PIOT/ConstrainedDevice/SensorMsg'
```

Figure 11-15. Creating an AWS IoT rules query

So what does `SELECT * FROM 'PIOT/ConstrainedDevice/SensorMsg'` do? Not much —yet. It will fire whenever a new `SensorData` JSON payload is published to the *PIOT/ConstrainedDevice/SensorMsg* topic. From here, you can assign an action.

Here's where you need to think a bit about your overall design (and budget!). What do you want to happen? Which service is best designed to handle that action? Is there anything else that should happen when this rule is fired? If you're in the process of designing a system, you may have already answered those questions. The "Add action" button will, well, add the action.

At this point, you'll have many different options available. You can simply insert the data into a DynamoDB table, store the JSON within an S3 bucket, pass the content on to another Lambda function, and so forth.

> Using existing provisioned services or provisioning a new service may incur charges. Be sure to review the costs before deciding on a course of action.

Once you've settled on the "what" (store the data), choose the service to which you'd like to pass the message (invoke a Lambda function) and click "Configure action." From here, you can configure the resource however you'd like.

The final step is to create the rule by clicking on the "Create rule" button and then enable it (assuming you want it to *actually* fire). The next page allows you to do so by clicking on the "..." next to the rule name and selecting Enable.

The no-code approach involves passing the data to an existing service that can process (or store) JSON messages natively, such as DynamoDB or S3. If you want greater control over the behavior of the event, you can trigger a Lambda function like the one you just created, as shown in Figure 11-16.

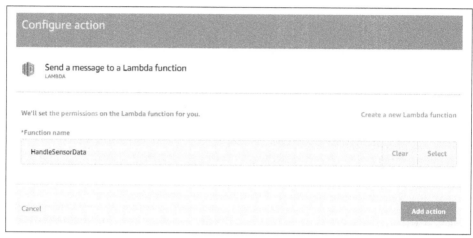

Figure 11-16. Snippet depicting the action configured to call the HandleSensorData *Lambda*

After completing the Chapter 11 Kanban board exercises and the AWS exercise described in PIOT-GDA-11-007 (*https://oreil.ly/JC81s*), you can test your implementation, monitoring activity using the AWS IoT Monitor to see whether IoT Core is receiving messages and triggering any rules.

Figure 11-17 shows the monitor once more, this time with the additional data—which now includes data within the "Rules executed" graph.

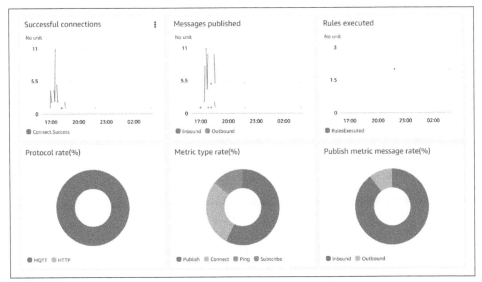

Figure 11-17. Snippet from the AWS IoT monitor showing rules executed

Further information

The example in PIOT is very basic and provides some initial ideas for managing IoT Core topic publish and subscribe events. One of the articles I found helpful for processing time-series data is described in the *AWS Database Blog*, titled "Patterns for AWS IoT time series data ingestion with Amazon Timestream" (*https://oreil.ly/XAI9w*).

For more information on the details of AWS IoT, see the developer's guide (*https://oreil.ly/edzWF*).

Additional Exercises

Lab Module 11 (*https://oreil.ly/RYrSe*) within the Programming the IoT Kanban board (*https://oreil.ly/programming-iot-kanban*) lists all the current exercises for this chapter, with more in the works. I'll be adding more exercises to the Kanban board in the future but have listed one you may want to tackle on your own.

Analyzing and Acting on Time-Series Performance Data

If you had access to hours, days, or even weeks of time-series data from your IoT devices, what would you want to know? How about the GDA's overall network utilization trends? If the data the GDA is sending to the cloud is not time-critical, and its network (and perhaps CPU) utilization is gradually increasing, would it be helpful to send it data streaming pacing instructions? Perhaps throttle back a bit (again, assuming the data it's sending can be more efficiently batched)?

Using the additional exercises from Chapter 2 for the GDA specifically, see if you can implement a cloud-based rule that observes GDA system performance trends and generates an event back to the GDA, instructing it to throttle back its data streaming (again, for noncritical data). This use case will require an advanced cloud-based rule, along with another topic the GDA can subscribe to related to system management. In fact, you may need to add another data type as well—perhaps you can call it `SystemMa nagementData` (also derived from `BaseIotData`)—that will contain the instructions the GDA will need to temper its data streaming activities a bit.

Conclusion

My objective with this chapter was to introduce you to some of the core concepts associated with connecting your GDA into the cloud. You learned how to create a simple cloud client abstraction layer within your code that uses MQTT to connect to two different CSP MQTT brokers. You also learned how to use some cloud services to interpret the data published by your GDA and to then publish an `ActuatorData` message back to the GDA.

Clearly, much more can be done in the cloud than I've explored in this chapter, so be sure to review the CSP documentation and use case examples provided in the various AWS developer guides for more detailed information on the various services and capabilities each service provides.

Taming the IoT

*A Discussion of Key IoT Enablement Principles
and Some Simple Use Cases*

Has my goal been reached?
Measure, Model, and Manage.
Now it all makes sense.

> **Fundamental concepts**: A way to tackle an IoT challenge and a few sample IoT scenarios are covered, including notional implementation approaches.

This is the chapter you've been waiting for, where we bounce out of the technical gobbledygook and look at the bigger picture of the IoT ecosystem. If you're planning on tackling a business problem, this chapter will help you bring together the concepts you've learned.

What You'll Learn in This Chapter

All technology-enabled systems *do* something, and they generally share some common characteristics. They also share a set of core requirements that—for the most part—can be abstracted into groups. I'll call these *IoT ecosystem enablers* and discuss them next.

IoT Ecosystem Enablers

Most systems comprise more than just categorized requirements and architecture, however, so it's helpful to think about the enablers that facilitate a robust, integrated platform—not only technically but also *systematically*. This requires considering a broader range of requirement categories, as well as processes to ensure consistency.

You can think of these requirement categories as *interdependent enablers*, as shown in Figure 12-1.

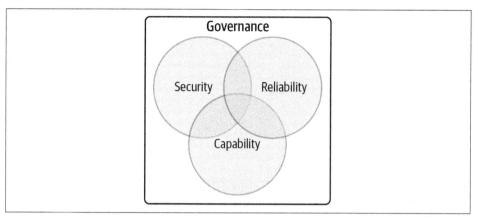

Figure 12-1. IoT ecosystem enablers and their relationships

At the center, where all of the enablers intersect, is a holistic, balanced, and effective IoT ecosystem—one that provides value for all stakeholders.

While these enablers might seem obvious, I find it helpful to keep them at the front of my mind to help me avoid focusing only on the technology solution. It's all about perspective.

Security

Not surprisingly, security is crucial to any technology ecosystem, and the IoT is no exception. Here is a brief and nonexhaustive high-level checklist of IoT ecosystem security categories that may help you think about potential gaps and resolutions.

System
> What is the software validation procedure (firmware, applicates, services, etc.)? What type of authentication and authorization will be used? How will tokens, certificates, secrets, and so on be protected on the system? How will the system data's provenance be ensured so you know you can trust it?

Administrative
> How will the system (devices and services) be physically and logically accessed? Who will be authorized to access and administer this system? What level of protection is required to keep each device safe?

Manageability
> How will system code or certificate updates be managed? How will the system recover from a failed management action? What happens if the system or any

part of it (such as keys, credentials, or data) is compromised? How will you protect your (or your customer's) intellectual property data within the ecosystem?

Capability

A secure and functioning system needs to meet business objectives and—most likely—to support future enhancements without negatively impacting either. It also needs to accept automated or manual instructions. Here are three general capability categories to keep in mind:

Functionality

What core functions must the system support? Who's responsible for defining these functions? What is the decision process for approving or changing system functionality?

Expandability

What future capabilities *may* be plausible? What's the timeline for system expansion? What does the system need *now* to support these activities?

Commandability

This extends beyond security manageability and centers on the ability of the system to receive instructions to start or stop a process. How will the ecosystem be managed? Who will manage it? What is your process for dealing with unintended management events?

Reliability

An effective IoT ecosystem needs to be secure and provide business value. It also needs to provide assurance that it is both robust and accurate, because your outcomes are only as good as the quality and robustness of your device interactions and the data they produce. If data is available sporadically or otherwise unreliably, it may be difficult to extract business value that informs the bigger picture. Here are some considerations to keep in mind regarding IoT ecosystem reliability:

Sustainability

How will the devices be powered? How will the ecosystem respond if one or more devices lose power? What is the duty cycle or longevity of each device? How will the devices be updated or replaced, and what's the process for doing so?

Connectivity

Where (physically and geographically) will the devices be deployed? How will they connect to the internet: wirelessly, wired, via a gateway, as the gateway? How will the ecosystem (and devices) respond if connectivity is lost?

Accessibility

What are the system responsiveness timelines? Are any devices within the IoT environment expected to send recurring "ping" messages? How will you know if a given device is accessible and available?

Governance

Good governance is important for a successful IoT ecosystem. At the end of the day, some stakeholder team needs to oversee the well-being of the current and future IoT ecosystem, including the processes and associated rules for managing its security, capability, and reliability enablers. This generally involves business unit stakeholders and the engineering team to ensure consistency in execution and system management. Here are some categories to consider:

Compatibility

How will system software updates be versioned? How will partner APIs be managed? How will all functions—including those that support interoperability—be tested and validated? What is the process for mapping these interdependencies and ensuring nothing breaks on update?

Data management

How will data element updates be decided? What data will be stored and where? Who *owns* the data at each capture point? What service level agreements (SLAs) will be put into place?

Regulatory

What, if any, regulatory constraints apply to the environment (devices, connections, data, access, etc.)? What, if any, local jurisdiction rules might apply now or in the future? Who is responsible for approvals and other sign-off activities?

These enablers are not exhaustive, of course; consider them a starting point, and add your own.

Now let's look at some sample IoT use cases that apply these enablers and touch on the key activities of an IoT ecosystem: Measure, Model, and Manage.

Sample IoT Use Cases

It seems there's no end to the potential benefits of an effective IoT ecosystem. Volumes can be (and have been) written about IoT use cases and their potential impact on business outcomes. This section covers a tiny sliver of this space, which I hope is helpful in establishing a mental map of how an IoT ecosystem comes together.

These sample IoT use cases serve merely as notional high-level design concepts; they are not intended to be complete. Many details—including but not limited to Cloud

Tier and Edge Tier security, data management considerations, and system management and control—are either left out completely or only marginally referenced.

The three use cases I'll discuss are:

- Home environment monitoring and temperature adjustment (manual and automatic)
- Garden monitoring and water adjustment (manual)
- Pond water quality monitoring (automatic)

Shared Enablers and a Common Notional Design

It turns out these three use cases can all be based on the same notional high-level design (HLD). Figure 12-2 generalizes this design in a way that captures the key components and their interactions without diving into the details.

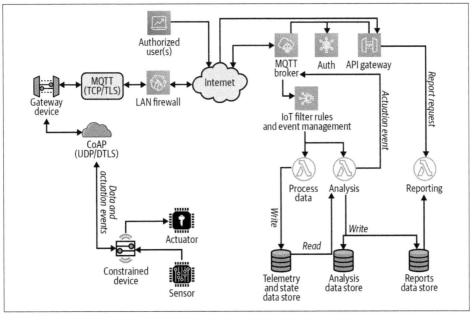

Figure 12-2. Notional HLD for generic edge to cloud IoT implementation

The enablers—security, capability, reliability, and governance—are related across each.

Enablers (security, capability, reliability, and governance)

Each use case incorporates the key enablers from the start:

Security

The Edge Tier is protected by a firewall. Messaging between the Edge Tier devices is encrypted (using TLS for MQTT messages or DTLS for CoAP messages). The Cloud Tier leverages the CSP's authorization and authentication capabilities, which require messaging traffic to be encrypted. Only authorized users can access the Cloud Tier through an API gateway that routes messages to the appropriate destination. Any data stored is encrypted and accessible only by authorized functions.

Capability

Each use case will impose its own capability requirements, but many will still be shared across all use cases. These requirements might include telemetry storage and analysis, or trend reporting that's available for authorized and authenticated end users to retrieve and view. Scalability is also important, since more Edge Tier devices may be added in the future. The cloud design—using a scalable microservices design for collecting data and triggering actions—supports this, along with the ability to distribute workloads across regions. Rules-based event management provides the ability to manage and scale new process flows using existing and future services.

Reliability

While not explicitly called out in Figure 12-2, features within the MQTT client library in the gateway device allow automatic reconnects, should the device lose its connection to the MQTT broker hosted by the CSP. Constrained devices rely on the connectionless CoAP over UDP (and DTLS) protocol, which means it is possible to lose a message; however, the CDA and GDA should be implemented to handle this type of situation.

Governance

Governance (though not covered in Figure 12-2) can be partially built into the rules and event management functionality. In addition to the organization's operations objectives and processes, this helps ensure that any significant changes that could influence organizational outcomes are approved before execution.

Now that we have a baseline established, let's move on to the use cases before analysis paralysis sets in!

Use Case 1: Home Environment Monitoring and Temperature Adjustment

Wouldn't it be wonderful to come home and find the lighting, music, temperature, and humidity at optimal comfort levels? The home automation market is growing rapidly, and opportunities to add even more "smart" features to your living environment seem to grow by leaps and bounds each year. How can you align these home automation ideas and your own monitoring needs with the knowledge you've gleaned here?

Let's go all the way back to that first problem statement in Chapter 1:

> I want to understand the environment in my home, how it changes over time, and make adjustments to enhance comfort while saving money.

Figure 12-3 aligns a notional HLD to the problem statement but is still based on Figure 12-2.

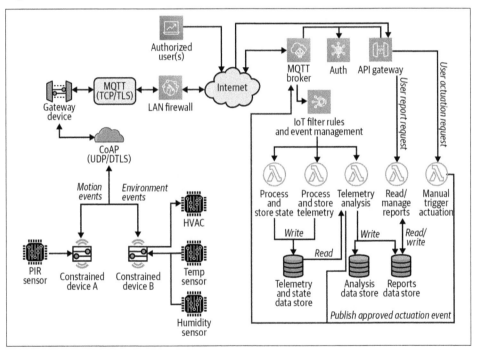

Figure 12-3. Notional HLD for home environment monitoring and temperature adjustment

Let's briefly unpack this diagram.

Measure, Model, and Manage

At the Edge Tier, the diagram depicts the measurement of temperature and humidity. It also uses a *passive infrared (PIR) sensor* to capture basic movement within a given space, such as when someone enters or exits a room. The PIR sensor simply reports a boolean—True or False—if it detects IR motion within its range.

We need a model to ensure that the right baselines are in place and that the measured data has some meaning. I discussed this process at length in Chapters 3 and 4, so I won't revisit it here; let's just assume that the appropriate measurement model and floor/ceiling configurations exist and are available within both the Edge Tier and the Cloud Tier.

This leaves the management activity, which will be active within the following components:

Constrained device B
> If the measured temperature "settles" above or below the threshold set by the local model (via a simple hysteresis analysis process), the HVAC actuation will be triggered to reduce or increase the temperature accordingly. Measurement activities continue, enabling the gateway device to track updates and pass these along to the cloud.

Gateway device
> This is receiving measurements from the PIR sensor attached to constrained device A, along with temperature and humidity readings (and HVAC actuation responses) from constrained device B. These readings let the gateway device determine whether it should send an actuation event to constrained device B that will raise or lower the temperature in a given area. It might do this if, for example, no movement is detected in a room or heating zone for a period of time yet its temperature is set to "high."

Cloud services
> The reporting function can generate temperature and humidity usage across a larger range of devices (not shown in Figure 12-3), showing the bigger picture of how the HVAC is engaged, how long it's active, and whether it's heating or cooling unused space. The user can manually adjust the model (if desired) or even permit automatic adjustments.

You can see how you might be able to add even more home automation capabilities to the system.

Use Case 2: Garden Monitoring and Water Adjustment

Let's say you like to travel, but you also keep houseplants, or perhaps a small indoor vegetable garden. You'd like your plants to thrive even when you're away from home. Figure 12-4 provides a notional HLD IoT system that may be helpful.

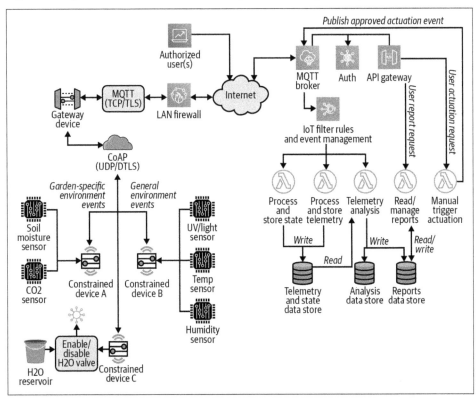

Figure 12-4. Notional HLD for garden monitoring and water adjustment

You'll notice this figure's similarity with Figure 12-3, but there are a few key differences—for example, the third constrained device (C), which is solely responsible for activating or deactivating a watering event. Let's dig in.

Measure, Model, and Manage

At the Edge Tier, Figure 12-4 depicts constrained device B's measurement of temperature, humidity, and light (UV and visible). Constrained device A measures carbon dioxide levels and soil moisture content. These sensor readings are passed along to the gateway device for further processing and transmission to the Cloud Tier. No analysis is really required at this point.

The model for this notional HLD is represented in two locations: within the Edge Tier's gateway device and the Cloud Tier. The Edge Tier model only needs access to the model representing the minimum and maximum (floor and ceiling) soil moisture levels for the constrained device instances and their paired plants, while the Cloud Tier model represents this information for all monitored plants (if, for example, there are multiple Edge Tier instances in play).

The management activity is generally confined to two components:

Gateway device
If the measured soil moisture level settles at or above the ceiling, the gateway device can instruct constrained device C to disable all watering until further instructions. If the level falls to or below the floor, it can either signal a watering actuation event to constrained device C or report back to the Cloud Tier that a given plant needs to be watered.

Cloud services
The reporting function can generate garden monitoring statistics across all managed devices, and potentially across many Edge Tier instances. When paired with plant-specific data and optimal soil moisture rules, it can produce human-readable reports recommending manual actions, which the human user can then trigger through the trigger actuation function (such as sending a water actuation event to the Edge Tier).

I purposely excluded the automatic watering actuation event within the Cloud Tier to show how, in some cases, it may be more appropriate for a human to review a report and manually trigger an action, even if the IoT ecosystem is capable of managing it automatically.

Use Case 3: Pond Quality Monitoring

This use case focuses solely on monitoring various quality metrics within a small body of water, such as a fishpond or tank. Figure 12-5 provides a notional HLD representing this type of monitoring system.

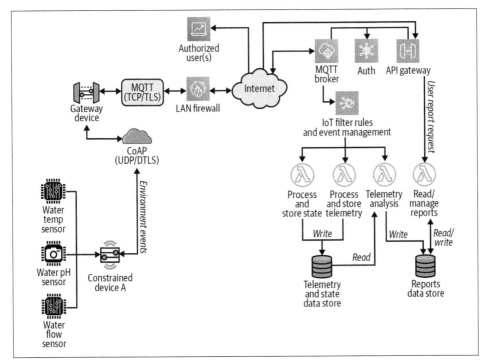

Figure 12-5. Notional HLD for pond quality monitoring

This is clearly less complicated than the other use cases, since it's monitoring only a few water properties and reporting back within a cloud service.

Measure, Model, and Manage

At the Edge Tier, the diagram depicts only measurement capabilities using a single constrained device: water temperature, water pH level, and water flow (via an appropriately placed water flow sensor). These measurements are collected by constrained device A, transmitted to the gateway device, and finally sent up to the cloud.

The only model needed for this use case is hosted exclusively within the Cloud Tier—it will provide comparative statistics and possibly some recommended floor and ceiling values for water temperature and pH (both important to the health of aquatic life) and water flow (to determine filtration activity).

The management activity is equally straightforward. It needs only to generate reports, not to trigger any actuation events.

Consider how you might want to incorporate actuation within this design. What additional measurements, if any, might be needed to facilitate automatic actuation of a feature at the Edge Tier?

Conclusion

Did these IoT use cases resonate with you? They represent some of the first IoT problems I tackled as personal projects. There are numerous use cases that could benefit from an IoT ecosystem, of course!

For my Connected Devices course, I've documented some basic requirements for a simple use case in Lab Module 12 (*https://oreil.ly/NECYa*). I'd encourage you to consider whether any of these requirements may be relevant for you, and how you might apply the concepts presented in this book to help you design and build an IoT solution for your own unique use case.

I hope you've enjoyed *Programming the Internet of Things* and have found it educational and useful. It has been a labor of love.

If you're interested in expanding your IoT technical knowledge, be sure to check the Programming the IoT Kanban board (*https://oreil.ly/programming-iot-kanban*) regularly. I expect to continuously refine and update the cards and even add new exercises.

Thanks for reading!

Design Road Maps

A view of the whole,
Shown as a system of parts
Assembled for all.

This appendix serves as the overarching detailed design road map for each chapter, leading up to your end-state IoT solution. It contains references to each application and to the applications' respective tie-ins to each other and the cloud, viewed step by step, starting from the exercises in Chapter 1 through those in Chapter 11.

As you walk through each diagram, you'll notice that the overall design remains the same, but each chapter's components are highlighted in the same manner as their related exercises discussed previously in the book. You can use this as a reference to assist with your understanding of the technical road map for each exercise, or even as a general guide to build a completely new solution.

Each of the UML designs in this section are notional, representing only class names (sometimes abbreviated to save page space) and the general associations with other classes. None of the diagrams explicitly call out instance multiplicity or declare internal members or their visibility.

These diagrams are best used as a guide to assist you with understanding the design principles outlined in each chapter. Please feel free to modify these and even change the names to suit your specific needs.

Part I, "Getting Started"—Design Road Maps

Chapter 1 Designs

The initial application shells are already written and included as part of the python-components and java-components repositories, but you can certainly add or change whatever features you'd like. Figures A-1 and A-2 represent this chapter's notional UML designs for the CDA and GDA, respectively.

Constrained Device Application design

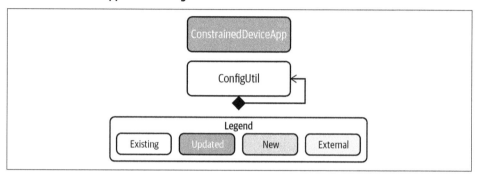

Figure A-1. CDA notional UML for Chapter 1

Gateway Device Application design

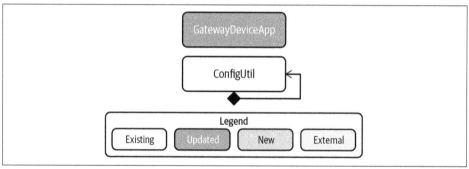

Figure A-2. GDA notional UML for Chapter 1

Chapter 2 Designs

With your development environment established and the initial application shells functioning, the next phase of the design for each application is to add system performance monitoring. This affects both the Gateway Device App and the Constrained Device App. Figures A-3 and A-4 represent this chapter's notional UML designs for the CDA and GDA, respectively.

Constrained Device Application design

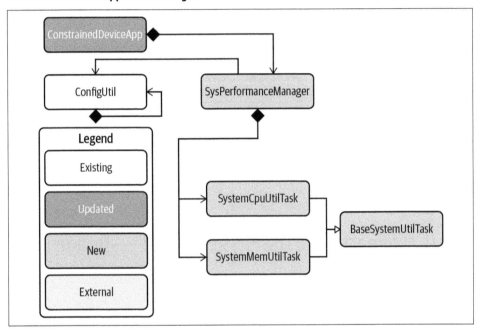

Figure A-3. CDA notional UML for Chapter 2

Gateway Device Application design

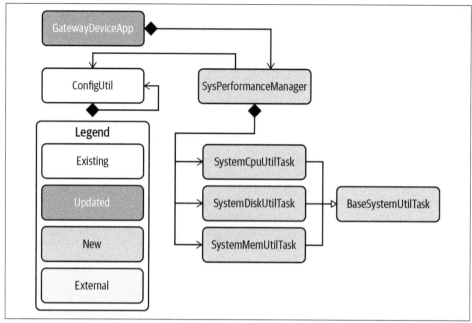

Figure A-4. GDA notional UML for Chapter 2

Part II, "Connecting to the Physical World"—Design Road Maps

Chapter 3 Design

For this chapter's design (and the next), only the CDA will be updated. In this exercise, the CDA design is focused on generating simulated data for sensing and simple commands that can be sent to a simulated actuator. Figure A-5 represents this chapter's notional UML design for the CDA.

Constrained Device Application design

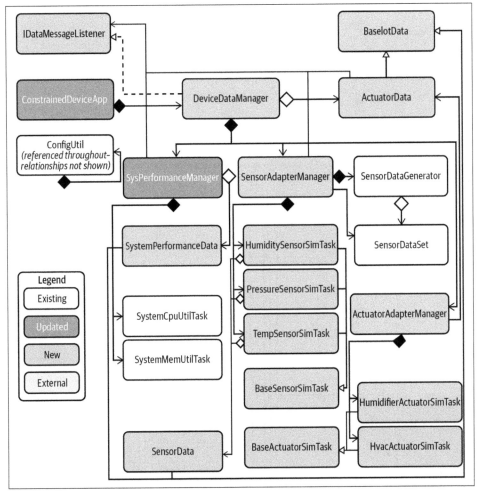

Figure A-5. CDA notional UML for Chapter 3

Chapter 4 Design

With your development environment established and the initial application shells functioning, the next phase of the design for each application is to add system performance monitoring. As with Chapter 3, only the CDA is affected. Figure A-6 represents this chapter's notional UML design for the CDA.

Constrained Device Application design

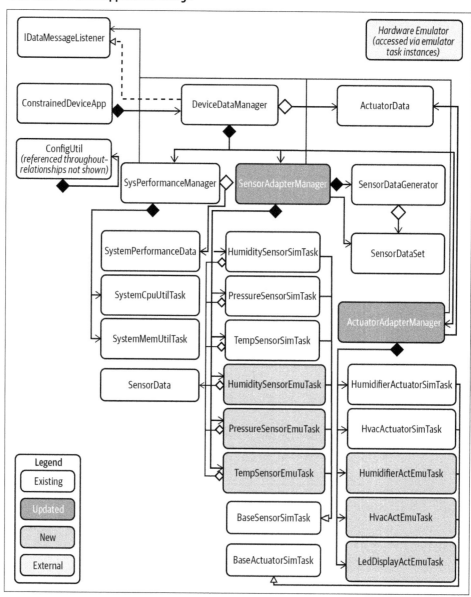

Figure A-6. CDA notional UML for Chapter 4

Chapter 5 Designs

Now that you've updated the CDA with sensing and actuation simulators and emulators, it's time to focus on data management for both applications. Included in this section are the designs for each application with these components highlighted, as well as the additional persistence functionality added into the GDA. Figures A-7 and A-8 represent this chapter's notional UML designs for the CDA and GDA, respectively.

Constrained Device Application design

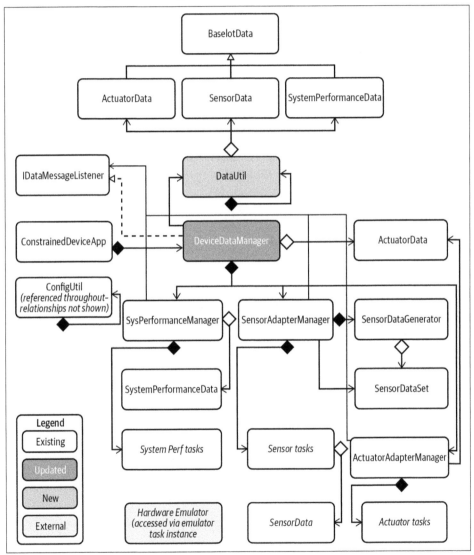

Figure A-7. CDA notional UML for Chapter 5

Gateway Device Application design

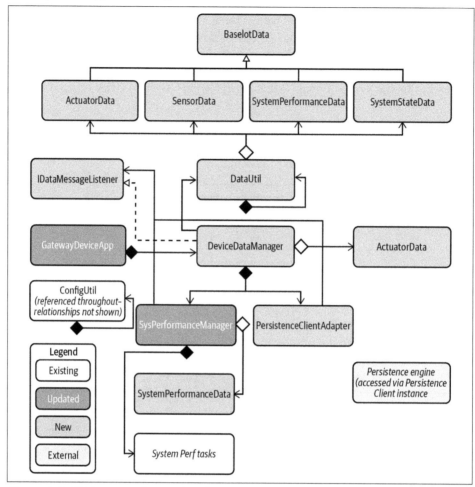

Figure A-8. GDA notional UML for Chapter 5

Part III, "Connecting to Other Things"—Design Road Maps

Chapter 6 Design

Part III moves your solution into the communications realm, where your CDA and GDA will use common IoT messaging protocols to pass messages among themselves. This chapter focuses on MQTT and CDA. Figure A-9 represents this chapter's notional UML design for the CDA.

Constrained Device Application design

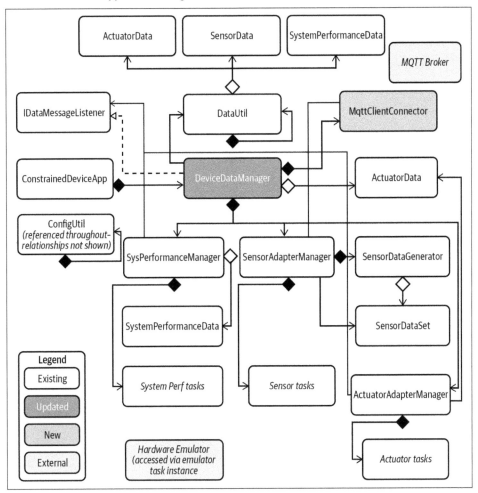

Figure A-9. CDA notional UML for Chapter 6

Chapter 7 Design

The previous chapter's exercises focused on building an MQTT connector within the CDA. This chapter does the same but for the GDA. Once this is complete, both the CDA and the GDA will be able to communicate using MQTT through a separate MQTT broker (server) application. Figure A-10 represents this chapter's notional UML design for GDA.

Gateway Device Application design

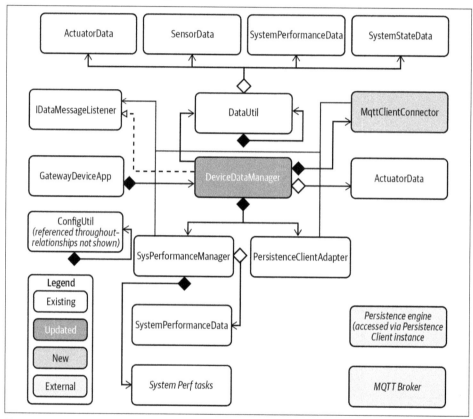

Figure A-10. GDA notional UML for Chapter 7

Chapter 8 Designs

The next two chapters focus on the design road map for CoAP integration. This introduces the request/response paradigm and focuses on building your own server using CoAP within the GDA.

As an optional Chapter 8 exercise, you can build your CoAP server adapter in Python and integrate it with your CDA. Figure A-12 depicts this approach in UML. Figures A-11 and A-12 represent this chapter's notional UML designs for the GDA and optional CDA, respectively.

Gateway Device Application design

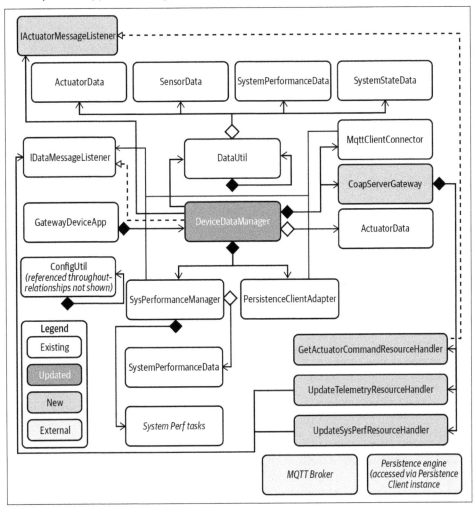

Figure A-11. GDA notional UML for Chapter 8

Constrained Device Application design (optional)

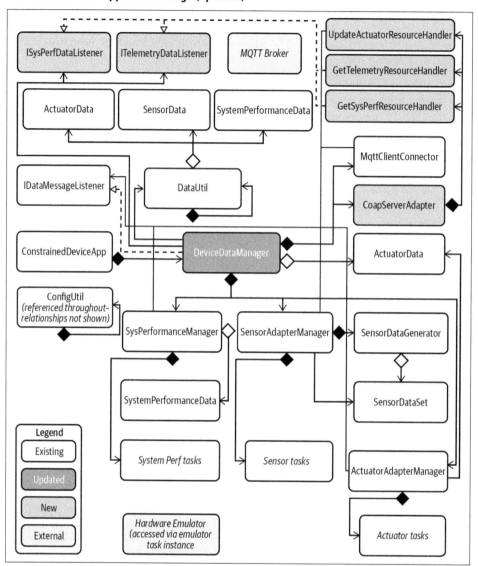

Figure A-12. CDA notional UML for Chapter 8 (optional)

Chapter 9 Designs

A CoAP server is great to have, but it's not very useful to your overall design unless you have a client that can use it. In this chapter's exercises, the design road maps show the components that will be used to create a CoAP client for the CDA that can connect to the GDA CoAP server.

As an optional exercise, the GDA can also implement a CoAP client. Figures A-13 and A-14 represent this chapter's notional UML designs for the CDA and optional GDA, respectively.

Constrained Device Application design

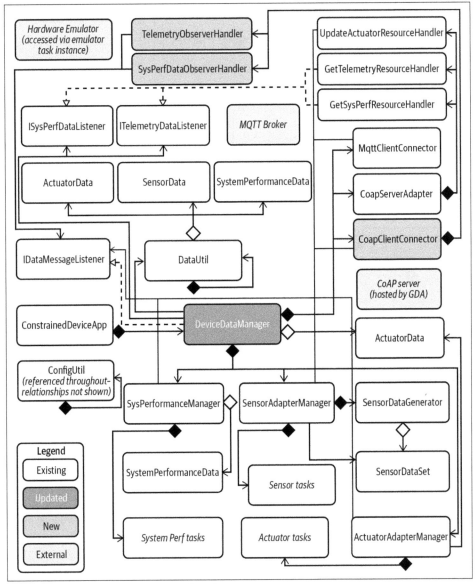

Figure A-13. CDA notional UML for Chapter 9

Gateway Device Application design (optional)

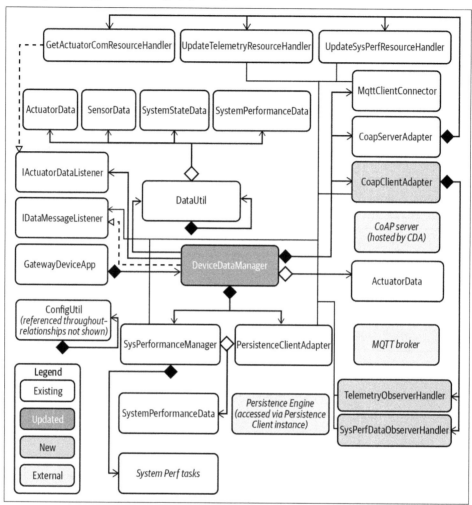

Figure A-14. GDA notional UML for Chapter 9 (optional)

Chapter 10 Designs

At long last, it's time to implement the business logic that connects all these pieces together! You'll use your choice of MQTT or CoAP (or both). The design road maps in this chapter show how to do this for both the CDA and the GDA. Figures A-15 and A-16 represent this chapter's notional UML designs for the CDA and GDA, respectively.

Constrained Device Application design

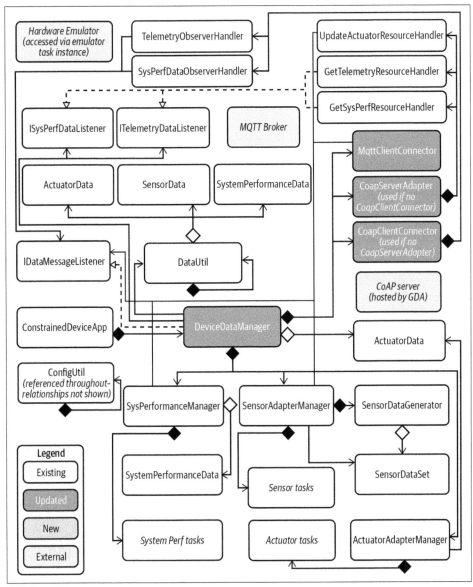

Figure A-15. CDA notional UML for Chapter 10

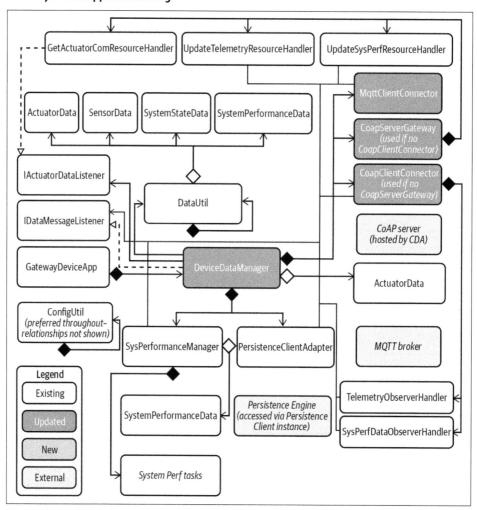

Figure A-16. GDA notional UML for Chapter 10

Part IV, "Connecting to the Cloud"—Design Road Maps

Chapter 11 Designs

Neither last nor least: it's time to connect your GDA into the cloud. (This is one of many ways to design a solution in the cloud.) The GDA will be updated to include a cloud connector that uses the existing MQTT client connector functionality, and the cloud implementation will draw on some of the data management functionality built to support the CDA. (Yes, that means the cloud functions will be written in Python.)

Figures A-16 and A-17 represent two notional UML designs—a basic design for the GDA using a single `CloudClientConnector` type, and an optional design for the GDA using a `CloudClientConnector` Factory to instance unique types specific to a given cloud service provider. Figure A-18 represents a notional UML design for the optional cloud service functions (CSF).

Gateway Device Application design (basic)

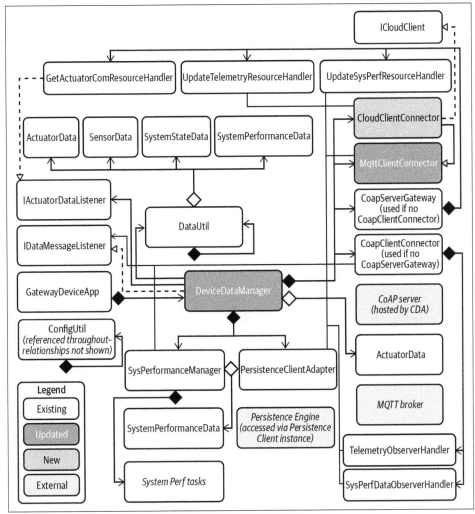

Figure A-17. GDA notional UML for Chapter 11 (basic)

Gateway Device Application design (optional)

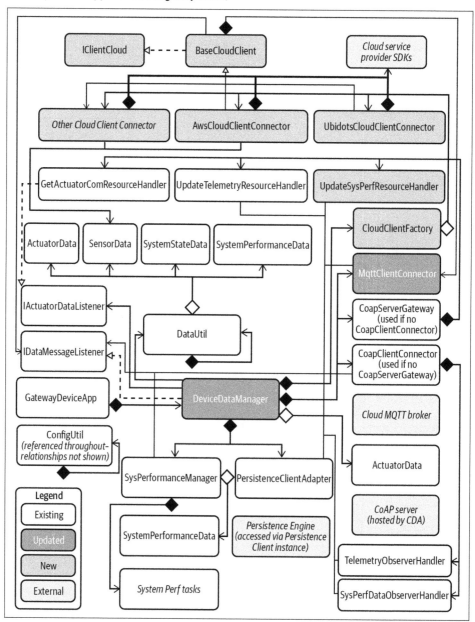

Figure A-18. GDA notional UML for Chapter 11 (optional)

Cloud Service Functions design (optional)

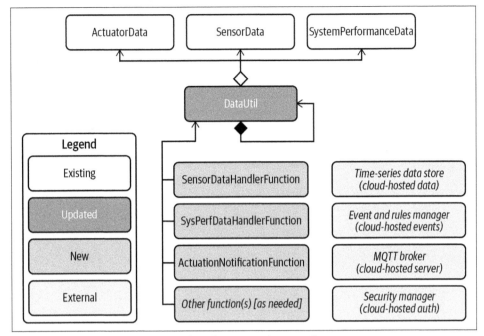

Figure A-19. CSF notional UML for Chapter 11 (optional)

Bibliography

Antón, Simon Duque, Daniel Fraunholz, Christopher Lipps, Frederic Pohl, Marc Zimmermann, and Hans. D. Schotten. "Two Decades of SCADA Exploitation: A Brief History." *2017 IEEE Conference on Application, Information and Network Security (AINS)* (New York: IEEE, 2017): 98–104. 10.1109/AINS.2017.8270432.

The Apache Software Foundation. "Commons CLI." (2019) [Online]. Available: *https://commons.apache.org/proper/commons-cli*.

The Apache Software Foundation. "Commons Configuration." (2020) [Online]. Available: *https://commons.apache.org/proper/commons-configuration*.

Ashton, Kevin. "That 'Internet of Things' Thing." *RFID Journal* (June 22, 2009).

Amsüss, Christian and Wasilak, Maciej. "aiocoap: Python CoAP Library". Energy Harvesting Solutions, 2013– . *http://github.com/chrysn/aiocoap*.

AWS (2021). AWS IoT Core – Developer Guide. "Try the AWS Iot quick connect."*https://docs.aws.amazon.com/iot/latest/developerguide/iot-quick-start.html*.

AWS (2021). AWS IoT Core – Developer Guide. "Explore AWS IoT Core services in hands-on tutorial."*https://docs.aws.amazon.com/iot/latest/developerguide/iot-gs-first-thing.html*.

AWS (2021). AWS IoT Core – Developer Guide. "Security in AWS IoT." *https://docs.aws.amazon.com/iot/latest/developerguide/security.html*.

AWS (2021). AWS Identity and Access Management – User Guide. "What is IAM?" *https://docs.aws.amazon.com/IAM/latest/UserGuide/introduction.html*.

Banks, Antón and Rahul Gupta. MQTT Version 3.1.1. OASIS Standard, 2014.

Berners-Lee, Tim, Roy T. Fielding, and Larry Masinter. "Uniform Resource Identifier (URI): Generic Syntax." IETF Internet Standard RFC 3986, (January 2005).

Bormann, Carsten, Mehmet Ersue, and Ari Keränen. "Terminology for Constrained-Node Networks." IETF Informational RFC 7228, (May 2014): 8–10.

Bormann, Carsten, Simon Lemay, Hannes Tschofenig, Klaus Hartke, and Bilhanan Silverajan. "CoAP (Constrained Application Protocol) over TCP, TLS, and Web-Sockets." IETF Proposed Standard RFC 8323, (February 2018).

Braden, Robert. "Requirements for Internet Hosts – Communication Layers." IETF Internet Standard RFC 1122, (October 1989).

Brooks, Tyson T. *Cyber-Assurance for the Internet of Things*. IEEE Press, 2017.

Crockford, Douglas. "The application/json Media Type for JavaScript Object Notation (JSON)." IETF Informational Memo RFC 4627, (July 2006).

Eclipse Foundation, Inc. "Californium (Cf) - CoAP for Java." (2020) [Online]. Available: *https://github.com/eclipse/californium*.

Eclipse Foundation, Inc. "Eclipse Paho Java Client." (2020) [Online]. Available: *https://github.com/eclipse/paho.mqtt.java*.

Eclipse Foundation, Inc. "Eclipse Paho™ MQTT Python Client." (2020) [Online]. Available: *https://github.com/eclipse/paho.mqtt.python*.

Eclipse Foundation, Inc. "Scandium (Sc) - Security for Californium." (2021) [Online]. Available. *https://github.com/eclipse/californium/tree/master/scandium-core*.

Oracle. "JavaMail." (2020) [Online]. Available: *https://javaee.github.io/javamail*.

Encyclopaedia Britannica Online, s.v. "Moore's law," by the editors of Encyclopaedia Britannica, last updated December 26, 2019.

Encyclopaedia Britannica Online, s.v. "ARPANET," by Kevin Featherly, last updated March 23, 2021.

Encyclopaedia Britannica Online, "Know Your Joe: 5 Things You Didn't Know About Coffee" (2. The Watched Pot), by Alison Eldridge, accessed January 18, 2021.

Gamma, Erich et al. *Design Patterns: Elements of Reusable Object-Oriented Software*. Boston: Addison-Wesley, 1994.

Google. "Gson." (2008) [Online]. Available: *https://github.com/google/gson*.

Grönholm, Alex. "Advanced Python Scheduler (APScheduler)." (2020) [Online]. Available: *https://github.com/agronholm/apscheduler*.

Hartke, Klaus. "Observing Resources in the Constrained Application Protocol (CoAP)." IETF Proposed Standard RFC 7641, (September 2015).

Herrero, Rolando. *Fundamentals of IoT Communication Technologies*. 1st ed., Springer International Publishing, 2022.

Hunter, John D. "Matplotlib: A 2D Graphics Environment." *Computing in Science & Engineering* 9, no. 3 (2007): 90–95.

The Industrial Internet of Things, Volume G1: Reference Architecture, Version 1.9. Needham, MA: Industrial Internet Consortium, 2019.

The Industrial Internet of Things, Volume G5: Connectivity Framework, Version 1.0.1. Needham, MA: Industrial Internet Consortium, 2017.

Jones, Dave. "pisense." (2015 – 2018) [Online]. Available: *https://github.com/waveform80/pisense*.

JUnit. "JUnit 4." (2020) [Online]. Available: *https://junit.org/junit4*.

King, Andrew D. "Programming the IoT – Source Code, Documentation, and Task Repositories." (2020) [Online]. Available: *https://github.com/programming-the-iot*.

King, Andrew D. "Programming the IoT – Exercises Kanban Board." (2020) [Online]. Available: *https://github.com/orgs/programming-the-iot/projects/1*.

Kucherawy, Murray. "Message Header Field for Indicating Message Authentication Status." IETF Proposed Standard RFC 8601, (May 2019).

Laster, Brent. *Jenkins 2 Up & Running*. O'Reilly Media, Inc., 2018.

Lea, Perry. *Internet of Things for Architects: Architecting IoT Solutions by Implementing Sensors, Communication Infrastructure, Edge Computing, Analytics, and Security*. Packt Publishing, 2018.

Light, Roger A. "Mosquitto: Server and Client Implementation of the MQTT Protocol." *Journal of Open Source Software* 2, no. 13 (2017): 265.

Linn, John. "Privacy Enhancement for Internet Electronic Mail: Part I: Message Encryption and Authentication Procedures." IETF Historic RFC 1421, (February 1993).

Leibiusky, Jonathan. "Jedis." (2020) [Online]. Available: *https://github.com/redis/jedis*.

Mijic, Dejan, Draško Draškovic, and Ervin Varga. *Scalable Architecture for the Internet of Things*. O'Reilly Media, Inc., 2018.

Monk, Simon. *Raspberry Pi Cookbook*. 3rd ed., O'Reilly Media, Inc., 2019.

Montenegro, Gabriel, Nandakishore Kushalnagar, Jonathan W. Hui, and David E. Culler. "Transmission of IPv6 Packets over IEEE 802.15.4 Networks." IETF Proposed Standard RFC 4944, (September 2007).

NumPy. "NumPy." (2020) [Online]. Available: *https://numpy.org*.

Postel, Jon. "Transmission Control Protocol." IETF Internet Standard RFC 793, (September 1981).

Postel, John. "User Datagram Protocol." Internet Standard RFC 768, (August 1980).

Quote Investigator (2021). "With Great Power Comes Great Responsibility." *https://quoteinvestigator.com/2015/07/23/great-power* [Online; accessed 05 June 2021].

The Raspberry Pi Foundation. "Sense HAT Emulator." (2016) [Online]. Available: *https://github.com/astro-pi/python-sense-emu*.

Rescorla, Eric and Nagendra Modadugu. "Datagram Transport Layer Security Version 1.2." IETF Proposed Standard RFC 6347, (January 2012).

Rescorla, Eric. "The Transport Layer Security (TLS) Protocol Version 1.3." IETF Proposed Standard RFC 8446, (August 2018).

Rodola, Giampaolo, Jay Loden, and Dave Daeschler. "Process and system utilities (psutil)." (2009 – 2020) [Online]. Available: *https://github.com/giampaolo/psutil*.

Selander, Goeran, John Mattsson, Francesca Palombini, and Ludwig Seitz. "Object Security for Constrained RESTful Environments (OSCORE)." IETF Proposed Standard RFC 8613, (July 2019).

Shelby, Zach, Klaus Hartke, and Carsten Bormann. *The Constrained Application Protocol (CoAP)*. IETF Proposed Standard RFC 7252, (2014): 68.

Smith, Sean. *Internet of Risky Things. Trusting the Devices That Surround Us*. O'Reilly Media, Inc., 2017.

Song, Jimmy. *Programming Bitcoin. Learn How to Program Bitcoin from Scratch*. O'Reilly Media, Inc., 2019.

Tanganelli, Giacomo, Carlo Vallati, and Enzo Mingozzi. "CoAPthon: Easy Development of CoAP-Based IoT Applications with Python." *2015 IEEE 2nd World Forum on Internet of Things (WF-IoT)* (Milan: IEEE, 2015), 63–68.

The Unified Modeling Language, Version 2.5.1. Milford, MA: Object Management Group, 2017.

Ubidots (2021). Ubidots API docs. "[hardware engineers]." Available: *https://ubidots.com/docs/hw*.

Ubidots (2021). Ubidots Developer Guides. "API Authentication." Available: *https://help.ubidots.com/en/articles/570026-api-authentication*.

Ubidots (2021). Ubidots Developer Guides. "Ubidots MQTT Broker." Available: *https://help.ubidots.com/en/articles/570008-ubidots-mqtt-broker*.

Vieru, Catalin, Massimiliano Angelino, and Philipp Sacha. "Patterns for AWS IoT time series data ingestion with Amazon Timestream." AWS Database Blog. *https://aws.amazon.com/blogs/database/patterns-for-aws-iot-time-series-data-ingestion-with-amazon-timestream* [Online; accessed 05 June 2021].

Index

About the Author

Andy King is a seasoned computer scientist, educator, and technology consultant with more than 20 years of experience designing and building complex software systems, ranging from network management tools to Internet of Things platforms. He advises clients across North America and Internationally on IoT fundamentals, technology strategy, cloud integration, and system design. As an Adjunct Faculty member in Northeastern University's College of Engineering, Andy teaches practical approaches to implementing IoT solutions through his Connected Devices class.

Colophon

The animal on the cover of *Programming the Internet of Things* is the purple gallinule (*Porphyrio martinicus*), also known as the American purple gallinule or the yellow-legged gallinule. This crane-like swamp hen is typically found in wet marshes, lakes, and waterways in the southeastern United States and along coastal regions of Mexico, Central America, and northern South America.

Purple gallinules have medium-sized deep blue bodies with white undertails, topped with iridescent green and turquoise feathers. This bird's bill is yellow and red tipped, and its forehead is a striking pale blue. The gallinule's legs and feet resemble those of a chicken—yellow with long toes—and help them walk on floating vegetation by better distributing their weight. Not the strongest of fliers, purple gallinules prefer swimming, walking, and taking short flights during which their legs dangle awkwardly.

This bird's omnivorous diet consists of fruits, seeds, and leaves as well as insects, spiders, frogs, worms, fish, and snails. It's also been known to eat the eggs and young of other birds. They often use their feet to hold food while they are eating.

Purple gallinules form monogamous long-lasting bonds; courtship rituals occur when birds of a bonded pair reunite after a separation. Both sexes bend forward, with wings angled down and necks outstretched. One bird will strut across the path of the other or both birds will bow as they approach each other.

While the purple gallinule's conservation status is currently listed as of Least Concern, many of the animals on O'Reilly covers are endangered; all of them are important to the world.

The cover illustration is by Karen Montgomery, based on a black and white engraving from *Wood's Animate Creation*. The cover fonts are Gilroy Semibold and Guardian Sans. The text font is Adobe Minion Pro; the heading font is Adobe Myriad Condensed; and the code font is Dalton Maag's Ubuntu Mono.

www.ingramcontent.com/pod-product-compliance
Ingram Content Group UK Ltd.
Pitfield, Milton Keynes, MK11 3LW, UK
UKHW010222060125
453221UK00006B/10